The Death Care Industries
in the United States

The Death Care
Industries in
the United States

by

Ronald G.E. Smith

McFarland & Company, Inc., Publishers
Jefferson, North Carolina, and London

British Library Cataloguing-in-Publication data are available

Library of Congress Cataloguing-in-Publication Data

Smith, Ronald G. E., 1943–
    The death care industries in the United States /
by Ronald G. E. Smith.
        p.   cm.
    Includes bibliographical references and index.
    ISBN 0-7864-0118-4 (lib. bdg.: 50# alk. paper)
    1. Undertakers and undertaking—United States. I. Title.
HD9999.U53U574   1996
363.7'5'0973—dc20   96-453
                                           CIP

Manufactured in the United States of America

McFarland & Company, Inc., Publishers
  Box 611, Jefferson, North Carolina 28640

Table of Contents

Preface

An economy consists of all the producing and consuming activities that go on within a society. For purposes of classification and study, the larger economy is commonly divided into a series of smaller economies or economic sectors. Each of these sectors includes all the economic activities that are associated with the production and consumption of a particular category of related goods and services. In many societies one of these sectors consists of an extensive variety of death-related goods and services that are produced by funeral homes, cemeteries, and related enterprises. For reasons discussed later, we speak here of all the activities associated with the production and consumption of these particular goods and services, taken together, as the death care sector of the economy, or simply "the death care economy."

As consumers we all are occasionally or eventually participants in the death care economy, but few of us have any cause to study its organization and operations. My interest in the subject is due to a long acquaintance with the late Gerard L. Schoen, Jr., former vice president and treasurer of Jacob Schoen & Son, Inc., the largest funeral service firm in New Orleans for many years. In 1975, Schoen and I began to examine a series of trends and developments which appeared likely to affect the future of family firms like his. By 1977, following a great deal of study which included visits to numerous death care facilities throughout the United States, we were convinced that conditions in many markets strongly favored the development of cemetery-mortuary combinations, especially in distinctive cemeteries capable of promoting pre-need sales of funeral services along with their cemetery products.

We were not surprised therefore when in late 1977 plans were announced for the establishment of the first cemetery-mortuary combination in the state of Louisiana, to be located on the contiguous grounds of Metairie Cemetery and Lake Lawn Park, two of five cemeteries then owned by Stewart Enterprises, Inc., in New Orleans. Soon thereafter the Schoen family entered into negotiations with Stewart Enterprises leading to participation of the Schoen firm as an equal partner in the development and operation of Lake Lawn Metairie Funeral Home. This partnership ended when the Schoen family sold its firm in 1985 and Stewart acquired their interest.

By 1992 Lake Lawn Metairie Funeral Home had become a mature facility.

The merits of combined operations were widely recognized within the death care economy. Stewart itself had become a public company, based partly on the strength of those merits. Since the history of Lake Lawn Metairie's growth from inception to maturity demonstrated fully the case for combined operations, I proposed a case study of the operating history of the facility for the purpose of understanding the economic impact of combinations. I asked Frank B. Stewart, Jr., chairman of Stewart Enterprises, if he would provide the data needed to document the case, and he agreed. The case was then published as a series of articles in *American Cemetery* in 1993. A revised version of the series is included here as parts of chapters 16 and 17. An article appearing in *The American Funeral Director* and *American Cemetery* during 1993 formed the basis in part for Chapter 18. Thanks are extended to the editor and publisher of those magazines for permission to reuse that material here.

The publication of those articles stimulated my curiosity about trends in the death care economy beyond the spread of combined operations. One of these trends is the continual consolidation of establishments at a rapid pace. Both trends have worked together to alter the traditional manner in which death care has been provided to consumers as a set of discrete products obtained in a series of separate transactions with different types of providers (funeral directors, cemeterians, and memorial dealers). Now two or more of these discrete parts of death care are often provided together as a package by a combined facility or a cluster of separate facilities. For this and other reasons, including the tendency for traditionally specialized providers to expand their scale and scope, the terms formerly used to classify discrete death care establishments, firms, and industries have become less adequate as technical descriptions of combined or clustered facilities which blur the lines of demarcation among different production processes and products. A comprehensive descriptive term is needed, and the term "death care" has emerged to fill that need.

Whether or not "death care" ever becomes accepted in the vernacular, its adoption as a technical description of the products and activities it comprises is indicated by the results of the analysis presented in this book. One result, presented in Chapter 6, is an extensive (but not exhaustive) product/market classification system for death care goods and services of all types. Corresponding to that system, a proposal is made for the collection and reporting of death care expenditures classified by major groups and by classes of expenditures within each major group. Further, a classification system for establishments engaged in the production and sale of death care goods and services is presented in Chapter 7 as a proposed revision of the Standard Industrial Classification (SIC) system employed by the U.S. Department of Commerce.

As it happens, this system is currently the subject of a comprehensive review by the U.S. Office of Management and Budget (OMB) with a view to replacing the current SIC system with a North American Industry Classification System (NAICS). The existing Canadian and Mexican industrial classification systems are under review along with the U.S. system. As a part of this review, an Economic Classification Policy Committee (ECPC) was established by OMB and "charged with a 'fresh slate' examination of economic classifications for statistical purposes, including industrial classification, product classifications, and product code groupings" (*Federal Register*, July 26, 1994, p. 38093). Following a series of steps in the review process, the implementation of NAICS is projected to begin in January 1997.

In the course of its review of the existing SIC system, the ECPC called for proposals "for new or revised 4-digit industries ... consistent with the production-oriented conceptual framework incorporated into the principles of NAICS" (p. 38095). Simultaneously, the ECPC called for proposals for an alternative market-oriented product grouping system to be implemented after 1997. In response to these calls, the relevant portions of chapters 6 and 7 were submitted for consideration by the ECPC prior to publication of this book. It is hoped that the committee will see fit to adopt the concept of "death care" as a category of related economic activities performed by a series of "industries" comprised of establishments with similar production processes as described in Chapter 7.

It appears that those industries meet the production-oriented criteria established by the ECPC for inclusion within a revised four-digit industrial classification system to be used in NAICS. Not all of the specific measures described in ECPC working papers (e.g., the specialization ratio and the heterogeneity index) were used in our analysis, but the ECPC has formally recognized that "other measures of the similarity among establishments will be considered and developed where necessary." Furthermore, the committee has stated that various "statistical measures will supplement, not supplant, industry expertise and expert judgments about industry production processes and similarities" (p. 38096).

The total market value of all the death care goods and services produced in the U.S. economy is unknown, but it has been estimated that it exceeds $15 billion annually. The economic significance of this category of goods and services seems to require appropriate recognition for the establishments and industries which produce them. Previously such recognition has been lacking in part because the variety of death care goods and services and the different types of death care establishments have not generally been perceived or comprehended as part of a large sector of the economy called "death care." Most funeral homes and cemeteries appear to be small neighborhood businesses in separate locations with no obvious links between their ownership and operations. Lately, however, the continued consolidation of the sector has privately linked more and more funeral homes and cemeteries together, and the development of many cemetery-mortuary combinations has publicly symbolized the close relationships among death care goods and services and the processes of producing them. Nevertheless, the operation of death care facilities as local establishments with distinctive identities has resulted in widespread misconceptions about the economic significance of the industries they collectively represent.

The industrial classification system and the product grouping system offered in this book provide a coherent framework for the comprehension of the death care economy as a whole and for the classification and collection of data which will indicate to the fullest extent the economic characteristics of death care establishments and markets. It may be hoped, then, that these systems will eventually be adopted for incorporation within the structure of NAICS. In any event, they provide a useful framework for understanding the nature of death care goods and services, the relationships among them, and the distinctive features of the establishments and firms that provide them.

In the interest of promoting a better understanding of these phenomena, this book has been written as a springboard for others to pursue further many of the issues raised within it. Some of the analysis is tentative and exploratory; many issues raised are unresolved. It is hoped that others will be moved to explore those issues further, perhaps even to resolve them. What I have attempted to do is to integrate the disparate elements of the death care economy into a total system of interrelated parts. The study of any of those parts and of the system as a whole is what I refer to here as the subject of death care.

My own study of the subject has been facilitated by others in various ways. Gerard Schoen, Jr., shared with me his knowledge and experience. Frank B. Stewart, Jr., provided data not otherwise available, but his chief contribution was his insistence over many years upon the concept of death care as a complete process. This stimulated my interest in exploring that concept in a serious way. Dr. Lawrence H. Falk contributed directly to the construction of the framework employed in Chapter 8 and to the development of ideas expressed in Chapter 6. Steven Saltzman and Gregory Capelli made available to me the fruits of their labor as "death care" analysts at the Chicago Corporation. Like their work, mine has relied at various points on data collected by the U.S. Census Bureau, where I was ably assisted by Jack B. Moody, chief of the Service Branch of the Business Division. Other persons and organizations provided a great deal of illustrative material, and their contributions are acknowledged where the illustrations appear in the text. My greatest debt is to Dr. Nova Catherine Thriffiley, who labored mightily to help me produce a presentable manuscript. If it may be said that a book is an embalmed and restored "body" of thought, then it is she who performed the procedures on this one. Her continued support, along with that of several others, through thick and thin, will long be remembered — perhaps even after I too have received death care.

Having said all that, I hasten to add, after the manner of an epitaph, that I alone am responsible for the views expressed in what follows. Although positively stated, these views represent an initial attempt to comprehend a largely unstudied sector of the U.S. economy. In spite of all the generous support I have received, it is inevitable that such an attempt will suffer from sundry errors of omission and commission. But, like life, books must come to an end. It remains for others to point out the flaws, to correct the errors, and to resolve the issues raised herein as best they can.

Ronald G.E. Smith
New York,
December 1995

PART I

Non ridere, non lugere, neque detestari, sed intelligere.
(Not to laugh, not to lament, not to curse, but to understand.)
Spinoza

1. *The Subject of Death Care*

Parts of the Book

This book is an attempt to examine the sector of the U.S. economy that includes funeral homes, cemeteries, and related enterprises. The point of view is strictly that of an observer. What is observed is the manner in which these firms operate and interact in order to provide death care goods and services to American consumers. While the book deals primarily with commercial providers in the United States, it includes some references to noncommercial operators of death care facilities, to firms in other sectors of the domestic economy, and to death care practices in other countries.

The twenty chapters fall into seven distinct parts, the contents of which are summarized briefly as follows:

Part I introduces the subject of death care as a field of study. It explores the isolation and fragmentation of the death care economy as qualities that are related to the lack of any comprehensive survey of the sector, a survey which this book seeks to provide. Part I then sets the stage for what follows by identifying some distinctive features of the death care process.

Part II presents an analysis of the variety of goods and services that death care establishments provide. It then examines some characteristics of the providers of those goods and services.

Part III first describes the markets in which consumers interact with providers as buyers and sellers of an extensive variety of death care goods and services. It then surveys the different types of businesses that constitute the death care sector of the U.S. economy.

Part IV examines some features of the operations of funeral homes, cemeteries, crematories, and firms selling memorial products. It also examines the conditions under which the outputs of the different types of death care providers are produced and sold to consumers.

Part V discusses the influence of some aspects of the role of the clergy and the use of religious facilities in the death care process. It also discusses alternative forms of death care and the individuals who choose them, the organizations which advocate some of them, and the views of those voicing an opinion on this controversial topic.

Part VI deals with the economic structure of the death care sector — its historical fragmentation, the consolidation movement within it, and the formation of cemetery-mortuary combination establishments. Then the operation and impact of the latter are illustrated by a case history of a modern cemetery-mortuary combination: its planning and development, its growth from inception to maturity, and the impact of its operation on rival funeral homes.

Part VII identifies and compares some distinctive features of the three largest investor-owned death care companies. It then attempts to assess the factors that will influence prospective demand for death care in this country. Finally, it speculates on a number of future trends and developments in the death care economy based on conclusions reached from the previous analysis.

As an aid to readers and researchers, the federal Funeral Rule is included in an appendix, and a list of references is presented at the end of the text and cited throughout in an abbreviated manner.

Different Audiences

The above brief summary of the parts of this book suggests that it is addressed to several groups. One of these consists of death care practitioners — funeral directors, cemeterians, memorial dealers, and the owners, managers, and employees of funeral homes, cemeteries, memorial dealerships, and related enterprises. It is hoped that they will obtain from the book a better understanding of their business and the economic underpinnings of the sector to which many have devoted their working lives. At the very least, they will be shown an unconventional treatment of their industries and their place within the death care economy.

Even more important than the current generation of death care practitioners and executives is the next generation of them, who are now being groomed in mortuary colleges, family-run businesses, and the management ranks of regional and international death care companies. It is the lot of the next generation of death care providers to cope with the consequences of current trends and developments which will have their greatest impact in the years to come. It is the future generation of owner-operators more than the present one that will face the gnawing issues of whether and how to continue as owners of independent establishments in the tradition of earlier generations. Some will be moved to form or to join regional, national, or international companies, assuming new responsibilities within those organizations. Others will seek the best ways to meet the challenges of operating in an environment unlike that of the past, which has formed the attitudes of the present generation. It is hoped that this book will be of help especially to the future leaders of the death care economy.

A third group to which the book is addressed consists of financial analysts and journalists, as well as investors of all types, who are increasingly interested in the securities of the few publicly owned death care companies. By becoming more fully acquainted with the operational and financial aspects of the death care sector as a whole, individual and institutional investors and their advisers may be better equipped to assess the relative prospects and risks of investment in death care firms. In what follows they will find a framework within which to form their own appraisals of the potential for expansion in death care markets and to assess the future stability or instability of demand for different types of death care goods and services.

The book may provide a useful backdrop for a fourth group broadly composed of professionals who deal with death care firms in the specialized capacities of accountants, attorneys, and consultants of various sorts. No attempt will be made to pursue any such specialized areas of the operations of death care providers, but the presentation of their general features as businesses may provide useful background for specialists. Another group that may fall into this category of interest consists of government officials and employees of federal, state, and local government agencies involved in the regulation of the death care sector or some part of it. Another group that may find something of value along these lines consist of members of the clergy and medical professionals and social workers who are called upon to participate directly or indirectly in the death care process.

Although not addressed to the general public, the book may be of use to a wider audience interested more in economic and social issues surrounding the production and delivery of death care to consumers. Finally, while no attempt is made to inform or to instruct consumers directly, their interest lies at the heart of this book. As Adam Smith correctly observed long ago: "Consumption is the sole end and purpose of all production; and the interest of the producer ought to be attended to only so far as it may be necessary for promoting that of the consumer." In precisely this spirit, the basic purpose of the book is to promote the effectiveness and efficiency with which firms in the death care economy serve the interest of consumers. In this respect the analysis of some topics may also interest social commentators and members of the general press who have tended to be critical of death care practitioners, often without fully understanding them or appreciating their role in the larger economy and in society as a whole.

This book seeks to provide the basis for such understanding and appreciation. Toward this end it attempts to examine how funeral homes, cemeteries, memorial dealers, and related enterprises produce and provide death care goods and services of all types. Many of the things they do are similar to what other businesses do, yet one cannot help but think that there is something "different" about them because of what they do.

Terminology

Symptomatic of this "difference" is the fact that there was a time when anyone who managed a business for himself was called an "undertaker," meaning simply a "man of business" or "businessman" (Ely, 1919, pp. 123–24). The term "undertaker" as such was employed by those in every line of business, including those engaged in providing the mortuary services component of what is here called death care. Because the term proved especially apt for the latter group, it gradually ceased to be used by those in other lines of business who wanted to distance themselves from those in the "dismal trade." Even the latter have now abandoned the term as "unprofessional," and perhaps too suggestive. For a time they experimented with "mortician," which appeared to have a scientific sound reminiscent of "physician." That attracted the fire of critics who charged them with playing "semantic games." Gradually they settled on the designation "funeral director" (Sloane, 1991, p. 202). Out of deference that term is adopted here, although "funeral home" and "mortuary" are used interchangeably for the establishments operated by funeral directors. The term "casket" is used rather than the once-common "coffin" to refer to the standard burial container.

The term "cemetery" seems to have replaced "graveyard," and the terms "cemetery man" or the gender-neutral "cemeterian" have generally been adopted by those who operate cemeteries. "Stone-cutters" who once plied their trade in "marble shops" have now mostly been replaced by purveyors of monuments who generally refer to themselves as "monument men" or "monument dealers" or even "memorial counselors" who operate out of "memorial studios." In conformity with these common usages, the gender-neutral versions of them are used throughout for the different types of death care providers to whom they refer. "Cemetery" refers generally to burial grounds of all types, including "memorial parks," although at times the term "monumented cemeteries" is used to indicate a cemetery with monuments as opposed to a memorial park with flat markers. Both types of facilities usually allow for burial or entombment as different means of disposing of human remains. Distinctions will sometimes be drawn between these different forms of final disposition, but at times no distinction is necessary. To inter a dead body is to put it into either a grave or a tomb; an interment may involve a burial or an entombment.

The variation in terms used above to describe death care providers and facilities may suggest to the reader that the death care economy traditionally has been fragmented. This is so, and as a result there has been no adequate generic term which includes all of the activities commonly associated with the demands brought on by the death of a person in society. The terms "funeral industry" and "funeral service industry" are insufficient in that they appear to exclude crematories, cemeteries, and memorial dealerships, which do not perform funeral services. The term "burial industry" is inadequate for the reason that it appears to exclude mortuaries, crematories and memorial dealerships, none of which performs burials. The term "memorialization industry" is likewise inadequate in that it seems restricted to memorial providers only. The term "death care sector" groups these related types of industries together under one heading. The use of the comprehensive term "death care" refers to outputs of all those industries in the sector. This is consistent with the use of "health care" to refer to a variety of goods and services made available to consumers by different providers. As with the use of "health care," the adoption of "death care" as a generic classification does not replace the separate identities of funeral homes, cemeteries, and monument dealerships as subclasses of death care establishments and firms, but it stands for the sum of all of them. By the same token, "death care practitioners" does not replace the occupational classifications of funeral directors, cemeterians, monument dealers, and so on, but it refers to them all, as a class, after the manner of "health care practitioners," which encompasses doctors, nurses, and other occupational specialists.

"Death care providers" will be used here to refer to either persons or entities engaged in the production or sale of death care goods and services. In this respect the term "providers" includes establishments and firms as well as the practitioners associated with these. This is consistent with the common usage of the term in the phrase "health care providers." The boundaries between health care and death care will concern us from time to time, but at this time it is sufficient to indicate the inevitable interaction between them, effectively at the point when the outer boundaries of each sphere meet.

Death care begins when health care ceases to extend life, and it is often provided initially by health care practitioners. They are usually in attendance when the life of the dying patient ends, and they perform the initial tasks of "death care" within their sphere. Typically, in a health care facility a doctor pronounces the patient dead and signs the death certificate; the body is then taken by an attendant to a morgue to await the services of a funeral home. If a patient dies at a residence or in a nursing home typically a funeral home is called directly to fetch the corpse. In every case, some "death care" is administered immediately after the event of death, no matter who performs the services rendered. When initial death care is rendered in a hospital, its cost is covered by the prices charged for health care goods and services by a health care provider. In this way a modicum of death care costs is subsumed within the health care economy.

Commercial death care providers enter the scene when the representative from a funeral home picks up the corpse from the morgue, hospital, hospice, nursing home, or residence. The dead body then begins its journey through the American death care delivery system. If the deceased has not arranged in advance for the provision of the desired death care goods and services, the arrangements must be made by survivors. The term "at-need" is used to describe such arrangements made by survivors after the event of death. Death care goods and services of all types may be purchased also in advance of need from a funeral home, cemetery, or memorial dealership. Such purchases are said to be made on a "pre-planned" or "pre-need" basis, and they require some form of funding or pre-payment. Mortuary services may also be "pre-arranged" without pre-funding. This is said to occur when a consumer's preferences for particular goods and services, to be delivered after her death, are placed on file at a funeral home as a matter of record.

The terms "funeral" or "traditional funeral" are generally used to describe a series of informal and formal social events, ordinarily including visitation and ceremonies at which the body is present in an open or closed casket. The formal ceremonies included with "the funeral" are generally described as "funeral services," wherever they are held and whatever form they take. To describe death-related social events and ceremonies at which the body is not present, the term "memorial service" is commonly used.

The terms "body" and "dead body" are generally used to describe the bodily remains, although "corpse," "cadaver," "decedent," "deceased party," or simply "the deceased" are also used at times. This seems preferable to the use of euphemistic terms such as "the departed" or "the loved one" which are used in the trade.

During cremation the bodily remains are reduced to cremated remains, some of which evaporate. By common practice the remaining ashes and skeletal material are then processed into a uniform matter for which the term "cremains" has emerged in the trade. In spite of possible objections to that term, it is adopted here for lack of any alternative in the language to describe the kind of matter that remains after complete cremation processing occurs.

The significance of the distinction between bodily remains and cremains will be explored at length in later chapters. The focus of this and other explorations will be to understand fully the basic process of death care and the system through which it is delivered to American consumers. In keeping with this focus, an attempt will be made to use consistently the terms introduced here, to define newly introduced terms adequately, and to revisit the meanings of certain terms in different contexts and from different perspectives. Although this may seem repetitive at times, its purpose is to reinforce the importance of a uniform terminology in the development of death care as a subject of serious study.

Limitations of the Subject

This book has a limited scope. Its subject is the group of economic activities associated with the death care process. This process is the outcome of the process of dying, and it triggers the process of grieving. These two related processes will not concern us here. They have been the subject of other books, including the recently published study *How We Die: Reflections on Life's Final Chapter* (1994) by Sherwin B. Nuland, M.D., and the popular classic by Dr. Elisabeth Kübler-Ross, *On Death and Dying* (1969), the first of a series on this topic. Death and related topics have been covered by numerous writers from many different backgrounds. Yet little of what has been written is concerned with "death care" as such. It is mainly devoted to topics like the legal and medical criteria of when death occurs, human organ transplants, euthanasia, assisted and unassisted suicide, dying patients and their doctors, grief and bereavement, the effect of death upon children, cryonic suspension of dead bodies, near-death experiences, life after death, and so on. These matters do not concern us, except as peripheral issues.

Our concern is with death as an event which initiates a series of economic transactions and activities here called "death care," and our major concern is the economic activities entailed in the delivery of death care goods and services. The history of the development of death care providers and their business practices will concern us only for the light it sheds on present and future conditions. Historical treatments are available from works such as *The History of American Funeral Directing* (1955) by Habenstein and Lamers and *The Last Great Necessity: Cemeteries in American History* (1991) by Sloane. We have drawn upon these as needed, but historical accounts of death care practices as such do not concern us. It is hardly relevant today that embalming was practiced by the ancient Egyptians and rediscovered as a result of the need to preserve bodies during the Civil War. What is important here is how the capability to embalm bodies serves consumer needs in contemporary America. The various means by which different societies have disposed of human bodies may be interesting to some, but they will be mentioned only in passing in this book. The pyramids and the Taj Mahal represent outstanding examples of the human impulse to memorialize, but they add little to our understanding of the memorialization component of the death care process as it exists in modern society.

Throughout history, death care practices have been a part of the social life of every human society. The impact of death and its aftermath has involved the services of priests and shamans, and more recently of psychologists, psychiatrists, and social and religious counselors. These professionals have tended to focus on the emotional well-being of survivors by offering them solace or therapy during the grieving process. The performance of these professional roles is not a subject of this book. Nevertheless, there is a sense in which the influence of religious and psychological factors cannot be separated from a consideration of the death care economy because they are an integral part of consumer demand for ways to dispose of the corpse, to allow survivors to deal with the grief of loss, and to enable them to memorialize the deceased. For their part, death care providers generally recognize and incorporate psychological and religious factors in the production and delivery of death care goods and services in their attempt to satisfy consumer demand.

Death Care as Ceremony

Underlying most contemporary death care is the concept of a funeral as a rite of passage which disposes of the body, socially acknowledges the death, and helps survivors adjust to the loss of a member of the community. The importance of the ceremonial content of death care is explicitly recognized in a slogan favored by providers which states that "funerals are for the living." In other words, death care is not simply a matter of taking care of the preparation of the body for final disposition and memorialization; it is also a matter of providing an opportunity for survivors to participate in the process of adjusting to the reality of the death.

The three different forms of death care with ceremonial options among which American consumers customarily choose are (1) a funeral service before final disposition of the body, (2) a memorial service after final disposition of the body, and (3) "direct" final disposition of the body with no ceremony before or after. Most deaths are accompanied by some sort of funeral (involving the presence of the body), and the economic underpinnings of the death care economy are based on this fact. For example, the modern funeral home as we know it is an establishment that exists basically for the purpose of holding funeral ceremonies. It is equipped with appropriate facilities "for the 'in-state' period during which a visitation, wake, or shiva is conducted — and in which funeral rites may be performed in whole or in part. The modern funeral home is designed and equipped to relieve the burden of the sorrow of death in comfortable and convenient surroundings" (Raether and Slater, 1977, p. 236). The economic justification for the investment required in such facilities and the costs of operating them depends in no small measure on the continued demand in this country for death care that includes a significant ceremonial element, which has traditionally characterized the disposal of the dead in most cultures.

Clearly, any significant trend away from the traditional American practice of arranging funerals which are social events is fraught with consequences for the death care economy as it is presently organized. The presence of the body prepared for viewing in a casket during funeral ceremonies is the backbone of the operation of funeral homes as death care providers. It is also the part of the American death care process that has attracted the sharpest criticism by those who associate the practice with excessive ceremonial displays involving costly caskets in which the preserved and restored corpse reposes during viewing. Alternative practices, such as direct disposition with no services and bodiless services have been advocated as logical alternatives to traditional services with the body present. It is necessary to consider briefly the strength of the case against the presence of the body in light of psycho-logical and socio-logical as well as purely "logical" factors.

The Presence of the Body

It is in one sense difficult and in another sense not so difficult to conceive of the dead body of a person as an object which plays a critical role in funeral ceremonies desired by many. It is difficult if we suppose that a dead body is something awful or repugnant to be disposed of as quickly as possible. It is not so difficult if we understand that death is a natural outcome of living and that the loss of life does not destroy the body or negate its significance for those who knew or loved the deceased. As someone has said, "Death ends a life, but it does not end a relationship." Even after death there may still be a relationship with the lifeless body of a parent, a child, or a spouse. It may be extremely difficult to dissociate oneself from the body of that person. To be in the presence of the body of the dead person may be a source of comfort for survivors. This has been explained by industry participants in the following way:

The finite mind requires evidence that an earthly existence has ended. With the body present, opportunity is also provided for recall and reminiscence, for the sharing of experiences with others who have related to the life that was lived by the person now dead. With the body present, the dead person can be viewed. This is perhaps of greater importance today than ever before. Most people die away from home, often in distant medical institutions. There are more deaths which follow a devastating lingering illness. There are more people whose lives end under tragic circumstances [Raether and Slater, 1977, pp. 243–44].

What, then, is the nature of the case against funerals which are based on the presence of the body? Mostly it involves objections to the need and expense of death care merchandise and ceremonies. Some of these objections appear to miss the point that viewing the body is a practice which is intended to satisfy consumer demand based on emotional needs, not logical ones. Thus it is not to the point for critics to claim that the practice is "illogical." To make such a claim is to fail to comprehend that funerals are social occasions which are psychological, not logical, in nature. The difficulty of explaining the logic of them may lie in the difficulties of explaining psychological and emotional phenomena generally.

Through death care choices, consumers give expression to social, cultural, religious, and personal sentiments, all of which may be difficult to explain in purely logical terms. For similar reasons, it is difficult to explain logically the artistic and decorative articles people prefer and buy, the styles of clothing they choose, or the forms of entertainment they enjoy. Criticism of death care practices because they are illogical is no more applicable here than it is for any practice which involves a preference for goods and services intended to satisfy complex psychological needs.

The Preservation of the Body

Beyond the need to preserve the body for the temporary period of the funeral, there is a desire on the part of many to preserve and to protect the body for a lengthy period after death. Again, it is in one sense difficult and in another sense not so difficult to understand this desire. It is difficult to understand it in intellectual or logical terms. It is easy to argue, as some have done, that the dead body is of no significance and that the logical thing to do is to dispose of it quickly and efficiently by cremating or burying it as soon as possible. This is the "rational" argument made by proponents of immediate disposition. Yet it is not necessarily the most emotionally and psychologically satisfying thing for many people to do. It is difficult for them to conceive of the body as an insignificant object to be destroyed quickly following death. They rather desire to provide some protection for the bodily remains, wherever they are to rest in perpetuity. It appears from the burial practices of earlier civilizations that this long-term concern for the protection of the remains has existed for centuries.

Against this background it is less difficult to understand that even under modern conditions many continue to experience a desire to preserve and to protect the dead body of a loved one. The economic consequence of this is the demand for cemetery facilities which are permanent in nature and for caskets and other burial containers with preservative and protective features. In the long run, of course, none of these features can prevent the eventual decomposition of the body, and it is a deceptive practice under federal regulation for funeral directors to (1) "Represent that funeral goods or services will delay the natural decomposition of human remains for a long-term or indefinite time," or (2) "Represent that funeral goods have protective features or will protect the body from gravesite substances, when such is not the case" (*Federal Register*, January 11, 1994, p. 1613). Subject to these legal provisions, death care providers are properly concerned with the desires of some consumers to preserve and to protect the bodily remains after death.

In this respect the preference for preserving and protecting the body permanently after death is analogous to the preference for having it present temporarily during the funeral. There are some respects, however, in which the two sentiments differ. The latter preference involves the demand for immediate postdeath activities performed as private social affairs in a funeral home, religious facility, or cemetery. There is little if any public impact from the private decisions of families either to have the body present during these ceremonies or not. The whole of the effect is limited to the psychological impact on the participants in such services and to some economic consequences in the form of the demand created for different types of caskets, the use of mortuary and other facilities, and the like. In addition to the psychological and economic impact of private decisions to preserve and to protect dead bodies permanently, there is a social impact which extends to the development of cemeteries which occupy large tracts of land in perpetuity. The repercussions of this will receive some attention insofar as they may affect the relative strength and stability of the preferences for burial, entombment, cremation, and memorialization.

Appropriate Death Care

Since the desires to preserve and to protect the body are matters of personal preference, they are largely a matter of taste. So is the desire to have the preserved and restored body present during funeral ceremonies. It is not reasonable to criticize such practices as "inappropriate." It is hardly to the point to say that viewing a restored body is morbid or ghoulish. Even if this is so, many people desire to have the dead body present during a funeral service because it brings comfort, it helps them come to terms with the death, or it eases the adjustment in some other way. Some have said that funeral ceremonies with the body present are "pagan." Is this so because pagans also performed rituals involving dead bodies? Even so, this does not make every ritual performed with a dead body present a pagan practice. Because pagans ate meat or used fire, are meat-eating and fire-using also pagan practices? Some have said that funerals involving the presence of the body in a casket are "vulgar" displays and "conspicuous consumption." Such socially critical terms may be applied as well to a great many forms of consumption in affluent societies, and even in unaffluent ones, but what weight do they carry? The validity of social criticism is not absolute. Spending on housing, automobiles, clothing, restaurants, pets, and other goods and services is affected by the socioeconomic status or aspirations of consumers. Spending on death care is hardly unique in this regard.

Some critics have pointed out that funerals are different in England or in Switzerland or in Japan than they are in the United States. As cultural phenomena these differences are not unexpected, but this also is beside the point. The fact that the great majority of Japanese are cremated does not create an imperative for most Americans to follow. Because Japanese eat more sushi and enjoy Sumo wrestling, should Americans give up turkey and baseball? The absurdity of criticizing death care practices along these lines is obvious. Those practices, as expressions of ethnic customs, religious sentiments, and personal preferences, are beyond such criticism. To object to them, to be critical of them, even to laugh at them, may be the prerogative of insensitive people with different tastes, but only someone who is socially and intellectually naive, in both an anthropological and a psychological sense, could fail to comprehend the desires of many for traditional funerals with the body present. It may be a source of some elite or avant-garde satisfaction to reject popular tastes in funeral practices as in other aspects of social life, but it is impossible to demonstrate that putting a corpse in a body bag and taking it to a crematory in a truck is an inherently superior means of caring for the dead. Cheaper, yes. More decent, no. Simpler, yes. More dignified, no. Easier, yes. More appropriate, no. Minimalism may be an aesthetic ideal and at times a political movement, but it is neither a "logical" nor an economic imperative.

In no area of American life are "cheap" and "simple" the only viable criteria of what is decent, dignified, or appropriate. It is hard to understand by what line of thought some have come to regard these criteria as the standards for judging what forms of death care are appropriate in American society. The components of a dignified funeral, a decent burial, and an appropriate form of memorialization are economic goods which, no less than any other goods, we all are entitled to regard and to choose as the objects of desire. There is no criterion by which "decent" must mean cheap, "dignified" must mean simple, or "appropriate" must mean a memorial service without the presence of the body. Such interpretations of the meaning of the words "decent," "dignified," and "appropriate" may be a cause for concern in the death care sector, but they are explicitly rejected in this book. The position taken here is that death care is a set of economic products, like any other products made available in different qualities, among which consumers may choose for themselves in accordance with their own criteria of choice, based on their individual means, tastes, and preferences.

Foreign Death Care

We are primarily concerned here with the death care economy of the United States, not with the global death care economy. Even so, a short digression will help to provide some perspective and to correct possible misconceptions about the peculiarities of American death care. Death care practices in other countries are discussed for the sake of comparison because critics have sometimes contrasted them to those in the United States.

In *The American Way of Death* (1963), for example, Jessica Mitford speaks admiringly of the French system of "offering several classes of state funerals in a wide range of prices that may be purchased directly from the government." Better still, she wrote, is the case of "Switzerland, where there have been no private undertakers since 1890 and where a free state funeral, carried out by municipal attendants, with free grave, free coffin and free hearse, is the right of every citizen regardless of his financial status" (p. 228).

In a chapter devoted to "Funerals in England," the situation described by Mitford leads her to express concern that "There are those within the [undertaking] trade who are envious of their American counterparts, who would love nothing better than to transplant the American way in England's unreceptive soil" (p. 164). By "American way" is meant such advances as embalming, restoration, viewing, and funeral ceremonies attended by friends, neighbors, and co-workers as well as close relatives. The rest of the death care process in England is protected by the extent to which "The great majority of cemeteries and many of the crematoria are municipally owned" (p. 171). No such protection prevented the largest American death care firm from acquiring the two largest funeral providers in England during 1994. The company now provides death care to more than 14 percent of those who die on English soil. At this point, however, it is still too early to conclude to what extent this will lead to a transplantation of the American way in that country.

Clearly, the trend of today is away from Mitford's theme, which extolled government-provided death care. The reason for revisiting this somewhat dated theme is to draw attention to recent developments in France which resulted in the repeal of a 1904 law that created a funeral monopoly in that country. The impetus for this repeal was the organization by Michel Leclerc, a French entrepreneur, of a network of several hundred franchised mortuaries along with his development of dozens of so-called "supermarkets of death — warehouses where individuals can pick out headstones and coffins and fill shopping carts with granite angels, urns and artificial daisies. According to Leclerc, smart shoppers can cut 50% from what a funeral would have cost before the law was changed." To accomplish this feat, Leclerc had to fend off 1800 court cases and to march in the streets of Paris protesting the legal monopoly. After his victory, a poll showed that "three out of four French citizens approve the idea of a funeral supermarket" (Doody, 1994, p. 12). He next plans to franchise the supermarkets in England.

In Japan, cremation is the universal custom, reflecting its uniform culture.

Cremation is customarily preceded by traditional funeral rites and followed by memorialization of the inurned cremated remains. Lack of space in large cities like Tokyo has led to the development of high-rise buildings to house cremated remains. Sunray Co., a Japanese death care firm, has proposed the development of a cemetery on the moon at some point in the future. In another use of modern technology, an Osaka Temple provides funeral ceremonies incorporating laser-beam light displays, electronic music, and a motorized platform which conveys the casket slowly down an aisle between mourners to the cemetery (Thornton, *Fortune*, March 8, 1993).

In China, as in many other countries, the dead body is rarely embalmed. Instead it is washed, dressed, and cosmetized, without embalming, all within a twenty-four hour period. A brief visitation period is held, followed by cremation or burial. The cemeteries around cities like Beijing are large, in order to handle large numbers of deaths, and some crematories are required to work overtime. The "funeral houses" also are large, surpassing the size of even Rose Hills, Forest Lawn, and other large American facilities. These state-operated funeral houses perform all the tasks of Chinese death care in facilities which combine the mortuary, cemetery, crematory, columbarium, floral sales, and administrative activities in the manner of privately operated combined facilities in the United States. The difference, of course, is that the Chinese counterparts of American combinations are operated under the Ministry of Civil Affairs, which oversees welfare, marriages, and death care, among other aspects of domestic activities in China (*The American Funeral Director*, November 1993).

Death care practices in Australia are similar to those in the United Kingdom, where the general practice is for cremation to be preceded by a funeral service and followed by permanent memorialization of the cremains. Since embalming is rare, refrigeration is commonly used to permit private viewing of the body preceding formal funeral services with the casketed body present.

In Israel the appropriate form of death care is prescribed by the Hebrew religion. Display of any kind is forbidden along with embalming and cremation. Earth burial is required, and the custom is to use a burial shroud or plain wooden box instead of a casket. In Mexico the government provides traditional funeral services to deceased citizens who cannot afford privately purchased death care. As a social phenomenon, however, there is a stigma associated with state-provided funerals, thus privately provided funerals are preferred by those who can afford them (Carlisle, *Wall Street Journal*, December 9, 1993).

This brief survey of the conditions under which death care is provided around the world serves to suggest that death care as desired and provided in many societies is an evolved response by the members of those societies to the event of death as they perceive it in light of the cultural, religious, and socioeconomic influences to which their tastes and choices are subject. All of these influences are recognized throughout this book. In the United States, they are clearly reflected in the organization and operation of the death care delivery system.

Death Care Businesses

As with businesses which produce other types of consumer products (both goods and services), death care providers promote their products in order to encourage consumers to buy them. The peculiar features of different types of death care goods and services may influence the business practices and marketing methods of firms which produce and sell them; but as businesses they are in no sense any less entitled to promote and to sell their particular goods and services than are any other profit-oriented businesses. At least that is the point of view of this book.

The general framework for the analyses within the book is provided by basic economic considerations which apply to the production and sale of distinctive types of goods and services under prevailing conditions. To prepare the way for consideration of the subject matter in later chapters, most readers should carefully read the first seven chapters in sequence. These chapters set the stage for an intensive examination of some aspects of the operations of death care providers in chapters 8, 9, and 10. It is in connection with some of this material, especially in Chapter 8, that the reader may encounter some difficulties with the character of the exposition and the clarity of the illustrations used. Readers not interested in the pricing process of mortuaries may be satisfied to skim the examination of this topic in Chapter 8. With the exception of the analysis in that chapter, most of the rest of the exposition of the book is in very general nontechnical terms and is based on personal observation of conditions and developments in the death care economy over a period of the last twenty years. During this period the industrial organization of the economy has been characterized by a consolidation phase driven by a few regional and international companies. The process and consequences of this consolidation will be a principal concern of our examination.

Of equal or greater concern will be the consequences of the combination phase in which different types of providers are brought together under one roof, so to speak. The case for such combined establishments is presented *in extenso* precisely because they are tangible manifestations of the unified view of death care presented here. This view is not limited to combined death care establishments which are physically integrated providers. It encompasses all of the establishments and firms engaged in producing any part or parts of death care goods and services. It is a theoretical view based on the observable behavior of consumers and providers of goods and services who participate in the economic sector we call "death care." As a concept, therefore, this view embraces all facilities participating in the death care process.

Demythologization

A necessary step in the direction of illuminating the death care process is to demythologize it by treating it as we treat other producing and consuming activities in the economy and society at large. There are signs noted by observers in the press that death is losing its status as a taboo subject. Perhaps. But as Dr. Nuland reminds us in his book devoted to how we die:

> Nowadays, the style is to hide death from view. In his classic exposition of the customs associated with dying, the French social historian Philippe Ariès calls this modern phenomenon the "Invisible Death." Dying is ugly and dirty, he points out, and we do not easily tolerate anymore what is ugly and dirty. Death is therefore to be secluded and to occur in sequestered places:
> "The hidden death in the hospital began very discreetly in the 1930's and 1940's and became widespread after 1950. ... Our senses can no longer tolerate the sights and smells that in the early nineteenth century were part of daily life, along with suffering and illness. The physiological effects have passed from daily life to the aseptic world of hygiene, medicine and morality. The perfect manifestation of this world is the hospital, with its cellular discipline.... Although it is not always admitted, the hospital has offered families a place where they can hide the unseemly invalid whom neither the world nor they can endure.... The hospital has become the place of solitary death."
> Eighty percent of American deaths now occur in the hospital. The figure has gradually risen since 1949, when it was 50 percent; in 1958, it reached 61 percent, and in 1977, it was 70 percent. The increase is not only because so many of the dying have needed the high level of acute care that can be provided only within the hospital's walls. The cultural symbolism of sequestering the dying is here as meaningful as the strictly clinical perspective of improved access to specialized facilities and personnel, and for most patients even more so [1994, pp. 254–55].

In response to the "sequestration" or "medicalization" of death, Dr. Nuland identifies his motive for providing vivid descriptions of dying in the following passage:

> I have written this book to demythologize the process of dying. My intention is not to depict it as a horror-filled sequence of painful and disgusting degradations, but to present it in its biological and clinical reality, as seen by those who are witness to it and felt by those who experience it. Only by a frank discussion of the very details of dying can we best deal with those aspects that frighten us the most. It is by knowing the truth and being prepared for it that we rid ourselves of that fear of the terra incognita of death that leads to self-deception and disillusions. There is a vast literature on death and dying. Virtually all of it is intended to help people cope with the emotional trauma involved in the process and its aftermath; the details of physical deterioration have for the most part not been much stressed. Only within the pages of professional journals are to be found descriptions of the actual processes by which various diseases drain us of vitality and take away our lives [p. xvii].

Death care is initiated by the completion of the process of dying which Dr. Nuland describes in compassionate but clinical terms. In fact, this book is a modest attempt to extend the "demythologization" of dying to the activities which follow in the wake of death. As Dr. Nuland said of dying, "Only by a frank discussion of the details of death care can we best deal with those aspects that frighten us." Like dying, death care is discussed in detail and without equivocation only in trade publications which are neither widely read nor commonly available. Yet, like dying, death care is a process through which we all must pass.

As we do, leaving the indignities and miseries of dying behind us, it is safe to assume that our corpse is blissfully unaware of whatever death care it receives. Our survivors may suffer grief related to our passing, but there is no factual basis for the view that the state of being dead is miserable for the corpse. On the contrary, death puts an end to the often laborious and degrading process of dying. Traditional death care practices involving restoration attempt to accentuate the state of rest and repose of the corpse. Yet a lifeless body moves most living observers nonetheless, owing perhaps to a shared propensity for human beings to sympathize with fellow members of their communities, even the dead ones. At least that is the explanation put forward by Adam Smith in this remarkable passage from his *Theory of Moral Sentiments*:

> We sympathize even with the dead, and overlooking what is of real importance in their situation, that awful futurity which awaits them, we are chiefly affected by those circumstances which strike our senses, but can have no influence upon their happiness. It is miserable, we think, to be deprived of the light of the sun; to be shut out from life and conversation; to be laid in the cold grave, a prey to corruption and the reptiles of the earth; to be no more thought of in this world, but to be obliterated, in a little time, from the affections, and almost from the memory, of their dearest friends and relations.... That our sympathy can afford them no consolation seems to be an addition to their calamity; and to think that all we can do is unavailing, and that, what alleviates all other distress, the regret, the love, and the lamentations of their friends, can yield no comfort to them, serves only to exasperate our sense of their misery [pp. 8–9].

Smith recognized, of course, that this view of the miserable corpse is based on an illusion. That is, it is entirely a product of the imagination of the living human mind as it contemplates the drastically diminished circumstances of the lifeless corpse confined in an open or closed casket and destined for the grave, the tomb or the crematory. Smith speculates that this powerful image lies behind a widespread human "dread of death" which has little or nothing to do with the actual state of being dead:

> The happiness of the dead, however, most assuredly is affected by none of these circumstances; nor is it the thought of these things which can ever disturb the profound security of their repose. The idea of that dreary and endless melancholy, which the fancy naturally ascribes to their condition, arises altogether from our joining to the change which has been produced upon them, our own consciousness of that change; from our putting ourselves in their situation, and from our lodging, if I may be allowed to say so, our own living souls in their inanimated bodies, and thence conceiving

what would be our emotions in this case. It is from this very illusion of the imagination, that the foresight of our own dissolution is so terrible to us, and that the idea of those circumstances, which undoubtedly can give us no pain when we are dead, makes us miserable while we are alive [p. 9].

According to Smith, this awful "dread of death" engenders a shared reverence for life that permeates the principles and institutions of enlightened societies. As a corollary, this theory appears to provide a highly plausible explanation for human concern with the care of the dead which is observed almost everywhere. If in our imaginations we feel a profound sympathy for the dead, as Smith suggests, we are loath to regard the corpse as human waste to be disposed of in callous if sanitary ways without marking the occasion and the place. In this respect, the fear of death on the part of the living members of a society may be said to underlie the "tender sympathies" with which it cares for its dead. These sympathetic feelings bring forth the efforts devoted to the care of the dead within virtually every society, regardless of wide differences in the cultures and economies of those societies.

In American society the prevalence of such sympathetic feelings toward the dead and the bereaved has shaped and sustained the death care industries as we know them. This book is an attempt to "demythologize" the ways in which death care is delivered to consumers by the operators of commercial enterprises in those industries.

2. The Isolation of Death Care

Ambivalence Toward Death Care Providers

We may begin by noting a certain ambivalence on the part of most of us toward the few who, like funeral directors, tend to the death care needs of us all. On the one hand, we regard them as practitioners of a trade we depend on at critical times in our lives. Although our needs for their goods and services fortunately are infrequent, we expect and even demand that they stand at the ready — literally around the clock — awaiting our call. We expect and even demand that they provide us with personal attention.

For all of these services, we reward them with our respect and trust, consistently ranking them in the top third of public opinion polls on the status of various professions. As customers of their establishments, we are also incredibly loyal, more so perhaps than to establishments in any other industry, a basic sign of our satisfaction with the quality and prices of the services they have rendered in the past. Funeral directors often point with justifiable pride to the loyal support they receive from generations of families in their communities — support which has allowed funeral homes to set enviable records of longevity as establishments and businesses.

On the other hand, there is evidence of a different sort to the effect that for various reasons — some of which may be of very complex psychological origins — the line of business in which funeral directors engage is not one with which the public is entirely comfortable. As discussed more fully in Chapter 5, sociologists have described it as "stigmatized" (or have more often used their technical term "polluted"). Clearly, it is not a calling to which many people are drawn who are not born into it. In the eyes of the public, it is probably true that there is something "unclean and distasteful" about the job (Gordon and Lee, 1972, p. 105).

Affected by a certain revulsion toward the work which funeral directors do, most of us can easily appreciate caricatures of them. The classic illustration of this is the portrayal of Mr. Joyboy, the quintessential embalmer in Evelyn Waugh's *The Loved One*, but it is hard to recall an occasion when a funeral director is portrayed as anything other than a caricature. None comes to mind. Observe the satanic looking version of Digger O'Dell, your friendly undertaker,

Caricature of a funeral director. A funeral director is depicted as a satanic figure hawking his wares in this illustration which appeared in an article entitled "Ten Things Your Funeral Director Won't Tell You" in the May 1994 issue of *Smart Money*, a monthly magazine published by Dow-Jones & Co. and the Hearst Corp.

in the sketch above which illustrated a *Smart Money* article entitled "Ten Things Your Undertaker Won't Tell You" (Assail, May 1994). There is a side of us that likes — or needs — to laugh at those who undertake the tasks we do not want to handle, and it is probably easy for many of us to agree with scathing criticism of "the American way of death" by social commentators like Mitford. It is likely that many approve the attempts made in the press and on TV to blow up the occasional indiscretion of a single funeral director into a blanket indictment of everyone who has ever attended mortuary college.

An Isolated Sector of the Economy

This mixed reaction of the public has contributed to a split personality on the part of many funeral directors. To reinforce positive public attitudes and counteract negative ones, they typically have striven to become active participants if not leaders in their communities. They are often active in their churches, in social clubs, in civic pursuits, and sometimes in local politics. Nevertheless, even in such community environments they have generally acquiesced to the common view that theirs is unlike any other business whose owners and managers are at liberty to discuss what they do and how successful they are at it. It would hardly sit well at a party to hear the local funeral director express satisfaction that so many customers are dying to get through his doors, take pride in the masterful use of his skills as a restorative artist in a particularly difficult case, or even complain about a hard day's work dealing with the unreasonable demands of hordes of grief-stricken survivors. It is clear that the freedom to discuss their work is largely denied to funeral directors and other death care providers, the effect of which has been to isolate them from the rest of the business world.

As an indication of the latter effect, it is noted that funeral homes and cemeteries serve as one of the few remaining examples in the U.S. economy of a sector populated predominantly by small, family-owned and -operated businesses. Even the few very large investor-owned firms in the death care sector are the creations of men who are second- or third-generation funeral directors or cemeterians. And, in spite of the success of their firms, they have not achieved the status of straightforward entrepreneurs in mainstream businesses. They too have tended to be caricatured as mass merchants of death, to which image their defensive behavior may sometimes have contributed. Thus, in an interview with *Fortune*, Robert Waltrip, chairman of the largest such firm, is described as "making a decorous effort to control his glee" over the growth in the population of the number of those more than 75 years old. This group is expected to increase by 26 percent in the decade of the 1990s, filling "God's waiting room," so to speak. In anticipation of this increase, Waltrip is quoted as saying: "When the death rate starts increasing, we don't have to do anything but be a recipient of the windfall" (Jacob, November 16, 1993).

In *Business Week*, Waltrip sums up his firm's difficulties in promoting its services thus: "We can't very well run an ad that says, 'Big Sale'" (Davis, August 25, 1986). As if testifying to this, the title of a lead article on the front page of the Sunday business section of the *New York Times* above a large picture of Waltrip exclaims: "This Man Wants to Bury You" (Myerson, August 1, 1993). Encouraged by such treatments in the business press, the popular impression remains that what death care firms do is different. The very large firms simply do more of it. Basically, then, their development has done little to reduce the walls that separate funeral directors from other more usual businesspeople in the public perception.

Effectively isolated as businessmen, funeral directors have tended to form various associations for their own kind, with whom they can frankly discuss the technical side of their trade. Like many such groups, they have sought to protect their turf and to defend it against the criticism of outsiders, especially the critics of American death care practices. Usually they have responded to such criticism, but their defenses have rarely matched the attacks of their critics. As a result of such criticism, consumers have been at times moved to question their own preference for traditional funerals and to experiment with less expensive alternatives. Following occasional investigations, government agencies have sometimes regulated death care providers in various ways, such as by federal regulation of the marketing practices of funeral directors.

Cemeterians, a less stigmatized class of death care providers, have so far avoided federal regulation, but some of them have coveted the exclusive franchises that funeral directors control in their common areas. Few in other businesses have been inclined to enter into competition with established funeral directors, but as fellow death care providers, cemeterians have been so inclined. Pursuing opportunities to extend their scope, some cemeterians have breached the wall of protection erected by funeral directors to bar entry to them and others. Some have become direct competitors by acquiring funeral homes near, or adding mortuaries to, their properties and taking business away from rival funeral homes. One large death care company has made a strategy of acquiring cemeteries and building funeral homes in them, shaking up the local markets for funeral services in the process.

But the threat to the status quo anywhere is not only from cemeterians. Some funeral directors themselves have disturbed the status quo in their local markets by striking bargains with memorial societies which act as consumer cooperatives, negotiating reduced prices for the limited demands their members have of funeral homes, usually in connection with cremation. A few funeral homes have even entered directly into the business of operating facilities designed specifically for the purpose of providing memorial services rather than traditional funerals. Further, there are "storefront" operators who specialize in graveside services and compete with their traditional counterparts by advertising messages such as: "Why pay $1,000 to $2,000 more for a funeral home with a chapel if the funeral doesn't have to be held at a chapel" (Levine and Lubove, *Forbes*, May 11, 1992). Others have become "aggressive cremators."

Still other funeral directors have not been satisfied with their roles as stigmatized small business owners. Some of them have set out to form local, regional, and national chains consisting of multiple units. A few of these have become public companies, breaking with the tradition of holding to private, family-run establishments. As publicly owned firms subject to the securities laws, the finances of these companies have become public information, providing a glimpse behind the veil of mystery which private ownership permits. This glimpse has revealed uniformly high profit margins and high management compensation at each of the public firms. Without in any way implying that these are undeserved, it must be suggested that this fact may eventually provide additional ammunition for critics of the death care sector.

Beyond forming chains of funeral homes, some of the regional companies and all of the national ones have expanded into the operation of cemeteries, joining these two traditionally separately owned and operated businesses under common ownership and management. Backed by the greater resources of the national firms, their units have retained the appearance of local, family-run establishments, but behind the scenes their operations have been altered to increase efficiency and compete more effectively in their markets. In their quest for expansion, primarily achieved through acquisitions financed by their ready access to the capital market, these firms have steadily increased their share of the U.S. market in recent years, and they seem likely to continue to do so in the years ahead.

All of these developments have begun to alter the traditions and conditions governing the ways in which death care has been provided to American consumers since the existing delivery system evolved during the nineteenth century. This is rending the veil of mystery behind which small family-owned establishments were able to operate without much scrutiny. The growth of publicly owned firms has created new and continual interest on the part of the investing public and financial analysts. These developments are forcing the death care economy out of isolation.

A Neglected Economic Sector

There is no doubt about the economic and social significance of the operations of establishments engaged in providing consumers with death care goods and services. In keeping with prevailing laws and customs, most of these products fall into one of three groups according to the three distinct components of the "death care process." These, again, are (1) mortuary services, (2) final (including pre-final) disposition, and (3) memorialization.

Each of these groups of death care products has traditionally been provided by separate types of establishments corresponding to the three components mentioned above — funeral homes or mortuaries, crematories and cemeteries, and marble shops and memorial dealerships. Historically, the scope of such establishments has been limited because they have been owned and operated by differentiated practitioners of the trade serving in each establishment — funeral directors or undertakers, cemeterians, and stone cutters or monument dealers. The scale of operations for these establishments has likewise been limited to the communities in which their physical facilities are located. This has led to a proliferation of the number of establishments of each type. According to eclectic estimates, there are more than 22,000 funeral homes, 7,500 commercial cemeteries, 1,000 crematories, and countless monument dealerships in this country. For the most part, these are small owner-operated establishments that employ technologies little changed over the years (e.g., embalming, grave-digging, cremation, and stone-cutting). The business practices of many are varied and unsophisticated, and reliable data relating to their prices, costs, and profits are unavailable.

For all these reasons, compounded by a number of features peculiar to death care providers, the death care economy has attracted little rigorous inquiry utilizing the concepts of economic analysis. There is no serious attempt on record to even elucidate the economics of cemeteries, and the last serious analysis of funeral costs was undertaken by Gebhart in the 1920s. A rigorous study by Knapp of the economies of scale in publicly operated crematories was published in Britain in 1985. In this country, however, the few modern studies of death care providers have been very limited in scope and conducted mostly by associations of different kinds of death care providers and consultants to those associations.

To be sure, some of the business practices of death care providers — especially of funeral homes, but also of cemeteries and crematories — have been the topic of journalistic exposés of alleged widespread abuses by practitioners. These have ranged from wholesale indictments of "the American way of death" to reports of occasional indiscretions of isolated funeral directors. Such indiscretions usually fall within the jurisdiction of the regulatory apparatuses of each state. Funeral homes in particular were the subject of a congressional investigation in 1964 (following the publication of *The American Way of Death* in 1963), and during the 1970s they were the subject of a lengthy investigation by the Federal Trade Commission which led to the promulgation of a federal trade rule applicable to them. Following an FTC review concluded in 1993, the rule was extended.

Most of the material accumulated during the FTC's original investigation and subsequent review, as well as material available from trade sources, has been examined in order to utilize it wherever possible in the present analysis. Nevertheless, much of it is so anecdotal or so lacking in rigor that even though it makes useful points, it can hardly be considered a proper contribution to a well-formed view of death care providers in general, or even of funeral homes as providers of one component of death care.

Reasons for Neglect

It is true that death itself has become a popular subject of books and articles in recent years. Some have attributed this to the aging of the American population, which is said to have raised the interest of readers in death as an approaching event. In addition to a general fascination with what follows the end of life, there is also a desire on the part of an aging population to prepare for the disruptive experience of losing older relatives and friends. These same factors would seem to operate to increase interest in the death care process. But none of the recently published books are concerned with the consumption and production of death care goods and services. Judging from their titles, they are mostly devoted to dying and grieving. The same is true of a recently announced "Project on Death in America" to be undertaken by the Open Society Institute. In a description of the project by the Institute, it is clear that what is to be studied is not death itself or its immediate aftermath during which death care is provided. The Project on Death in America is focused on "understanding and transforming the culture and experience of dying and bereavement in the United States" (program announcement, 1994). Yet the death care process is entirely neglected in spite of its importance immediately following a death and its impact on bereavement for better or worse. Such neglect is not uncharacteristic of the attitudes of health care practitioners and others whose tendency has been to avoid the subject of death care practices for the most part.

This may be explained in part in terms of the lengths of the intervals involved in activities surrounding death. Often the event itself is preceded by a long interval of dying, and for survivors it is followed by an extended interval of grieving. By comparison with these lengthy processes, death care is compressed into a relatively short period of time immediately following death. For many people this brief interval is programmed with activities prescribed by custom and religion which are "directed" by the funeral home selected. As a short, highly structured sequence of events through which people are guided by the funeral director, death care is not a process to which people ordinarily devote much attention as a matter for contemplation in itself. In this respect, death care is different from dying and grieving, which themselves are seen as processes with which people feel the need to know how to cope individually.

Death and dying are events which characteristically produce emotional strife and inspire aesthetic expression as well as philosophical, theological, and teleological rumination. Providing death care goods and services is a pragmatic response to the event of death, which may be likened to the performance of the housekeeping function in that it is necessary even if uninspiring because it keeps our world orderly and more habitable. The technical features of these activities are studied by would-be practitioners in vocational schools where funeral directors acquire the tools of their trade. Such tools are rarely acquired or even fully understood and appreciated by outsiders.

Nevertheless, the operations of death care firms also need to be understood by those concerned with them as interested observers — financial analysts, regulators, and others. For many types of firms, this understanding is acquired in the study of economics and various business subjects taught in colleges and universities. These subjects treat of a variety of different types of firms and the industries associated with them, but firms engaged in the delivery of death care are rarely if ever mentioned in mainstream books used in courses dealing with business and economics. In *The Competitive Advantage of Nations* (1990), for example, Michael Porter provides an extensive analysis of industries, including the "service industries." In addition to many major industries, he mentions the "cut flower industry," the "embroidery machine industry," the "thread industry," and even the "wig industry." His only mention of even one of the death care industries, however, is in the following sentence: "Large multi-unit service firms have emerged in fields as disparate as laundry and dry cleaning, hotels, hospital management, and mortuaries" (p. 245). Furthermore, in his investigation of processes affecting industries and firms, he neglects to cite any elements of the process of integration occurring in the death care industries, which constitutes an exception to the rule emerging from his analysis — the tendency toward "de-integration" in the service industries.

A wider examination of textbook treatments of death care firms and industries will illustrate further the general neglect to which they have been subject.

Textbook Treatments of Death Care

In spite of the extent to which the economic aspects of death care providers have been neglected, the commercial enterprises which they operate comprise a part of the private sector of the economy. Like the firms in other sectors, their outputs contribute to the gross domestic product, national income, nonfarm employment, and the cost of living (or dying, in their case). As private businesses, their operations have to be financed and managed in appropriate ways if they are to perform their economic function effectively and efficiently.

For this reason the operations of most types of business which comprise a sector of the economy are the subject of study by economists, financial analysts, and management specialists, among other "professionals." Yet there have been few, if any, attempts to study the financial and economic aspects of the operations of death care providers by members of these groups. Likewise they are not mentioned in numerous books advising people on how to start, manage, and finance small businesses, in spite of the fact that most funeral homes, commercial cemeteries, and memorial dealerships are small businesses existing in great number. There is a general lack of attention to facts about the sector of the economy to which death care firms and industries belong, about the trends within that sector, and about the effects of those trends on the welfare of consumers. One looks in vain for any reference to the business of funeral homes or cemeteries in any book on economics, finance, or management. It is as if those businesses did not exist, or that if they did, their operations would defy economic analysis or the principles of management and finance would not apply to them.

Perhaps the authors of college textbooks feel it would be inappropriate or insensitive to call attention to funeral homes or cemeteries as businesses in their discussions of supply and demand, stocks and bonds, managerial economics, marketing, and so on. Death is a business, but it is an unpleasant one. Textbook authors may feel that it would not be appropriate to talk about funeral homes and cemeteries as if they were merely another example of commercial businesses subject to the same unemotional examination as, say, fast-food restaurants or amusement parks.

There are, of course, mortuary colleges which train funeral directors and embalmers. But mortuary colleges are devoted primarily to imparting technical and interpersonal skills. It is unlikely that they are capable of preparing the professional managements required by the large death care firms. On the other hand, it is unlikely that managers recruited by such firms from other colleges or business schools will have learned anything about the operations of death care providers. Nor will they find any reference to the sales and marketing of death care goods and services in specialized books on such subjects as "niche-manship" and "relationship marketing," both of which funeral homes pioneered, or on direct marketing, at which cemeteries have excelled, or on marketing to the aging, who are prime candidates for death care. None of the popular books on these topics deal with their application to the field of death care.

As a regulated sector of the economy, it would seem that the operations of funeral homes and cemeteries would at least be discussed in textbooks about industrial organization and the social control of business. But none of the latest texts even mention the existence of such firms. Here is the full extent of the reference to cemeteries in one of the older texts, which appear under the heading of "Urban Enterprises," referring to municipal services: "These units range from subways and water systems to zoos, parks, and libraries. Many of them are quite necessary and utilitarian — and as dull as only sewage, garbage disposal, and cemeteries can seem" (Shepherd and Wilcox, 1979, p. 459). Even if inadvertent, comments such as this in a textbook are unfortunate; as intentional remarks, they are a slur on the efforts of the men and women who toil in the maligned fields to serve the needs of us all, including those who make such comments.

Consumer Economics

It is more difficult for textbooks of consumer economics to dismiss the existence of funeral homes and cemeteries. The authors of most of these, evidently influenced by the feeling that something has to be said about consumer expenditures on death care, usually offer a few tables of outdated statistics on spending on funerals and some basic generalities on the difficulties faced by consumers when dealing with funeral directors. They then quickly move on to more appealing goods and services on which consumers spend. A notable exception to this general tendency is provided by several editions of a textbook entitled *Economics for Consumers* by Leland A. Gordon and Stewart M. Lee (1972). In a lengthy chapter devoted to "Ceremonial Custom-Made Wants," Gordon and Lee present a lengthy introduction to the full range of death care goods and services provided by funeral homes, cemeteries, and monument dealers. Their presentation is informed by a variety of sources balanced between death care providers and their critics. Among their observations are the following:

> Ceremonies are elaborate ways of satisfying important emotional needs. The primary events in life are birth, coming of age, marriage and death.... All ceremonial events could be ignored. But life would be drab and dull without them.... What lies beyond death? No one knows. Because no one knows, death instills awe, fear, and superstition, or hope, according to the individual.... When a person dies it is the responsibility of the family to arrange for burial. At such a moment many people discover that they have no real freedom of choice. The method of disposing of the body is prescribed by one's religion, by one's lodge, and by one's community.... A funeral is a ceremony which disposes of the body of the deceased, helps the survivors adjust, and publicly acknowledges and commemorates the death. At the same time it demonstrates the viability of the group.... Death is a rite of passage, not only for the deceased, but for the survivors also. All — the living and the dead — assume new roles, and funeral ceremonies are affected by this fact.... Funerals help keep the community intact [pp. 101–4].

On the role of the funeral director in this process, the comments of Gordon and Lee seem overly dramatic but reasonably descriptive:

> The funeral director has been described as a ceremonial producer who stages a performance, sees that the participants play their parts, that properties are provided, and that all the arrangements are made. He is a private enterpriser willing to do the unclean and distasteful job of preparing dead bodies for burial. As an embalmer he closes the staring eyes, the gaping mouth, and reinforces the dead muscles. As a cosmetician he performs the last toilette. All of these services are rendered to soften the revulsion felt by the survivors. And for these services he collects his price [p. 105].

Unfortunately, some of their observations border on popular cliches:

> Psychiatry has partially displaced religion in the funeral service. Except for reading the Scripture and the eulogy, which is the responsibility of the clergy, the modern-day funeral director is prepared to assume all activities associated with death. He finds himself in a dilemma. Survivors who have no theology to sustain them encourage him to disguise the reality of death. At the same time as a businessman he is impelled to call attention to his special service. "Thus he both blunts and sharpens the reality of death." The bluntness stresses death, the made-up corpse in the slumber room denies the reality of death. In rejecting the reality of death modern society embraces all the accouterments of the burial service and the grave, including artificial grass.... Funeral directors have succeeded in conditioning the minds of people to associate established funeral customs with all that is desirable in "the American way of life." The industry promotes the belief that a funeral service is a status symbol. So instead of reducing prices the industry has succeeded in raising prices high enough to permit all firms in the industry to continue [pp. 103, 109].

As might be expected in a text addressed to consumers, an obligatory section entitled "The Sordid Side of the Burial Business" enumerates a litany of practices about which consumers should be aware, such as "false and misleading price claims, deceptive selling, fictitious pricing, false invoicing, substituting inferior products, and tie-in purchases," payoffs to members of the clergy and nursing home operators for referrals, the use of casket selection rooms equipped with two-way mirrors and wired for sound "so that the salesman can hear what prospective buyers are saying," and other questionable practices (pp. 110–11).

To be fair, however, Gordon and Lee point out that "in all businesses and professions there are marginal operators whose practices are a discredit to the honest and conscientious firms and practitioners" (p. 110). On the whole, their presentation throughout many editions of the book represented a thorough introduction of the subject to consumers. To a large extent, it seems likely that this was due to an idiosyncratic interest in the subject on the part of Prof. Gordon, and with his passing later editions under new authorship provide less coverage of the topic.

Grievous Ceremony and Symbolism

One of the passages of Gordon and Lee which was quoted above emphasizes the admittedly ceremonial nature of funeral services. This is proper enough,
for the notion of a funeral includes that of rites or observances performed in
connection with the death of a person. Without some sort of ceremony, there
is no "funeral" as such. Of necessity there is a measure of death care involved
in removing a body from the place of death and disposing of it in some fashion, but it hardly makes sense to describe the performance of these tasks as "a
funeral."

The funeral is a social event involving a ceremony of a very special kind,
however simple or complex. As a social event marking a rite of passage, it is a
ceremony like a wedding or a christening, but it is absolutely different from these
in one all-important respect: it is characterized by grief rather than joy. Unlike
joyful ceremonies, which are called celebrations, funerals are grievous ceremonies most often fraught with symbolism of the saddest human kind, of loss,
separation, and death. The funeral is symbolic of the end of the social relationship between the deceased and the survivors and friends.

As a symbolic event, the choice of a particular type of funeral is more emotional than rational or intellectual. The choice expresses personal attitudes based
on aesthetic tastes, customs, sentiments, feelings, morals, and even internal
compulsions about what is appropriate — or inappropriate — under the circumstances. The "sense of fitness" involved in the choice is evident in the symbolic
features of a state funeral for a president or former president, the protocol for
which includes lying in state, the service, the procession, the monument, and
other trappings. On a smaller scale, this sense is evident in military services
and those held for uniformed officers killed in the line of duty, an event which
underscores every person's vulnerability.

The latter point is made in a recent *New York Times* article entitled "Police
Funeral: Sorrowful Rite and Potent Symbol," which states: "And with its attendant rituals of thousands of blue uniforms closing ranks behind a fallen colleague
and elected officials letting no seat go unfilled, a police funeral ranks high
in the nation's iconography, as potent in symbolism and tradition as the fare-
wells for the nation's most revered heroes" (Roberts, March 20, 1994). For other
individuals the symbols are different in kind, but in all such arrangements there
is a symbolic statement that this is the way in which the deceased or the survivors chose to ceremonialize the death and to memorialize the life of a person.

As providers of the goods and services used in the enactment of symbolic
events and the symbolic processes of final disposition and memorialization, the
owners and operators of funeral homes and cemeteries necessarily lead symbolic
lives as people who care for and bury the dead. They hold out their establishments as symbolic places of trusted service and perpetual care. They are not
anonymous operators of ordinary businesses whose involvement with their customers is limited. As businesses to which families entrust the care of a cherished

person's body, temporarily or permanently, it is reasonable to say that funeral directors and cemeterians occupy positions of trust in their communities.

We are well aware, however, that not all business firms are to be trusted, at least not equally. It follows that the choice of a funeral home or a cemetery is often based on our experience with it, or the experience of those we know who recommend it, or the appearance that it is well-established in the community. All of the nonprice factors of this sort that enter into the choice of an establishment are encompassed in what is described as "reputation." As the basis on which consumers choose among alternative death care establishments, reputation is the chief means of competition among them. To attract and to retain the support of consumers, it is necessary for firms to build and to maintain their reputations as signs or symbols of their trustworthiness. The longevity and volume of certain facilities are such signs because it is reasonable for consumers to assume that firms which have persisted and those which attract a large number of customers are effective providers of goods and services. This creates a competitive advantage for those establishments over many small firms in a given area, so that there is a hierarchy of firms ranging from the leading "heritage" establishments to a variety of small ethnic funeral homes, local cemeteries, and monument dealerships.

Taken together on a local, state, or national level, these firms have tended to be identified with the status quo, that is, with traditional death care goods and services, particularly the traditional funeral service. Like other keepers of the status quo, of the religious, political, and business kind, death care providers have come to be seen as creators and promoters of the so-called "American way of death." As such, they have been condemned as "merchants of death" who profit handsomely from misery and grief. Their business methods are believed to exploit grief by promoting "denial" and the "beautification of death." This point of view has subjected funeral directors, even more than other death care providers, to intense criticism, further isolating them.

Social Criticism

In a previous section, reference was made to the discussion of "the sordid side of the funeral business" in a textbook of consumer economics. As a matter of consumer education, there is something to be said for describing the way in which death care providers deal with their customers, including the ways in which unscrupulous operators may attempt to take advantage of them. Discussions of that sort belong in books addressed to consumers and will contribute to more informed decisions on their part, thereby forcing providers to respond to a more informed market. Scrupulous providers have nothing to fear from informed consumers, and they themselves are the beneficiaries of attempts to identify and to criticize unscrupulous ones.

Quite a different kind of criticism is represented by the attacks of critics specifically against the scrupulous operators of a whole class of businesses. In most fields this phenomenon does not occur. No one has any reason to criticize the ethical members of an industry, but death care industries are different in more ways than one. In particular, their products are matters of varied customs and personal tastes. As a result, it is possible for critics to claim that consumers spend more on traditional funerals, burial or entombment, and memorials than the critic deems appropriate. Rather than attack consumers for spending on these things, the critic derides the businesses which sell them. This is shown in the following words in the foreword to Jessica Mitford's critical classic, *The American Way of Death* (1963):

> This would normally be the place to say (as critics of the American funeral trade invariably do), "I am not, of course, speaking of the vast majority of ethical undertakers." But the vast majority of ethical undertakers is precisely the subject of this book.... Scandals, although they frequently erupt (misuse by undertakers of the coroner's office to secure business, bribery of hospital personnel to "steer" cases, the illegal reuse of coffins, fraudulent double charges in welfare cases), are not typical of the trade as a whole, and therefore are not part of the subject matter of this book.

There can be no doubt about it, the object of Mitford's disdain is not "the sordid side of the burial business," described by Gordon and Lee. Her attack is directed toward the best side of the business — that is, at the successful efforts of death care providers to satisfy consumer demands. She elaborates, claiming that it is the providers rather than the consumers who are responsible for consumer demands: "Another point often made by critics of the modern American funeral is that, if there are excesses in funerary matters, the public is to blame. I am unwilling on the basis of present evidence to find the public guilty; this defendant has only recently begun to present his case."

Can a sector of the economy continue decade after decade to provide goods and services which its customers do not want, especially a sector which does not generally advertise its products extensively? We shall consider this question fully later, but it is sufficient to point out here that it has been more than thirty years since Mitford's book was published. Although it was well received by reviewers, it appears doubtful that her wholesale criticism, or that of subsequent critics, has had any significant impact on consumer demands and spending on death care goods and services.

Consumer spending on all sorts of goods and services has long been a favorite subject of crusading writers and journalists whose tastes differ from those of the consuming public. Rarely are their views of how consumers ought to spend taken seriously. Even Mitford admitted this about previous attacks on spending on funerals (p. 38). In her case, however, more influence than usual was exerted because she furnished a basis for extensive federal regulation of funeral service providers in the supposed interest of consumers. In this respect her influence continues to be felt in the death care economy in spite of the fact that she failed to present solid statistical and economic data to support her case against "the vast majority of ethical undertakers."

Consumer Education and Consumerism

It is noteworthy that, while making serious charges, the style of Mitford's treatment of her subject was that of a witty observer of an industry for which she appears to have bemused disdain. In the tradition of *The Loved One* (Waugh, 1948), her approach as a writer was to treat the subjects of death and death care as something so dull or so frightening, or both, that discussions of them must be laced with satire and humor to make them entertaining. The difference, of course, is that *The Loved One* was a work of satirical fiction in which humor has a place. In a nonfiction work on a serious subject like "the American way of death," humor seems misplaced, and there is always the possibility that a desire to entertain may interfere with the serious analysis of a subject. That is why the serious analysis of conditions in an industry is not ordinarily a subject of popular books. It is too tedious to be palatable to the popular taste. Serious treatments of any technical subject have a limited audience consisting mainly of those whose interest in the subject is so compelling they are willing to endure this tedium.

To entertain is not the purpose of this book. Here death is seen as a very serious matter, as are the ways in which people attempt to cope with its occurrence and the ways in which death care providers help them to do so. These are considered to be important social and economic phenomena in modern society, not objects of humor. They may be the subject of black humor which amuses us when we are far removed from the experience of death, but not when we are close to it. Death does not often touch us directly, but when it does it is a grievous affair fraught with distress, even if its horror is diminished by the dignity with which some endure it. Nevertheless, the macabre fascination with death, perhaps resulting from the denial of death and its dreadful aspects, has turned it into a popular genre of entertainment which appeals to large segments of the public, especially children. It is remarkable that horror stories and movies are a common part of our culture, whereas serious death education is not. An indication of this is the ease with which a course entitled "Death and Dying" is lumped together with one entitled "Witches, Werewolves, and Ouija Boards" in a list of "off-beat" college courses presented in the *Wall Street Journal* (Frank, October 5, 1994).

Many of us are introduced to death and funeral homes and cemeteries in the horror movies we see as children. It is unlikely that these first impressions are ever completely expunged by mature understandings of these subjects. This is unfortunate because normal death and its consequences are an inevitable part of real life — the very price of life, as it were. Like sex, death is a part of life, and like sex, it appears to be a subject about which misinformation and disinformation abound among children, if not among adults. It would seem, therefore, that if sex education has a place in school curriculums, then death education does also. But as yet there has been no general campaign in that direction. To their credit, it would seem, there have been some efforts by funeral directors to participate in programs of death education in schools and community organizations. Even these efforts have been attacked by some critics on the grounds that they are self-serving (Arvio, 1974, p. 65).

According to one critic, it is not consumer education that is needed, but consumerism: "Consumer educationists would argue: inform the consumer. Show him the score card. But, as everyone will readily admit, the impact of sorrow and pressure at the time of death is indeed great: one's education and training and consumer instincts tend to fall by the wayside. The answer for society is not here" (Arvio, 1974, p. 65).

On the contrary, it would seem that consumer education about the availability of pre-need planning and pre-funding of pre-arranged funerals are ideal ways to address concerns about "the impact of sorrow and pressure at the time of death." This point is not made by this particular critic. Instead he describes consumer education as a solution which puts "the burden on the consumer." His "consumerist" solution is "to refocus on caveat venditor, putting the responsibility on the shoulders of the seller," organizing consumers into local groups which negotiate with death care providers (Arvio, 1974, p. 65).

One wonders if this process always results in lower prices for the kinds of services many consumers want. Since not all consumers have experienced alleged abuses of the marketplace in their dealings with funeral directors, it is possible that consumers want to engage in pre-planning with the funeral home of their choice and arrange the funeral of their choice at the best possible price. In any case, the consumer alliance option is one that may not suit the needs and desires of every consumer.

Consumerism and Regulation

As it happened, the publication of *The American Way of Death* and *The High Cost of Dying*, both in 1963, focused the attention of the nascent consumerist movement on the death care sector of the economy. Based largely on concerns expressed by Rachel Carson about environmental pollution and by Ralph Nader about automobile safety, the movement spawned a variety of efforts on the part of government and independent organizations designed to protect so-called consumer rights, including the right to safety, to information, to choice, and to be heard during legislative and regulatory hearings involved in the formulation of governmental policy (see, for example, Aaker and Day, 1974, pp. xvii–xviii).

Once established, the thrust of this movement was to extend the sphere of commerce which was covered under specific legislative and regulatory initiatives. In the 1970s an investigation of the funeral industry was begun by the Federal Trade Commission which ended in 1982 with the promulgation of a federal trade rule applicable to funeral homes. Major provisions of the rule will be discussed later. The point to be made here is that under the rule the operation of funeral homes became subject to federal regulation on top of the regulation by state boards to which they had long been subject.

It would now be a fruitless exercise to revisit the arguments for and against such regulation which were aired during the investigation and hearings which preceded promulgation of the rule. Suffice it to say that funeral providers and their industry and its trade associations vigorously opposed the advent of additional regulation. In the process there is little doubt that a sense of isolation on the part of many in the industry was reinforced by the impact of the investigation and the hearings leading up to promulgation of the rule.

Consequences of Isolation and Neglect

The general neglect of the death care sector in the technical literature of economics, finance, and management has contributed to its isolation from other businesses and the rest of the economy. The treatment of death care providers and their industries by social critics and fiction writers has further isolated them as operators of businesses that are in some ways unusual and unlike the rest of the business world. While understandable perhaps, this isolation of death care providers has probably contributed to the rigidity and insecurity that some of them exhibit. It has cut them off from the vitality of new blood and new ideas. In a few cases, where the large companies have attracted management talent from outside the death care sector, these managers have sometimes been reluctant to associate themselves with the technical side of the business of those firms. More than once they have been heard to say something to the effect that "Here at headquarters we try not to think very much about death and grief; we're mainly concerned with the figures that look like those of any other business." The attitude revealed by such statements toward the technical side of death care is a dangerous sign in any company or industry. It may lead to conditions in which the "head" or "brains" of an organization is isolated from its "body." This is isolation within firms, within an isolated economic sector.

No such phenomenon has characterized death care establishments and firms whose owners are directly involved in the technical operations of their businesses, but those owner-operated firms are subject to other consequences of isolation. For example, the operations of companies under private owner-management are removed from any source of organized pressure to perform financially. Without this pressure, they may tend to drift along.

Although the ownership of businesses by investors is not an unmixed blessing, it does at least expose firms to outside scrutiny and pressures to perform financially. Investor-owned death care companies are subject to these pressures; they are obliged to provide a flow of data about their operating performance to the securities market. It is the function of securities analysts to interpret these data for investors, but few analysts specialize in the sector due to the small number of public death care companies and the unusual nature of the area in which they operate. Most of these analysts have been impressed by the general finan-cial results of the public companies, but it is possible that they have missed some finer points of their operations. Furthermore, analysts frequently focus on the short-term results and prospects of companies, so that their assessments do not always fully reflect differences in such long-term strategies as pre-need sell-ing and the development of combinations. Even extensive analyses with a long-term orientation have tended to concentrate on the funeral service side of death care, rather than on the sector as a whole and on the relationships among its parts.

One of the reasons for this focus is the difficulty of analyzing the sector as a whole because of its complexity, comprising as it does so many different types of establishments and firms. Many of these are privately owned and operated and are therefore not required to make public any data on their operating and financial performance. To obtain reliable data about the revenues and costs of such firms is a difficult task — one that has not been made much easier by the aggregate nature of the data made available by the few publicly owned firms. There is another reason, however, for the historical lack of interest in the death care sector. Until recently, the operations of funeral homes, cemeteries, and monument dealers did not constitute a dynamic economic sector which attracted much interest. The process of death care went on decade after decade without any substantive changes occurring within the sector. Consequently, it was largely ignored.

In recent decades, however, several forces at work within the sector have gained momentum, adding currents of vitality just below the surface of its placid exterior. One of these forces, dating from the 1960s, is the continued consoli-dation of small firms in the sector into regional and even national chains of funeral homes and cemeteries. Another force is the development of new facil-ities by cemeteries which have acted as agents of change in the death care econ-omy by offering more options to consumers, including community mausoleums, crematories, and even mortuaries. The availability of these options has affected consumer behavior, which in turn has had dynamic repercussions within the whole sector. As these forces have gained momentum, they have set in motion further forces which only now have begun to work themselves out in manifest changes in the operations of death care providers on one side and in the behav-ior of consumers on the other.

To clear the way for an examination of these and other developments in the death care economy generally, it will be the purpose of the next chapter to identify those factors which are unique, or at least distinctive, about the sec-tor.

3. *The Distinctiveness of Death Care*

Death Care Under Stress

As a rough estimate, it may be said that a death occurs about once in every fifteen years in the average family. The infrequency of the event and the emotional circumstances surrounding it are a source of stress for families at such times. Most of them have arranged a site for final disposition in advance of the event, and some of them have arranged for mortuary services, but most have not. As a consequence, they are forced to make arrangements for these required and desired services at the time of need and stress. These unique conditions have long attracted the attention of critics, who recently have provided the basis for greater regulation of the way in which funeral directors deal with their customers.

The effect of this criticism has been to subject funeral directors to the stress of regulatory burdens and costs in their dealings with customers. These costs must ultimately be borne by consumers, for whom the value of any benefits obtained from regulation is difficult to measure. Yet the effect of federal regulation has been to impose on the funeral homes an elaborate set of rules, involving substantial paperwork and bureaucratic oversight which are in some respects distinctive. Although there are other industries in which dealings with customers are regulated, the extent of the regulation of the business practices of funeral homes is unusual. This will concern us insofar as it affects the operation of funeral homes as death care providers. Of less or no concern to us are the effects of regulations to which death care providers are subjected, along with most other businesses and industries, such as the Truth in Lending Law, Occupational Safety and Health Administration regulations, the Fair Labor Standards Act, and others.

There are, in addition to the laws and regulations mentioned so far, a variety of state and local regulations which apply to the circumstances of death, the handling of dead bodies, their disposal and subsequent disinterment, and so on. These include the following forms required by local bureaus of vital statistics or health departments: death certificates, burial transit permits, cremation permits, and disinterment permits. These will not concern us; neither will the paperwork involved with applications to the Social Security Administration or the Veterans Administration in connection with death benefit payments, interment in national cemeteries, markers for veterans graves, and flags for their caskets (for such details, see *Mortuary Administration and Funeral Management*, 1991).

Nor will we be concerned with specific forms and records required or used by funeral homes in the performance of their technical functions, such as forms granting "permission to embalm," "authorizations to restore" when extensive work is involved, and billing forms, among others. All of these are dealt with at great length in technical textbooks addressed to practitioners and mortuary students. The significance of reciting the litany of forms required in connection with the operation of death care establishments is simply to convey the extent to which they are affected by the legal environment of business. In effect, they are operated under considerable legislative and regulatory stress. This is distinctive, but it is mostly beyond the scope of our concern.

Business and Technical Functions

By training and experience, death care providers learn to live with the stress of their occupations as those in other fields do. It is to be expected that an examination of the death care economy along the lines proposed here will find that it is a microcosm of the larger economic system of which it forms a part.

Like businesses in every sector of the economy, death care providers have to attract customers, serve them, and charge them prices which cover the providers' costs and yield a profit for their owners, whether proprietors or stockholders. The managers of death care firms have to hire workers with the appropriate qualifications, supervise them, and pay the wages and salaries which their occupations command in the marketplace. Death care firms must invest in facilities and equipment used in their business and purchase supplies for use and merchandise for resale. They must pay rent, utility bills, and interest on mortgages and borrowed funds and pay income and other taxes. They have to contend with the burdens of regulation and the effects of inflation. Here we will be far less concerned with all the features which death care firms have in common with other businesses than we will with their features peculiar to death care. Some of the latter features pertain to a general lack of knowledge about the products and services and methods of operation of death care firms.

As consumers, most of us are accustomed to dealing with various types of businesses which provide us with the various kinds of goods and services we need or desire. Our expectations of the goods and services we seek are standards for judging the adequacy of those we receive from the firms with which we deal. In some respects perhaps this is true of our dealings with death care providers. There may be some differences in the way we approach those dealings, but most of us are not unaware of how death care is arranged and delivered. We know, for example, that we order flowers from a florist and he delivers them to the funeral home. We select a memorial from a monument dealer, and he installs it and perhaps maintains it. We buy a lot or a plot or a mausoleum crypt from a cemetery, and when the time comes we are buried or entombed in it, after which it may be perpetually maintained in keeping with our wishes and our contract with the cemetery. We know that if we select cremation, the crematory will cremate the body and return the cremated remains to us, usually in a container of some sort for further disposition.

We know that there are usually several different funeral homes scattered throughout the neighborhoods in which we live. We attend funerals occasionally, and we arrange them infrequently. We know that the funeral director "directs" the funeral services, and we have some idea of what that entails. If we have ever arranged a funeral, we may recall some of the services the funeral home performed on our behalf. As set out in the promotional brochure of a typical full-service funeral home, its personnel provide the following services in connection with a traditional funeral:

1. Assist in making and coordinating all funeral arrangements and schedules.

2. Obtain vital statistics information necessary for filing the Death Certificate and securing the necessary burial permits. The funeral director will specifically need the deceased's exact date and place of birth, social security number, father's name, mother's maiden name, and the place of the birth of both parents.

3. Secure certified copies of the Death Certificate from the Bureau of Vital Records for insurance policies and for other purposes.

4. Place funeral notices in the local newspapers as well as in out of town newspapers in accordance with family wishes.

5. Help secure any burial allowances or benefits to which the deceased may be entitled through the Veterans Administration, or under the Social Security Act or Railroad Retirement Act.

6. Assist in completing life and burial insurance claims.

7. Contact the cemetery or crematory and assist in coordinating arrangements for cremation, interment or entombment.

8. Contact the clergyman or priest of the family's choice and coordinate the religious ceremony and arrangements with the clergy and the family.

9. Provide the technical staff, facilities and equipment necessary for preparation of the body for burial.

10. Assist in selection of a casket or burial container.

11. Arrange for the family's transportation by scheduling the appropriate and desired number of cars and limousines.

12. If the family requests, the funeral director will call the friends they have listed and ask them to be pallbearers.

13. Notify any fraternal order or organization of the death.

14. Handle all arrangements, and coordination of travel when it is necessary for burial to take place in another city.

Simply reading the above list provides some idea of the variety of tasks performed by a full-service funeral home. In addition to the paperwork performed in connection with many of those items, there appear to be three "core" tasks: (1) the handling and preparation of the remains, including the provision of a suitable container, (2) the provision of facilities in which ceremonialization occurs, and (3) the direction of the funeral service leading to final disposition. Reference in item #7 to coordination with the cemetery for burial, entombment, and with the crematory for cremation, suggests that mortuary activities are linked sequentially or coincidentally to final disposition and memorialization, which complete the death care process, but which are performed by other providers unless the funeral home is combined with or operated in conjunction with a cemetery, a memorial dealership, a flower shop, and so on.

Such a list is indicative of some of the various parts of the mortuary services provided by funeral homes, and most of the items it includes are distinctive elements of the tasks involved in the death care process. Most of them relate to the technical side of the business. For funeral homes, these include handling, preserving, restoring, and transporting the remains; conducting the funeral, if any; and arranging and overseeing whatever form of final disposition is involved. For cemeteries, crematories, and monument dealers, they include opening and closing the grave or tomb, the process of cremation, and stonecutting. Because few other firms may do these things, they are distinctive functions performed in the death care sector, but as technical matters they are of interest mainly to those who perform them.

We will be concerned mostly with the results of their performance, but it is necessary briefly to describe how consumer needs and desires give rise to demand for the services of death care providers. Any distinctiveness of the services they provide derives from these needs and desires, some of which involve the treatment of human remains, a matter of considerable concern on the part of consumers.

Significance of the Body

During life, the human body is universally revered as the physical persona and, by some, as the seat of the soul; after death, it quickly becomes a nuisance. Yet because of its previous association with life, it remains an object of reverence. It is the role of the funeral director to dispatch with the nuisance of the remains while providing the means for regarding the body as an object of reverence.

The desires leading to consumer demand for this service are not necessarily based on religious sentiments. They seem to reflect a distinctly human attitude toward the dead body, based in the emotions, which is widely observed. This attitude is manifested in different ways and degrees by the members of particular societies. In contemporary American society, the range of behavior extends from desires on the part of some for direct disposal, consistent with legal requirements, to desires on the part of others to have the body present for a certain period of time following death. For the latter, it is often a component of the funeral ceremonies performed by survivors in connection with death. Since some of these ceremonies involve a period of several days during which the body is present, the need to preserve the body arises, hence the practice of embalming. "If the body were not embalmed, the fetid remains would be so unpleasant as to be upsetting to those in attendance. In some countries where embalming is not commonplace, it is not unusual to obtain reports of nausea and other unpleasant reactions to the malodorous remains" (Blackwell 1971, p. 157). Not to mention the public health issues involved, for which the death care provider is responsible. Nevertheless, the practice of embalming has been criticized, and it is necessary to consider it further.

To Embalm or Not to Embalm

At earlier times in American society, the family of a person was frequently at hand when he or she died. This is true also today in some countries, but it is less true in the case of American deaths. The mobility of the population has separated families and created conditions under which family events such as funerals often require a period of time during which survivors may gather. If the body itself is to be shipped, then either it must be embalmed or a special container must be used for health reasons. The cost of the container usually exceeds the cost of embalming.

The primary role of embalming the body in cases which do not involve shipment is to afford a period during which visitation can occur with the body present prior to the funeral service and final disposition. A secondary role of embalming is to allow this process to extend over a period during which those who wish to attend the services can travel and arrange the necessary accommodations. Death is rarely, if ever, convenient, and those affected by it often require time to adjust to it and to arrange their schedules to allow them to participate in appropriate ways.

It is true that bodies may be kept refrigerated for as long as required to accommodate the attendance of survivors and the participation of the desired parties, including members of the clergy, in funeral services. But even refrigeration is not costless and the investment in and operation of body coolers contributes to mortuary costs. It is understandable, therefore, that American funeral directors have tended to be advocates of the practice of embalming.

Historians of death care attribute the origin of embalming in America to the Civil War, during which it was a necessary procedure if bodies were to be repatriated from distant battlefields (Sloane, 1991, p. 174). Critics of American death care are fond of pointing out that embalming is a distinctly American practice, unheard of in many other countries. Both of these concise observations are largely beside the point. Under modern conditions embalming is a useful procedure because it disinfects the body so that it may be handled or shipped safely. Embalming also retards decomposition of the body and "provides a normal degree of firmness and fullness" to the corpse (Hopke, vol. 4, 1990, p. 223). These effects are important for the purpose of allowing the restored body to be present for viewing during visitation and funeral services and for the purpose of allowing the necessary interval of time to elapse during which the attendance of survivors and the participation of desired parties may be arranged. Otherwise, embalming is not necessary, and under FTC rules it is against the law for funeral directors to represent that it is required. In fact, they must specifically obtain permission to embalm.

Even so, the great majority of American bodies are embalmed at death. This represents most of those that are not are the subject of immediate disposition, usually involving direct cremation. This appears to suggest that consumers are aware of the uses of embalming in the death care process and that the demand for it is derived from their desire to have the body present during visitation and funeral services or to allow final disposition to be delayed for various reasons. When embalming is used to preserve the body for viewing during funeral services, it does not interfere with cremation of the body. It does inhibit natural decomposition following burial, and the burial container(s) may further inhibit the process. As noted, these effects may be desired by many, but they also have been the subject of criticism by those who believe that the act of disposal is properly to facilitate rather than inhibit decomposition of the body.

Restoration

By itself, embalming merely preserves the body and disinfects it as an extension of the traditional washing of the corpse. Although complications may arise when autopsies have been performed previously, the embalming of unautopsied bodies is a simple post-mortem procedure. In an occupational manual, it is described in the following manner:

> The body is positioned in a comfortable-appearing manner, and an incision is made either at the base of the neck or in the groin to secure access to a major artery and vein. The tube in the artery is attached to a mechanical pump that introduces a preservative and disinfectant solution into the blood vascular system. Circulation of the chemical solution into the arterial network eventually forces the blood out of the drainage tube in the vein. The treatment is concluded by another procedure that removes gases and fluids from the trunk organs and introduces an additional disinfectant chemical into the area. The preparation of an autopsied body is much more complex, depending on the extent of the post-mortem examination and the skills of the pathologist [Hopke, vol. 2, 1990, p. 249].

In any case, additional steps must be taken to restore the appearance of the corpse when viewing is incorporated into funeral rites and observances. There is also a need or at least a desire for the body to be restored to a more acceptable ("life-like") appearance. This is understandable in view of the noticeable changes that occur in the body after death occurs and the vital functions cease. In short order the skin becomes discolored due to the cessation of circulation (livor mortis). The muscles become rigid as rigor mortis sets in. Liquefaction of the tissues and the bodily organs begins the process of putrefaction or decay. Embalming inhibits these natural processes and allows the body to be restored to a more attractive appearance.

In a meticulous description of the product of funeral homes, Blackwell (1971) explains the desire for restoration as follows:

> The art of restoration is considered to have psychological importance in the effect death has upon people who see the dead remains. Funeral directors and some psychologists report that a natural looking corpse tends to evoke stable emotions and remembrances of the pleasant experiences in the life of the deceased, whereas a gruesome or mangled corpse tends to evoke a memory picture of the pain and unpleasantness of death. It is reasoned that the mental health of the survivors is likely to be better if he can view a "slumbering" corpse rather than a deteriorated one. The reputation of a funeral firm may be partially based on its skill in restorative art [p. 161].

Once embalmed and restored, the corpse must be dressed and placed in a casket, the available types of which may vary widely in quality and cost. The funeral home customarily provides the casket, and it may also sell vaults and graveliners which may be desired by consumers or required by cemeteries to protect the casket — especially an expensive one. The sale of these products by funeral homes for use in funeral services involves them in the merchandising business, and it gives them a stake in the types of services and the quality of merchandise selected by consumers. In particular, they have been said to promote more elaborate funerals and to discourage direct disposal and "simple" services without the body present.

The prices and sales methods of cemeteries, crematories, and monument dealers have attracted less attention than those of funeral homes, but they also reflect the technical nature of the goods and services provided by such establishments. As elements of death care which follow in the train of the provision of mortuary services, the active involvement of the cemetery or crematory begins with the delivery of the body to such a facility.

The common forms of final disposition are not affected by the prior preparation of the body for its role in the funeral services provided by funeral homes, although there may be a degree of interrelatedness among some elements of consumer desires. For example, the desire for cremation may affect the choice of a casket, insofar as it is destined to be destroyed by the process. Generally speaking, unembalmed bodies contained in minimal ways may be cremated, interred, or entombed, subject only to the technical and legal requirements of crematories and cemeteries. Nevertheless, it is not unusual for survivors to desire to preserve the body after death and well beyond the time of the funeral. This leads some to select a form of final disposition which is expected to have some preservative effect, for example, entombment or earth burial in protective caskets and outer burial containers.

Memorial products used in connection with the form of final disposition selected do not contribute to the preservation of the body, but they may be said to preserve the memory of the deceased. The desires or urges of people to memorialize the dead, to preserve the memory of the deceased and even, in some cases, the actual body are distinctive factors that are at the heart of the technical functions performed by death care providers.

Dependence on the Random Event of Death

Beyond such technical factors, moreover, there are several things about the operations of death care providers that are different from the operations of other businesses with which most of us are more familiar and comfortable. One has to do with the nature of the demand for their services. Death is a unique event which ends the life of a person. For any individual, when and how death occurs is proverbially uncertain, but for populations of hundreds of thousands or millions of lives, mortality tables are capable of such accurate predictions that the number of deaths can be estimated with virtual certainty.

Mortality tables are based on the death rate of a given population at any time. The death rate is equal to the number of people who die annually divided by the number alive during the year. The rate varies with the demographic characteristics of the population, such as age and sex, and with the conditions under which those in different societies live. It varies over time with changes in those demographic characteristics and living conditions. In the United States, this rate has hovered in the neighborhood of 8.2 per 1,000 in recent years. For the population of the United States in 1995, the annual number of deaths is more than 2.2 million.

Each of these individuals who die annually requires some form of death care. At the very least the body has to be removed from the place of death to the site of final disposition. In addition to this minimal requirement, a number of death-related goods and services are customarily desired. Arrangements for these required or desired elements of death care may be made by the deceased in advance of death or by survivors in the event of death. In any case, they are delivered at death. For some, the event of death is a sad occasion, but for death care providers it is a business opportunity for which an establishment must be prepared at all times in spite of wide variations in daily, weekly, or monthly demand for its services. Jacob reports that even for a huge death care provider like Riverside Memorial Chapels in New York, which performs 2,400 funerals annually at four locations, the daily case load varies "from zero to 20" (*Fortune*, November 16, 1992). For the general run of small establishments, there may be days or even weeks between "calls," the largest number of which occur on average during the winter months. The revenues and profits of most death care providers are thus subject to some seasonal fluctuation.

Even the random event-related nature of the demand for death care is not distinctive in and of itself; it is similar to the demand for health care which results from illness and to the demand for various types of goods and services desired in connection with life events like births or weddings or bar mitzvahs. In the latter cases appropriate ceremonies are usually desired. These are analogous to the ceremonies customarily desired at death. Insofar as the ceremonies desired are not required, they are mostly luxuries, although the role they play in fulfilling custom and social conventions creates an element of necessity. This influences consumer expenditures on death care, making them less dependent on income, or even wealth, and more dependent on ethnic customs and religious beliefs than is common for most other goods and services. The extent of the influence of socioeconomic factors on the consumption of death care goods and services is distinctive and will concern us herein.

The Demand for Death Care

In economics the quantity of a good that consumers demand is presumed to be related to its price. At lower prices more of the good is demanded than at higher prices. The degree to which the demand for a good is responsive to a change in its price is called its price elasticity of demand. The demand for some goods is highly elastic or dependent on their prices; the demand for others is relatively inelastic. The demand for death care is one of the latter. People do not buy fewer funerals because their prices rise; nor do they buy more if prices fall. Ordinarily only one is desired, and one is enough.

Although the demand for the mortuary services and final disposition components of death care, is relatively inelastic, the demand for memorialization products, because they are not absolutely essential at death, is somewhat more elastic. This is demonstrated by their historical sales patterns (Sloane, 1991, p. 203), yet some form of memorial is commonly desired by consumers to complete the death care process. Reinforced by the sales methods of cemeteries, the complementary nature of a memorial makes the demand for such products relatively inelastic when the forms of final disposition chosen by consumers lend themselves to it (e.g., burial).

The inelasticity of the demand for some products and services is not necessarily a sign that providers can charge any prices they please, however. Where consumers who require those goods and services have a choice among different providers, as they usually do, competition for customers causes prices to approach the cost of production, including an allowance for some profit. This is a feature of the markets for death care in which providers compete on the basis of prices charged for its components, as in local markets for final disposition and memorialization, but it is less frequently observed in markets for mortuary services.

For various reasons, funeral homes that provide such services do not often engage in price competition, and consumers do not usually choose among funeral homes on the basis of their prices. Other factors strongly influence their choice of an establishment. Once they have chosen a funeral home on the basis of other factors, it may seem that they are at the mercy of that provider who is free to overcharge for his services. This situation is similar to the position of consumers who selects a doctor or a lawyer on the basis of his general reputation or recommendations from others. Having selected a provider in which they have confidence, they then pay whatever rates they are charged. The freedom to decline the services offered at those rates exists in various degrees in these cases, as with funeral homes, but switching firms is often inhibited.

A distinctive feature of funeral homes which differentiates their position vis-à-vis consumers is their universal practice of offering consumers a line of related products and related services which substantially affects their pricing behavior. This is not entirely distinctive, of course. It is also observed in other types of firms like automobile dealerships which offer a line of different models of one or more types of automobiles. Consumers may choose among various alternatives which differ widely in price and quality. This is characteristic of the operations of most types of death care providers, each of which offers a broad line of caskets, final disposition, and memorial products to consumers. Given the opportunity of consumers to choose among alternatives, it is obvious that the prices of death care products are not determined unilaterally by their providers but by the interaction of buyers and sellers in death care markets. The intricacies of this process are distinctive and will be the subject of later chapters.

Another distinctive feature of the sale and delivery of death care goods and services is that they involve a subject and event about which people often have strong feelings. They may dread their own death or that of others so much that it is uncomfortable or even impossible for them to talk about such matters rationally in connection with the purchase of death care goods and services. They may be emotionally distressed or even overwhelmed with grief during the sale or delivery of the merchandise and services of a funeral home. It is customary for people affected by the occurrence of a death to take comfort in the company of family and friends with whom they may seek solace in ways which reflect the cultural traditions and religious sentiments they share.

Required as they are to deal with people affected with such feelings and desires, the operators of funeral homes and their personnel must perhaps depend more heavily than those in other businesses on some knowledge of the kind provided by psychology, sociology, religion, and other fields which inform their sale and delivery of funeral services.

As with funeral directors and embalmers, most professional groups and skilled tradesmen are subject to licensing requirements, and there may be other legal limitations to which their practices are subjected as there are with funeral homes and cemeteries. Thus, in some jurisdictions the establishment of hospitals and other facilities require "certificates of need," which are also required for the establishment of new funeral homes and cemeteries in some cases. Cemeteries, in particular, are subject to zoning and other land-use requirements of the law that affect other businesses. These, then, are not highly distinctive features of their establishment and operation which will be our primary concern.

It is their association with death and the disposition of human remains which primarily distinguishes funeral homes and cemeteries from many other businesses. Stripped of these, a cemetery is essentially a real estate development operation *cum* sales organization *cum* property maintenance system. In this respect it is not unlike other real estate development businesses or amusement park development companies or golf and country club operations. The distinctive feature is, however, the use of its property for the perpetual interment of human remains.

Associations with Death and Dying

All of the distinctive features of death care providers seem to relate to the association of their products and services with death. As a corollary, the facilities at which such goods and services are provided also are associated with death in the eyes of the public. Consider, for example, the place of business of a typical funeral home. Whether operated in an urban, suburban, or rural area, there is little that is distinctive about its facilities except that it is a place where human remains are processed and visitation and funeral services are conducted.

The facilities of cemeteries and memorial parks are not unlike those of other businesses requiring large tracts of developed land, like golf courses, except that the land of a cemetery is used as the permanent "resting place" for human remains. Crematories are similar in many respects to facilities that incinerate wastes; their operations are distinctive in that their facilities are used to incinerate human remains.

Because of the associations of all such facilities with these distinctive functions, communities commonly authorize or restrict the locations and operations of death care providers. Concerns about public health and safety, employee qualifications, vehicular traffic and parking, neighborhood characteristics, or even superstition may properly play a role in the governmental processes by which communities regulate death care firms.

Of particular interest in connection with the nature and function of death care facilities is their relationship to those of health care providers. As a corollary of their concern with health, the practitioners of health care also oversee dying. When death occurs, it must be confirmed by a doctor. At one time this usually occurred at home, but now most deaths occur in hospitals, which are to that extent engaged in death care.

Without malicious intent it may be said that the input into the death care process may logically be described in terms of the "failure rate" of the health care process. The effectiveness of the health care process is therefore an inhibiting factor in relation to the death care production process. In spite of a close, interlocking relationship between the two processes, integration of them does not ordinarily occur, presumably because it would create conditions of extreme "moral hazard" in which the doctor or hospital would stand to benefit from their errors. Clearly, the public would not look favorably upon a hospital with a mortuary attached; even the morgue is usually hidden or disguised in hospital design. Such considerations provide an explanation, apart from tradition, for the existence of a separation between health care and death care facilities and occupations.

Without such an explanation based on moral hazard, it would be difficult to understand why the process of dying falls within the province of physicians and hospitals, while the actual death — the outcome of dying — does not. The training of doctors and the facilities of hospitals would appear to equip them to provide mortuary services as an extension of their existing production processes. Indeed, it is necessary for hospitals to include a morgue where dead bodies are kept and autopsies performed. These facilities may also be used to deliver some mortuary services, such as embalming. In general, however, it would be unacceptable for hospitals to dispose of human bodies in the manner of veterinary establishments. This limitation on the ability of health care providers to expand their production process establishes a need for the existence of an independent source of the goods and services of the mortuary services and final disposition industries which are provided by funeral homes, crematories, and cemeteries.

To resort to the kind of reasoning employed in the preceding paragraphs may seem unnecessary to some, but it is a proper part of the analysis of the relationship between industries. It provides an economic case based on moral hazard for a distinctive feature of death care industries which distinguishes them from other industries which have not been similarly protected. Because of their association with death, industries in the death care sector seem also to be protected from incursions by firms in industries unrelated to the health care field, such as unrelated conglomerates. Superficially the stability of death care firms — and to some extent also their earnings and growth prospects — would appear to be attractive to large firms which often seek to diversify their operations by investing in unrelated businesses and industries. An early case of this is illustrated by the operation of a chain of funeral homes by Kinney Services, which also operated parking lots and other businesses. It later sold its funeral operations to Service Corporation International, the death care firm here called "SCI." In general, the tendency has been for funeral homes and cemeteries to be owned by firms which are not affiliated with companies outside the death care sector.

Although this situation may change in the future, it appears to reflect a general perception of the uniqueness of death care which seems to inhibit the desire of many to be involved in it, at least publicly. Behind the scenes, many firms in various industries are associated with death care firms as suppliers of goods and services ranging from hearses to accounting and legal services, especially the latter. Furthermore, commercial banks and insurance companies have been closely associated with death care firms, and investment bankers have been eager to underwrite the frequent issues of securities by the national companies. Finally, institutional investors, as well as individuals, have been more than willing to hold their stocks in spite of, or rather because of, their association with death. Apparently there are no unsavory associations with the dividends and capital gains provided from investments in the death care sector. In these respects there is nothing distinctive about death care companies.

In terms of public perceptions, however, they are different. It is noteworthy, for example, that there are no companies in the death care sector which have names that include any reference to death or death care. Individual establishments often call themselves names that refer to "rest" or "park" or the families of their founders. The three largest firms in the sector are SCI, the Loewen Group, and Stewart Enterprises. It is true that these public companies which own both funeral homes and cemeteries have recently begun to refer to themselves in prospectuses and annual reports as "death care providers," but, significantly, there is no Death Care Industries or U.S. Deathcare, Inc.

Neither individual funeral directors and cemeterians nor their trade associations refer to themselves as death care providers or in any way that connotes death. Death still has unpleasant associations which, even in this age of enlightenment and liberation, must often be avoided by euphemism.

The reason for these euphemistic tendencies is unique and distinctive, but the tendency is not. It has characterized many occupations and firms as they have evolved through the years. It may be entertaining to poke fun at those in any line of business who play such euphemistic games, as some critics have done, but the practice does not reveal anything distinctive about the death care economy. What it seems to reveal on the part of the critics is a certain contempt for, or insensitivity to, public attitudes toward death. It is clear that these attitudes reflect a desire on the part of many people not to be confronted with death. If there is reason to be critical of this, then the critics might attempt to educate the members of the public who hold these attitudes. Perhaps they can encourage the public to accept death on blunt terms. Until they do, it is pointless to criticize death care practitioners for attempting to deal with consumers on terms which public attitudes and desires seem to demand. Consumers themselves are inclined to use euphemisms when death is involved. People do not "die"; they "pass on" or "expire." Military strategists plan in terms of "acceptable losses" rather than "mangled corpses." Even within the underworld, hired killers are known as "hit men" and people are "taken out." There is something about death which seems to require us to adjust our vocabulary to cope with the stark reality of it.

In dealing with death care consumers, it would be insensitive for funeral directors to ignore the desire of many to be spared confrontation with the harsh realities of death. For the same reason that doctors do not practice "in your face" health care by confronting their patients with the cruel realities of morbidity, funeral directors do not practice "in your face" death care by confronting their customers with the stark realities of mortality. Psychiatrists may confront their clients with death, but it is not the role of funeral directors to do so. The role of the latter as death care providers is to assist the survivors at a difficult time, not to assault them with gross references to the "corpse" or "cadaver." The use of a vocabulary of terms such as "the departed" or even "the loved one" has been adopted over time in an attempt to spare their customers unnecessary hardship. Criticism of death care practitioners for failing to force consumers to confront death starkly contrasts ironically with the criticism of health care practitioners for their failure to take the feelings of their patients and the families of their patients into account. The expectation that death care providers will be receptive to the wants of survivors and sympathetic is a distinctive feature of their roles, which is to provide the kind of death care their customers desire. To do otherwise would be offensive on their part, not to mention detrimental to their business.

More so than for any type of firm in any sector of the economy, the reputation of a funeral home depends on manifestations of receptivity and sensitivity to such special needs and desires of its customers as its stock-in-trade. The comfort of survivors is stressed in the education and training of funeral directors and other funeral home personnel. Even etiquette is still a topic for discussion in the classrooms of mortuary colleges. Where else are these attitudes inculcated as a vital part of the conduct of business today? There is something distinctive about the education and socialization of funeral directors, and these processes will receive their share of attention at a later point. So will the related question of whether the occupation of funeral directing is a skilled trade or a profession.

A Regulated Economy

In other countries, death care establishments are often owned and operated by the government at some level. In this country this is true of some municipal and national cemeteries, but many death care establishments here are privately owned and operated. At the federal level, their operations are subject to various laws which affect businesses generally, and some features of the operations of funeral homes are subject to regulation by the Federal Trade Commission. Insofar as the latter applies to funeral homes in particular, it is highly distinctive and will concern us.

This book, though, is not the place to examine critically the rationale for regulation of the type represented by the federal trade rule. Following its promulgation and subsequent review, the existence of the rule is a matter of fact to which funeral homes have been required to adapt their operations. Whatever the benefits of the rule, its costs are a burden for both large and small establishments, more so perhaps for the latter. Regulatory costs and risks of noncompliance are some of the factors which have encouraged many of them to affiliate with a regional or national firm, thus contributing to the consolidation movement within the death care economy.

In addition to federal regulation, the operations of funeral homes and cemeteries are subject to regulation by state boards composed of members of the regulated trade group (e.g., cemeterians or embalmers and funeral directors). Over the years this form of "self-regulation" by state boards has developed for a number of trades and professions over which the states otherwise exercise little or no control. The extent of the power of these boards varies from state to state, but a common exercise of their power is to establish licensing requirements for establishments and practitioners. Every state requires licenses for embalmers, and most of them require licenses for funeral directors as well. Such is the case for dozens of occupations which also are licensed. Clearly there is nothing unusual about this form of regulation which extends to several death care occupations. Nor is it unusual for state boards of most trades and professions to be dominated by representatives of the regulated field. Nevertheless, regulation of this sort is somewhat distinctive, and some of the effects of its influence within the death care economy will be noted.

Objections to Government Ownership

Apart from the regulation that now exists at the state and federal levels, it may appear feasible that government ownership and operation of death care facilities along the lines seen in other countries might be considered in the United States. While this might once have seemed unimaginable, so did a national health care program. At this stage in our history, government-provided death care is an issue, and actually it has been for some time. A decade before Mitford declared her war on funeral directors, a distinguished supporter of free enterprise, Professor W.A. Paton of the University of Michigan, expressed his frustration with government enterprises by suggesting tongue-in-cheek that government "tackle" the undertaking business:

> If it is desired to have further experimenting in government operation of business undertakings I have a candidate to suggest. Instead of setting up additional TVA's and other government utility enterprises let's give government a crack at the undertaking and cemetery business. Here's a field — burying people — that might conceivably be handled more economically by government monopoly than by private concerns. Of course this would probably introduce a considerable degree of standardization and drabness, but curbing the desire of relatives to squander money on lavish funerals for the deceased would hardly be an intolerable interference with personal liberty. And *since deceased people have no vote the danger that the enterprise would become primarily a vote-coddling device would be lessened.* By undertaking undertaking, moreover, government would be adding a nice touch in the direction of implementing the "security-from-cradle-to-grave" slogan. The state's traditional interest in births and deaths could also be used as an excuse for taking over in this area [Paton, 1952, p. 284].

Obviously the good professor was joking. Even the critics of death care providers recognize the lack of wisdom in such a proposal. To avoid any appearance of bias in the argument presented here against direct government involvement in the industry, we quote the argument of an industry critic:

Perhaps the answer is government ownership.... Proposals for government ownership and operation have to be considered in their context. Many people would oppose such a move because it denies the right of a person to enter a field and to make a profit in it. Others remind us of the overblown and inefficient bureaucracies that characterize much government operation today. Some would say that the government owned funeral business would not be able to pay for itself and thus consumers would be contributing to yet another welfare-state operation, in which the extra funds needed to operate the facilities (beyond consumer payment for their use) would need to come from our taxes. And still others would say that our government is traditionally designed to support private business operations and is not likely to take over a major industry in that way, particularly if it is succeeding.... Were the funeral parlors failing, and the practitioners flying to other work, that would be another matter. No, the answer is not here [Arvio, 1972, pp. 63, 65].

In another place the same critic points out that under government ownership and operation the consumer "would have only those choices prescribed him by government" (Arvio, p. 63). All told, this represents an effective argument against direct government involvement in the death care field.

The Mystique of Death Care

Obviously, there are many similarities and relationships between death care establishments and other business establishments of any kind. This book will attend to some of these similarities. Comparisons and contrasts will guide the subsequent analysis. This approach will afford an explanation for many unexamined aspects of the death care economy which are similar to those in other parts of the larger economy which are better understood. It is hoped that attention to similarities in the analysis will serve to eliminate some of the mystique surrounding the death care sector.

One of the sources of this mystique is undoubtedly the sanctity and solemnity with which the events of death, death care, and bereavement are treated by most people. Nevertheless, in a technical work such as this, a straightforward examination of the inner-workings of the death care economy, without emotional overtones, is what is required, for this is the procedure followed for all other profit-oriented industries.

Popular treatments of the subject have contributed to the mystique of death care by failing to treat it like other sectors of the economy. A case in point is Mitford's treatment of death care providers as operators of Disneylands for the dead. In the world she describes, the cemetery becomes "God's Little Million Dollar Acre" and Forest Lawn Memorial Park becomes "Shroudland." Whatever the motives behind such a treatment, its effect is to further isolate death care providers as businesses, removing them from the realm of reality in a world where people have long sought to preserve bodies, ceremonialize death, and commemorate and memorialize the dead. Merely to describe the ways in which these things are done today, or were done in the past, without relating them to the context of the needs and desires of the people who do them, is to trivialize the roles of those who help them to do so. Taken out of this real-world context, anecdotes about what funeral directors and cemeterians do may seem bizarre or absurd.

The humorous style of relating such anecdotes surely permitted Mitford to reach a wider audience than a serious treatment of her subject might have done, but it probably also contributed to the further cultivation of a mythical view of a death care culture in America that is somehow separate and apart from American culture as a whole. It is easy to believe that death care providers are somehow separate and apart from other types of businesses, but in fact this view is a myth. The business of providing death care has many features in common with other types of businesses engaged in delivering products and services to consumers for a profit. The ceremonial part of the death care process, for example, may be likened to the ceremonial events directed by convention managers in the hotel industry or by "special events directors" in many industries or by party planners of weddings, bar mitzvahs, and other ceremonial occasions. This parallel is clearly indicated in the title "funeral director," although "funeral director and producer" might be more apt for describing the role performed.

Some may object to making such a parallel because of the difference in mood and attitude characteristic of a ceremony involving death and grief, but it seems appropriate in the attempt to demystify the business to the point where it may be analyzed like any other. In defense of this procedure, one need only recall the point of transition at which the conception of cemeteries as businesses required that cemeterians adopt a view of themselves as "producers" of goods and services like producers in any other types of profit-oriented firm. Sloane (1991) describes the onset of this process in the 1940s:

> The cemetery business was changing. In 1944 a colleague reminded cemeterians that the burial of the dead was a business: "We are manufacturers. Instead of coke, slag, pig-iron, etc., we take ground, fertilizer, seed, shrubs, trees, flowers, water, stones, top dressing, etc. and with equipment and men we manufacture a 'product' known as a cemetery. Then we divide this product into individual lots — 'packages' — and there you have it" [p. 208].

With greater recognition of this view, came a more businesslike focus in the industry. As Sloane notes, "Labor relations, installment sales, even pre-need sales and legislation were new topics at state cemetery conventions in the 1940s" (p. 208). The operation of cemeteries had emerged from an earlier age into the modern era in which more of them were operated like other businesses to which they were analogous. Thus, in a similar way, we may liken funeral homes to art galleries, cemeteries to golf courses, crematories to incinerators, casket makers to furniture manufacturers, monument dealers to purveyors of garden ornaments, and so on. To some extent, such comparisons may help to demystify death care firms and raise the level of our understanding of them to that of other businesses we understand better. As a consequence we can ignore many unremarkable aspects of death care businesses and concentrate most of our attention on the distinctive aspects of the sector of the economy they comprise.

The first steps in this process appear to require an examination of the distinctive qualities of death care goods and services and the distinctive qualifications of those who provide them. The next part of this book is devoted to those two subjects.

PART II

There are not unfrequently substantial reasons underneath for customs that appear to us absurd.

Charlotte Brontë

4. *Death Care Goods and Services*

The Death Care Process

Allusion has been made to the death care process as a series of three sequentially linked components of care provided in connection with death: mortuary services, final disposition, and memorialization. For reasons which emerge in the course of this chapter, it is appropriate to think of the death care process as a complete product comprised of and assembled from these component parts, each of which may result from separate and distinct transactions between consumers and providers of death care. It would be ideal if an unequivocal descriptive term for each part were used by consumers and providers alike. But this has not occurred for several reasons.

One reason has to do with the variety of death care practices which coexist in American society. In most cases these practices involve some sort of ceremony or "funeral services," but not all do. To use the term "funeral" in descriptions of the providers of mortuary services generally is to fail to recognize the more extensive nature of the services provided by "funeral" homes and "funeral" directors. Nevertheless, we employ these commonly understood terms here as technical descriptions of providers of mortuary services products (goods and services). The terms "undertaking establishment" and "undertaker" were once used to describe the providers of such services, but their use has been discouraged by funeral directors. Thus, as explained in Chapter 1, the terms "funeral home" and "funeral director" are used here in spite of their inadequacy in a technical sense.

As a technically descriptive term, "mortuary services" avoids complications of this sort, but its use is not without its complications. In particular, it is open to the criticism that its reference to "services" does not adequately recognize the role of the sale of tangible products, such as caskets, garments, and other merchandise. "Mortuary goods and services" might be more fully descriptive, but it is cumbersome and unnecessary. Just as "food services" involves the sale of food, mortuary services may be understood to involve the sale of merchandise, either directly to consumers or via the production of the services delivered to them.

56

"Final disposition" also is open to some objections or problems. It obviously describes the stage in the death care process which disposes of the body in some acceptable final manner. Both burial and entombment are legally and actually the final disposition of the body. Cremation is legally considered to be a form of final disposition in most states (Sloane, 1991, p. 228), but it does not actually dispose of the cremated remains in a final manner. In actuality, cremation consists of a stage in the process of final disposition which reduces the bodily remains to a small corpus of cremated remains and then "cremains" that require further disposition, either final or nonfinal. Due to the manageability and portability of the cremains, the procedure adopted following cremation may be formal or informal. An example of the latter is the delivery of the container of cremains to survivors for their further disposition of the remains through scattering, placement in the home, or other courses of action allowed by law.

An example of formal procedure is the inurnment of the cremated remains for burial, entombment, or columbarium interment. Alternatively, the cremains may be formally scattered by designated personnel on cemetery grounds or other designated areas on land or at sea. Strictly speaking, this implies that cremation is an incomplete means of final disposition; it is in fact "pre-final" disposition, requiring a further step which may or may not involve memorialization. Cremation is thus a distinct part of the final disposition component of the death care process, not to be confused with final disposition as such.

As with mortuary services and final disposition, the memorialization component of death care poses some difficulties in the classification scheme adopted here. The difficulties arise from the attempt to separate and distinguish the parts of a process which are logically and practically linked. In an important respect, the process of memorialization is tied to the act and form of final disposition selected. This is illustrated in the case of monuments and markers as memorial products. Such memorials are an integral part of most cemeteries in which final disposition occurs. Without monuments, a cemetery becomes a memorial garden or park (with flush markers). Furthermore, the common site of memorialization is the final resting place of the body in a cemetery. But cremated remains may be memorialized at any site, affecting the processes of memorialization associated with them and the nature of the goods and services desired by consumers.

There is such a close relationship between memorialization and final disposition that the reasons for treating them separately require explanation. The most important reason perhaps is the logical distinction between the two activities: to dispose of the body is not to memorialize it. Each activity has a specific function of its own, and one does not accomplish the other. Memorialization is thus a separate and distinct part of the complete death care process. It is different in kind from both mortuary services and final disposition, including the pre-final stage of cremation. For example, memorialization is the only part of the death care process that can be postponed (or eliminated). Some measure of the other two components is required in every case. All three have a particular function in relation to the complete process that neither of the others performs.

Moreover, as a practical matter it is not necessarily the case that memorial products are obtainable from the providers of final disposition. Many cemeteries do not provide monuments, although some of them do. Memorial firms have a long tradition in the death care field, dating from its earliest days when they were operated by artisans who manufactured their own products in marble shops. Now those products are mainly provided by monument dealers who purchase memorials and resell them to consumers in the same manner as cemeteries which also do so. Even when provided by cemeteries, however, memorialization is a distinct stage in the process of death care.

As mentioned before, memorialization is also unique in that it is the only avoidable or postponable part of the process. Some sort of mortuary services and final disposition are required by laws governing the treatment and disposal of human remains. Beyond such minimum legal limits, the types and extent of the different components of death care desired may vary widely among different segments of the community and among different individuals and families within those segments. Specific expenditures on each of these categories and the proportion of each to the whole depend on the tastes and preferences of the consumer or consuming unit, which in turn depend on such factors as the age, ethnicity, religion, and social status of the deceased and the survivors. The level of spending on each depends on the level of consumer income, wealth, and life insurance proceeds received at death. None of these is constant from case to case.

Types of Death Care Goods and Services

In connection with each of these components of death care mentioned above, a variety of goods and services may be used, as described in the following decomposition of the complete process:

(1) *Mortuary services* consist of two types of activities:

(a) Those services used to care for and prepare human remains for final disposition by burial or entombment or by cremation followed by some further disposal of the cremated remains.

(b) Those services used to arrange, to supervise, to direct or to conduct services prior to final disposition of the remains.

Both types of services must be performed in order to come within the definition of the term "funeral services" as it is commonly used, and in connection with this term, a variety of goods may be provided by the establishment that performs the services, namely a funeral home. On the other hand, a direct disposition firm which merely transports bodies to a crematory is a death care provider but not a provider of "funeral services." Moreover, funeral services entail some form of ceremony with the body present in an open or closed casket, whereas a memorial service is a form of ceremony conducted without the presence of the body.

The traditional funeral services provided by funeral homes involve removal of the body from the place of death and preparing it for final disposition. The preparation of the body may involve efforts to preserve (embalm), restore, and display it in connection with public or private ceremonies desired in conformity with prevailing social customs and conventions. These ceremonies may be conducted in mortuary facilities or at churches, crematories, cemeteries, or elsewhere, involving the conveyance of the body between facilities. Because of the role played by the casket in these ceremonies and because of its use in the final disposition of the body, it is an important product provided in conjunction with mortuary services. The quality and style of the casket and its preservative features may be of concern to consumers.

The ceremonial activities performed vary with such factors as the cultural, religious, and educational backgrounds of particular segments of the population. Insofar as these activities serve as a source of comfort to the bereaved, it may be said that they are grief-reducing in nature. To this extent there is a psychological effect of their performance. It is sometimes said that funeral directors provide grief therapy to their customers, but it is noteworthy that they have never seen fit to charge a fee for whatever psychological services they provide. For that reason these services are similar in nature to the ministrations of clergy and the emotional support of family members and friends. Professional grief therapy provided to survivors for a fee by psychologists, psychiatrists, or others is not "death care" in the sense discussed here; it is a part of health care rendered to the living.

Not all of the elements of mortuary services included above are provided in every case, and even if they are available from the provider the consumer may be free to decline some of them under regulations imposed on providers. Furthermore, the ways in which prices are determined and quoted by providers do not depend on the use of all of these services, but they all are a part of what is here called mortuary services. Regardless of variations in these services selected by consumers, the "full-service" funeral home must be equipped to provide them. As such, it is a full-service provider of mortuary services only, not of complete death care. The traditional stand-alone funeral home is not equipped to provide the final disposition component of death care toward which the mortuary services are directed. Funeral directors may assist in arranging final disposition as a part of their services, but the only way they can provide this service directly is if their facilities include a cemetery or crematory, which is not ordinarily the case. They may, of course, seek to provide merchandise and services related to final disposition and memorialization which are not strictly a part of mortuary services themselves. This is often the case.

In some cases, the regional and national death care companies include funeral homes which are operated together with a cemetery or cemeteries as parts of a cluster of facilities in a common service area. Moreover, a funeral home may be operated together with the facilities of a cemetery, resulting in a combined establishment capable of providing all three components of death care in a single location. The mortuary services may then be provided at the site of final disposition, with repercussions for those elements of mortuary services that have to be coordinated with final disposition. These include production schedules, conveyance of the remains between funeral home and cemetery or crematory, and transportation of family and flowers from funeral home to cemetery.

(2) *Final disposition* consists of various steps taken to dispose of the body in some more or less permanent manner. At various times in the past, these steps have included such exotic methods as exposure to the elements, water burial, animal consumption, and cannibalism, some of which are still practiced under certain circumstances and in other societies (Adler, 1972, p. 7). In American society at present, the basic modes of final disposition are earth burial in a cemetery, entombment in a mausoleum, or cremation followed by some further disposition. The latter, as discussed, is a form of final disposition only in the legal sense; actually the process of cremation does not finally dispose of the remains. It decomposes them quickly into "cremated remains," some of which after pulverization of teeth and bone fragments become "cremains," a residue which must subsequently be disposed of by scattering or inurnment and perhaps niche interment in a columbarium or some other means.

Accordingly, the goods and services used in the process of final disposition are of two types: (a) tangible products such as lots, crypts, and mausoleum spaces along with the vaults, markers, and other items used in conjunction with those products and (b) services, such as those involved in cremating remains, opening and closing graves and tombs, and various forms of perpetual care for graves, mausoleums, and columbariums. By common practice, these goods and services are usually provided by cemeteries and crematories, or combinations of these establishments. In addition, cemeteries and crematories may provide other goods and services which are not technically a part of final disposition, particularly memorialization products such as markers and monuments, urns, vases, flowers, and the like.

(3) *Memorialization* entails any activities with the object of commemorating the life of the deceased. These may include "social" memorials, such as memorial services of various types, and "durable" memorials, such as markers or monuments. In addition, we may include flowers as "perishable" memorials, usually sent in memory of the deceased. As memorial products, however, flowers are different from durable memorials in that they are a means by which individuals and groups express caring or sympathy. They are purchased from florists by those who send them to the funeral home or take them to the cemetery. Florists provide flowers, which are used in the death care process, but they themselves are not death care providers. They are therefore not extensively considered in this book. Neither are firms which produce sympathy cards, mourning jewelry, and similar memorial products.

Also excluded from consideration in this book are financial memorials or gifts of money or other property in the name of a deceased person. It is clear that these frequently used forms of memorialization are consistent with the spirit of "death care" embodied in the use of that term in this book. As a rule, however, we will be less concerned with the highly discretionary and varied forms of memorialization which occur in connection with death and more concerned with the memorialization products and services commonly associated with the choice of mortuary services and final disposition.

Confusion of Mortuary Services and Final Disposition

This elucidation of the goods and services provided in connection with each component of death care appears to conform with public perceptions of what is necessary or desirable when a death occurs: mortuary services, final disposition, memorialization. It is likely, however, that careful distinctions between these components of death care are not made by consumers. In their minds "the funeral" probably includes (1) and (2) above even though the ceremonial content of death care is largely limited to (1). As used by consumers, the meaning of "funeral expenses" or sometimes "final expenses" may include the cost of (1), (2), and (3) even though "death care expenses" would be more fully descriptive.

Fine distinctions between closely related goods and services are not expected of consumers, but they are a necessary part of the study and description of the operation of firms of all types. Those operations cannot be identified, much less understood, unless their outputs are fully defined in terms of their technical characteristics. But while the outputs of most types of firms are well defined and understood, there have been few attempts to describe the outputs of death care firms, either by practitioners or independent observers. This accounts for the existence of a certain amount of confusion about the outputs of death care providers.

One source of confusion has also been the looseness of the methods used in earlier attempts to define and describe death care goods and services. None of these has focused on the death care process in order to delineate the goods and services associated with each part of the process. Instead, they have focused on the goods and services produced by particular types of death care providers, especially funeral homes. This is true, for example, of Blackwell's early attempt to describe fully "The Product of the Funeral Director" (1971). This was a valuable exercise, unusual in the literature before or since, and he did an admirable job of describing fully what funeral directors do, or may do, for consumers. The problem is that by framing his subject in terms of the funeral director, he shifts his focus away from the question of "what the product is" to the question of "what the funeral director does." In effect, this leads him to confuse the distinction between the mortuary services and final disposition components of death care identified above.

This is evident from the introductory paragraph in Blackwell's study (pp. 155–56):

> The product offered by the funeral director is primarily one of service. This service has two distinct dimensions:

1. Disposal of human remains.
2. Assistance to survivors in their efforts to adjust to death. While performing both of these services, the funeral director becomes involved in the sale of merchandise connected with both elements of the service.

Blackwell quotes in support of this position "one commentator" who "has described funeral service reduced to its lowest common divisors as the remains, the facilities for handling them and a place for interment. These are the essential elements which are found in almost all funerals but *their exact nature may vary considerably*" (p. 156, emphasis added).

The error in this presentation of the product of the funeral director is obvious. The funeral director who operates a funeral home and conducts the funeral does not provide "a place for interment" or for "the disposal of human remains." This is not a part of the mortuary services component of death care traditionally provided by funeral directors. It is rather the essential part of the death care product traditionally provided by cemeteries and crematories. The facilities they operate are highly specialized for providing final disposition which the facilities of funeral homes are incapable of providing.

This is not to suggest that Blackwell or the "commentator" he cites are unaware of this distinction. It is simply to draw attention to the fact that mortuary services and final disposition are distinct but closely related parts of the death care process. In his subsequent presentation of the elements of the product of the funeral director, Blackwell recognizes explicitly the point to which attention has been drawn here. Thus, under the heading of "Interment" he says: "The funeral director provides the service of making arrangements for grave preparation and in many instances advances the fees for this. If the family has not previously purchased a plot, the funeral director assists in procuring a place for the burial" (p. 159). Under the heading of "Cremation," he repeats the point: "When cremation is elected by the deceased or his survivors, the funeral director makes arrangements in much the same manner that he would in the case of earth interment. 'Graveside' services may be arranged with a committal at the facilities of the crematory handled in the same way as any other funeral" (p. 159).

In other words, the mortuary services provided by funeral homes involve the funeral director in arranging for whatever final disposition of the body is desired by those who have engaged the services of the funeral home. Final disposition itself is not to be confused with the funeral service, however; it is a distinct part of the death care process. The involvement of the funeral director with the final disposition part of the process — his assistance to his customers in arranging for it and even advancing the funds for them to do so — is an important indication of how closely connected the mortuary services and final disposition components of death care are. And this raises the question of why they should be provided separately by different firms, rather than together by a single provider of both components of the death care process. A single provider would, of course, have to be a cemetery (including a crematory).

Sources of Death Care Goods and Services

In primitive societies most or all of the components of death care are provided by members of the family of the deceased person. This was once true in the United States, but in contemporary American society few families are inclined to transport, prepare, and dispose of dead bodies themselves. Even if they were so inclined, they are not equipped to undertake these tasks. When a death occurs, families are obliged to seek the services of those who are prepared and equipped to perform them. Ordinarily they must hire a funeral home to provide mortuary services, and they must purchase final disposition goods and services from a cemetery or crematory or both. In connection with their choices of final disposition, they commonly require or desire an appropriate marker or monument, and they may desire floral tributes for the final services.

These obligations and desires of families give rise to a number of different types of producers or providers of death care goods and services of the types and in the quantities required or desired by consumers. By common practice, these goods and services are produced and provided by funeral homes, cemeteries, and crematories, and related enterprises whose operations overlap one another, creating points of contact between them. For example, funeral homes conduct funeral services and oversee the final disposition of the body in the cemetery; monument dealers sell monuments for use in cemeteries, and so on.

On the one hand, the relationships among the different goods and services these firms produce and provide requires them to coordinate their production schedules and cooperate in various ways. On the other hand, those relationships create potential conflicts of interest among them over the sale and marketing of competing products and services, such as vaults, graveliners, markers and monuments, among others. In an economic sense, the integration of the operations of the providers of different types of death care goods and services increases the coordination of their production processes and reduces the conflict among them.

Yet, for various reasons, some of which will be discussed later, most death care establishments are not integrated "full-service" facilities capable of providing complete death care to consumers in one location. The bulk of the death care economy consists of "stand-alone" funeral homes, cemeteries, and monument dealers who operate facilities that are only partially integrated, if that. Because of this, it is ordinarily necessary for a consumer to deal with more than one provider of death care at the time of need or when death care is pre-planned. Although a funeral home may assist consumers in this process, it is only the modern combination establishments in the sector which offer one-stop shopping and provide complete death care to consumers at facilities which are located together. For the most part, therefore, death care goods and services are acquired by consumers from different sources, often at different times and in different ways.

Death Care and Its Parts

Until very recently, death care has not been widely available "as a whole" from a single provider. Instead, it has usually been purchased by consumers in parts available only from different providers. The difficulties of doing this, particularly in the circumstances under which funerals are arranged at-need, have led to the development of cemetery-mortuary combinations capable of providing complete death care to consumers. The array of death care goods and services available, even from these combined establishments, may nevertheless be classified in terms of the death care process which is comprised of a series of separate and distinct steps or parts of the process. Combined facilities allow consumers to obtain all the component parts of the complete process or product from a single provider. In such cases the nature of the complete product is clear; it may be less clear when consumers obtain each component of the product from different providers and assemble it themselves, so to speak.

Let us illustrate the basic concept of death care as a complex product assembled from distinct parts with the case of a death involving, say, entombment as a form of final disposition. What else is required besides the tomb? Obviously the answer is a body. But that is not all. Some kind of marker is required to identify the person whose body lies within. A tomb without either a body or a marker is an incomplete product. What is required to complete it is both a body and a marker. The former is provided by the mortuary services which deliver the body to the tomb. The latter is provided by a marker with the name, dates of birth and death, and perhaps an epitaph, which memorialize the deceased, completing the process.

The assembly of the product requires the inputs of land, capital, and labor, as occurs in the production of any other product. The death care product is assembled from raw materials of various types — casket, vault, tomb, grave — as occurs in the production of other goods. The forms of labor involved in producing and assembling the parts of the product are varied as occurs in the case of other products. In short, the death care product is no different in its essential respects from most other goods and services. It is different only in the respect that its "parts" have traditionally been produced and provided to consumers piecemeal by separate providers who are generally different firms. The historical reasons for this have been mentioned, and their consequences will be discussed at length, but they should not be allowed to obscure the validity of viewing death care as a complete product comprised of three components, each of which is an integral part of the whole. Because of the fragmented production system that exists within the death care economy, however, the consumer is usually forced to "assemble" his own death care from separate parts purchased from different "partial" providers.

Who Is the Consumer?

Just as the stigma of death affects public attitudes towards death care providers and facilities, it affects the attitudes of consumers towards death care goods and services. For the most part those attitudes reflect a need or desire on the part of many people to postpone purchasing or even selecting (without funding the purchase of) such products until it is too late. Even in those cases where some or all of the items required or desired by an individual at death are selected or purchased in advance of the event, the actual goods and services themselves are delivered — and therefore "consumed" — following the person's death. Who then is the consumer?

The use of the term "consumer" in connection with death care goods and services refers to the person or persons who purchase them. This is the way in which the term is commonly used in economic analysis. The consumer may be the deceased person who purchased cemetery property, a funeral service, or memorialization products in advance of need. Approximately two-thirds of the deaths which occur annually result in some form of final disposition which was pre-arranged and pre-funded; the rest involve at-need purchases. In the case of funeral services, the statistics are reversed.

In the at-need cases, it is usually the survivor or survivors of the deceased who comprise the consuming or purchasing unit. In this latter respect, the purchase of death care differs from most consumer expenditures, but it is not unlike others which involve decisions to purchase, say, a house or a car, in which family members participate.

Of course, the purchase of death care, even if it is done prior to death, is frequently surrounded by psychological difficulties which are not present to the same extent in the purchase of most other products and services. It is fraught with emotional overtones, but this may actually be a factor which tends to promote solidarity and agreement within a consuming unit based on shared religious traditions and family values. Not necessarily, of course, but it is a matter of fact that a large number of funerals are arranged every day, suggesting that, whatever difficulties may be involved, it is possible for families to work them out and to choose. Any complications resulting from joint decision making by consumers may therefore be ignored.

What cannot be ignored, however, is the position of the consumer whose choices are affected by earlier death care decisions made by relatives and others. These decisions have often involved interment in commercial and noncommercial cemeteries; the operations of the latter are not strictly a part of the subject matter of this book. From the standpoint of consumers, those noncommercial facilities are operated as alternatives to commercial providers of final disposition. Most of them have coexisted for many years with their commercial counterparts; some have pre-existed them for many years. Together they have sold or otherwise allocated large quantities of burial space and other forms of final disposition products to generations of families, both at-need and in advance of need.

The upshot of this is that a large number of death care consumers already possess burial property at the time of death. Even if they do not, many families are strongly inclined to select a particular cemetery because it is the site at which relatives are buried or entombed. Thus many consumers have ties to a cemetery which affect their death care expenditures.

It is true that consumers often have strong ties also to funeral homes at which the funerals of family members have been held. A smaller number of consumers have pre-arranged or pre-funded funerals, further tying them to particular funeral homes. Such ties can be broken, of course, but because of permanence of final disposition and memorialization in cemeteries, the ties that bind families to cemeteries are more difficult to break.

Consumer Expenditures on Death Care

Expenditures within the death care category must be allocated to goods and services which are used in the death care process, consisting of mortuary services, final disposition, and memorialization. This may be demonstrated by expressing total death care expenditures as a sum of the expenditures on each of the three components of the complete process:

Total Death Care Expenditures=
Expenditures on Mortuary services
+Expenditures on Final Disposition
+Expenditures on Memorialization.

It will be clear from this formulation that the total amount available to consumers must be allocated among the three components. If the allocation among all three components is to be optimal, it would seem to be important for the allocation to be made in a single transaction or in a series of related transactions to allow consumers to consider alternative packages involving different amounts of each of the related parts. Only in this way is the complete package likely to be balanced among the three components to achieve the greatest total satisfaction from expenditures on death care.

This is not, however, the way in which consumers ordinarily have shopped for and purchased death care, although the opportunity is now available for them to do so in some markets. The traditional separation between death care providers has contributed to a tendency on the part of consumers to purchase death care in separate transactions with each type of provider, often entered into at different times under different conditions, subject to different degrees of sales pressure from the purveyors of each component. It seems highly unlikely that this disjointed approach to a set of component parts of a complex product is as conducive to ultimate satisfaction as the purchase of a complete package which represents a deliberate consideration of the extent of each element included in the whole purchase.

Establishment of Consumer Customs

The existing framework of separate businesses providing only their particular part or parts of the death care goods and services desired by consumers results from historical conditions favoring fragmentation of death care providers. The behavior of consumers has adapted to those conditions. As consumers, we are accustomed to buying cemetery property from a cemetery, possibly in advance of need. We are accustomed to buying mortuary goods and services from a funeral home at the time of need. And we are accustomed to selecting and purchasing a monument following interment. The allocation of our personal expenditures on these elements of death care in these disorganized and uncoordinated ways has become customary, and customary ways of doing things are slow to change, even for the better. This does not mean that customary spending patterns never change, however, particularly if consumers are offered alternatives to established ways of spending their funds. Thus supermarkets offered them a more economical and convenient "one-stop-shopping" alternative to the myriad small shops where consumers were in the habit of shopping.

Like the customers of supermarkets, death care consumers also respond to economy and convenience. But funeral homes and cemeteries are not grocery stores. They are not places we frequent in our daily lives, based on custom or habit. On the contrary, they are places to which we go only when we must, in the extraordinary event of death. Something transcending convenience and economy attracts customers again and again to a funeral home or cemetery. This is what inspires customer loyalty and sustains the business of death care establishments to a remarkable degree. There is something about what they do for their customers which is different from services of other businesses. It seems related to the care and attention they have provided or which they have a reputation for providing. Is it death care?

Is It Death "Care"?

In generic terms, the goods and services which consumers require or desire in connection with death are referred to here as "death care." The needs and desires of consumers for death care goods and services are in many respects similar to their needs and desires for most other products.

But in some important respects they are different. Because funeral services are provided at a time of loss and grief, the relationship between consumers and a funeral home, although its services may be required infrequently, is an intimate, extremely personal one. Consumers ordinarily expect the atmosphere created by a funeral home and its personnel to be one of comfort and dignity. The creation of this atmosphere is a part of the product it provides along with a set of goods and services. These services, as enumerated initially by Blackwell in "The Product of the Funeral Director" (1971), may be classified here in terms of the type of care they represent, as follows:

(1) *Care and handling of the remains.* These include (a) removal of the body from the place of death, (b) conveyance of the body during the final services, (c) embalming of the body if required or desired, and (d) restoration of the corpse to give it a slumbering appearance which is not shocking to the survivors. There is a widespread concern regarding the importance of treating human remains in appropriate ways. For whatever reasons this is a highly sensitive matter for many people. It is important for them to know, or at least to believe, that it is done with appropriate care.

(2) *Care and assistance to survivors.* These include (a) preliminary counseling about various aspects of mortuary services, (b) the arrangements conference in which the funeral service is arranged and the casket is selected, (c) arranging for final disposition of the remains, (d) providing transportation between funeral home and cemetery, (e) overseeing interment or cremation of the remains, and (f) aftercare programs designed to assist survivors in dealing with their loss.

(3) *Auxiliary services.* These include (a) coordinating with clergy, (b) preparing death notices, and (c) providing a record of attendees and floral tributes. Some of these are unfamiliar tasks, and others are small details which may be overlooked by the family in the circumstances surrounding a death. To insure that they are done, and done properly, it is customary for the funeral director to take care of all necessary details at the time of death. This is the sense in which "undertaker" became a common occupational title for practitioners of the trade, and it is entailed in the meaning of "death care."

In consideration of these aspects of the tasks performed by funeral home personnel, it seems not inappropriate to describe what they provide to consumers as a form of "death care." In a similar way, the relationship between consumers and cemeteries which provide a permanent "resting place" for a deceased family member is a close, continuing one. Family members frequently wish to be interred or entombed together, and one of the needs or desires of many people is to return to the site where remains are interred or entombed. As consumers, they expect the site of a cemetery to be a permanently secure place of appropriate appearance. A related desire is to conserve places of interment and entombment so that they perform their function in perpetuity. Graves and mausoleums must therefore be the object of ongoing maintenance which families can rarely provide themselves, hence the development of "perpetual care" as a part of the product provided by cemeteries in connection with the sale of burial space and mausoleum crypts.

Likewise, crematories — because they provide services which entail the handling of remains — have a special relationship with their customers. Family members may not be present during the process of cremation, but they are entitled to assume that the remains are handled with dignity and care throughout the incineration process. Afterwards, they are entitled to receive the cremains in an appropriate container, based on their subsequent plans for scattering or further disposition whether formal or informal. The manner in which a crematory performs these activities is properly the concern of funeral homes through which arrangements for cremation are ordinarily made on behalf of consumers. Under this influence, crematories may be expected to exercise "care," and the failure to do so is illegal in some states.

Even the work of monument dealers may be said to involve goods and services which require them to demonstrate appropriate care for the wishes and desires of families to memorialize the dead. In keeping with the permanence of cemeteries and with the nature of memorialization, consumers expect the markers and monuments they erect to the memory of those interred or entombed in a place should be of such quality as to last in perpetuity. In view of the desire of families for memorials which endure and are expected to continue to reflect well upon the memory of the dead, there is a modicum of care involved in the activities performed on their behalf by those who sell, install, and maintain monuments, markers, and similar products. Furthermore, the memorials they make or sell become installed on the premises of a cemetery, and their work is performed, at least in part, on those premises. The operator of the cemetery thus has a stake in ensuring that the memorial provider exercises appropriate care.

For all these reasons, the firms which provide death care goods and services to consumers may properly be said to be providers of care. A community depends on its funeral homes, cemeteries, memorial dealers, and related enterprises to provide goods and services which serve the special needs and desires of their customers following death. The care provided by such establishments must be in keeping with the laws, customs, religious sentiments, emotional needs, and desires of their customers. Only by paying careful attention to those needs and desires can such establishments expect to survive and to thrive. Recognition of this underlies the use of the term "death care" as a description of the goods and services such firms provide to consumers.

In adopting this usage, we do not wish to appear to elevate the status of the businesses included within it by claiming that they are "caregivers" or "caretakers" in any sense other than that they care for the remains, comfort the survivors, take care of the details surrounding an important life event, and maintain the facilities at which remains are perpetually interred and memorialized. In the use of "death care" to describe a sector of the economy, and the establishments, firms and industries which comprise it, there can be no implication that death care providers "care" for their customers in a literal way. The implication is rather that they dispense care at the time of death. Death care signifies appropriate care for the needs of consumers at the time of death, nothing more and nothing less.

Death Care in a Diverse Society

Many countries, like Japan and Taiwan, have much more homogeneous populations than does the United States. The members of such societies share a common ethnic, religious, and cultural tradition. Because these factors influence, or dictate some would say, the choice of death care practices within a society, there is less variation in those practices in such societies, although there may be wide variation in spending on similar practices.

For historical reasons the population of the United States is one of the most diverse societies in the world. According to demographic details in the 1990 census, the U.S. population includes members of 110 racial and ethnic groups, many of whom practice a large variety of religions. Its culture has long been and will long continue to be influenced by its basic diversity. Not surprisingly, then, it is a country in which a great variety of death care practices exist, none of which is distinctively American but all of which reflect the unique history of the United States, which never developed a uniform culture, much less a uniform culture of death. The U.S. death care economy therefore consists of numerous economies within numerous communities, many of which are multicultural. Thus it is a country with no truly national form of death care. In this respect, the American way of death which Mitford described does not exist in reality.

American diversity leads to a number of distinctive features of the death care economy which differ substantially from the organization and operation of other "economies." This diversity affects the variety of goods and services desired by consumers as a part of the death care process. It affects the character and size of death care establishments. It affects the characteristics required on the part of those who operate them. It affects the markets for death care in an area and the relationships among them. It affects the business practices adopted by establishments and their ability to consolidate or to integrate effectively. In all these respects and others, the death care economy has been and continues to be a reflection of the diversity of the society in which it exists. In other cases the communities which comprise the society have been at odds with one another, but this does not appear to have been true within the death care economy where the members of different communities have been content to pursue their own varied ideas of what is appropriate. This is distinctive and raises questions about how well past criticism of American death care practices would be received today.

One of the significant cultural developments of the last few decades in the United States has been a growing awareness of the social value of multiculturalism in a diverse society. Central to this sense of awareness has been an appreciation of the distinctive features of ethnic and cultural traditions. Among these traditions are the death care customs and practices of diverse groups. Just as the members of any such group are entitled to express pride in their ethnicity and cultural heritage, so they are entitled to engage in the death care practices which derive from their respective origins and shared beliefs.

Under conditions of enhanced sensibilities about cultural differences in a diverse society, it is far less likely today that the criticism of death care preferences and choices would receive the kind of treatment it received in the early 1960s when Mitford made such fun of "the American way of death." Indeed, it is difficult to imagine today that an attack on the death care practices of any group, whether in other societies or our own, would be critically well received or even acceptable. This is not the 1960s, and in the last thirty years it is to be hoped that our tolerances for differences among cultures has progressed to the point where the ceremonies we desire at death, reflecting our ethnic, religious, and other differences, are not open to ridicule by those who hold different views about what constitutes appropriate death care. Judged by today's standards, there is an intolerant ring to such anachronistic statements as this, made some thirty years ago: "Cremation sounds like a simple, tidy solution to the disposal of the dead.... It is applauded by ... those who would like to see an end to all the malarky [*sic*] that surrounds the usual kind of funeral" (Mitford, 1963, p. 129).

It is possible that one may still hear ethnic, religious and cultural practices described as "malarkey," but it is less likely that such characterizations are to be regarded as praiseworthy. Of course, those who make such statements are free to hide behind the claim that they are attacking the ones who sell "malarkey," not the ones who purchase it. On careful consideration, however, it is obvious that this is analogous to claiming that Chinese restaurants are responsible for the fact that their customers prefer Chinese food.

Death Care Preferences

Like personal preferences generally, the death care preferences of consumers in this society and elsewhere are complex phenomena for which there is no entirely rational or logical explanation. Take, for example, the preference for cremation over earth burial, or vice versa. It is not possible to prove that one is more or less "logical," even if cremation is simpler, quicker, less expensive, or whatever else it may be. Some people simply prefer one practice over another for various reasons, including but not limited to their psychological reactions to the thought of bodies being burned, or buried, or entombed, or otherwise disposed of. Any of these alternatives may be preferable to an individual, but not more logical. By a similar process of thinking, the ceremonies and services preferred by consumers are not more or less logical choices. Nevertheless, such preferences are experienced by consumers in ways which express themselves as demand for alternative forms of death care.

For whatever reasons, people want different things. They often want to be interred next to one another or in the family plot or tomb. When they choose cremation, they often want their cremated remains to be scattered in a common location or to be held in adjoining columbarium niches. They sometimes want to lie in state in the same parlor of the same funeral home where their parents were laid out, or they want others to do so. They prefer to use a mortuary that caters to their racial or ethnic group or to members of their socioeconomic class or the one to which they aspire. The prominence and ambiance of a facility may be valued by them; so may its location, the stateliness or modernity of its architecture, the elegance of its furnishings, the personality of its owners, and many other qualities too numerous to mention. But not too numerous for consumers somehow to bring into juxtaposition in the process of choosing the death care they prefer for themselves in advance of need, or for others at the time of need.

The Value of Death Care

The variety of death care goods and services made available in the marketplace reflects the variety of human needs and wants associated with the death of a person in our society. The "value" of a good in this context refers to what it is worth to a consumer based on her expectation that it will yield satisfaction ("utility"). Any such expectation of satisfaction or utility is a personal judgment. It is temporal for any individual and it is noncomparable. People want what they want at any particular time.

When a member of the society dies, the body must be removed from the place of death and prepared for final disposition, something that most consumers are ill prepared to do. They must instead arrange to have it done by a death care provider. Beyond this, however, when a death occurs there are those who knew the deceased party who wish to pay their respects and extend their sympathies to his or her family. To do this does not necessarily require the services of any business. There are "how-to" books for those who desire to care for their own dead (e.g., Carlson's *Caring for Your Own Dead*, 1988). As a social matter, friends, neighbors, and others might call on relatives of the deceased at their home at different times. Or one of their number might arrange a get-together, without the body present, in their home or another location. Even if this were all that were done, it would involve costs associated with arranging the event, and the difficulties of doing so on short notice make it unlikely that it would allow the broadest circle of those who wish to attend to do so.

Adding to the difficulties of such homemade arrangements are the dictates of custom in many communities regarding the presence of the body. To prepare and preserve the body, to display it in a proper receptacle, to provide facilities which accommodate visitation, to obtain equipment with which to transport the casketed remains to the church for religious ceremonies, to remove them to the cemetery for graveside services and interment or entombment or to the crematory — all of these actions are impractical or impossible for most consumers to do on their own. If they want them done at death, they must purchase them from a firm whose business it is to provide them. The fact that they do is proof of the value they attach to mortuary goods and services.

Whether or not the full range of mortuary services and products described above is desired, a death necessitates that the body be disposed of in some manner. In primitive societies this duty may be performed by the family and friends of the deceased. The body may be buried or cremated or allowed to deteriorate from exposure to the elements. In modern societies, public health regulations and local ordinances limit the means by which bodies may be disposed of; hence the need to provide for earth burial, entombment, or cremation of the remains. Again, the fact that consumers arrange for the forms of final disposition of their choice is proof of the value they attach to this component of death care. The final act set in train by a death in our society is the need or desire to memorialize the deceased party. The fact that consumers erect stone or metal markers and monuments in commemoration of the dead is proof that they value these products.

It is beyond our concern to consider the reasons the members of a society may have for wanting to preserve the body and to restore it following death — to have it present for a time, to gather around it, to dispose of it in particular ways, to return to the place where it lays, to mark the spot or to erect a monument over it, and to do any of the other things that they do in the process of confronting death. It is sufficient to observe that people want to do these things in connection with death and to realize that death care goods and services are among the things that many people want and on which they are willing to spend. This observation is the starting point of the present analysis.

The willingness of consumers to spend on death care sets in motion a continuous series of processes to produce such goods and services, so that the demand for them may be satisfied. Death care establishments, firms, and industries employ labor and capital in order to produce and distribute these goods and services. Taken together, the array of death care establishments, firms, and industries whose outputs are used to provide death care to consumers constitute the death care sector of the economy. Like other sectors which provide goods and services to consumers according to market demand, the constituents of the death care sector are themselves consumers, who use or resell the goods and services of other firms. They hire workers, borrow money, earn profits, pay taxes, conform to regulatory requirements, and generally do all the things that other firms do. Like other businesses they provide opportunities for men and women to excel in a trade or the operation of a small business. They have provided a few with the opportunity to earn considerable wealth and power as the developers of local, regional, and national chains of death care establishments. In all these ways and others, the economic activities of the death care sector contribute directly and indirectly to the economy as a whole. The outputs of those activities satisfy human needs and desires for death care goods and services. Some characteristics of the providers of those outputs to consumers are examined in the following chapter.

5. *Death Care Providers*

Origins of Different Types of Death Care Providers

From the description of the death care goods and services presented in the previous chapter, it will be clear that those products have traditionally been made available to consumers by several different types of establishments, namely funeral homes, cemeteries and crematories, monument dealers, and perhaps others. Each of these different types of establishments has its particular form and function in relation to the death care process. In general, mortuary services are provided by funeral homes, final disposition is provided in part by crematories and in full by cemeteries, and memorialization products are provided by monument dealers, florists, and other enterprises. Although there are some establishments which provide combinations of products which relate to different components of the death care process, the different parts of the process have traditionally been provided by different types of firms. But this is a historical artifact, not an inherent condition. It reflects circumstances that prevailed in particular places at particular times in the past. In many respects those early conditions were vastly different from conditions which prevail today, but their influence is still seen in the structure of the death care economy.

Perhaps this is true to some extent in other economic sectors, but nowhere to the same degree. There are several features peculiar to the death care economy which make past conditions and developments especially influential on the present state of the sector. One of these features is the permanence of death care facilities such as cemeteries, which in principle remain in place forever, through all kinds of conditions. Secondly, the facilities of funeral homes are not permanent, but the stability of their operations as businesses has contributed to the persistence of some mortuaries over generations, often under the continuous ownership of one family at the original facilities or locations that date from their founding.

These features have created a rigid infrastructure of death care providers, especially in the oldest urban areas of the United States. It is largely in the more recently developed suburban areas of the East Coast and in the growing metropolitan areas of the South and West that new investments in death care facilities have led to an infrastructure consistent with modern conditions. Thus it is in those areas that the modern phenomena of commercial cemeteries, memorial parks, and cemetery-mortuary combinations originated as modern forms of death care establishments unlike the older types that predominate in the eastern part of the country. In all areas, however, the occupational specializations of funeral directors, cemeterians, and monument dealers and the investment required to establish firms of each type have tended to limit the scope of new firms to one type or another.

The upshot is that most death care firms are not integrated providers of complete death care. Instead they are small, locally owned and operated establishments which provide either mortuary services or final disposition to consumers, but not both. The sale of memorials has been added to the products sold by many cemeteries and some funeral homes, and cemeteries have also expanded the types of final disposition they provide, but only a relatively small number of them have become fully integrated by adding a mortuary. Even where this has been done, the identities of the facilities have remained separate, so that they are comprised of a funeral home and a cemetery, reflecting the inherent distinction between the mortuary services and final disposition components of death care. Some equipment and personnel may be jointly used by the two facilities, and the arrangement and conduct of mortuary services, final disposition, and memorialization can be coordinated internally by the funeral director, or death care counselor. This differs in significant respects from the typical situation involving several stand-alone providers of death care goods and services.

The Relationships Among Death Care Providers

The manner in which death care goods and services are delivered to consumers obviously depends in large measure on the qualifications of those who deliver them. Unless the death care facility selected by the consumer is a full-service combination establishment, several different providers are typically required, including a funeral home, a crematory or cemetery, a monument dealer, florists, and perhaps others. Inevitably, the delivery of a complete set of goods and services requires these different providers to interact.

To facilitate their interaction, it is customary for the funeral home to be in charge of arrangements. The funeral home thus becomes the focal point of death care activities, and the funeral director becomes the coordinator of all the various elements of death care. Funeral directors have thus attracted relatively more attention and criticism than other death care providers. In public hearings on the "funeral" industry, for example, cemetery charges have usually been regarded as "add-ons" to the charges of funeral homes, and memorialization has commonly been ignored as a process. Although this is understandable in light of the pivotal role played by the funeral director, this view of his relative importance may distort the true picture in which the cemetery is the essential facility in the death care process. That is to say, it is the facility toward which many of the activities coordinated by the funeral director are oriented. Thus the casket and the flowers are ultimately transported to the cemetery, along with the funeral party, in the funeral procession. Furthermore, since the cemetery is the site of interment or entombment, the memorialization process is logically related to the cemetery product. The only exception to this is the case of financial and other memorials that are not associated with the grave site, mausoleum, or columbarium.

The significance of the facilities at which final disposition occurs is indicated by the necessity of the funeral director to become involved with arranging for burial or entombment of the body or cremains. As described by Blackwell in "The Product of the Funeral Director," he "provides the service of making arrangements for grave preparation and in many instances he advances the fees for this. If the family has not previously purchased a plot, the funeral director assists in procuring a place for burial" (1971, p. 159). He must do this, of course, in order to complete the part of the death care process he provides. To bring his services to a close, he must deliver the body to a cemetery or a crematory. In the latter case, some arrangement for the final disposition of the cremains in a cemetery or elsewhere must also be made by the funeral director. In a sense, therefore, the services of the funeral director are in preparation for the act of final disposition. If necessary or desired, the mortuary services may be reduced to a limited set of activities involved in transporting the body in a suitable container to the cemetery/crematory, which is the essential facility where the final disposition occurs.

The Pivotal Role of the Funeral Director

In spite of the essential role of the cemetery or crematory, at least two factors are responsible for the attention focused on the funeral director as the pivotal figure in the death care process: (1) he physically takes custody of the remains immediately following death at a time when public health concerns are the most critical, and (2) he undertakes a large number of activities legally required or commonly desired at death. As described in the previous chapter, the role of the funeral director begins with the removal of the body from the place of death and continues until the final disposition is underway or complete at the cemetery or crematory. If the funeral home is a provider of memorial products and "aftercare" services to survivors, the funeral director's role may extend beyond the act of final disposition itself.

Throughout this process, the funeral director interacts with the providers of final disposition and memorialization as the agent of the family of the deceased person, a role which enhances his status among death care providers and creates the potential for conflicts of interest with them. In effect, the role of the funeral director is similar to that of the physician as the primary health care provider, directing the total care of the patient, which requires the use of the hospital and drugs provided by others.

This pivotal role of funeral directors, together with their reputation as handlers of human remains, has secured their social status as specialists in all aspects of death care, including final disposition and memorialization, which are traditionally provided by others. In fact, the involvement of funeral directors with human remains and the survivors is limited in duration to a short interval when compared to the permanent interment or committal of remains to cemeteries for perpetual care. It seems likely that two factors have contributed to this state of affairs. One is the perception of a cemetery as a place for the disposition of human remains; the other is the role of cemeteries as suppliers of goods rather than services, such as perpetual care. Greater emphasis on the latter by commercial cemeteries in recent years has probably not yet been sufficient to create an image of cemeterians as care providers rather than purveyors of lots and other products which are associated with death, but not with death "care." Although this may change in the future, it is unlikely that the role of the funeral director as the primary provider of death care will be altered.

Women as Death Care Providers

Historically the death care field, like many others, was dominated by men. This is clearly reflected in the earlier descriptions of "monument men" and "cemetery men." The origins of these trades and the tasks they involve are both responsible for the prevalence of males in each. For similar reasons the field of funeral directing once seemed to require men, who were better able than most women to perform the tasks involved in lifting and moving dead bodies. The development of mechanized equipment to assist in the performance of these tasks has reduced substantially the need for physical strength on the part of funeral directors. As a consequence of this and the general tendency for women to become involved in a wider variety of occupations, the number of women funeral directors has increased steadily over several decades. To some extent this trend represents the increased participation of females in family-owned funeral home businesses, but it also reflects a growing attraction to women of the field as a career. While currently only 5 percent of the members of the largest trade association of funeral directors are women, more than 25 percent of the graduates of mortuary colleges during 1991 were females, compared to only 6 percent in 1976. These figures indicate a continued increase in the proportion of women funeral directors in the future (Goldman, *New York Times*, February 13, 1993).

As this occurs, it has been suggested that the field will undergo changes "because women will bring a different sense of style and a different sensitivity" to the performance of the role of funeral director. Whatever these changes may be, they are unlikely to affect the roles of death care providers that are under consideration here. For the record, however, the masculine pronouns used throughout this book are intended to signify men and women equally. This is consistent with the increased representation of women in the funeral service field and in the sales forces of cemeteries, where they are recognized as highly effective. Their greater participation in the ranks of death care practitioners may eventually alter the public perception of those trades, but it does little to change their strong association with death. As two sisters who operate a successful funeral home told the *New York Times*, they prefer "not to talk about their work at parties or other social situations; it tended to provoke too much black humor and too many squeamish remarks" (Goldman, February 13, 1993).

Stigmatization

The problem for both men and women who become death care providers, especially funeral directors and embalmers, is that the stigma of death is attached to those occupations in the eyes of the larger society. Anthropologists refer to this as a situation in which those who perform certain tasks, such as caring for the dead, are "polluted" or "tainted" by their occupations. Stephenson cites as an example of this attitude a study by David Sudnow in which a morgue attendant in a large hospital "who was trapped in that role worked very hard to disassociate himself from his job in order to mask the stigma of polluted work" (1985, p. 222).

Stephenson concludes that "this description applies to the role of the funeral director, who is also polluted by his occupation." As evidence, he cites some work by Vanderlyn Pine, a sociologist and funeral director, who found that "in some cases, urban funeral directors who live at a distance from their work will seek to hide their occupation from their suburban neighbor's [*sic*]. This becomes more difficult in smaller communities where such anonymity is not as easily attained" (cited in Stephenson, p. 222).

Based on personal observations, Pine detected a significant difference between "urban" and "rural" funeral directors. The urban funeral director is viewed as an anonymous bureaucrat whose role is more impersonal than that of his rural counterpart. The urban practitioner is thus more often the object of public criticism, whereas the rural funeral director is characterized as a member of the community who "enjoys high social status, considerable community prestige, political power, and personal respect" (cited in Stephenson, p. 141).

Stephenson attributes this to a standard "rural-urban" dichotomy "wherein the urbanite is seen as cold, calculating, and mercenary, while the rural dweller is warm, caring and altruistic" (pp. 222–23). It is difficult to avoid the extrapolation of this dichotomy from rural-urban to chain-operated versus family-run, and to utilize this dichotomy to explain why the large companies which operate chains of funeral homes have sought to retain the image of their units as family firms. Furthermore, it is a universal feature of the operation of the large firms to encourage the personnel of their units to engage in social and civic activities in their communities. These efforts resemble closely the use of such methods by local funeral directors "to counter the stigma of his or her occupation by being active in the community, thereby counteracting some of the negative images associated with the job of funeral directing" (p. 223).

In conclusion, Stephenson provides the following portrait of the treatment of the funeral director in modern America:

> An important aspect of being labeled as having a polluted occupation is the victimization of the individual or occupation which may occur. As a means of venting society's anxieties, the unclean may be set upon, as if punishing them will punish (or rid the world of) the unwanted, dirty image they represent. One form of this victimization of the funeral director is the low esteem in which the occupation is held by the public; another is the use of the role as a negative or comic relief character in the media.
>
> In a society that seeks to deny the reality of death, the funeral director is a living symbol of this dreaded subject. At the same time, the funeral director may be seen by some as one who profits from another's loss. The anger that is a fundamental part of the grieving process may be projected onto the funeral director, who is a prominent figure in the process of social affirmation that the death has occurred.
>
> In addition to the external strains associated with the occupation of funeral director, there are internal strains as well. Wishing for more funerals, which would spell success, also means wishing for death to strike more often. Most obviously, the funeral director is surrounded by death and grief. Many hours each day are spent dealing with the bereaved, as well as performing tasks that most people would react to with abhorrence. The role of these "dismal traders," and the resulting psychological stress have been neglected areas of research. That work which has been done, however, does not lead to the conclusion that funeral directors are necessarily ghoulish, profit-mad, or unethical characters, as some would like to label them.
>
> In a society that views the corpse with horror, the funeral director reduces those feelings of revulsion by making the body "acceptable" again in the process, the illusion that is presented again restores a kind of manageability to death. Contemporary people have contended with death by means of science and technology. When these fail, then death reasserts itself as of old; replete with all its primal terror and images. To proceed from a technological battle with death to a direct confrontation with a rotting corpse is too much for us. As a result, we require of the funeral director an intercession to soften the blow. This is not a true denial of death, for if it were so, then the funeral industry would be inventing more and more lifelike presentations of the body. The corpse may look "at rest," but this does not imply "alive." What the public desires is a blunted representation of death, to make its reality easier to confront. When death appears, we avoid it in the abstract, and attempt to mute it in the concrete in order to make it somehow more manageable. The job — making the reality of death more manageable — we delegate to the funeral director. It is a job few of us would take on ourselves [pp. 223–24].

Because of the stigma associated with caring for dead bodies, the funeral director's role attracts more attention: By contrast, the cemeterian and monument dealer are not involved in embalming and restoring dead bodies, and this obscures to a degree their roles as actual death care providers. The funeral director's role is more directly associated with issues of public health and legal compliance, which has contributed to a greater public interest in the qualifications of those who perform this role. As with other occupations connected with such issues, the tendency of the states has been to regulate entry into funeral directing by requiring practitioners to be licensed, a condition that does not extend to cemeterians and other death care providers. The result has been to institutionalize the pivotal position of funeral director in the pecking order of death care providers. One of the causes and consequences of this enhanced status has been that funeral directors are generally required to satisfy an approved program of education designed to ensure a minimum proficiency in performing their duties and responsibilities.

Educational Requirements for Funeral Directors

The licensing procedures established for embalmers and funeral directors commonly provide for minimum educational requirements that vary considerably from state to state. The wide disparity in these requirements among the several states is indicated in this profile (Bigelow, October 1992):

> One year of mortuary college beyond high school, 17 states;
> Two years of college (including mortuary science), 14 states;
> Three years of college (including mortuary science), 16 states;
> Four years of college (including mortuary science), 1 state;
> Sliding scale requirement, 1 state; and
> No educational requirements, 1 state.

The spread of these requirements is interesting in that most states requiring only one year of study beyond high school are in the Southeast, in the Southwest, and on the West Coast. Two-year states are more often found in the Northeast and three-year states in the North Central regions.

Allowing for the variations indicated by this profile, the general nature of the educational requirements required for licensure as funeral directors may be gleaned from a brief look at the form and substance of the curriculum endorsed by the American Board of Funeral Service Education, the national accrediting agency for funeral service education in the United States. There are 42 college and university programs which are approved by the board, which oversees the curriculums taught in the 42 programs. The recommended curriculum requires a concentration or major in funeral service of 50 semester credits covering the following four areas plus electives:

> 1. *Public Health and Technical*: 14–22 semester (21–33 quarter) credits.
>   The aforesaid credits of work must be taken in the application of the sciences to work in the funeral service professional. The curriculum must involve a distribution of work in the following content areas: Chemistry, Micro-Biology and Public Health, Anatomy, Pathology, Restorative Art.
>   Clinical requirements: **a.** Each student shall actively participate

in the arterial cavity embalming, either on campus or in a practicum experience, of at least ten dead human bodies, under the supervision of an approved clinical teacher who is a certified member of the faculty. **b.** In addition, each student must participate in an on campus course, including a lab portion, in which the application of Restorative Art principles is practiced in a laboratory setting.

Throughout this section, the student must be exposed to the application of the above to the profession with special emphasis placed throughout on the public health aspects involved.

2. *Business management*: 14–22 semester (21–33 quarter) credits.

   Accounting, Funeral Home Management and Merchandising, Computer Application, Funeral Directing, Small Business Management.

3. *Social Sciences*: 8–12 semester (12–18 quarter) credits.

   The aforesaid credits must be taken in the application of the social sciences to the work of the funeral service professional. The curriculum must involve a distribution of work in the following content areas: Dynamics of Grief, Counseling, Sociology of Funeral Service, History of Funeral Service, Communication Skills (oral or written).

4. *Legal, Ethical, Regulatory*: 3–6 semester (4–9 quarter) credits.

   The aforesaid credits of work must be taken in the consideration of legal, ethical, and regulatory ramifications for the funeral service professional. The curriculum must involve a distribution of work in the following content areas: Mortuary Law, Business Law, Ethics.

5. *Electives* sufficient to meet graduation requirements for the Associate Degree or Baccalaureate Degree as prescribed by each state and institution, if the student is enrolled in a degree program.

In addition to such minimal education requirements recommended by the American Board of Funeral Service Education (*Manual of Accreditation*, 1990, p. iv), *The Encyclopedia of Careers and Vocational Guidance* (1990) states the following: "Tact, understanding, and a genuine desire to help people at a time of great stress are essential qualities for anyone wishing to enter the funeral service field. Good physical health and emotional stability are also very important" (Hopke, vol. 2, p. 249). Reinforcing this, the encyclopedia concludes its discussion of funeral directing as an occupation with the following statement:

> Funeral directors, as stated above, must be tactful, discreet, and compassionate in dealing with people at a time of great emotional stress. They must be able to provide firm guidance to those who may be confused and upset, while at the same time respecting their wishes and, often, their financial limitations. They must be especially tolerant toward a diversity of religious and philosophical beliefs.
>
> Funeral directors, especially in smaller communities, are looked upon as respected professionals who provide an essential service. They have the satisfaction of helping people through a time of crisis and enabling them to express their grief over the loss of a loved one [vol. 2, p. 251].

These social and psychological qualifications are not mentioned in descriptions of the occupations of cemetery supervisors or memorial designers. "*Supervisors of cemetery workers* coordinate the activities of workers engaged in maintaining cemetery grounds and in related activities, such as grave digging and lining, grave marker placement, and disinterments. They draw up plans for the work to be done, determine personnel and equipment requirements for each task, and hire and train workers" (Hopke, vol. 2, pp. 309–10). "*Memorial designers* design stone memorials such as monuments, statues, and mausoleums" (Hopke, vol. 2, p. 166). Such occupations are farther removed from the handling of remains, which stigmatizes the occupations of embalmers and funeral directors and from the tasks of dealing with bereaved survivors in the immediate aftermath of a death, which leads to the characterization of funeral directors as the primary providers of death care who require special social skills.

Is It a Profession?

In addition to learning how to embalm dead bodies, to deal tactfully with bereaved families, and to run a small business subject to regulatory burdens, the education of funeral directors involves socialization into the death care culture. In the course of this socialization process, funeral directors acquire the skills and status associated with "occupational stratification" in American society. As described in the literature of sociology, this process of socialization is a necessary and useful means for ensuring that essential tasks are well performed and properly compensated in societies. As a part of this process, some occupations become recognized officially as "professions" based on public perception. Once this recognition occurs, additional features of "professionalism" arise (Cockerham, 1989, pp. 173–74). Some or most of these features are associated with the occupation of funeral directing to some extent. Funeral directors have traditionally shared a service orientation, and they have generally been trained in a specialized body of knowledge, consisting of the elements of embalming and dealing with bereaved persons. The extent of such training has never been prolonged, however, as it is in the case of medical, legal, or other "professional" studies. One reason for this is that funeral directing and embalming are purely practical arts that do not have or require an abstract body of knowledge of their own. The practice of embalming is based on the body of knowledge provided by the medical science of pathology. The body of knowledge on which the practice of funeral directing is based is provided by the fields of psychology, psychiatry, and theology, among others. The purely clinical nature of funeral directing and embalming appears to rebut the claim of funeral directors to full professional status.

In terms of educational preparation, the status of funeral directors appears to rank far below the status of practitioners of established professions such as physicians, surgeons, attorneys, or even registered nurses. For example, the educational and training programs for funeral directors are still offered mostly at vocational-technical colleges which have lower academic standards for admission than do other colleges and universities. The contrast is even greater when one considers that graduate and professional schools of medicine, law, business, and other fields generally seek the best-performing college graduates for further education and training as physicians and surgeons, attorneys, college professors, executive managers, and other such highly trained specialists.

In terms of length and cost of education and training, there is also a vast difference between the investment and commitment by students with a professional orientation and those with a vocational orientation. It is unrealistic to regard as comparable the educational and training requirements for funeral directors — two years or less at a vocational college with emphasis on practical techniques and interpersonal behavior — with the educational and training requirements for accepted professions — three years of law school after college or four years of medical school after college followed by internship and residency or four to six years of graduate school followed by the dissertation for university professors. Thus, it seems that the education acquired in most mortuary college programs is vocational rather than professional.

Death Care Providers as Complex Specialists

This discussion is not meant to suggest that the role performed by funeral directors is not complex and highly specialized, with outputs valued by American consumers. Their comprehensive social role as death care specialists — often combining the roles of embalmer, counselor to bereaved families, and funeral director — requires a certain personality and a set of specific technical, interpersonal, and managerial skills. Consumers desire to be served in a way that inspires three responses: (1) trust that someone competent will assume the burden and the horror of dealing with the dead body, (2) expectation of compassionate treatment at a time of bewilderment and grief, and (3) a sense of security that the death care process, most often including grievous ceremonies and religious services of the appropriate kind, will be completed satisfactorily.

Those who doubt the complexity and difficulty of meeting this set of demands might recall their own difficulty when dealing with the members of a family which has experienced a death. Even in the role of friend, most of us find ourselves groping for the right words and the right ways to express them. We are uncomfortable because we are untrained and inexperienced in the role of caregiver to the bereaved when it is forced upon us by circumstances.

Because he is a stranger hired by the family, the attention of the funeral director may mean less to family members, however, than the untrained utterances of friends and acquaintances. It may be less meaningful than the comfort provided by clergy with whom the family is familiar. But the availability of these sources of comfort is often limited. For the most part, the counsel which is available "on call" to the family is that of the funeral director selected. When communities were small and families were extended, the event of death rallied voluntary support. But these are not the conditions under which most of us live and most deaths occur today. Under modern conditions, the only support on which many families can rely is that purchased from the providers of death care.

It is this claim to the role of death care specialists, not to the dubious status of professionals, that secures the position of death care providers in contemporary society. Most of us do not know how to do the things that funeral directors and cemeterians do. We rely upon them to do such things for us, not because they are highly complex tasks like brain surgery or constitutional law or civil engineering, but because they are serious tasks in their own right.

Even apart from the technical tasks of handling dead bodies, the arrangement of ceremonies is something which most of us do not do often enough to do very well, whether the arrangements involve a funeral or a memorial service. Obviously, we are not prepared to bury or to cremate a body ourselves. To perform on demand these specialized activities is the raison d'être of the death care economy; its structure is consistently maintained by the ability of death care specialists to supply the goods and services that members of our society need, expect, and are willing to pay for. Given the required ability, a high degree of "professionalism" may be said to apply to the role of funeral directors only insofar as it relates to their performance, most especially their conduct. And it is by their conduct that they are judged. As someone has said, "The integrity of men is measured by their conduct, not by their professions."

Adherence to "Traditional" Funerals

One likely outcome of the socialization of funeral directors which reflects their training and experience is their widespread belief in the value of traditional funerals involving ceremonies that are based on viewing the body. This practice, which requires embalming, restoration, and display of the remains in a casket for viewing during funeral ceremonies and rituals, is the backbone of the mortuary services component of death care that is traditionally provided by funeral homes. Without it, the extent of the mortuary services required is effectively reduced to transporting the body from the place of death to the site of final disposition. The significance of the role of the funeral home and the funeral director in the death care process depends on the extent of the ceremonies desired following death and prior to final disposition of the body. It is no exaggeration to say that the provision of these ceremonial services is the bread and butter of the business in which funeral homes are engaged.

As a result, it is not surprising that funeral directors and their trade associations have consistently sought to defend the traditional funeral against its critics. Indeed, it seems likely that many funeral directors, based on their training and experience, sincerely believe that traditional funerals involving viewing and religious observances are the most effective means of dealing socially and psychologically with death in modern society. This is probably why they enter into and remain in such a stigmatized line of business and even consider it a "profession," a "calling," or a (priestly) "vocation." It should not be surprising therefore that they have tended to advocate traditional funerals with the restored body present for viewing during a ritual period. Even many laymen strongly believe that traditional funeral services are an appropriate part of modern death care. Based on the common sense proposition that "seeing is believing," there is something to be said for the belief that viewing promotes acceptance and closure.

If funeral directors truly believe this, as a result of their training and experience, their adherence to and advocacy of traditional funerals may be attributed to a desire to serve their clients best. Because such a belief is consistent with the sale of services and merchandise in which they specialize as death care providers, it is entirely understandable that they have tended to promote traditional funerals as their principal product. Even so, as a commercial matter, funeral homes commonly offer nontraditional services and in fact are required to do so by the funeral rule which applies to all of them.

Under this rule, funeral homes are required to provide customers with only the mortuary services they choose, based on an itemized list of the merchandise and services the establishment provides. As businesses, funeral homes have adapted to this requirement, but the nature of their operations remains based on their role as providers of traditional funerals. The demand for caskets, vaults, viewing, visitation, and other components of traditional funerals is the main source of their revenues and incomes as death care providers. This demand has tended to remain so stable for many funeral homes that they have experienced little stimulus to change the nature of the goods and services offered or their methods of selling to consumers. While some firms have now begun to experiment with new merchandise and selling techniques, no radically new goods and services have been introduced by funeral homes in this century. This is a distinctive feature of their operation which clearly distinguishes funeral homes from other businesses and even from other death care providers.

Commercial cemeteries, in particular, have made evolutionary progress from urban and church graveyards to monumented rural cemeteries to lawn-parks to memorial park facilities. New goods and services have been offered: community mausoleums, crematories, columbariums, and others. As a result of changes in the memorialization products associated with different types of cemetery facilities, the products of monument dealers have been altered or eliminated to some extent. The operators of cemeteries and monument dealerships have been forced to adapt their operations to the changes occurring around them.

Adaptation and Maladaptation

Funeral homes until recently have been largely insulated from changes requiring them to adapt. As has been pointed out several times, this insulated status has changed or is in the process of changing. Funeral homes are being forced to respond to such factors as increased regulation, increased competition from cemeteries and crematories, increased consolidation, and the increased threat of power shifts due to rapid dynamic social and economic change. In response to these forces, some independent operators have sold their firms to regional and national chains, and this has led to the rise of large corporations whose interests threaten to dominate the sector. The remaining independent operators and the trade associations they dominate have sought to preserve the status quo in ways that are often at odds with the interests of consolidators. Their methods have involved fostering regulation that impedes consolidation and combinations as well as pre-need selling, and they have sought to restrict new sources of competition while proclaiming their concern for the interests of consumers.

Funeral directors usually frame their support for particular public policies and restrictive legislation in terms of the need to protect public health and safety as well as the interests of consumers and even the sacredness of burial grounds. Similar attempts by practitioners in a trade or industry are common in our society, used as a device by entrenched business interests to bar entry to potential competitors. The potential for this abuse exists in the death care sector as much or even more than it does in other sectors because death care goods and services are highly varied and complex. Thus consumers do indeed require a measure of protection from practices involving misrepresentation, abuse, and fraud. Nevertheless, if this is used as a rationale for laws and regulations unnecessarily limiting the choices of consumers and the degree of competition among death care providers, the result is not consumer protection. On the contrary, a kind of consumer abuse results from spurious "protective" legislation, which effectively denies consumers freedom of choice. This includes laws which prohibit cemetery-mortuary combination establishments, pre-need sales solicitation, the ownership of multiple establishments, and the use of centralized embalming facilities by local clusters of establishments. Such laws are a striking example of the abuse of power by funeral directors who have the power to restrict competition through their control of state boards.

Beyond such questionable competitive practices, the unethical practices of clearly unscrupulous providers serve to raise doubts about the integrity of even the most honest and conscientious providers and to sully the reputation of death care providers generally. There seems to be little that ethical practitioners can do about the unethical ones except to support a variety of codes of conduct and standards of ethical practice which deal harshly with unscrupulous operators by stripping them of their association memberships and licenses. But even this fails to address the basic issue of what is expected of death care providers generally because the associations and boards are still provincial and their judgments are still susceptible to the influence of powerful personalities and special interests.

In addition, it is clear that no amount of piecemeal legislation or regulation at the state or local levels will solve these problems. It may appear that what is needed is wider federal regulation of death care providers of all types, especially since the regional, national, and even international scope of the operations of large death care companies exposes them to a wide variety of regulations imposed by the many jurisdictions in which their facilities are located. Even small death care establishments are subject to a variety of regulations when they ship remains from state to state and internationally. Uniform requirements concerning education, licensing, transportation, health issues, pre-need sales solicitation, and funding arrangements might well be achieved under a federal "Death Care Act" similar to the Mortuaries and Cemeteries Acts of some other countries. In a sense the federal regulation of funeral home marketing practices by the FTC represents a partial imposition of such regulation in the United States. Consideration has even been given to extending federal regulation to other providers of death care.

A better solution would seem to be for death care providers themselves to create a united representational body for self-governance. Since the boundaries of their businesses overlap, all different types of death care providers engage in various forms of cooperation and rivalry while often working side by side to serve the same customers. It would therefore seem desirable for all of them to establish a common basis for ethical competition consistent with their special status individually and jointly. To accomplish this would require cooperative action among members of their separate associations and state boards. Beyond that, perhaps the separate associations and boards in each state could be consolidated into a single Death Care Association or Board of Death Care Providers with balanced representation from, and coordinated responsibility for, all types of occupations and establishments which comprise the death care sector of the economy in each and every state.

To support the thesis that it is the raison d'être of death care providers to serve the needs of consumers, it would be wise for such consolidated boards to include consumer representation. Furthermore, such boards might well include a pathologist or public health professional who brings technical expertise and scientific knowledge to bear on the issues affecting death care providers. This would help to allay criticism and to heighten the credibility of associations and boards of death care providers.

Criticism and Response

The publication of Jessica Mitford's book was a watershed event in the history of death care in the United States. As a commercial exploitation of its subject, it was a huge success. Some thirty years later it is still in print, and Mitford remains the quintessential critic of "the American way of death." Yet her analysis showed little appreciation for the value which American consumers attach to the variety of death care goods and services they receive in transactions with death care providers. Her claims that the death care they receive is imposed on them against their will is patently absurd. It flies in the face of common experience and overwhelming evidence that human needs and social factors play a dominant role in determining the forms of death care that consumers prefer and freely choose in this country.

The weakness of Mitford's case provided an invitation for the associations of death care providers to defend their performance by demonstrating that the value of "the American way of death" is based on the manifest demand by American consumers for death care goods and services. But they appear to have been incapable of presenting a strong defense against even a weak attack. Few industries have suffered from a similar inability to defend themselves against their critics by presenting a strong case for the positive value of their ways and means. The tobacco industry, for example, whose critics are much better supported by the evidence, has defended its products and actions to the hilt. Gunmakers and pornographers defend themselves against their critics. Why, then, have death care providers failed to defend themselves effectively, since presumably the value of death care goods and services is demonstrable and defensible? More so than with many other products and services on the market, the desire and demand for death care goods and services are deeply rooted in the nature of man as a social, religious, and rational being.

Death care practitioners are mainly concerned with the performance of their roles at the concrete level of the practitioner, whose performance sometimes attracts attention at the abstract level of social criticism and debate. This situation parallels that occurring in other controversial fields of business that are the subject of criticism because their goods and services are objectionable to many for social reasons; a prime example is birth control clinics. Where the goal of critics is to modify consumer behavior, typically the supplier has been condemned for pushing the objectionable product onto consumers, in effect "creating" consumer demand. This was Mitford's charge against funeral directors in particular, and by association against providers of death care goods and services generally.

Criticism of death care practices on the abstract level places stress on practitioners at the concrete level, but their primary concern is to provide the kind of death care that consumers want as demonstrated by their purchases, which are based on their individual desires and means. The restrained ways in which most of them have tended to advocate the forms of death care in which they have the greatest confidence can probably be attributed to the special status that death occupies in our society as an unresolved issue in the lives of many people, even otherwise sophisticated ones. Because of this special status, it is deemed inappropriate for death care providers, and especially funeral homes, to push their goods and services or even to draw much attention to them.

Critics have exploited this taboo, and there has been no easy way for the providers to stand up and say: "It's okay to spend money on a funeral service, a cemetery plot, and a monument of your choice. It makes sense. It satisfies basic human needs and desires. It serves an important social function. There's a strong case for it. It costs money like everything else, but there is a wide range of choices at different prices from which everyone can select according to their individual means and desires, well in advance of need if such is desired. For most people, the money they spend on death care is well spent. It provides value, everlasting value, a footprint, so to speak, in the sands of time."

For death care providers to present a convincing case for this view, two courses of action seem to be required. First, it must be recognized and publicly acknowledged that commercial death care providers are businesses engaged in the production and delivery of goods and services to consumers. In this respect they are the same as other legitimate businesses and are therefore entitled to engage in standard business practices. Second, the value of death care goods and services to consumers must be demonstrated by evidence drawn from the fields of anthropology, sociology, psychology, philosophy, theology, art, music, and literature, among other disciplines. An effective defense of this value is rooted in these branches of human knowledge, but because differences in human practices provoke disagreement, it will be difficult for death care providers ever to answer their critics satisfactorily.

PART III

Show me the manner in which a nation or a community cares for its dead and I will measure with mathematical exactness the tender sympathies of its people, their respect for the law of the land, and their loyalty to high ideals.

William Gladstone

6. *Death Care Markets*

Overview of Death Care Markets

In the terminology of economics, a market is the area within which buyers and sellers of particular goods and services interact and transactions take place between them. When sellers interact with customers and potential customers throughout the world, the market is global. At the other extreme, the sellers of goods and services such as death care commonly interact with customers and potential customers within a very limited area. To serve as accessible sites for traditional forms of funeral services, final disposition, and memorialization, funeral homes and cemeteries must be located close to their customers. For this reason the markets for their products are largely restricted to more or less well-defined geographic areas surrounding the location of death care facilities. Bodies may be shipped between establishments serving different markets, but this involves an operational link between death care establishments in different geographic areas. It does not entail competition between establishments that are geographically separated. Even within a limited geographic area, the interaction of some death care providers may be effectively limited to a particular ethnic, religious, or socioeconomic segment of the local population which comprises the market they serve.

Within a growing number of local markets, there are now one or more establishments which provide all of the components of the death care process to consumers, but this has not traditionally been the case. The firms providing death care goods and services within most local markets have traditionally specialized in providing a limited range of death care. This has led to a confusing variety of partial providers in most areas. There are thus funeral homes operated by funeral directors who provide mortuary services but not final disposition to consumers. There are cemeteries which provide final disposition but not mortuary services. There are monument dealers who provide only memorialization goods and services. And there are firms which provide various combinations of goods and services short of the complete set provided by full-service combined establishments. Inevitably the operations of these partial providers overlap one another as they provide separate parts of a complete package of death care to the same customers. In addition to the inconvenience it causes consumers, this disjointed way in which death care is delivered by separate providers involves operational inefficiencies and occasional friction among them over jurisdictional matters such as who is in charge after the funeral procession enters the cemetery gates.

This awkward manner in which death care is provided in most local areas finds its historical causes in conditions under which people lived as many cities and metropolitan areas developed. These conditions generally favored the establishment of numerous small, local funeral homes which served their immediate neighborhoods by providing conveniently accessible locations for funeral services and visitation at wakes. Final disposition then occurred in less convenient locations on the outskirts of towns where cemeteries were generally situated.

The resulting separation of death care facilities created a corresponding separation of ownership of firms operating different types of death care facilities which serve a common set of customers comprising a single local market for complete death care.

It may appear that each such local market further comprises a market for mortuary services, a market for cremation, a market for final disposition, a market for memorialization, and so on. In theory this may be true, but in practice a set of these products is commonly purchased together by consumers in connection with or in anticipation of the event of death. In making such purchases, consumers deal with various providers because different types of death care establishments have traditionally provided only their separate and distinct parts of complete death care. To accommodate the desires of consumers for the complete "product," however, more establishments of each type have tended to expand their scope by integrating their operations so that many of them now provide a combination of mortuary services and memorial products, cemetery products and cremation services, or other combined outputs. Further integration has resulted from the operation of crematories by funeral homes and the operation of mortuaries and cemeteries under common ownership and management. The epitome of integration is the modern "mortuary-crematory-cemetery-memorial dealer" combination establishment which physically integrates the facilities for providing all parts of the death care process at a single location.

These combined death care establishments are comparable to modern supermarkets, department stores, or medical centers which provide a full complement of related goods and services to a common market. Integrated establishments of these types coexist in most market areas with nonintegrated establishments which provide only a limited variety of goods and services in which they specialize. Such is also the case in most local death care markets. As a result of the emergence of combined death care establishments, the economic organization of many local markets for death care is comprised of one or more full-service operations and a number of traditional stand-alone funeral homes, cemeteries, and monument dealerships which exist side by side with them. In most cases some of the same goods and services are also offered by both funeral homes and cemeteries, and cemeteries generally offer memorialization products which are offered also by memorial dealers. In general, this has represented the direction in which establishments have been driven as a means of providing the complete death care desired by consumers. The few exceptions to this include the emergence of direct disposition firms and discount providers of graveside services in some large metropolitan areas and the creation of independently owned "casket stores" which provide merchandise only in a few isolated markets. In a similar way, the service of opening and closing graves may be viewed as a component of death care which may be independently provided, as are flowers, death notices, and a few others. For the most part however, the bulk of death care is provided by mortuaries, crematories, cemeteries, memorial dealers, and combinations of two or more of these different establishments.

Substitutability Among Death Care Components

In an article entitled "The Relationship Between Mortuaries and Cemeteries," the substitutability of death care products was initially considered by Smith and Falk (1979). The article began by introducing the general concept of product substitution as follows:

> In economics two goods or services are said to be substitutes if an increase (decrease) in the price of one leads to an increase (decrease) in the quantity purchased of the other. This relationship is called the "cross-elasticity" of demand between two products. High cross-elasticity indicates a high degree of substitutability between them....
>
> Following this notion, the outputs of mortuaries and cemeteries may be said to belong to the same industry if their "products" are close substitutes in the eyes of consumers. It would not appear, however, that this is the case for the two types of firms. That is, the services of a mortuary — funeral services — are not a "substitute for" interment or cremation. It is true that the amount spent by consumers must be allocated between mortuaries and cemeteries, so that if more is spent on funeral services, there is less available to spend on burial or cremation. But, realistically, there is no reason why a mortuary price change would ever lead to a change in the number of burials and cremations, though it might lead to some substitution of cremation for relatively more expensive earth burial. This, however, is substitution between types of final disposition generally furnished by cemeteries, not between mortuary services and final disposition as such [pp. 24–25].

Based on this line of thought, the article concluded:

> Since a price change by mortuaries cannot lead to a change in the number of interments and cremations, the outputs of mortuaries and cemeteries cannot be said to be close (or even distant) substitutes for one another. Of course a change in the prices charged by mortuaries for the so-called "complete" funeral might occasion some substitution of less-than-complete funerals. To this extent the latter "products" are substitutes for the complete

funeral product, even though the degree of product differentiation is great [p. 25].

In this last respect, mortuaries not only compete among themselves by offering funeral services that are substitutes for one another; they also compete with themselves in the sense that they offer a line of caskets that are substitutes for one another. Likewise, the sale of graveliners, vaults, and markers by mortuaries brings them into direct competition with cemeteries, which commonly sell these types of merchandise. By the same token, cemeteries compete with one another because their outputs — earth burial, crypt interment, mausoleum entombment — are substitutable forms of final disposition.

Furthermore, cemeteries and crematories are direct competitors insofar as their outputs are substitutes in a technological sense. This is so even when the crematory is jointly owned and operated in connection with a cemetery, as is often the case. The competition between them results from the fact that consumers may regard their outputs as partially or fully substitutable. This explains why cemeteries have developed their own crematories to avoid the loss of customers to alternative providers of cremation in their areas. The willingness of customers to substitute among forms of final disposition depends on prices and other factors. If the prices of interment or entombment increase greatly relative to that of cremation, more consumers may take the latter as a substitute for the former in spite of their previous preference for burial or entombment and in spite of the fact that it is not a perfect substitute. What is more, if consumers regard cremation alone as a substitute for a combination of burial or entombment plus memorialization, then they may be even more sensitive to changes in the prices of the combination relative to the former alone. Consumers, of course, differ greatly in their willingness to switch from earth burial or entombment to cremation for various reasons.

Given the significant difference between cremating a body versus burying or entombing it, as techniques, consumers seem unlikely to switch among alternatives on the basis of price alone. But, in general, as the prices of alternative forms of final disposition (and memorialization) rise, it is reasonable to expect some substitution of cremation for those other forms. In other words, the cross-elasticity of demand between cremation and earth burial or mausoleum entombment (with or without memorialization) is positive (if not high) (Smith and Falk, 1979, p. 25).

At the extreme, some consumers may regard cremation as a substitute not only for burial or entombment, but also for a funeral service or memorialization. This appears to be true of consumers who use immediate disposition firms and dispense with a funeral service, formal disposition of the cremated remains, and even a memorial service. Yet it must be realized that in fact the cremation process cannot "substitute" for a funeral or memorial service or for formal memorialization of the cremains. How could the act of cremation possibly be a substitute for a social ceremony or memorialization of the inurned cremains? In such a case the consumer simply chooses to dispense with those elements of the complete death care product by selecting to incur the cost of only the "necessary" part of the complete product, i.e. the part which reduces the body to a manageable package of sanitized remains. In such cases the consumer actually forgoes most of the mortuary services and all of the memorialization components of death care. Nothing is substituted for them in a technological sense.

In contrast, if cremation is seen as a mere stage in the final disposition process, the decision consumers make between alternative forms of final disposition will reasonably be taken together with the respective forms of mortuary services and memorialization they consider to be appropriate. Since their choice of final disposition affects their choice of memorialization, they will actually choose among such alternatives as "cremation plus inurnment then niche interment," "earth burial plus a monument," "mausoleum entombment plus a plaque," and so on.

Complementarity of Death Care Components

These combined forms of alternatives raise the issue of complementarities among death care goods and services of different types. In economics, two goods are said to be "complements" when they are used together by consumers. The classic example is gin and tonic. Thus it is clear that cremation urns and columbarium niches are complements to cremation as a form of final disposition. Similarly, monuments are complements to earth burial in monumented cemeteries, flush markers are complements to interments in memorial parks, plaques are complements to entombments in garden mausoleums, and so on. Based on the economic notion that a fall in the price of a good spurs the demand for its complement, a decrease in the price of any particular form of final disposition spurs the demand for the complementary form of memorialization, and vice versa.

As a technical matter, therefore, the memorialization product is not in any sense a substitute for the primary product of any other component of the death care process. Memorialization represents the third and final part of the "complete" death care process. Technologically, it appears that none of the goods and services falling within the separate component parts of death care is a substitute for the goods and services in any other component part, although there are substitute forms within each component part. Each of the three component parts of the total death care process consists of a group of goods and services, some of which are close substitutes and some of which are complements.

The goods and services grouped under different components of the death care process are not substitutes, but some of them appear to be complements in the sense that they are "used together" by consumers. For example, the principal products supplied by mortuaries (mortuary outputs) and cemeteries (final disposition outputs) are not substitutes, and the two different types of establishments do not compete directly, unless these establishments cross each other's product lines as they have tended to do in some cases.

"Complete" Death Care

Although mortuary outputs and final disposition outputs are complementary in nature, in a technical sense, the cross-elasticity of the demand between complementary products is negative. Using the complements gin and tonic as an example, when the price of gin (a good) goes down, the quantity of tonic (its complement) purchased by consumers goes up. But this is not the case for the outputs of mortuaries and cemeteries. Consumers do not necessarily buy fewer (more) graves or monuments because the prices of mortuary services rise (decline).

What this implies is not that the three components of death care are unrelated; they are obviously closely related. In fact, they are parts of a single complete product. The parts of the product are technological complements in the sense that they are used together when they are needed, but the fact is that our needs for the product and its components are strictly limited. Most of us need only one funeral service, one form of final disposition, and one primary memorial to fulfill our desires. When the need is experienced, the mortuary services–final disposition–memorialization complex of goods and services may be treated by consumers as a total product. Mathematically, the sum of these parts is 1.0 or 100 percent of the death care desired by the consumer, which implies that the three parts are complements, not in the economic sense but in the ordinary intuitive sense of that word. This is to say that the different types of death care goods and services appear to comprise a package of the three parts of a total product which is complete only when taken together as a whole.

This view of the matter appears to be consistent with popular expectations and social perceptions. What, for example, could be as incomplete as an unmarked grave or an urn of cremated remains stored in the hall closet? The former is a popular metaphor for a sad, unremembered end to a life, and the latter is the source of comedy skits. At the root of both of these reactions is a fundamental recognition of the incomplete product. Even without the emotional connotations, the unmarked grave, the unidentified urn of cremains, the death which is not accompanied by a funeral service or memorial service attended by mourners — all of these are analogous to a car without an engine or a house without a roof. One cannot escape the feeling that there is something essential that is missing from the picture of the product as a whole.

The Production of Death Care Goods and Services

In spite of the obviously close relationship between the three parts of death care, the production of the goods and services which comprise these parts has not generally been combined or integrated in a single establishment or firm, although this has occasionally occurred as more cemeteries have sought to provide markers and monuments, to offer cremation, and even to operate mortuaries. Funeral homes have not generally entered the cemetery business, although some operate crematories and many offer vaults and memorial products. The important point to keep in mind, however, is that the market for death care in an area consists primarily of all the death care goods and services offered to consumers, perhaps by many different establishments and firms.

Technically speaking, then, the firms in the death care economy operate mortuaries, crematories, cemeteries, monument dealerships, and combinations of these types of businesses. There are, in addition, many other firms in the economy which furnish goods and services that are directly or indirectly related to the death care process: casket manufacturers, florists, and newspapers, to name only a few. These firms are suppliers to death care providers on the one hand and the sellers of death-related merchandise and services to consumers on the other. Although a mortuary, a cemetery, or a monument dealer may use or sell these products in connection with providing death care or consumers may buy them directly, it is clear that they are produced by separate and independent industries, such as the casket, flower, and newspaper industries. The outputs of these industries are not close substitutes to buyers (death care providers or consumers), and there is no direct competition (or negligible competition) between them. For example, there is no close substitution by consumers among flowers and death notices, at least not in the sense that small or moderate changes in the relative prices of these goods would cause consumers to shift expenditure significantly from one good to the other. Similarly, caskets, embalming fluids, and hearses cannot be substituted for each other by death care providers who use them in the process of production (Smith and Falk, 1979, p. 26). On the contrary, they are highly complementary products used in the production of mortuary services.

The opposite is true of some of the inputs used by other types of death care providers. Cemeteries construct mausoleums on their grounds rather than use the space for earth burials. Cemeteries and memorial dealers may offer consumers bronze markers instead of upright monuments made of either granite or marble. The resulting shifts in consumer preferences for the complementary and substitutable outputs of different establishments in the death care sector thus affect the inputs of those establishments which are purchased from suppliers, whose outputs are thereby affected.

For example, an increase in the demand for cremation affects the number and quality of caskets sold by mortuaries, which affects the number and quality of caskets produced by suppliers. It affects the number of urns and memorial products of different types which are produced and sold. It also affects the production rate of firms which manufacture and upgrade crematory equipment, using inputs from other industries. When all such effects are taken into account, it is clear that shifts in the demand for goods and services produced (provided) in the death care sector of the economy has repercussions throughout industries in other sectors of the United States and even the global economy (insofar as imports of materials are involved).

Multiple Markets for Death Care

A very large number of establishments comprise the death care economy, but not all of these establishments serve the same customers. Although there are some multiunit firms which operate more than one funeral home or cemetery, each of the units of these firms usually serves a limited geographic market. In this respect, then, there are many death care markets in the United States, each of which consists of a common group of customers in a given area served by death care providers. As Smith and Falk have noted:

> Even in the same community the customers served by one or more mortuaries or cemeteries may be limited largely to a particular ethnic, religious or socio-economic group, so that such establishments are not really in competition with those that serve other groups. Local groups of funeral homes that are ordinarily non-competing because they cater to different consumers may nevertheless be potential competitors since they sell a similar (if not identical) product and since there are no legal barriers preventing consumers from shifting their purchases to rival establishments if there is some perceived advantage to them from doing so. Even where funeral services have been pre-arranged and pre-funded, the contract can generally be transferred to another mortuary. In a given geographic area, this situation gives rise to a number of semi-separate and semi-independent markets for the funeral service component of death care which are related by the ever present threat of substitution among them [Smith and Falk, 1979, p. 26].

In economic analysis, this last point seems to be the critical one. In a local market for particular goods and services, it is obvious that the availability and prices of similar or even identical goods and services in other localities do not directly affect consumer behavior because it is difficult and costly for local consumers to switch their purchases to another geographic market. For death care goods and services, it is especially difficult for consumers to switch between geographic markets because the location of the funeral home, the site of final disposition, and the kind of memorialization chosen usually must be accessible to survivors. Even in the case where burial is available free of charge elsewhere, as it is for veterans entitled to use a national cemetery, consumers often opt for local private facilities. Within a given area consumers are free to shift their purchases among available establishments for reasons other than price.

In a purely economic sense, this represents a marketplace in which there is mostly nonprice competition. Advertising is used to introduce or to reinforce the name and availability of local establishments, to emphasize their reputations for providing "family-to-family" care to members of the community they serve, or to promote their pre-need sales programs. For the most part, however, funeral homes depend on repeat business from families who return to an establishment based on their experience with it as survivors on a previous occasion. In an analogous way, a cemetery depends on the pre-need and at-need business of generations of family members who choose it because earlier generations are buried or entombed there.

The strength of such ties to a particular establishment varies among consumers, and some of those who prefer a particular establishment based on these and other noneconomic reasons, such as its specific ethnic, religious, or socioeconomic orientations, may be induced to switch to a different provider under the influence of pre-need selling or the added availability of a funeral home in the cemetery where interment is anticipated. These forces may overcome long-standing consumer loyalty to a particular establishment, including even one that is distinctive by virtue of its ethnic or socioeconomic orientation. As a rule, however, a heritage establishment which caters to the "carriage trade" may be better able to retain its clientele based on the strength of its location and its reputation as a premier provider. Even a reputation for charging higher prices than other providers may actually reinforce the distinctiveness and attractiveness of such establishments. But at some point the prices charged by even those providers do potentially become a critical factor in the thinking of consumers who must ask themselves whether the privilege of being served by the "undertaker to the stars" or being buried in a "premier" cemetery is worth the increased cost that confers this privilege. In these various respects, competition plays a role in local death care markets which are served by several providers even when those providers do not appear to compete with one another.

The Death Care Industries

Death care markets are served by a local economy consisting of all the establishments in an area that provide any part of the death care process to consumers. Each local economy is composed of a mortuary services industry composed of funeral homes and related providers, a final disposition industry composed of cemeteries and memorial parks with or without mausoleums and a memorialization industry composed of memorial dealers and related enterprises. In some areas there also exists a sort of pre-final disposition industry composed of crematories which process human remains into cremains requiring further disposition. It is worthy of note that although crematories constitute a separate death care industry, these facilities are almost always operated in connection with either mortuaries or cemeteries. The death care sector of the U.S. economy entails the sum of these local death care economies. The sum of outputs of all the local death care providers is their contribution to the U.S. economy in terms of goods and services sold, employment, and other measures of industrial performance.

This conception of the death care sector is consistent with the way in which economic sectors are generally conceived by economists and the way in which they generally operate in practice. Like other economic sectors, death care is organized into a set of related "industries" comprised of establishments which have similar production functions or techniques. Several establishments of any one of these four different types represent collectively a separate death care "industry" of that type. The boundaries between the types of death care industries are obscured by the practice of death care providers operating across industry boundaries, whether through usurpation of product lines of competing industries or through physically integrated operations. Thus, stand-alone funeral homes and cemeteries often sell memorial products in competition with memorial dealers and stand-alone cemeteries may sell mortuary products such as caskets. Moreover, firms may own and operate more than one type of establishment — mortuaries together with cemeteries, mortuaries or cemeteries together with crematories, memorial dealerships together with crematories. Such practices result from the demand by most consumers for complete death care which includes some of each part of the death care process.

In other economic sectors, such complete products are often assembled by firms before they are provided to consumers, but death care has traditionally been provided by separate firms and "assembled" by consumers themselves, yielding the total combined (complete) product we call "death care," consisting of mortuary services, final (including pre-final) disposition, and memorialization. It is clear that the production of each of these three distinct components is linked sequentially to the others because the funeral service ends at the cemetery, which is also where the memorial part of the complete product is "assembled" (installed). All three parts are commonly desired by consumers, although often in different proportions.

Comprehensive death care has not traditionally been provided to consumers as an integrated product, and its production has not been perceived as an integrated process. As a result, most death care establishments are not fully integrated facilities capable of providing all three components of the complete process in one location. This does not appear to be due to any inherent advantages of separated production and distribution facilities. It has to do rather with various external factors which have favored a fragmented form of economic organization to which consumers have become accustomed in spite of the inconvenience and inefficiency it entails. It seems correct to view this fragmentation of the sector as an artificial device designed to accommodate consumers in customary ways.

The joint production of complete death care in physically unified establishments governed by a single provider appears to be the natural form of organization of the death care sector based on the economic criteria of effectiveness and efficiency. It is not without strategic intent that memorial dealers have traditionally located their establishments as close as possible to cemeteries. It was a small step but an important one for commercial cemeteries to add monuments and other memorialization products to the line of cemetery products they sold. As suburbanization has increased the accessibility of cemeteries, it is no wonder that many of them have developed their own mortuaries, forming unified facilities for the efficient delivery of complete death care to consumers at one location. The success of these developments demonstrates the economic advantages of combining in a single location the production processes involved in delivering the three components of death care as a combined (complete) product.

These integrated providers straddle the death care industries, obscuring the traditional boundaries separating them from one another. To a lesser extent this is true of cemetery-crematory combinations, mortuary-memorial outlet combinations, and cemetery-memorial outlet combinations, and so on. To which "industry" do these combined establishments belong? To which industry do firms which own both funeral homes and cemeteries belong? To which industry do direct disposition establishments belong? At a later point these questions will be considered in the course of a discussion of an industrial classification system for what has obviously become a "death care sector." The title of this book recognizes this fact, and it is hoped that the case presented within it may contribute to the widespread adoption of the term "death care" as the most appropriate one for describing the sector of the economy examined here, the goods and services produced within that sector, the markets in which those goods and services are provided to consumers, and the industries and firms to which the establishments providing those goods and services belong.

Intrasector Rivalry

Death care markets are many and varied, often consisting of overlapping segments served by different types of death care establishments in a given geographic area. On the one hand, there appears to be limited competition among establishments of different types because their primary outputs are not close substitutes for one another. On the other hand, the goods and services they produce are sold to the same consumers in a common area. Moreover, those goods and services are parts of a complete death care package comprising substitutable or complementary component parts to which the limited funds of consumers may be variously allocated. Assuming that consumers approach the purchase of complete death care (including mortuary services, final disposition, and memorialization) with a fixed sum in mind, it follows that the greater the amount they spend on one element, the less there is available for another, according to the rules of zero-sum conditions.

Under such conditions there may be vigorous rivalry between funeral homes and cemeteries even though they supply different products to the market. This intrasector rivalry is seldom a matter of competition in terms of prices; it more often takes the form of legal and political maneuvers by those in one death care industry to restrict competition from those in another one. For example, the laws of some states limit the right of cemeteries to sell funeral merchandise and to solicit business on a pre-need basis. The laws of four states — Texas, Michigan, Massachusetts, and New Jersey — still require crematories to be located in cemeteries. In others, the law gives to funeral directors alone the right to control the process of cremation through further disposition of cremains. In some states there are requirements that the operation of a mortuary must not be combined with that of a cemetery or that two such facilities may not be jointly owned and operated. The principal effect of such restrictions is that they serve to protect the competitive position of the death care providers who support them, no matter why they are deemed to be necessary.

Take, for example, the antisolicitation laws which limit the ability of firms to sell funeral services or memorial products on a pre-need basis. These laws clearly protect the at-need sales programs of funeral homes from the pre-need sales efforts of cemeteries. This is important insofar as both types of establishments commonly sell some substitutable products such as vaults and memorial products and thus directly compete in this regard. But even as purveyors of only complementary products — mortuary services and final disposition — mortuaries and cemeteries are in direct competition for shares of the total sum of dollars spent by consumers on death care.

When the consumer purchases both mortuary services and final disposition together at the time of need (at-need), mortuaries are in the choice position in the competitive process because they are the primary provider with whom the consumer deals at the time of need. But the adoption of pre-need selling by cemeteries redresses this imbalance, allowing them to improve their competitive position vis-à-vis funeral homes by selling to consumers in advance of need, often long before funeral directors serve them. Because of the advantage this affords, the strategic use of a pre-need sales program tends to secure the strategic sales advantage to the establishment it represents. This advantage has tended to lie with commercial cemeteries because funeral homes have been slow to embrace pre-need selling, and small facilities are economically less able to do so. This has left them particularly vulnerable in those markets where a combined establishment or a cluster of funeral homes that includes a cemetery is engaged in the pre-need sale of funeral services along with cemetery property. Hence the efforts of funeral directors to protect themselves from such competition by legally restraining the use of pre-need selling, as well as cemetery-mortuary combinations and the joint ownership of cemeteries and mortuaries.

Market Characteristics

The analysis to this point has established the existence of very numerous separate and distinguishable death care markets in the U.S. economy. Each of these markets is served by several types of local establishments which provide death care in whole or in part to some or all of the consumers in a given area. Not all of these establishments compete directly with one another, but they are actually or potentially in competition to the extent that their outputs are substitutes and to the extent that the complementary goods and services they sell compete for the consumer's dollars within the total sum to be allocated. From an economic standpoint, therefore, the relevant death care market in an area consists of all the funeral homes, cemeteries, and related enterprises in a given area among which consumers allocate their spending in accordance with their preferences for different packages of complete death care consisting of the three basic elements: mortuary services, final (including pre-final) disposition, and memorialization.

Within any such market, the prices of particular death care goods and services depend on the conditions of supply and demand, both actual and anticipated, for different types of substitutable and complementary components of the death care process. As a rule, the prevailing prices for death care goods and services are established by sellers making offers at levels which they expect their customers to accept based on their particular means and tastes. Some aspects of the process by which prices are determined will be the subject of later chapters.

It is necessary at this point only to observe that the variety and prices of death care goods and services provided to the market are determined not by death care providers unilaterally, but by buyers and sellers interacting together within their relevant market areas. In all such market areas, there is generally a high degree of product differentiation based on the different locations, reputations, community affiliations, and distinctive features of particular establishments. This differentiation obviously affects the marketing and pricing strategies of firms very significantly. It also tends to divide each geographic market for death care into a series of separate, though closely related, submarkets bound together by their accessibility to a common group of consumers, some or all of whom are subject to switching their purchases among rival firms serving different submarkets within a given market area.

The most diverse subdivision of death care markets is found in large urban areas, where many small, stand-alone funeral homes cater to the ethnic, religious, and socioeconomic characteristics of different segments of the local population. Commercial cemeteries typically cater to multiple segments, not only because of their size, but also because of their tendency to subdivide sales territories along the lines of market segmentation. This latter is based naturally on the traditional cemeterian practice of subdividing their property into sections designed to appeal to different market segments.

In some cases a single firm owns and operates funeral homes, cemeteries, and crematories and sells memorial products in the same and different locations. Their emergence of such "death care" companies supports the view adopted here of a "death care economy" which consists of all of the establishments providing death care goods and services to the market. In numerous cases these firms have sought to integrate the operations of mortuaries and cemeteries, removing the barriers which have traditionally separated those establishments.

Nevertheless, the death care sector will probably continue to be dominated by several different types of establishments serving fragmented markets subject to highly varied state and local regulations. It is likely that even the regional and national chains will continue to consist of large numbers of different establishments serving highly varied and dispersed local markets. The fragmentation of the death care economy will continue to result in a confusing variety of death care providers and markets, which will interfere with integration and with attempts to reach a general conclusion on the unified concept of the "death care sector of the economy."

A Product (Market) Classification System

It may help to provide a substantial framework for the analysis that follows if we ignore temporarily the fragmented manner in which death care is provided by different types of establishments serving overlapping markets with various local characteristics. One way to do this is to shift the focus of attention from the different types of establishments serving those markets to the particular types of goods and services produced and sold by establishments of whatever type and wherever they are located. Regardless of whether such establishments are funeral homes, crematories, cemeteries, or memorial dealers, whether large or small, independently owned and operated or the units of chains, and so on, the particular outputs produced and sold by them will be our only focus of attention. For purposes of classification, these outputs may be classified in terms of the uses to which they are put by consumers.

Some of those outputs are used in connection with the death care process. Previously this process was divided into three complementary parts based on the way these parts are viewed by consumers who comprise the market for such products. Accordingly, the variety of death care goods and services produced and consumed as a part of each successive stage in the process may be grouped together into one of three categories: mortuary goods and services, final disposition goods and services, and memorial goods and services. The latter two of these are further divisible. Since final disposition may entail pre-final disposition (cremation), final disposition products are divided into (a) cremation goods and services and (b) cemetery goods and services. Memorial goods and services are divided into a variety of types of memorial products. The extant set of death care products (goods and services) may be briefly described and summarized in the following manner:

Death Care Products (Goods and Services)

    I. *"Mortuary services" products (goods and services)*
        These consist of death care goods and services used in the process of handling dead bodies prior to final disposition, preparing them in various ways, conducting ceremonies and rites at which they are present, transporting them from place to place, and generally caring for the remains and attending to the needs of survivors that result from the death. All such goods and services are either substitutes for one another or complementary parts of a total set of mortuary services customarily desired by consumers. A preliminary indication, but not necessarily a final determination, of the full range of the goods and services of this sort is the list of items required by the FTC (see Appendix) to be included in a "general price list" if they are offered for sale by a mortuary: Forwarding remains to, or receiving remains from, another funeral home; Services in connection with direct creations and immediate burials; Transfer of remains to funeral home; Embalming and other preparation of the body; Use of facilities and staff for viewing, funeral ceremony, memorial service or

graveside service; Hearse and limousine(s); Caskets and alternative containers; Outer burial containers; Burial garments; Other merchandise, etc.

The use of the elements of an itemized price list to enumerate the variety of mortuary goods and services has the advantage of concentrating attention on the items for which mortuaries charge a price or fee, paid by consumers. It omits any transcendental elements of the product of mortuaries, such as "grief therapy," for which consumers do not pay directly even though some costs may be incurred by firms to provide those services and their total revenues must cover those costs as well as others. As pointed out in an earlier chapter, any benefits of these services accrue to the general well-being of death care consumers. To the extent that this enhances the attractiveness of particular mortuaries, such expenditures are analogous to advertising and other promotional expenses incurred by firms, but one does not ordinarily regard advertising as a consumer product.

II. *"Final disposition" products (goods and services)*
These consist of death care goods and services used in connection with the process of physically disposing of dead bodies, maintaining and safeguarding the remains, and generally providing and "caring" for the final "resting place" of one sort or another. All these goods and services are either substitute forms of final disposition (e.g., a grave or a mausoleum crypt) or parts of a total set of goods and services commonly used together to accomplish final disposition. For example, cremation services are a pre-final stage in the process of final disposition which may involve scattering, or burial, or inurnment followed by niche interment in a columbarium. A partial itemization of the goods and services which serve these purposes includes, but is not limited to, the following items provided by cemeteries or crematories:

A. Cremation goods and services: Crematory services; Scattering gardens; Scattering services (land or sea); Urns and boxes (for cremains).
B. Cemetery goods and services: Cemetery lots, plots, crypts, and tombs; Family mausoleums and tombs; Community mausoleums and tombs; Columbariums niches, scattering gardens; Urns for burial or niche interment; Vaults, graveliners, copings; Opening, closing, and committal services; Maintenance and upkeep services; Perpetual care; Exhumation services; Vases.

This list is made up of groups representative of the limited range of disposal options acceptable in contemporary American society. Thus it does not include some additional options which are not widely practiced in the United States. Those options might properly be included in an international product classification system.

III. *"Memorialization" products (goods and services)*
These consist of death care goods and services used in connection with the process of memorializing the life and death of a deceased

person or persons. The form of memorialization may be essentially impermanent (e.g., a memorial service) or permanent (e.g., a monument). It is convenient to distinguish further between several basic forms of memorialization: (a) social (e.g., a memorial service), (b) published (e.g., obituaries, articles in memoriam), (c) physical (e.g., a monument, marker or plaque, a decorative urn), (d) financial (e.g., donations or gifts made in memory of a deceased person), (e) electronic (e.g., audio and video tributes), and (f) wearable (e.g., mourning jewelry). Physical memorials may be durable (e.g., monuments) or nondurable (e.g., flags) or even perishable (e.g., fresh flowers). Virtually all memorial goods and services are substitutes for one another, although they may be complementary (e.g., monuments and monument repair services). In addition, they may complement the choice of particular mortuary services (e.g., floral and videotaped tributes used at funeral services) and forms of final disposition (e.g., monuments used to mark graves following burial). Among these are the following:

Memorial services held without the presence of the body; Published death notices and tributes; Monuments, markers, plaques, decorative urns; Memorial repair and maintenance services; Donations in memory of the deceased; Photographs; Audiotaped and videotaped tributes; Televised memorials; Electronic memorials; Mourning jewelry; Flags and insignia; Sympathy cards; Floral tributes; Vesper lights.

Again the list consists of different classes of memorial goods and services. Within some classes there is a wide range of variation in particular types of memorials which consumers may prefer. This is also true within some of the different classes of items included in I and II. There is thus a wide range of options within some of the specific groups into which each of the three major groups are divided. Consumer expenditures may vary widely among and within each major group, and the amount of spending on any class of items in each group may exercise more or less influence on spending for related or unrelated items in the same or other classes and groups.

A Classification of Consumer Expenditures

The last point establishes a basis for the view that consumers are confronted simultaneously with a comprehensive set of markets from which they select the death care of their choice. In a technical sense, however, there is a separate and distinct "product market" for the death care goods and services of each type on which consumers spend. As a counterpart to the above product classification system, it is possible to divide consumer expenditures on death care into the various classes of goods and services in each of the three major groups of death care products. Such detailed breakdowns of spending on other major product groups are valued by market researchers who analyze the demand for particular goods and services. The collection and reporting of death care expenditures in this way would serve a similar function which, for lack of a comprehensive view of the death care process, has never been performed. Although several government agencies and trade organizations collect and report various market data related to death care expenditures, all of the methods used involve inadequate and incomplete descriptions of death care and its component parts. Accurate measurements of consumer expenditures and establishment data have been seriously hampered by faulty conceptions and incomplete descriptions of death care, by the atomistic structure of death care markets, and by the fragmented manner in which those markets are served. Wider adoption of a more fully explicit system will address the problems of proper definition and description, but the measurement or estimation of market data the system entails must be adjusted to the practical features of the market conditions under which death care is produced by firms and purchased by consumers. One of these features relates to the timing of expenditures by families.

In relation to the event of death, the production and sale of goods and services of each type may occur at various times which may be designated as a "preneed" market, an "at-need" market, and an "aftermarket." This is a complicating factor which necessitates allowing for a possible separation between the sale and delivery of death care products. Nevertheless, in any period a measurable quantity of the death care goods and services of each type is produced and sold. For macroeconomic and microeconomic purposes, it would be useful to obtain some idea of the unit and dollar volume of such goods and services sold and delivered in local, regional, national, and even international markets. No such precise indications currently exist, and to attempt to obtain them is not without its practical difficulties. Chief among these is the fact that the goods and services included in most classes of death care are produced and sold to consumers by different types of death care establishments and other firms. Memorial dealers may be largely restricted to providing memorial goods and services, but funeral homes and cemeteries may deal in a number of distinct varieties of goods and services which technically fall outside their respective products classes. Such firms handle these additional varieties of items because of buying or selling economies or because the items are substitutes for or complementary to the main varieties of merchandise and services they provide.

It will be recalled that in some cases a single enterprise in the form of a cemetery-mortuary establishment may provide all types of death care goods and services to consumers. The sales of such firms cut across all three classes of goods and services identified above. In other cases, mortuary goods (but not services) may commonly be provided by cemeteries, and memorial goods and services may be provided by mortuaries and cemeteries as well as by memorial dealers. In still other cases, certain products of each type may be provided by establishments other than mortuaries, cemeteries, memorial dealers, and combinations thereof. For example, florists provide flowers used during funeral services and thereafter as perishable memorials used to decorate graves. Various types of retail establishments sell sympathy cards used to express condolences, along with other products which may fall into the death care category of consumer goods as well.

As a further complicating factor, mortuaries commonly accommodate their customers by arranging for the purchase of various goods and services not provided directly by funeral homes. Newspaper notices, cemetery goods and services, and other items may be among the goods and services for which mortuaries advance the funds. This practice leads to the inclusion of various types of goods and services in the statements of mortuaries which are strictly to be regarded as final disposition and memorial goods and services. In addition, financial memorials are a personal expenditure that is unrelated to any particular class of firm or product.

For all these reasons, it is unlikely that the volume of consumer expenditures for death care goods and services of each type can be calculated from the accounting and reporting of the sales of establishments or firms of various types. Nor is it likely that consumers are able to make very clear distinctions among the types of death care goods and services on which they spend. It is more likely that they will distinguish among the amounts spent at each type of establishment. Since these may include some goods and services of each type, all such estimates are subject to some degree of imprecision in terms of the three classes of death care products. The greatest degree of precision would appear to be associated with consumer surveys which distinguish clearly between spending on each type of product described in detail and assigned to one of the three major classes of death care. This would appear to be possible to do in the Consumer Expenditure Survey of the Bureau of Labor Statistics (BLS).

Conducted under the auspices of the U.S. Department of Labor, this survey is a specialized study in which the primary emphasis is on collecting data relating to family expenditures for goods and services used in day-to-day living. A portion of these expenditures is devoted to death care goods and services of various types. As currently conducted, the BLS uses two independent surveys, a Diary Survey and an Interview Panel Survey, to collect information on family expenditures and other demographic and economic characteristics of the population. As a part of its survey of consumer expenditures, it currently includes two categories of expenditures on death care goods and services described as "funeral expenses" and "cemetery lots, vaults, maintenance fees" ("Consumer Expenditures and Income" in BLS *Handbook of Methods*, undated, Chapter 18).

This appears, however, to be an inadequate description of the components of death care expenditures. Accordingly, we propose a revision of the survey items to include a category described as "death care" comprised of spending on "mortuary goods and services," "final disposition goods and services," and "memorial goods and services." Clearly, this breakdown is more consistent with the purposes for which families spend on this general category of goods and services, and it is representative of the conceptual distinctions among the major components of death care.

It would also be useful in such a survey to differentiate between death care expenditures as "pre-need" or "at-need." For complex categories in other economic areas, allocation routines are currently used to transform consumer reports of nonspecific items into specific ones. For example, when survey respondents report expenditures for "meat" instead of "beef" or "pork" allocations are performed using proportions derived from specific reports in other completed diaries to distribute the expenditure reported for "meat" to the specific items such as beef or pork (Chapter 18). Analogous allocative routines might be used to distribute reports of nonspecific expenditures on "death care" among the three major groups and among the various classes within each major group.

The adoption of the data collection and reporting format proposed here would add clarity and specificity to the section of the Consumer Expenditure Survey conducted by the BLS. The resulting scheme would fully survey and report annual spending on death care and its components as distinctive categories of consumer expenditures. The proposed format is explicit at all points, and it conforms with the treatment of such comparable categories of consumer spending as, say, "medical services." Most death care expenditures are made by consumers in the U.S. economy, but government and other organizations also spend on death care of several types. Public and private expenditures on morgues, military death care, municipal cemeteries, and government memorials would not be included in the results of a consumer survey of households. For purposes of obtaining some indication of total spending represented by the death care markets, it would be necessary to add these to estimates of consumer expenditures.

Markets and Population

In the analysis of consumer goods markets generally, the influence of population is brought out by Gentry and Taff (1966, pp. 305–6). For death care goods and services, as with other goods and services, markets are comprised of the people and groups of people who desire such items and are willing to spend for them. As a general rule, the extent of the market for death care goods and services varies with the population of an area. Population is thus the primary indicator of potential sales volume. An exception to this rule may be found in the case of cremation and goods related thereto. For cultural, religious, or other reasons, the number of people who prefer cremation does not vary directly with the population. For the general run of items that comprise death care, however, population is an important indicator of the potential demand for the goods and services provided by death care establishments. In this respect, the situation for death care is similar to that of most retail stores, for which "population is the primary indicator of the potential sales volume" (Gentry and Taff, 1966, p. 305).

Throughout this century the United States has experienced continued changes in the size, distribution, and composition of its population. From 1965 to 1993, the total population of the country has increased from 190 million to more than 258 million people, who live in 96 million households, 25 percent of which now consist of only one person. Changes in the geographic distribution of the population are exemplified by the movement from rural to urban areas, followed by the growth of the suburbs where large cemeteries had often previously located. Mortuaries and other firms followed people to the suburbs by relocating or opening branches in areas to which their traditional customer base had moved. These shifts also produced changes in patterns of living which affected the consumption of death care.

Accompanying these changes has been a simultaneous shift upward in the age composition of the U.S. population. With the gradual aging of the postwar baby-boom generation, large numbers of Americans are expected to swell the ranks of the elderly in the early decades of the twenty-first century, leading to an increase in the number of people who die annually. This development will create growing markets for death care goods and services in many areas of the United States. A similar aging of the populations of most developed countries will produce an increase in the numbers of persons who die annually in most areas of the world.

In addition to this basic demographic factor, a variety of features of the populations of the United States and other countries may be expected to influence the growth of spending on death care and its components in the years ahead. Among these are changes in the levels and distributions of personal disposable income, wealth, and life insurance in force, all of which may exert some influence on family expenditures on death care. Even more important from a marketing standpoint is the increasing diversity of the populations of the United States and other countries where the cultural traditions and religious customs of growing segments of those populations may exert a strong influence on the extent and forms of death care desired by consumers in the future.

In a later chapter, the prospective demand for death care will be discussed in greater detail. The present observations are meant to suggest only that the death care economy is driven primarily by demographic changes and secondarily by changes in various economic and noneconomic characteristics of the populations served. To adapt specifically to these changes, the operators of local establishments must respond to shifts in their markets as determined by the number of potential customers residing near the location of their facilities. Within the total population of this area, the potential customers of a given establishment are further delineated in terms of the ethnic, religious, and socioeconomic characteristics they possess in common. Given the limited extent of such markets, the mode of expansion by death care firms occurs by adding markets to their existing one(s). The markets added may consist of new customers to whom their existing line of goods and services is sold or of a new line of goods and services sold to their existing customers.

To provide consumers with all types of death care goods and services made available in markets throughout the United States, the death care sector of the economy has evolved into its present state of organization. The economic structure of the sector is in some respects similar to the economic structures of other sectors, but like other economic sectors, it is unique in some respects to be discussed in subsequent chapters.

7. *The Death Care Sector of the Economy*

Death Care as an Economic Sector

The modern death care sector includes some combined establishments which provide various types of death care products made available to consumers at a single location or from separate establishments operated together in different locations of a metropolitan area. For the most part, however, establishments in the death care sector are small, "stand-alone" establishments that are independently owned and operated and are capable of providing only incomplete death care.

Each of these firms has tended to be identified closely with the separate component of death care it provides and with the occupational specializations or trade associations which represent each component. In spite of, or perhaps because of, the associations of such firms with death, they have never been known as "death care" providers. Yet the term is apt. It rings truer than the euphemistic terms used by those in the business in order to distance themselves from death. This may be necessary when dealing with consumers, but euphemism has no place in the technical terminology adopted to describe this sector of the economy.

The necessity for death care activities arises from basic natural phenomena. Life spans are limited, people die, and something must be done with their remains. Those who knew the deceased, and perhaps loved them, wish to honor their dead in ways appropriate to their individual values, judgment, and means. Whatever forms these ways may take, their accomplishment requires the assistance of those who are in the death care business. Whether such businesses are viewed collectively as death care providers or as funeral homes, crematories, cemeteries, monument dealerships, or other types of specialized establishments, the sector of the economy to which they belong is indicated by the outputs of their operations and the use to which such outputs are put by consumers. To the extent that some part, or all, of the outputs of such firms are used in the death care process, they fall within the sector treated here as "the death care economy."

Comparison of the health care sector and the death care sector shows the fragmented manner in which such major categories of consumer goods and services have tended to be provided and have tended to be purchased by consumers. Health care is obtained in part from community-based physicians, capital-intensive hospitals operated by governmental, religious, commercial, and other organizations, and local pharmacies. In a similar fashion, death care traditionally has been provided by community-based funeral homes, capital-intensive cemeteries operated by governmental, religious, commercial and other organizations, and local monument dealerships. Other local establishments like florists provide certain goods and services which are used in the death care process.

Like the health care sector, the death care sector is populated by a large number of separate entities which tend to exhibit a high degree of stability. Further, just as there is a distinctive aura of morbidity about doctors' offices, clinics, hospitals, and pharmacies, there is a distinctive aura of mortality about the facilities of firms that provide the components of death care to consumers. That aura is a manifestation of the common bond among them: they all deal in death.

Stability of the Death Care Sector

During the twentieth century, almost every aspect of life in the United States has undergone dramatic changes as a consequence of the impact of technology, urban decline and suburban development, and modifications in cultural values, among other factors. For example, consider the impact which advances in modern medicine, computers, communications techniques, governmental deficit financing, women's liberation, the sexual revolution, and the dissolution of families — to name only a few forces at work during the last half of the century — have had on the lives of us all.

In a period during which so much change has swept through our society, it is not surprising that there have been changes also in the types of death care desired by consumers. For example, cremation as a legal form of final disposition and as a form of preparation before actual disposition has become more widely acceptable. Compared to the sweeping changes experienced in other areas, however, the death care sector of the economy has been characterized by remarkable stability. This is true in spite of occasional criticism of the American funeral as an institution and of funeral homes and cemeteries as businesses.

In other industries there have been periods during which vocal critics have produced gradual changes in the attitudes of consumers towards products previously desired by a large proportion of the population. Tobacco products are one example. Consumer attitudes toward death care appear to be more resistant to criticism of the sort directed toward it so far. The effect of criticism mainly has been to induce federal regulation of funeral homes, which does not appear to have affected greatly their operations or their relationships with their customers. This point was confirmed by two econometric analyses of the effects of the Funeral Rule that were performed by the Bureau of Economic Analysis in the course of the FTC's 1990 review. First, a time-series analysis was performed to compare a sample of funeral expenditures from 1981 with a similar sample from 1987. The second approach involved the use of cross-section analysis of the sample of 1987 data to determine if the average expenditure of those who received "compliant" treatment was different from those who did not receive the required price disclosure or other documents or who received otherwise "less than compliant" treatment from a mortuary.

The results of the cross-section analysis indicated that the respondents who were treated in compliance with the rule did not spend less than those whose treatment was not in full compliance as defined in the study (U.S. FTC, July 1990, p. 80). Following criticism, a further analysis also concluded that compliance had no statistically significant effect on funeral expenditures. The results of a time-series analysis of consumer expenditures strongly suggested that "the Rule has not contributed to a general reduction in consumer expenditures for funerals" (U.S. FTC, July 1990, p. 83). These results did not conform with the expectations of the FTC that consumer expenditures on funerals would decrease as a result of disclosure provisions in the rule. On the other hand, mortuary services costs appear to have increased "for personnel as a result of a 23-minute average increase in the duration of the arrangements, and for business expenses such as printing, accounting and legal service" related to the FTC rule (*Federal Register*, January 11, 1994, p. 160). The extent of these increases is a subject of debate, and it is not clear to what extent the higher costs of complying with the rule have been passed on to consumers. In any event, however, it appears that the industry as a whole has adapted successfully to federal regulation, and its effect has done little to alter the historical stability of funeral homes.

A Stable Population of Establishments

In many industries large numbers of firms come and go over the years. Some firms have also disappeared from the death care economy, but most of them go on and on, with the result that funeral homes are some of the longest-lived firms on record, and cemeteries seem to have perpetual existence. The number of funeral homes of all sizes probably exceeds 22,000, most of which are small establishments handling fewer than 200 cases annually. The number of establishments which handle more than 400 cases annually is small, and only a handful deal with more than 1,000 cases per year. The emphasis of this large majority of smaller firms has tended to be on providing mortuary services to a limited clientele defined in terms of specific ethnic, racial, and religious characteristics.

The number of named cemeteries in this country exceeds 100,000, many of which are small inactive facilities (*The American Funeral Director*, July 1993). There are approximately 7,500 commercial cemeteries which are privately owned and profit-oriented. Another 3,000 to 3,500 are religious cemeteries, a majority of which are affiliated with the Roman Catholic church. There are also thousands of municipal, state, fraternal, and military cemeteries, which differ widely in their orientations and characteristics. Even so, the different facilities in a local area have tended to compete actively for business, driven especially by the sales organizations of the commercially operated cemeteries. An emphasis on actively soliciting sales through the use of large sales organizations and methods has distinguished the operations of these commercial cemeteries from those of funeral homes. To some extent this has been a consequence of the nature of the facilities operated by cemeteries, but it reflects also the tendency of cemeteries to divide into sections which attract a diverse clientele. Funeral homes, on the other hand, have tended to cater to more homogeneous "niche" markets. The need for a separate sales force on their part was neither economically necessary nor desirable.

Given a strong sales orientation, the tendency of commercial cemeteries has been to seek products to sell. As a result, they have promoted different designs and products, including family tombs and community mausoleums. As logical sites for the location of crematories, they have responded also to markets in which there was a potential demand for crematories, most of which are operated by cemeteries. To accommodate the demand for the final disposition of cremated remains, they subsequently added columbariums, urn gardens, and scatter gardens. This is consistent with what has occurred in many other industries as firms have increased the variety of goods and services offered to consumers. By contrast, in the death care economy the extent of product innovation has been limited largely to the cemetery side of the sector. Few new mortuary services have been introduced by funeral homes, although there have been some changes in the variety of caskets and other merchandise they offer and the degree to which they accommodate the desires of consumers for limited services involving cremation without embalming or viewing. This change has resulted in part from the necessity to comply with federal regulations requiring the unbundling of mortuary products and services and growing consumer preference for less-than-complete funeral services.

A major change in the death care economy has involved the process of consolidation undergone in recent decades that has resulted in the emergence of a number of chains of death care establishments. The effect of this has been less noticeable to consumers, perhaps because it has occurred without much alteration in the ways in which establishments are operated, even after they have become part of a chain. Perhaps more noticeable to consumers has been the entry of cemeteries into the operation of funeral homes, creating a new entity: the combination establishment. We defer until later a full consideration of these trends in the sector.

Industrial Classification: A Suggested Revision

The Standard Industrial Classification (SIC) is the statistical classification standard underlying all establishment-based federal economic statistics classified by industry. Each class of establishments is identified by a four-digit code in which the first digit identifies the division of the economy (Manufacturing, Services, and so on), the second digit identifies the major group within a division (e.g., Business Services, Personal Services, and so on), the third digit identifies major groups of industries; and the fourth digit identifies each industry. These SIC codes are used to promote the comparability of establishment and firm data describing various facets of the U.S. economy. The classification covers the entire field of economic activities and defines industries in accordance with the composition and structure of the economy.

Accordingly, the activities of establishments which provide death care to consumers are included within the classification system along with the suppliers of goods and services used by death care providers. As presently designed, the manner in which death care establishments are represented in the standard industrial classification system is fragmented, like the sector itself, and spread over a wide variety of economic divisions, major groups, industry groups, and industries, as identified by SIC codes. This is a confusing way to account for the output of a sector of the economy that clearly consists of a set of closely related outputs produced by a class of firms whose production processes are sequentially linked and in some cases combined into one firm.

The classification system is revised periodically to reflect changes in industrial organization, including technological and institutional changes. In addition, changes are made to improve industry detail and coverage and to clarify classification concepts as well as the classification of individual activities. In 1987 the system was revised to incorporate the first major changes since 1972; no major changes were made, however, in the manner in which death care establishments were classified, in spite of the changes which had occurred in the death care economy during that period. To reflect those changes and to provide a classification system consistent with the views adopted here, we propose a revision in the manner in which death care establishments are classified.

Let us first consider the intricacies of the current classification scheme. Under the division of "Service Industries" (7XXX), the major group of "Personal Services" is identified by a 2. Thus the preliminary four-digit SIC code can be represented as 72XX. The SIC industry group 726X is described as "Funeral Service and Crematories," and funeral homes and crematories operated in connection with them are classified in this industry group under the SIC industry code 7261. According to the SIC system, this industry consists of a mixture of establishments which provide mortuary services (preparing the dead for final disposition and conducting funerals) and also the pre-final part of final disposition (cremating the dead). This seems inappropriate because crematories do not perform mortuary services; instead they perform a pre-final function in the final disposition process, the function relating to the incineration of bodily remains prior to their further final disposition. In this respect crematories properly belong to a "Pre-final Disposition Industry" which coexists with a "Final Disposition Industry" composed of cemeteries, a "Mortuary Services Industry" composed of funeral homes, and a "Memorialization Industry" composed of memorial dealerships. It is misleading to place crematories or their function under the mortuary services industry, and to do so is to ignore crematories which are operated by and in conjunction with cemeteries. Furthermore, the present industry grouping, "Funeral Services and Crematories," actually excludes those crematories that are operated by cemeteries, which includes approximately one-half of the crematories located in the United States.

Cemeteries, including crematories operated in conjunction with them, are classified under the division of "Finance, Insurance and Real Estate" (6XXX), the major group of "Real Estate" (65XX), the industry group of "Land Subdividers and Developers" (655X), and the industry of "Cemetery Subdividers and Developers" (SIC Code 6553). Crematories and burial services for pets, a growing sector, are classified in the Agriculture Division as industry 0752.

Establishments which produce and sell memorial products are included under the Manufacturing Division as "Cut Stone and Stone Products," the "Wholesale Trade Division," the "Retail Trade Division," and elsewhere. To the extent that these products are produced and sold by various types of manufacturing and wholesale establishments, this seems not inappropriate, but insofar as they are sold to consumers, they represent death care goods and services as defined in chapters 4 and 6. Their sale is analogous to the sale of merchandise such as caskets and burial clothing by funeral homes. Yet the latter are included in the receipts of funeral homes and crematories under "Personal Services."

Likewise, the goods and services sold by cemeteries and crematories represent examples of death care provided to consumers. Furthermore, it is often the case that funeral homes sell burial containers and vaults in competition with cemeteries, some cemeteries sell caskets in competition with funeral homes, and both sell memorial products in competition with monument dealers and each other. Indeed, combined establishments and clusters of separate establishments specialize in selling all of these. The SIC classification of such firms in different divisions and major groups fails to reflect these real conditions. The result is a confusing and misleading classification of the establishments which form the industries that provide death care consisting of mortuary services, final (including pre-final) disposition, and memorialization.

In recognition of the fact that there exists a family of industries which provide death care goods and services to consumers, it is here proposed that SIC Code 726X or its successor, representing a group of industries within Personal Services within the Services Division, be revised to represent "Death Care Providers" divided into four distinct industry groups, which reflect basic differences in the production processes they employ to produce the death care goods and services they provide. In general, based on their production functions, this results in four industry groupings consisting of providers of mortuary services (funeral homes), pre-final disposition (crematories), final disposition (cemeteries), and memorialization (memorial dealers). The four death care industries composed of similar establishments which together deliver the three component parts of the complete death care process, may be represented by the fourth digit of the four-digit SIC code for death care providers, as indicated below:

726 DEATH CARE PROVIDERS.

7261 Funeral Homes: Death care establishments primarily engaged in preparing dead bodies for pre-final or final disposition, in conducting funerals, and in merchandising products used in connection therewith. (Funeral directors, Morticians, Funeral homes, Mortuaries, Funeral parlors, Undertakers.)

7262 Crematories: Death care establishments primarily engaged in the operation of crematories, which perform a pre-final disposition function in the process of final disposition of dead bodies, and in merchandising products used in connection therewith. (Crematories, Scattering services.)

7263 Cemeteries: Death care establishments primarily engaged in the operation of cemeteries, mausoleums, columbariums, including the sale of vaults, grave liners, and other products and services used in connection therewith. (Cemeteries — commercial, Mausoleum operation, Cemetery associations, Memorial parks, Columbariums, Pet cemeteries.)

7264 Memorial Dealers: Death care establishments primarily engaged in buying, selling, installing, and servicing monuments, tombstones, grave markers, urns, and other products used to memorialize the dead. (Marble shops, Memorial studios, Memorial counselors, Monument dealerships.)

The logical consistency of this scheme is appealing. In terms of the argument of this book, it represents a classification of death care providers which is consistent with the view that the death care process consists of mortuary services, final disposition (including the pre-final stage), and memorialization. The proposed SIC classifications identify the four types of industries which provide each of the three complementary components of the complete process: funeral homes and related providers of mortuary services, crematories, cemeteries, and memorial dealers and related establishments. Not only are many of the goods and services produced or sold by each of these different types of establishments substitutable, the production processes by which those goods and services are produced or provided to consumers are similar or identical, in full or in part. As a result of both of these features, these establishments belong together and their output as a whole is properly treated as death care.

The proposed scheme is not open to the criticism that the firms included under the heading "Memorial Products and Services" are engaged in retailing, for which there is a separate industrial classification. It is also true that funeral homes, cemeteries, and crematories are engaged in the sale of products at retail. This is in the nature of the process of providing death care products, which includes goods as well as services. As a rule, most of these establishments are either funeral homes or cemeteries or memorial dealers. Most of these establishments are to be regarded as firms which are independently owned and operated, usually in a single location. Their outputs consist of both goods and services, although the proportions of these are different for establishments of each type. The proportion of services is highest for crematories, followed by funeral homes. Cemeteries involve the sale of a high proportion of goods, and memorial dealers are primarily goods providers. This raises the issue of whether it is appropriate to group them together under the division of Services and the major group of Personal Services in an industrial classification system.

The justification for doing so lies in the nature of death care as a complete process consisting of mortuary services, final disposition, and memorialization. As described in Chapter 4, each of these components entails some elements of "care" for the remains and the sensibilities of the deceased or surviving parties. For this reason it is proposed that the outputs of mortuaries, crematories, cemeteries, and memorial dealerships are properly classifiable as "personal services." The boundaries between goods-producing and services-producing sectors of the economy are often blurred by the sale of goods in connection with the delivery of services, as in the case of food services and health services. Few firms are exclusively providers of services entailing no sale of related goods. The complications of this problem are recognized in ECPC working papers, but there is no generally accepted means of coping with difficulties it poses for economic classification. In the interest of an industrial classification system which groups all death care providers together under a single group of related industries, the inclusion of cemeteries and memorial dealerships together with mortuaries and crematories under the major group of Personal Services seems justified. In any event, however, their status as death care providers is appropriate wherever they may be classified.

Establishments, Firms, and Industries

As mentioned in the Preface, the U.S. government is currently engaged in a lengthy review of the present SIC system in collaboration with the governments of Canada and Mexico. As a part of this ongoing review, the U.S. agencies involved have prepared an extensive set of guidelines for the development of a production-based industrial classification system and a demand-based product classification system. These two systems will form the basis of a uniform North American Industrial Classification System (NAICS) to be implemented successively over several years. The purpose of this section of text is to present the case for the view that the classification of death care industries set forth above and the classification of death care products (goods and services) set forth in Chapter 6 meet the criteria for inclusion as a sector of the economy in the classification system under development. Those criteria are stated in a series of papers prepared as a preliminary part of the review process (ECPC, *Issues Paper No. 1*, January 1993, p. 6) the general features of which may be summarized along the following lines:

> In the literature of economic classification it is commonly held that a classification system should reflect the structure of an economy. This presumably means that the system selected should allow for the collection and aggregation of data which are indicative of the variety of producing units which exists at any time. For purposes of the collection and aggregation of data, the establishment has historically been treated as the appropriate

concept of the producing unit. Establishments are identified and grouped together into "industries" based on the similarity of their production functions or processes. This treatment recognizes that establishment is to be distinguished from an enterprise as a whole, that is, the firm. As a legal as well as an economic entity, a firm may own one or more establishments engaged in one or more areas of economic activity which fall into one or more industries.

To separate and to aggregate data relating to the production and distribution of particular products (goods and services) in an economy, the establishment is thus regarded as the basic unit of economic activity. Independently of its ownership and financing, it represents a fixed location of operation where economic resources such as equipment, labor, materials, and techniques are combined in the production of goods and services. Under a supply-side or production-oriented concept of economic classification, establishments are grouped together into the same industry if they employ similar production processes to produce similar outputs from similar inputs. Under such circumstances the aggregation of economic data collected from similar establishments will reflect real input-output relationships, employment patterns, cost structures, price levels, and other economic characteristics of the industry they comprise and the markets they serve.

As discussed in the previous section, the variety of death care establishments may be classified into industries in terms of the production processes they employ to produce death care goods and services. On this basis four basic death care industries were distinguished, as follows:

I. Funeral homes or mortuaries use similar inputs of facilities, equipment, merchandise, supplies, and occupational skills and techniques to provide mortuary goods and services to consumers. Establishments of this type are to be clearly distinguished in terms of their production processes from crematories, cemeteries, and memorial dealers. For purposes of economic classification, this is the case even if such an establishment occupies the same or adjacent space with a crematory or cemetery.

II. Crematories use similar inputs to transform dead bodies into cremated remains, some of which become cremains requiring further disposition.

III. Cemeteries use similar inputs to provide final disposition goods and services to consumers.

The production processes of these last two types of establishments, crematories and cemeteries, differ in terms of the inputs used and the outputs produced. In particular, the production process of cemeteries entails the use of land and structures (tombs and community mausoleums) as principal inputs used to dispose of human remains, whereas the production process of crematories entails the use of energy as its principal input into the disposal process. The output of the cemetery is a site of final disposition (a grave or tomb with an interred body); the output of a crematory is a package of cremains. Interment and entombment of the body encourages the use of caskets and vaults which protect and preserve the body, whereas the process of cremation discourages the use of protective caskets, while permitting the use of other containers such as urns. These basic differences justify the separation of cemeteries and crematories as industries composed of establishments with different production functions. This is true in spite of the frequently close relationship between such establishments and the fact that they are often commonly owned and operated together as a unit, even in the same or adjacent locations. The economic significance of crematories as a distinctive industry comprising a class of business establishments is indicated by the fact that the cremation rate now exceeds 20 percent of U.S. deaths, and it is much higher in some local markets. The dollar volume of crematories represents a large and growing share of death care revenues.

IV. Memorial dealers use various kinds of technical skills to provide for the memorialization of the dead following burial, entombment, or cremation. None of the latter processes accomplishes memorialization in the sense of identifying and commemorating the life of the deceased person by marking the site of final disposition of the bodily remains or cremains or by other means not involving the remains directly. As discussed more fully in Chapter 6, the types of memorialization desired by consumers may be linked so closely with the final disposition process that the two may properly be regarded as complementary parts of a complex set of death care goods and services. Yet, even if the parts (e.g., the grave and the marker) are provided by the same firm (i.e., a cemetery which also erects monuments and markers), the use of different inputs and different techniques of providing the two products justifies their being considered different economic activities for purposes of an industrial classification system.

It is important to consider the implications of the latter point. Although the establishment is conceptually the appropriate unit for the classification of death care providers and the collection of data relating to them, its use is complicated by the interrelationships among the goods and services produced or distributed by the establishments of each type. As pointed out in Chapter 6, many of those establishments provide several parts of the death care process because those parts are either substitutes (e.g., cremation with or without inurnment vs. bodily burial/entombment) or complements (e.g., graves and markers) and because there are often economies associated with the joint production and distribution of related death care products (e.g., the operation of a crematory together with a cemetery or mortuary). In such cases it is possible for theoretically separate establishments to be operated together as if they were one business which its owners identified by its principal activity (based on sales volume, presumably). Thus a cemetery or a mortuary would be identified as such even it were to include a crematory, to sell memorial products, and so on. These cases of joint production or distribution inevitably lead to some distortion in the collection of economic data for death care establishments, firms, and industries.

The most extreme case of joint production and distribution is the "mortuary-crematory-cemetery-memorial dealer-florist" form of combined establishment or firm which owns and operates a full range of different death care facilities in the same location or in adjacent locations that are operated by shared personnel using common equipment. At least some of the labor, managerial, and other inputs into the operation of these combined facilities cannot be uniquely attributed to the mortuary, cemetery, crematory, and so on. Even if separate records on inputs and outputs are maintained for the different establishments within the same firm, the relationships between them may be distorted by the allocation methods adopted. The only way to avoid this would be to establish a separate classification for "Cemetery-Mortuary Combinations" as a distinct type of death care provider of multiple outputs consisting of a full range of death care goods and services. Based on estimates of the number and volume of such facilities that now exist throughout the country, the economic significance of this class of establishments would appear to justify this treatment in a revised economic classification system. In effect, it would be analogous to the economic classification of department stores and supermarkets as separate industries within the retail sector.

A less extreme form of joint production arises from the common ownership and operation of multiple establishments (funeral homes or cemeteries) as units of a chain. The U.S. Census Bureau classifies as chains those organizations consisting of four or more units over which some degree of centralized control is exercised. Even in such cases the establishment may represent separate production units which are more or less autonomous entities for which separate records are kept. In many cases, however, the units of chains are operated together within a common geographic area as clusters of separate facilities (funeral homes or cemeteries) which share personnel and equipment among several locations where funerals are conducted. In some cases they incorporate centralized production facilities (e.g., for embalming and preparation) or pre-need sales organizations. In these cases, major decisions may be made at the enterprise or firm level rather than at the local establishments, where very little autonomy resides. Where this is so, some of the local facilities of death care chains may well be viewed as similar to "automated teller machines" which do not represent banking "establishments" for economic classification purposes. For the largest chains, furthermore, the relevant autonomous units may well be the regional divisions of the total firm or some other organizational subdivision (ECPC, *Issues Paper No. 1*, January 1993, p. 7).

Sector Boundaries

For the vast majority of economic units in the death care economy, the establishment is clearly the autonomous entity. Most of those entities are to be regarded as firms which are independently owned and operated establishments. The operations of many of them are limited by the traditional boundaries between the three parts of the death care process. Within these boundaries the delivery system for each major type of death care product (including both goods and services) is highly fragmented. This fragmentation is due to two factors:

(1) the tendency for death care establishments to specialize in providing a limited (bounded) part of the complete death care process and (2) the tendency of such establishments to locate close to their clienteles. These factors have exerted their influence over many years, but in recent decades the effect of several countertrends in the sector has been to create interrelationships among providers which have altered the nature and extent of relationships among establishments, firms, and industries of each type.

One trend tending to bind together death care establishments, firms, and industries has been the tendency for memorial products to be sold by commercial cemeteries and by some funeral homes. Another such trend has been the tendency for crematories to be owned and operated either by funeral homes or by cemeteries as partially integrated death care providers. A further trend tending to integrate the sector has been the consolidation of establishments into local, regional, and national chains of funeral homes and cemeteries. This has linked these traditionally separate types of providers together under common ownership and management, breaking down the boundaries between them.

The precise extent to which these trends have altered the traditional boundaries between industries within the death care sector is difficult to assess, but some alteration is clearly indicated by estimates that there are from 900 to 1,450 locations at which a mortuary has been added to a cemetery, either within or adjacent to its grounds, physically integrating their operations. Further, the number of clusters of funeral homes, cemeteries, or both may be estimated to be in the hundreds. The number of multiunit operations probably exceeds 1,750. The number of regional chains has been estimated at 50 or more. There are, finally, several large investor-owned companies which together own and operate thousands of funeral homes and hundreds of cemeteries, including a large number of local clusters of those facilities.

These developments reinforce the case for the existence of a death care sector of the economy comprising a family of industries, firms, and establishments that together provide complete death care or any of its component parts directly to consumers. The revenues of these establishments, firms, and industries, taken together, represent the total value of the output of the death care sector in the gross domestic product of the larger economy. The total revenues of the sector derive from the sale of goods and services in two different ways which are distinguished as "pre-need" and "at-need." This necessitates a distinction in the measurement of revenues resulting from sales of each type, the proportions of which vary among death care providers according to the sales practices they employ. These practices involve differences in the promotion and marketing methods of death care industries and firms, but they do not affect the basic production and distribution processes of those firms and industries. For this reason, pre-need sales of death care goods and services cannot be said to represent a separate and distinct death care industry, notwithstanding the FTC's reference to a "Pre-need Sales Industry" in certain documents (U.S. FTC, July 1990, p. 259).

Further Strata of Economic Activity

The establishments, firms, and industries included in the death care sector of the U.S. economy represent the productive entities at its core. It appears from a glance back at the product classification system presented in Chapter 6 that there is a further stratum of economic activities associated with the production and distribution of death care goods and services. Many establishments and firms engage in these activities in one of two ways: (1) as producers and distributors of goods and services purchased directly by consumers who use them in connection with the death care process and (2) as suppliers of goods and services to death care providers for use as inputs in the production and distribution of death care.

Even further removed from the production of death care goods and services are a number of specialized educational institutions engaged in the process of instilling death care skills and techniques in students of mortuary science programs and colleges and upgrading the skills of practitioners through the continuing education programs. Also, it may be said that morgues are maintained by hospitals and municipalities for the purpose of providing death care. These activities peripheral to the actual death care sector will not concern us further; we instead will consider briefly the extent of the two major categories indicated above.

Some death care goods and services are sold directly to consumers by firms which properly belong to other industries, such as the flower industry (floral tributes), the greeting card industry (sympathy cards), the newspaper industry (death notices and published memorials), and others. The firms in these industries differ from those of death care providers in that only a portion of their outputs is used in the death care process. Since these goods and services are not produced or sold by death care providers in many cases, the revenues derived from them by firms in other industries must be added to the revenues of death care firms in order to obtain an estimate of the aggregate volume of death care goods and services produced in the economy. To some extent this is reflected in the receipts of funeral homes in the form of cash advances made to other establishments for funeral-related merchandise and services such as flowers and newspaper notices.

It is instructive to observe that cash advances of the sort involved here are not a feature of the operation of firms in other industries. They have developed and still persist as a business practice of mortuaries because of the fragmented manner in which death care is provided to consumers who deal with a funeral home but also require the services of a crematory, a cemetery, a memorial dealer, a florist, and other sources of death care goods and services. The funeral home is equipped to provide a limited variety of the items desired, so the rest of the necessary or desirable elements must be provided by others. As an adaptation to this fragmented form of economic structure and for the convenience of its clientele, the funeral home ordinarily advances the funds for these items. Even though such advances are a part of the total revenues generated in the death care economy, they are not properly a part of the revenues of death care establishments since they are paid to other firms and industries whose outputs are used by death care consumers.

Suppliers

In addition to the classes of firms described above, there is also a collection of firms which produce and sell supplies and merchandise used or sold by death care providers. These firms include manufacturers and distributors of caskets, vaults, graveliners, memorial products, embalming fluids, and various types of specialized equipment and vehicles (e.g., hearses), general business equipment and supplies, and business services. As the outputs of a variety of firms and industries, the revenues derived from the production of these products and services are included in the accounting for the sector of the economy to which each belongs. As inputs into the death care process, they are a part of the expenses incurred or investments made by death care providers.

It is not necessary to examine the operations of all of the different types of firms which are suppliers to death care providers. Many of them are as common as automobile manufacturers and electric or other utilities. There is nothing distinctive about most of these firms. Some of them are distinctive, however, in that their output is used by death care providers only. This is true of some manufacturers of cremation equipment, burial garments, caskets and outer burial receptacles, urns, and some other memorial products. We cannot profitably devote much space to each of these, but it is clear that the total dependence of casket manufacturers on the death care economy requires us to examine the implications of this for their operations. This dependence arises because the need for a casket is evident in all cases where a funeral ceremony is held, in cases of earth burial or mausoleum entombment whether or not a funeral is held, and in the case of cremation only if a funeral ceremony is held. Since the latter is not always the case, the shift toward cremation as a part of the final disposition process has had implications for casket manufacturers.

At one time more than five hundred casket manufacturers operated in local markets throughout the United States. The line of caskets produced by each was geared directly to the local conditions of demand for the outputs of such goods, which ranged from cloth-covered plywood models to numerous grades of hardwoods. Batesville Casket Company, a unit of Hillenbrand Industries, Inc., invented the first moisture-proof metal casket in the years before World War II. The protective features of metal caskets appealed to consumers. On the strength of this appeal, Batesville grew rapidly into the largest manufacturer of caskets in the United States, with manufacturing plants and distribution facilities throughout the country (Edmands, *Barron's*, April 2, 1971).

According to an article in *Forbes* (Lubove, February 28, 1994), Batesville's "share of the $1-billion-a-year (wholesale) casket market is around 40%, and much higher (60%) in the high-end caskets made of steel and hardwoods like mahogany." The article explores Hillenbrand's power to lock out competition through its established "strategic selling" relationship with a vast network of funeral directors and other casket buyers in the industry:

> Over the years Hillenbrand has seen the competitive threats coming and parried them brilliantly. When it comes to making your customer your partner, no company does it better than Hillenbrand.... It refuses to cut in any middlemen and sells only to funeral homes, which in turn sell Hillenbrand caskets to the bereaved at markups of 200% to 400%. For its customers, Hillenbrand finances beautifully appointed casket showrooms costing as much as $80,000. ... The idea, of course, is to give Hillenbrand and the funeral homes a common goal: preserve Hillenbrand's and the undertakers' margins by freezing out people like Russell Moore who attempt to sell coffins to consumers at a discount [p. 64].

Lubove also describes the process of adaptation in progress at Hillenbrand: "Further consolidating its grip, Hillenbrand is now the biggest underwriter of so-called pre-need funeral life insurance, ... and rather than fight the lively growth in cremations, Hillenbrand now offers a full selection of cremation caskets and urns" (p. 65). This latter is a major strategic accommodation to the shifting preferences of consumers in favor of cremation, with all that this implies for the final disposition and memorialization components of death care.

Similar practices characterize several other firms now engaged in casket manufacturing and distribution on a national scale, including the York Group and others. The growth of these firms, based on manufacturing economies and improved distribution channels, has added to the gradual decline of casket manufacturing as a local business activity. Fewer than 100 small firms remain in the industry, and many of these are jobbers who purchase metal or wooden shells from the national firms and customize them with interiors which appeal to tastes in their local markets. As a sign of the culmination of these developments in the casket manufacturing field, the Casket Manufacturers Association changed its name in 1993 to the Casket and Funeral Supply Association of America. According to trade reports, the change in name "reflected its changed membership brought about by consolidation within the casket-making industry and the outright loss of some prime manufacturers. Of the association's 160 members at the date of the change in its name, only 70 were manufacturers or distributors of caskets. The other 90 were suppliers to casket manufacturers themselves or suppliers of goods and services other than caskets to funeral homes. The change in name by the association, which broadened the groups it embraces, was expected to attract additional supplier firms as members, including suppliers of computer services, automobiles, and pre-need insurance products (*The American Funeral Director*, November 1993).

Even so, such a group is unlikely to attract many providers of business services, such as accounting and law firms, whose clients include an occasional funeral home or cemetery. Nor does the broadened base appear to enbrace florists, newspaper publishers, and greeting card manufacturers, a portion of whose revenues is derived from the sale of death care goods and services.

Insurance and Other Sources of Funds

The insurance industry is not, of course, a part of the death care sector of the economy. There is, however, a sense in which a significant connection exists between life insurance and death care. After all, life insurance is a euphemism for insurance policies which pay off when life ends, that is, at death. Burial policies are a special category of life insurance, the proceeds of which are specially designated for funeral expenses. Furthermore, life insurance policies are one of the means by which pre-planned funerals are funded, in which case a funeral home is itself the beneficiary of a policy purchased by the deceased as a means of paying for pre-arranged services.

Beyond these special uses of insurance for funding death care, it is generally true that the beneficiaries of life insurance policies are often the survivors who arrange and pay for the death care of the insured party upon death. In a similar way the death of a person leads to a legal process of succession by which legacies or inheritances flow to those who have the responsibility for arranging death care for the deceased person. Like life insurance proceeds, the average amounts received from legacies has tended to grow from generation to generation as a result of the growth of personal income and household wealth in the economy.

Whatever the extent of the funds made available in these ways at death, the effect of their receipt by parties responsible for death care expenses is to relax the degree to which income (or savings) is a constraint on death care expenditures. This does not imply that individuals will spend more freely or less carefully on death care than they spend on other categories of consumption goods and services. Nor does it imply that the nature and extent of the death care desired will be affected. It simply means that the ability of consumers to spend on the death care of their choice is supplemented by the receipt of funds associated directly with the event of death.

Viatical Settlements

A relatively recent innovation in the insurance field allows early payouts or accelerated benefits to insured persons who become terminally ill. A growing number of insurance companies provide such "living benefits" to policyholders, subject to various conditions, when there is a certifiable medical opinion that the insured party has less than six months or so to live. Moreover, for policyholders of insurers who do not offer living benefits, there are so-called "viatical" companies that specialize in buying the policies of terminally ill patients based on medical estimates of their life expectancies. In either case, the survivors of those who opt for the living benefits of life insurance policies are deprived of some or all of such funds at the time of the insured's death, reducing their ability to pay death care expenses in those cases (Flaherty, *New York Times*, October 16, 1993). On the other hand, early payouts allow the proceeds to be spent not only on medical and living expenses, but also on pre-planned death care purchased near need. This latter is important because adequate funds may not be available to cover death care expenses at the time of need. There would thus appear to be an opportunity, indeed an obligation, for death care providers to attempt to sell pre-planned death care to a near-need market as the popularity of living benefits and viatical arrangements grows in the future.

This brief survey is sufficient to indicate that funds become available to consumers from various sources at death. This is obviously a distinctive factor which supports consumer spending, thereby enhancing the stability of death care firms and the sector of the economy which comprises them. Unlike spending on other consumer goods and services which comes from income, death care expenditures are made from accumulated savings, or wealth, in an amount which is supplemented at death by the sources mentioned. In this respect, consumers are less constrained by their incomes in their role as death care customers than they are when spending otherwise. Even so, it may take them a month or more to liquidate assets or to collect insurance proceeds, so that funeral homes often must extend credit to their customers. They thus experience some bad debts in their day-to-day operations. While the use of collection agencies by mortuaries was once uncommon, it has become more acceptable in recent years. It is also a common practice for funeral homes to charge interest on unpaid balances. Some establishments accept credit cards, provide an installment plan, and offer discounts for cash payment (Smith and Schoen, February 1978, pp. 15–16).

Trade Associations

It has been claimed in government proceedings that "the development of the funeral industry has probably been influenced and directed more greatly by trade associations than by any other factor" (U.S. FTC, 1978, p. 52). Historians of the industry explain the strong influence of the trade associations in terms which conform with the earlier discussion in this chapter of the stigmatization of the work of funeral directors. The tendency to form strong associations among the practitioners of the trade represented an attempt to "rise above the traditional status of providers of funeral paraphernalia and factotums of burial" (Habenstein and Lamers, 1955, p. 449). To accomplish this goal, the National Funeral Directors' Association (NFDA), the largest association of death care providers in this country, has long taken the position that funeral directing is a profession. The NFDA adheres to this position today, but over the years it has modified its stance against advertising, sales solicitation, pre-need selling, and other practices. This prior stance was adopted in the name of professionalism, but was potentially anticompetitive in effect. In some cases the recent modifications have been voluntary, but in others they have been imposed legally (U.S. FTC, 1978, p. 58).

Another major trade association of over 950 funeral homes in more than a dozen countries is the National Selected Morticians (NSM), which adheres to the position of this book that funeral directors are engaged in a trade or business, not a profession. Because of this stand, NSM at times has taken positions on various issues that differ from those taken by NFDA, reflecting the former's view that funeral homes, as businesses, may reasonably engage in advertising, pre-need selling, and other accepted business practices without restraint. The NSM is also unlike NFDA, in that it is a restricted-membership organization. The restrictions have tended to create "an organization composed of larger, older, and better established funeral homes" (U.S. FTC, 1978, pp. 72–73)—heritage establishments, in the parlance of the industry.   .

As an indication of the different ethnic orientations of funeral homes, there are the National Funeral Directors and Morticians Association (NFDMA), an organization of black funeral directors, some of whom belong also to NFDA, and the Jewish Funeral Directors Association (JFDA), a group whose members abide by agreements negotiated with certain rabbinical groups regarding Jewish funeral practices. Other organizations of funeral directors provide business services to their members; these include the International Order of the Golden Rule and the Federated Funeral Directors of America. The Associated Funeral Directors is primarily a referral service used by members to arrange for shipments of human remains. Finally, the Academy of Professional Funeral Service, established in 1976, provides a voluntary continuing education program for funeral directors, leading to the designation of Certified Funeral Service Practitioner.

In addition to these associations of funeral directors, there are also several major associations of cemeterians. These include the American Cemetery Association (ACA) and the National Catholic Cemetery Conference (NCCC). Among other activities as a trade organization, the ACA provides certification of leading cemeterians as Certified Cemetery Executives, based on their demonstrated accomplishments in the field of cemetery management. The Cremation Association of North America (CANA) is the leading association of crematory operators, which includes a large number of cemeteries; the Monument Builders of North America (MBNA) is a major association of memorial dealers; and the Pre-arrangement Association of America (PAA) includes a number of cemeteries which engage in pre-need selling. Like the NFDA, each of these national groups — and various state and regional associations of each type — engage in a variety of activities, including lobbying, data gathering and dissemination, and educational and public relations programs. Each supports legislation and regulations favorable to the interests of its members.

"Balkanization" of the Sector

It is clear from the above discussion that in many cases the different associations represent conflicting interests potentially or actually. For example, within the major associations like NFDA, it is inevitable that the interests of the large multiunit firms differ in some respects from those of small independent establishments. Moreover, the interests of firms which operate in different areas do not always coincide. These differences create conflicts of interest within the separate associations — a balkanization of sorts, which divides the death care sector as a whole into fragmented interest groups. This "balkanization" has become institutionalized in the laws relating to death care in different jurisdictions, due to the past success of the lobbying efforts of groups with conflicting interests at various times and in various places.

Numerous differences have created and sustained the balkanization of the death care sector by pitting the interests of one association against another's. Although occasional friction among the different segments of any economic sector is inevitable, the extent to which it has been used as a means for securing competitive advantage in the death care sector has marked it as a distinctive expression of rivalry within the sector. This has tended to permit different types of death care providers and their trade associations to engage in the economically unproductive use of legal processes and regulatory channels in order to avoid having to compete economically. Reference will be made throughout to instances in which such a mentality and behavior has tended to characterize the relationships among different segments of the sector, positioning the different types of death care providers and their separate associations antagonistically. Clearly no common identity or unified sense of common purpose as "death care providers" has developed among these disparate groups.

On a smaller scale than that of the death care sector as a whole, the development of large death care companies embracing each and every component of death care has encouraged a unified identity subsuming their disparate units. This is clearly lacking in the sector as a whole, where there is no superstructure within which the existing trade associations can interact formally as participants in something on the order of a Death Care Association of North America. Perhaps, however, the formal organization of all death care practitioners into such an identifiable master group would represent a further step toward the official development of a degree of social status, solidarity, and unified strength that would better enable them to achieve their collective purposes.

Trade Publications

As in most industries, trade publications play a visible role in the death care economy. They include newsletters of suppliers, trade association journals addressed to their members, and independently published magazines aimed at specific groups of death care providers. Most of these publications carry extensive advertising by suppliers of merchandise and services used in the trade. The editorial policy of these journals tends to reinforce and to support the interests of their subscribers. Because these interests are often at odds, no *Journal of Death Care* has emerged in the sector. Indeed, the contents of *American Cemetery* and *The American Funeral Director* are scrupulously separated, in spite of the fact that they are published by the same company and editorial staff.

Not surprisingly, the contents of the trade publications are perhaps the most extensive source of the various positions of different death care providers and the conflicts among them. Mitford relied heavily on such sources and made use of them to her advantage. She could do this, of course, only because the material she found in trade sources provided her with examples of behavior and squabbling among death care providers which could be held up to ridicule. Apart from such uses, little of what goes on in most industries is of interest to consumers except insofar as it expresses itself in the variety of goods and services made available at various prices. We will consider these aspects of the death care sector at length in subsequent chapters. Even at this point, however, it is appropriate to provide some indication of the changes in the cost of death care to consumers that have occurred in past years.

The Cost of Death Care

For lack of an appropriate term, the cost of death care has heretofore been called "the cost of dying," but dying, insofar as it is an economic activity, falls within the province of health care providers. Most of us die in health care facilities and incur large costs. These medical costs are properly called "the cost of dying," but it is confusing to use that term to refer to the cost of mortuary services, final disposition, and memorialization. It is preferable to refer to the cost of these death-related activities and the merchandise used in connection with them as "the cost of death care."

The prices of the goods and services provided by an industry are key elements of performance in which consumers are interested. The prices paid in general for consumer products comprise the cost of living. The Consumer Price Index (CPI) computed by the U.S. Bureau of Labor Statistics (BLS) is a measure of the cost of living based on a weighted average of the prices of a representative "basket" of goods and services used by consumers at a given time, including some death care components.

Over time, increases in the index indicate a rising cost of living due to inflation. This has differential effects for consumers and businesses alike. Some segments of consumers and firms are more able than others to keep up with inflation. The prices of health care providers, for example, have been observed generally to rise at a rate exceeding the rate of inflation over a long period of time. Other industries, faced with more competitive conditions in their markets, have not been able to do this. Inflation thus has differential effects on particular firms and sectors of the economy. It is important, therefore, to examine the recent variation in the cost of death care goods and services in relation to that experienced in the cost of living generally. Unfortunately no index of death care costs, including the costs of mortuary services, final disposition, and memorialization, is calculated by the BLS. Instead, it prepares an index of funeral service prices of the merchandise and services sold by funeral homes. It is not entirely clear, therefore, whether this index is properly compared with an index

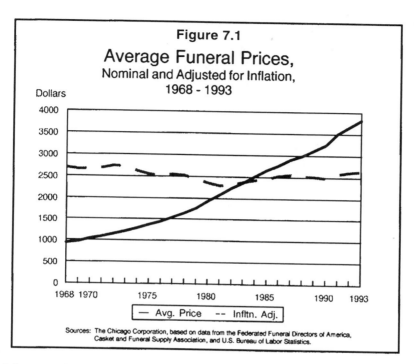

Figure 7.1
Average Funeral Prices,
Nominal and Adjusted for Inflation,
1968 - 1993

Sources: The Chicago Corporation, based on data from the Federated Funeral Directors of America, Casket and Funeral Supply Association, and U.S. Bureau of Labor Statistics.

of the cost of living generally for all urban consumers (CPI-U) or with a separate index of the cost of services (CPI-S). In any case, for the period between 1986 and 1993, based on BLS data, the cost of the funeral service component of death care has lagged behind the rising cost of living as measured by both indices; at other times it has outpaced the indices modestly. In general, this tends to confirm the view that death care providers are usually able to keep up with the rate of inflation by adjusting their prices as necessary, perhaps with a lag.

A longer-term view of trends in average funeral prices is revealed in an analysis of industry data by Steven Saltzman and Gregory Capelli of the Chicago Corporation as presented in Figure 7.1. The adjusted average prices shown by the broken line confirm that funeral homes have generally managed to hold their own against inflation during the last several decades, during which the inflation rate has varied widely.

Pricing Behavior

It is important to note, however, that death care providers are different types of establishments and firms subject to different conditions. In general, however, since cemeteries are sellers of real estate, or the rights to occupy real estate, and real estate prices show a tendency to rise during inflationary periods, it would seem that cemeteries are in a position to raise prices at a rate which allows their revenues to keep pace with inflation. Further, new entrants into the industry must charge prices which reflect current prices, and this allows existing firms to raise prices without necessarily attracting new competition. Furthermore, the basic operation of cemeteries is a perfect example of the operation of the scarcity principle. As the available burial space is used up, two factors operate together to drive up the value of the remaining lots. One of these factors is the growing number of families with links to the cemetery; the other is the smaller number of lots available for sale at all prices. The result of these conditions is an increase in demand for a smaller supply of available space that reinforces higher prices over time.

The pricing behavior of mortuaries will receive further scrutiny in the next part of this book, which is devoted to an examination of the operations of different types of death care providers and the major factors which influence them as businesses.

PART IV

Tombs are the clothes of the dead; a grave is but a plain suit;
a rich monument is an embroidered one.

Thomas Fuller

8. *Mortuary Economics*

Mortuaries as Businesses

Mortuaries, or funeral homes, are commercial businesses traditionally owned and operated by licensed funeral directors or undertakers who provide the mortuary services and merchandise required or desired prior to final disposition of a dead human body. Funeral homes are thus the death care providers with which consumers have the first contact at the time of a death. Funeral homes are called by consumers to pick up the body following death. Family members go to these establishments to make whatever arrangements are required or desired, including appropriate preparation of the body and selection of a casket or container. Funeral homes provide the facilities in which visitation and funeral services are held. They transport the body to the cemetery for burial, entombment, or cremation followed by disposal of the cremated remains. They oversee graveside or committal services, and in a number of ways coordinate or "direct" myriad activities required by law or desired by consumers as a part of "the funeral."

For all these services and for the merchandise they provide in connection with them, mortuaries charge prices which cover their costs and provide their profits, if any. The purpose of this chapter will be to develop a framework which describes the general conditions under which funeral homes operate and the influence of those conditions on their costs and prices. Our discussion will utilize some concepts and tools of analysis employed by economists, as presented, for example, by Gould and Ferguson (1980, Chapter 9). It will be shown that the economic behavior of mortuaries seems to follow generally recognizable lines, with minor variations arising from the particular characteristics of funeral homes as distinctive business firms in the mortuary services industry.

Market Structure

In order to understand the pricing behavior of the firms in an industry and to obtain some notion of how well the industry responds to consumer needs and desires, economists generally rely on one of several basic models of market

136

structure — perfect competition, monopolistic competition, oligopoly, or monopoly. It has been observed, however, that there are many distinguishable death care markets in the United States and that these markets differ widely. For example, in some local markets there are many funeral homes, cemeteries, and crematories offering death care goods and services in more or less direct rivalry with one another, suggesting perfect or at least workable competition. In others, the rival funeral homes, cemeteries, or crematories are few, suggesting oligopoly. In almost all markets, furthermore, there is a substantial degree of product differentiation in the outputs of funeral homes and cemeteries, suggesting monopolistic competition where there are many firms of each type, differentiated oligopoly where there are few firms of each type, and a price-discriminating monopolist where there is only one "active" firm of a particular type.

This wide variety of apparent market structures, together with a number of features peculiar to the death care sector, has led to a confusing variety of claims regarding the pricing behavior of funeral homes. As pointed out in FTC documents, for example, the structure of the market for funeral services has been variously described by one analyst as an "atomistic monopoly," by at least two economists as "monopolistic competition," and by an industry consultant as "a composite of local markets which possess the characteristics of oligopoly involving a differentiated product" (U.S. FTC, 1978, p. 86).

In contrast to all such characterizations, however, it appears from the analysis presented below that none of the usual economic models apply to markets for the mortuary component of death care goods and services, although there are elements of the models which seem to apply. In effect, it appears that all funeral homes follow a variation of second-degree price discrimination, regardless of how much or how little competition they face in their particular market area. Moreover, it appears that mortuary prices and costs are interdependent and that, accordingly, supply schedules are determined mainly by demand or, as it turns out, by what is called marginal revenue. This may be demonstrated by drawing on some basic concepts of economics.

Consumer Demand

It is a common practice to analyze consumer demand for a typical product by postulating an ordinal utility function and deriving an individual demand function with quantity demanded inversely related to price. The problem here is that this approach requires the assumption of nonsatiety, that is, the more of the product that is consumed by an individual, the higher the utility level he achieves. Clearly, this is not the case for the funeral service product of mortuaries. Only one unit of the product is ordinarily required (desired) per body, no more and no less.

By common practice, this "unit" consists of all the necessary or customary items of merchandise, facilities, and services which meet the needs and customs of the market served by a funeral home. In industry parlance this unit is referred to as the "traditional funeral"; since traditions differ, however, this unit will be referred to here as a "complete" funeral. Under federal regulation, funeral homes are required to itemize the prices of the major types of death care goods and services included as a part of a complete funeral, and the customers of a funeral home have the right to decline to purchase any particular components. The use of a single nondeclinable fee for limited mortuary services provided in connection with less-than-complete funerals is allowed by regulators. Beyond this, "The Funeral Rule does not govern or otherwise regulate how funeral directors set prices for various funeral goods and services.... Consequently the Rule permits funeral directors to recover overhead costs through the non-declinable professional service fee, by means of a mark-up on caskets, or by mark-ups on other goods and services" (U.S. FTC, July 1990, p. 164).

For various reasons to be discussed here, funeral directors generally believe "that it is more appropriate from an economic standpoint to allocate overhead expense and profit recovery to both merchandise and services rather than to rely on the professional fee to recoup costs and as a source of profits.... This method of accounting or pricing permits a funeral director to charge a lower professional service fee, which in turn enables him to provide full service funerals to those whose ability to pay is limited and who might not otherwise be able to afford them.... Use of this system of cost allocation is longstanding" (U.S. FTC, July 1990, p. 165). In keeping with this long-standing practice, the use of a nondeclinable professional service fee and itemized charges is not shown in the illustrations used throughout this chapter. The purpose of this is not to ignore these features, it is rather to focus attention on the pricing behavior of funeral homes as they are generally operated for a specific set of customers.

The specific items included in the complete funeral offered by funeral homes are those usually associated with the religious and cultural heritage of their customers. In spite of itemization requirements imposed on funeral homes, therefore, the funeral service is purchased as a unit and paid for as a unit in most cases. The exceptions are such individual items as burial clothing, vaults, and the like, the need or desire for which varies.

In addition to the funeral service, if any, purchased from a mortuary, the consuming unit (which is usually the family of the deceased) must provide also for final disposition of the body. In most cases this involves earth burial in a cemetery, entombment in a mausoleum, or cremation followed by appropriate disposition of the cremains. The family may also desire flowers, newspaper notices, the services of clergy, and other funeral-related merchandise and services. Although these items are not usually provided directly by mortuaries, most funeral directors assist in their purchase, and they even advance monies for their purchase as an accommodation to the family. The present analysis refers only to the pricing of the product provided by mortuaries directly, but it recognizes that there will be a maximum amount that any consumer will pay for death care goods and services in toto—an amount limited by the buyer's ability and willingness to spend in this way. Out of this amount, the expenditure on the funeral service product of mortuaries will be determined during the funeral transaction, as outlined below.

The At-Need Funeral Transaction

For various practical and psychological reasons, most individuals do not make funeral arrangements prior to actual need, even though the opportunity to do so is generally available. Most common is the arrangement of a funeral by survivors at the time of actual need. In most families this does not occur often enough for members to be familiar with the prices of death care goods and services. Once a death has occurred, survivors do not usually have the time or inclination to enter into a discriminating decision-making process. The funeral home that comes to mind because of its location or general reputation or because of past experience is likely to be chosen by survivors at the time of need, without careful regard for its prices.

It does not necessarily follow that the demand for funeral services is insensitive with respect to price. Even if price is not a critical factor in the choice of a funeral home, it may nevertheless be an important consideration once the choice of a funeral home has been made. Each funeral home typically offers a line of complete funerals over a wide range of prices, depending almost entirely on the quality of the casket selected by the family. These alternative caskets are highly substitutable elements of the traditional funeral among which consumers may choose after they have chosen a mortuary on the basis of considerations other than prices. The extent of the variations in casket quality is reflected here in the array of caskets manufactured by the York Group, Inc. In the photos on page 140 and 141, the variety of metal caskets is arranged from the high end (a) to the low end (h) of the line. In the photos on page 142 and 143, the variety of wooden caskets is shown arranged from high end (a) to low end (g). The casket line of a given funeral home would consist of a mixture of caskets like these, along with various minimal caskets and alternative containers.

Under FTC-imposed itemization requirements, a funeral home must quote separate prices for the major components of mortuary services, but since most of these items are the same for complete funerals, it is the price of the casket which ultimately determines how much the typical consumer pays as a total amount (i.e., the price of the funeral). Although this amount includes various charges for usual and customary services, the prices charged for items other than the casket may bear little or no relationship to their costs.

Instead, the quoted casket prices may be set to cover the costs of other items, as well as the cost of the casket. The prices paid by consumers for a complete funeral will thus vary primarily with casket quality (cost). A family is presumably free to select a casket on the basis of price alone; the choice is usually influenced, however, by the presentation techniques of mortuaries as well as by such variables as the age, education, socioeconomic status, ethnic membership, and religious beliefs of the deceased and the survivors.

b) 32-ounce solid copper

d) 16-gauge steel

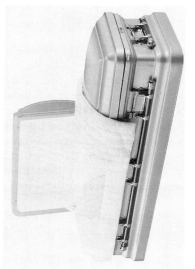

a) 48-ounce solid bronze

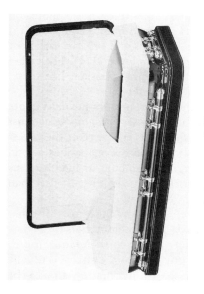

c) stainless steel

f) 18-gauge steel (alternate design)

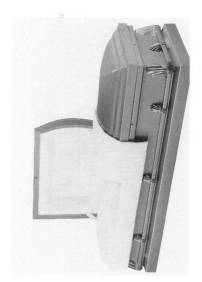

h) 20-gauge steel (non-protective)

e) 18-gauge steel

g) 20-gauge steel

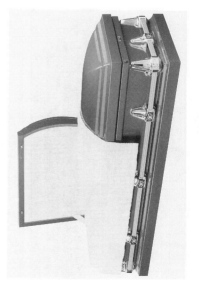

This page and previous: A line of metal caskets. Courtesy of the York Group, Inc.

a) solid mahogany

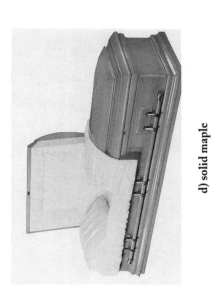

b) solid walnut

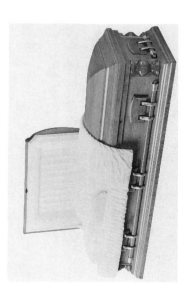

c) solid cherry

d) solid maple

e) solid oak

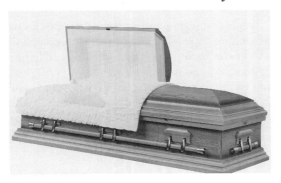

f) solid poplar

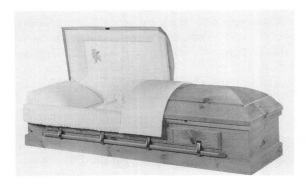

g) solid pine

This page and previous: A line of wooden caskets. Courtesy of the York Group, Inc.

Demand Formation

In terms of dollars expended, the purchase of a funeral service is one of the more important buying decisions in which consumers become involved. But in the absence of specific prepurchase planning, most of us have only some vague idea at best about funeral service prices when we enter into the arrangement conference at the funeral home. While complying with various price disclosure requirements during the conference (see Appendix), the funeral director collects a body of information that indicates such things as the religious affiliation and socioeconomic status of the deceased and ourselves.

At an appropriate moment, we are taken to the casket selection room, where we are confronted with an array of caskets at various prices. At this point presumably, some notion of a price range is formulated in our minds, based on what we think we can afford to spend and cannot avoid spending for the funeral service component of the total set of death care products and services we require or desire.

Allowing for the amount of spending for other components of death care, such as cemetery or cremation charges, each buyer may be thought of as demanding one funeral service at the time of need. The buyer is usually the bereaved family, even if the deceased has purchased a pre-need contract beforehand, for such a purchase simply creates a deferred demand for the delivery of death care goods and services at the time of need. In any event, there are two limits to the amount which may be spent for a funeral service — an upper limit that the consumer cannot exceed for financial or other reasons and a lower limit that the consumer will not go below, for whatever reasons. The entire "demand curve" for a hypothetical consumer is thus depicted by the unbroken vertical line segment in Figure 8.1.

Between the upper and lower limits of a consumer's demand for a funeral service, the point at which he settles will depend on his propensity to spend more than is minimally necessary, having regard for the fact that other expenditures (on cemetery space, a monument and so on) may be necessary or desirable. Now generally, there are many factors which influence this propensity. Some may arise from the survivor's own psychological predisposition to spend in expiation of guilt or out of sentiment, whether rational or irrational. Some may arise from social conventions and norms. Some may arise from the more or less subtle pressure that is brought to bear by the funeral director in the sales process. ("Don't forget, this is the last gift you will ever give your husband, Mrs. Jones.")

Under this set of psychological, conventional, and commercial influences, the consumer reaches a decision to spend the amount which seems to her most appropriate at the time, even though she may later regret that she did not spend more or less.

Firm and Market Demand

In a given period of time, a funeral home is approached by a number of customers, all of whom contemplate buying from the firm because of its location, reputation, or its ethnic or religious orientation, among other factors. The sum of individual demands activated during a period comprises the firm's demand curve during the period, but the individual maximum-minimum ranges

Figure 8.1

Individual Consumer's Demand Curve

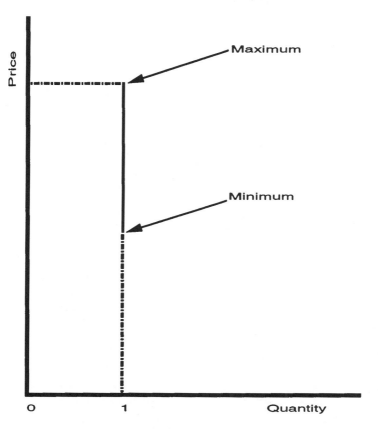

of Figure 8.1 must be reduced significantly to be viewed as demand by the firm. The tendency of a particular mortuary to view a price within each consumer's range as a feasible price will vary with the characteristics of the population of customers it serves and the extent of the rivalry within the market in which it operates.

But in general a mortuary will not view the maximum price to be a feasible price; attempting to extract the highest price possible from each customer is not in the best interest of the firm for two reasons. In the short run, unreasonably high minimum prices can cause a customer to turn to one of the firm's competitors, even if moving the body is required. In the long run, a mortuary may damage its reputation and resultant future business from family and friends by backing its current customers to the wall. Unless its prices are considered reasonable by its current customers, a mortuary may lose both present and future business to actual or potential rivals.

The importance of this factor in the market for funeral services has tended to be obscured by the traditional emphasis placed on nonprice competition in the industry, but its influence on consumers is borne out by evidence developed in the review of the Funeral Rule by the FTC. In a section entitled "Market price-sensitivity" in the final amended trade regulation rule, the commission staff commented as follows:

> Consumers' demand for funerals, of course, is price inelastic. Record evidence indicates, however, that consumers' selections of individual funeral providers, overall types of funeral service, and individual funeral goods and services are price-sensitive.
>
> Consumers value available price information in selecting a funeral home and in making specific funeral arrangements, particularly when they receive the price information early in selecting funeral goods and services. With respect to the selection of a provider, 52% of NSM [National Selected Morticians] survey respondents in the years 1983–1988 said that they considered price "very important" in their funeral home selection, although other factors appeared to be more important; only 19% considered price unimportant [*Federal Register*, January 11, 1994, p. 1598].

As noted by the FTC staff, the results of another survey are "remarkably similar" concerning the importance to consumers of the prices of funeral goods and services.

Given these considerations, a point at or near the lower limit of the maximum-minimum range of each consumer will be viewed by the firm as individual customer demand, when there is sufficient competition in the market. Under conditions of monopoly or monopolistic competition, prices in the inner reaches of the maximum-minimum ranges may be viewed as feasible demand prices, but even mortuaries with strong monopolistic features will not usually regard maximum prices as feasible, either from fear of attracting competition or from the desire to maintain goodwill, or both. In any case, an array of the feasible price-points in all the individual demand ranges of customers constitutes a mortuary's demand curve (Figure 8.2). It should be noted, and indeed stressed, that the curve is downward-sloping not necessarily because a mortuary has monopoly power over price, but because the maximum-minimum ranges, and hence the feasible demand prices, of different consumers are different. If there are sufficient sales in the time period covered (one year seems to be most useful period to consider), a line drawn through the feasible prices of its customers will closely represent firm demand.

Market demand is then the horizontal sum of all firm demand curves in the market, defined not only by geographical but also by ethnic, religious, and socioeconomic segments. The market demand quantity will be inversely related to price because it is the sum of individual arrays that are so related. As will be seen below, however, the market demand curve thus derived is not the usual demand curve of economic theory because it does not represent industry average revenue; instead, it follows closely the marginal revenue curve for the market.

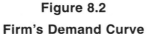

Figure 8.2

Firm's Demand Curve

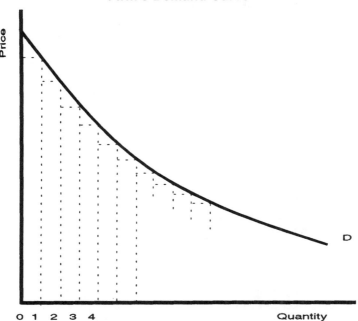

Satisfying Demand

In order to satisfy the varied demands of its customers, a funeral home typically offers a variety of caskets which may be incorporated in the desired funeral services, each carrying a different price based on the quality of casket included. In a single establishment, therefore, consumers may purchase funeral services offered in a wide range of prices.

Yet the cost of the casket accounts for less than 20 percent of the price of the average funeral service, and the remaining costs are essentially constant per service. Allowing for the variation in casket quality, therefore, differences in the prices of funeral services do not generally reflect differences in the total cost per unit of producing those services, so that there occurs a process of price discrimination. In other words, the prices of funeral services are differentiated by the prices of caskets subsumed under the total price of service — caskets which appeal to different buyers in such a way that those paying higher total prices (because they chose higher-priced caskets) secure a total funeral service substantially or exactly the same as that available to those paying lower total prices (because they chose lower-priced caskets).

In theory, a mortuary could obtain absolute maximum total revenue if it could charge each customer his particular demand price, that is, if it could apply what is essentially discrimination in the first-degree in pricing its differentiated product. In effect, the seller would move down the demand curve he faces, charging each customer his feasible demand price. The mortuary's demand curve then would be identical to its marginal revenue curve; total revenue would be the entire area under the demand curve and, logically, it could not be higher. But, as noted, it is customary for a funeral home to satisfy all demands of the customers who come to it, so that total revenue includes all the area under the demand curve, including a portion which represents "child," "welfare," and "less-than-complete" or "partial" adult cases which may not cover variable costs. To maximize total revenue in this fashion would require that the seller have full knowledge of each customer's demand — a condition that is never quite satisfied.

What does provide the funeral director with a fairly complete knowledge of the demand curve he faces, however, is the consumer's choice in response to his offering of variation in casket quality. When the buyer is presented with a range of casket quality (prices), he reveals his demand by selecting a casket (funeral service) which represents his feasible price. Thus, if the funeral director could offer infinite variation in his product, he could outline the entire demand curve and use the first-degree discrimination approach.

In practice, the funeral director cannot offer infinite variety, but he can and does offer a product line with a number of different prices — basically one price for each quality of casket to be found in his showroom. And in doing this, he is following a policy of second-degree price discrimination under these conditions: (1) the markets for funeral services cannot be kept substantially separate and therefore (2) the services are made to appear different by varying the quality of the casket included. By differentiating its services on the basis of casket quality, a funeral home is able to segregate the various components in the demand for its product to obtain higher prices from some of its customers. As a consequence, the firm may obtain larger total revenues than would be possible if a uniform price were to be charged for an undifferentiated funeral service output.

An Illustration

To illustrate how the revenue of a mortuary is enhanced by offering a product line, first assume that only one casket is offered with a complete funeral service, requiring that a single price be charged. In order to serve all customers (ignoring child, partial adult, and welfare services), the price of a funeral service would have to be equal to the lowest demand point in the firm's array as illustrated in Figure 8.3. Total revenue in this instance is represented by the rectangle OP_0DQ_0 (price times quantity). Additional revenue may be obtained by adding better quality caskets at higher prices, the case illustrated by Figure 8.4.

Adding two caskets to the line increases total revenue as follows: OQ_2 of one funeral category can now be sold at a price of OP_2; Q_2Q_1 of another can

Figure 8.3

One Casket—One Price

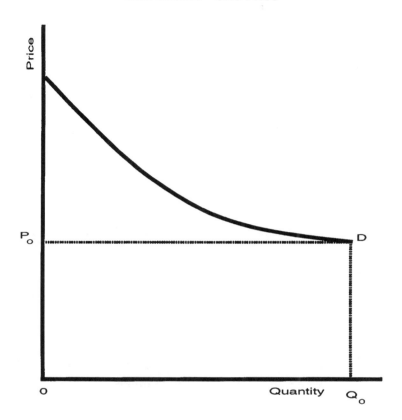

be sold at OP_1; the remaining funerals, Q_1Q_0, may still be sold at the old Figure 8.3 price of OP_0. The increase in total revenue, over the case illustrated by Figure 8.4, is the sum of the areas P_0P_2CA and ABEF. Additional revenue may be obtained by expanding the casket line even further. But adding caskets to the line involves increased merchandise and stockage costs, and it may involve a loss in revenue due to any "trading down" by customers who would otherwise have opted for a higher priced service. The best product line structure is achieved when no additional caskets can be added without the increment in costs being greater than the net change in total revenue.

We assume that the well-managed funeral home does in fact attempt to develop and to balance its casket line in the manner indicated. At least some crude comparison of the cost and gain from adding caskets is made by the funeral director, and additions to the line are discontinued when no further benefit can be foreseen. That, at least, is the impression one gets from the emphasis placed on balancing the casket line by the trade press and by casket

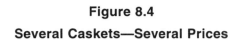

Figure 8.4

Several Caskets—Several Prices

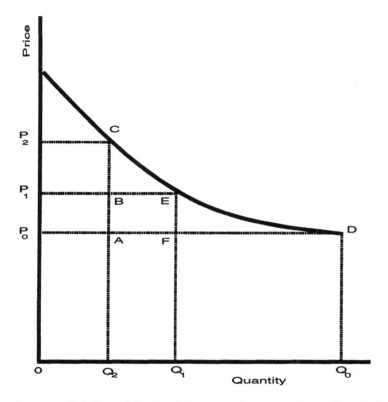

manufacturers. A balanced line in this context is essentially one in which price differences are clearly related to quality differences in the eyes of consumers. The difficulties of achieving this balance when a mortuary purchases its caskets from several suppliers has led to the development of casket companies which specialize in producing and supplying a mortuary's full line, for example, the Balanced Line Casket Co., Cambridge City, Indiana.

The upshot of the balancing process described here is that an extensive casket line is found in virtually all full-service funeral homes, that is, a large variety of casket styles and models is made available to the consumer. We therefore can expect the resulting demand-price relationship to look something like that shown in Figure 8.5. The illustration is limited to the full line of caskets associated with the total-adult funeral services offered by an establishment. As previously noted, the product line of a mortuary will also include child, partial-adult, and welfare services, the inclusion of which does not necessarily depend upon the adequacy of prices charged to cover the variable or overhead costs of providing the service. It often reflects more general considerations,

Figure 8.5

Product-Price Differentiation—Full Line of Caskets

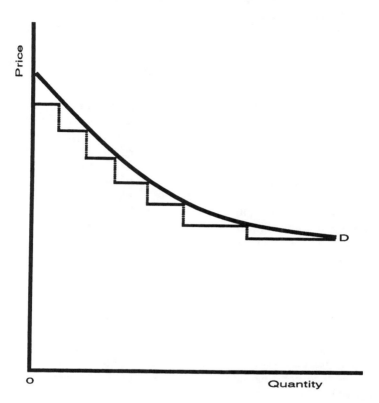

such as the reputation of an establishment in the community. This simply means, of course, that part of the costs of providing these services is borne by the business as a whole and represents, in effect, a form of investment in goodwill for the future.

Supply and Cost Functions

The supply curve for a firm shows the relationship between price and the quantity offered for sale. Normally the curve is expected to be upward-sloping because incremental costs of production generally rise with increased quantity. A funeral home, however, is not so much in the business of producing and selling a product as it is in the business of selling its available capacity (personnel and facilities). It will therefore supply its output (funeral services) at the various prices it has set to follow demand. This supply for the firm is represented by the "stairsteps" of varying length shown in Figure 8.5. Total market supply is downward-sloping, since it is the horizontal sum of the downward-sloping supply curves of individual mortuaries. Such a curious result is not a violation of the law of supply, since the law envisages a homogeneous product. Funeral homes sell a variety of caskets (funeral services), and each variation has its own cost. In general, the lowest-priced variation of the complete funeral service is also the lowest-cost variation.

In contrast to the cost functions of firms which produce a homogeneous product (and whose costs are determined by production functions subject to diminishing returns after a point), the cost functions of a funeral home depend on the manner in which its output is arrayed. The rationale for arraying mortuary demand on the basis of casket quality was discussed in previous sections. Demand for funeral services incorporating caskets of varying quality was arrayed from high to low in order to produce a mortuary's demand curve for a given period of time.

Logically, then, an analysis of mortuary costs should reflect the same output array. From left to right, the first units should measure the costs of producing the highest quality output, the next units should reflect next highest quality, and so on down the line to the lowest quality output. In order to relate prices to costs, it is necessary to consider the variation in costs that will occur, given such an array.

Costs and Prices

Since the complete funeral service offered by a mortuary varies primarily in terms of differences in the quality of casket included, variation in the costs of services incorporating caskets of different quality reflects primarily the differences in casket costs.

The remaining costs (of personnel, facilities, etc.) are in essence the fixed costs of having a mortuary ready to provide funeral services to almost anyone on demand. Given the sales of different units in the line of a funeral home during a period, therefore, its variable costs per service will appear as depicted in Figure 8.6.

Each flat portion of the variable cost-per-service stairsteps in Figure 8.6 is related to the analogous steps of the demand-price function developed previously (Figure 8.5).

The total area under the price steps in Figure 8.5 must be equal to at least the area under the cost steps in Figure 8.6 in order for total revenue to cover total variable costs. But merely to cover total variable costs implies a loss equal to total fixed costs, including the return that could be received on any alternative use of the realizable value of the firm's capital and, in the cases of proprietorships and partnerships, the services of the owner(s). The prices and resultant revenues of a mortuary must be sufficient to cover these costs in the long run.

Figure 8.6

Variable Costs Per Service

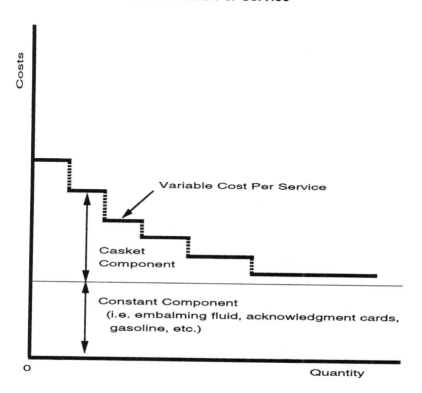

Consumer Welfare

Although we lack the systematic data to permit an evaluation of the profitability of the industry, we can make a tentative observation about how the industry's approach to demand satisfaction affects consumer welfare vis-à-vis a hypothetical alternative: one undifferentiated product sold at one price. While this comparison may seem to be unrealistic, it does serve to make a useful point. Plainly, the point is that the product-lining policies of mortuaries ensure more efficient demand satisfaction than a single-product, single-price approach. For in either case, total revenues would have to cover total costs. Under the single-price approach, the only way that this could possibly be achieved would be to price the standard service above the demand prices of some customers, so that some individuals would be forced to move toward their maximum prices (above what we have called their feasible prices) or to forgo a standard funeral service altogether.

Figure 8.7 illustrates the point. Figure 8.7(a) corresponds to the above-

Figure 8.7

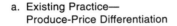

a. Existing Practice—
   Produce-Price Differentiation

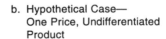

b. Hypothetical Case—
   One Price, Undifferentiated
   Product

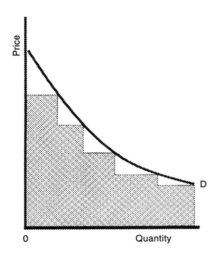

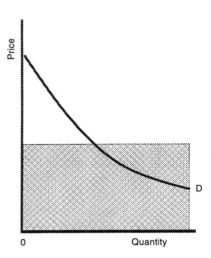

demonstrated demand-price relationship that exists for firms in the industry; 8.7(b) illustrates the hypothetical single-price alternative, given the same total firm demand. The two shaded areas must be equal because they cover the same total cost and target profit. Under sufficiently competitive conditions at least, the product-price differentiation which characterizes the mortuary services industry tends to ensure that each consumer pays a price close to his minimum theoretical demand price. In the hypothetical single-price case, some consumers would pay a price below their theoretical demand prices; others would have to pay a price above their maximum theoretical demand prices.

While we cannot draw any firm conclusions about consumer welfare from this analysis, we can reasonably speculate that the existing practice of product lining is beneficial to consumers. Most buyers are able to purchase the quality of funeral service (casket) they want at prices they are willing and able to pay. Alternative practice would leave some consumers less than satisfied with the quality of the product purchased, others would be forced into excessive casket quality at prices exceeding their "feasible" demand prices.

Pricing Practices

One of the characteristic features of mortuaries, regardless of the market conditions under which they operate, is that they must quote prices rather than sell at prices established by rival firms. They are then prepared to sell as many services as the market will take at the quoted prices. For the most part, therefore, they face a problem of deciding at what prices they will offer their services, not of deciding how many services they will provide. The practical effect of this is that each mortuary must estimate the demand for each unit in its line and adjust its prices to that demand.

Under FTC rules the charges of a funeral home must be itemized, and funeral directors are required to quote prices over the phone. In effect, this means that they are required to adopt a form of multipart pricing, where fixed service charges are quoted, plus a price for the casket, which varies with quality. Definitive answers as to how mortuaries establish prices for the major components of the complete funeral are not available. But it seems generally to be accepted throughout the industry that charges for the service components, which are virtually the same from firm to firm, are not based on their costs. Quoted service charges within a market may thus appear highly competitive, even though actual prices paid by consumers and averages per service may differ greatly among rivals. Likewise, the advertised minimum prices of complete funerals may be similar within a market, due to the common practice of advertising and quoting prices based on the low-end of the casket line.

The critical determinant of funeral prices undoubtedly is the casket price, and there is considerable evidence to indicate that most funeral homes base their prices on some variant of "mark-up" pricing based on casket or full costs. Since many such firms are in some respects distinctive (i.e., their establishments differ from those of rivals or they are geographically distant from rivals), they generally have some freedom in fixing their prices (mark-ups). They may set them as low as the break-even level, which they calculate in terms of estimated volume and costs, or as high as the market will bear. Of course, the mark-up they adopt must produce revenues which exceed the break-even level in order to yield a profit, and usually it will not be as high as the market will bear, in order to build goodwill and avoid attracting competition. Most mortuaries will fix their mark-ups within some narrower limits and usually — because they can estimate their volume — at a level which will produce an acceptable or "target" level of profit (absolute or as percentage of capital).

Assuming that the target profit is equal to the opportunity cost of capital and owners' services, achieving this objective is the equivalent of exactly covering short-run total cost. Where a mortuary has monopoly features, however, its mark-up can result in a set of prices which produce a rate of return on capital exceeding its opportunity cost. A lack of price competition in the market allows the firm to treat its demand curve as one which lies above the demand curve it would face under sufficiently competitive conditions. Only when there is sufficient price competition will the lowest points in the maximum-minimum ranges of its customers necessarily be viewed as individual demand by the firm, and only then will the firm's pricing procedures be constrained by the lowest points of all its clients.

There are perhaps some isolated markets in which the price competition among funeral homes is sufficient to constrain their pricing practices, but the widespread absence of pervasive price competition within the industry undoubtedly permits many mortuaries to establish prices to cover inefficiencies or to earn above-normal profits. Even if this is not the case, the effect of the pricing practices employed by them results in prices charged for caskets which reflect a mark-up higher than would ordinarily be associated with casket retailing as a separate line of business.

Ruhl (1993) explains this practice as follows:

> While families compare prices for the service portion of the traditional funeral, they normally do not compare prices for the merchandise portion of the traditional funeral. This is due to the fact that it is very difficult to compare one casket with another or one burial vault with another. There are a variety of casket and burial vault manufacturers, and the quality of their products is not easily compared. Therefore funeral directors feel more comfortable marking up the casket and burial vault rather than the service portion of the traditional funeral, which may be roughly compared across funeral homes [p. 39].

This practice of underpricing the service component of the death care provided by funeral homes allows them to quote similar service charges, but it is entirely based on the sale of complete funerals which include a casket. It is inherently unsound as a method of pricing when the mortuary services desired by consumers do not include a casket, or at least not an expensive one.

Cremation and Combustible Caskets

As a theoretical description of the pricing behavior of mortuaries, the preceding analysis does not in any way depend on the form of final disposition or memorialization chosen by consumers. In practice, of course, the choice of final disposition may affect the quality of casket selected. Indeed, it may eliminate the need for a casket altogether, replacing it with a minimal disposable container of some sort suitable for transporting the body to the crematory. The effects of these separate cases may be distinguished.

On the one hand, the preceding analysis allows for the case of cremation, provided a ceremony is held that requires the use of a casket. A so-called combustible subline of caskets, most suitable and sensible when cremation is selected, then becomes integrated into the complete line of caskets displayed by a funeral home. Again, this subline is differentiated, as illustrated in the photos on page 158 and 159, which show six combustible caskets ranging in quality from "high end" (top) to "low end" (bottom).

The analysis may be extended also to include the case in which cremation is selected and no ceremonies are desired. In this case a container, rather than a casket, is all that is required. In effect, this entails an additional step (or steps) in the variable costs of a mortuary, shown in Figure 8.6 on page 153. This added step represents the variable costs of whatever level of mortuary services is required in such cases, including the minimum container(s).

From the standpoint of economic behavior, it is profitable for a mortuary to take any case for which it is able to charge a price which exceeds the variable cost of providing the service. To quote a lower price would be unprofitable and to quote a higher one would be to actively discourage cases involving no funeral—a strategy which has sometimes been adopted by mortuaries. Thus, some firms have refused to negotiate rates for minimum services with memorial societies, whereas others have been willing to do so for various reasons to be discussed at a later point.

If the service charges in such cases are set at a level which does not cover the variable costs of providing them, then a portion of the costs must be covered by the prices charged for products or other services, specifically by the mark-ups applied on caskets used in services involving ceremonies. Yet, because the charges for direct cremation are comparable among mortuaries, there may be some competitive pressure on them to quote prices which are less than variable costs. To the extent that this is so, it is a further example of price discrimination generally employed by mortuaries, as examined earlier in this chapter.

Casket "Handling Charges"

Our analysis to this point clearly establishes the significance of the charge for caskets sold by a mortuary to its operating performance. Notwithstanding their role as providers of death care, consisting of many personal services, mortuaries have established pricing practices more akin to those of retailers and merchandisers than to those of professionals offering legal, medical, and other specialized services.

Underlying this practice, clearly, is the traditional conception that the output of mortuaries consists of complete funerals, requiring the use of a casket. It is a given that the casket is to be purchased from the funeral home providing the funeral service. Consumers customarily have expected this to be so, and caskets have not generally been available from other sources in most markets until recently. It is no surprise, therefore, that the pricing practices of mortuaries have resulted almost inevitably in higher mark-ups on caskets than would be found ordinarily in casket retailing as a separate line of business. In a few local markets, this has invited competition from so-called "casket stores," which sell caskets at retail to consumers who then take them to a funeral home from which they purchase its services. Confronted with this new form of competition, affected funeral homes have at times refused to handle third-party caskets, but some have consented to do so while imposing a handling charge on such caskets.

In 1990, during the "Mandatory Review of Funeral Industry Practices," the staff of the FTC recognized the emergence of third-party casket retailers as a healthy sign of increased competition in the industry. The number of such parties was estimated at 150 to 200 stores, operating in a handful of states. To encourage this form of competition, the staff proposed, and the commission

b) eastern black cherry

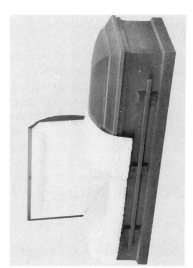

d) eastern poplar

a) American black walnut

c) Appalachian oak

e) selected hardwood

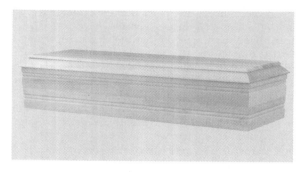

f) eastern poplar (unfinished)

This page and previous: A line of cremation-oriented hardwood caskets, all 100 percent combustible and environmentally safe for use in cremation. Courtesy of the York Group, Inc.

adopted, an amendment to the federal trade regulation rule which forbids funeral homes to impose a handling fee in connection with services involving third-party caskets. The amended rule took effect in July 1994, and presumably its effect has been to require funeral homes to absorb any loss of revenues associated with services involving third-party caskets.

Evidence presented during the FTC review provides a detailed look at the complications raised by the use of casket prices as a means of service cost recovery by funeral homes. The evidence established that the use of casket handling fees was widespread, and that the amount of the fee was often substantial (roughly equal in many cases to the wholesale cost of a casket). An industry consultant "concluded that handling fees are thus roughly equal to the amount that providers' non-declinable service fees are underpriced."

Based on such evidence, the FTC concluded:

> Concerning the amount of "casket handling fees" assessed, 81% of the PAA [Pre-arrangement Association of America] Survey respondents said that the average handling fee was over $300; 74% reported an average fee between

$300 and $500. Sixty-two percent of the PAA Survey respondents further reported that the highest fee charged was over $500; 35% said that the largest fee was over $700. A "handling fee" of $500 was nearly equal to the average wholesale cost of a casket in 1988 ($517) and 60% of the average casket mark-up in that year ($821). Wendell Hahn of the FFDA [Federated Funeral Directors of America], which provides financial advising services to 1,500 providers in 30 states, testified that handling fees are assessed because providers, who typically charge professional service fees "hundreds of dollars" below their true operation cost will try to recoup those costs that are lost by the third-party casket sale. Mr. Hahn concluded that handling fees are thus roughly equal to the amount that providers' non-declinable service fees are underpriced....

"Casket handling fees" prevent potential price competition and reduce consumer choice. Ninety-two percent of the casket seller respondents to the PAA Survey reported that their casket sales have declined as a result of handling fees; about one-third said that they have reduced or eliminated their casket marketing efforts as a result of those fees. One industry observer testified that "casket handling fees" have caused the exit from the casket market of five small businesses who thought they could gain market share by offering third-party caskets at lower prices. Several casket retailers and others also asserted that these so-called "handling fees" impede price competition by removing consumers' incentive to price-shop for less costly caskets, and penalize consumers who do shop.

Finally, third-party sellers testified that market forces will not effectively regulate "casket handling fees," and that the elimination of those discriminatory fees would result in increased competition in the sale of caskets and reduced casket prices. Mr. Royal Keith, a funeral provider appearing for the NFDA [National Funeral Directors Association], when asked on cross-examination about the effect of market forces on handling fees, responded that he is not aware of any cases where market forces have successfully reduced the amount of handling fees charged in a particular area [U.S. FTC, June 1990, pp. 125–27].

In rebuttal of this position, the basis for imposing casket handling fees was brought out in the testimony of industry representatives, who did not refute their prevalence or purpose but defended their use on several grounds. This testimony was summarized by the FTC:

> The industry [has a] long-standing tradition of recovering much of its overhead costs and profits through the casket mark-up, and not by increasing service fees; lower service fees allow funeral homes to provide full service funerals, including lower priced caskets, to those who might not otherwise be able to afford them. Although providers in recent years have shifted some of that casket mark-up to service fees, the shift has been very gradual. The industry groups concluded that providers who lose casket sales to third parties must, as a result, still forego [sic] the recovery of much of their costs and profits that would have been included in the casket sale.
>
> Those groups asserted that the imposition of "casket handling fees" is an isolated, non-discriminatory practice that fairly allocates providers'

overhead costs and profits; the purpose of the fee is to obtain from consumers who buy third-party caskets consumers' proportionate share of providers' costs and profits for rendering the funeral service. Providers' only alternative to handling fees, the industry groups argued, would be to raise service fees charged to all consumers, which, in effect, would require regular clients who purchase providers' caskets to subsidize the funerals of consumers who purchase their caskets elsewhere—by paying the mark-up on the casket as well as the higher service fee that would result from other consumers supplying their own caskets.

Those groups further asserted that handling fees are not assessed for shipins, outer burial containers sales traditionally lost to competing cemeteries, or for direct cremation/immediate burials where the consumer supplies the alternative container because, unlike the unexpected loss of a casket sale to a third-party seller, providers set prices for those services with the knowledge that they will not make a sale in those cases. Finally, the funeral groups concluded that the amount of "casket handling fees" is sufficiently regulated by the market, because providers that charge unreasonably high fees will offend consumers and lose market share [U.S. FTC, June 1990, pp. 123–24].

This kind of statement seeks to justify or to rationalize adherence to an irrational pricing mechanism. It is not a defensible pricing approach; it leads to extensive subsidization of some consumers by others as an inevitable result of undercharging for services and overcharging for caskets. Whether or not one supports the unbundling requirements imposed by the FTC on funeral homes, they do exist. It should be obvious that a pricing practice which results in overcharging for caskets sold by funeral homes invites consumers to unbundle their purchases for themselves and it invites casket stores to encourage them to do so. Indeed, this increased competition in the sector was an expressed goal of the FTC in adopting the Funeral Rule. Casket handling fees were a temporary expedient for the funeral providers which were destined to be outlawed by the FTC in its pursuit of this goal.

By taking this action, the FTC allows "one non-declinable service fee" to be charged by funeral homes. Presumably this fee will be set at a level which recoups more of the overhead costs of a mortuary. But there still may be a tendency for many of them to hold the line on the charges imposed as fees which can be compared easily by consumers. This may mean that most mortuaries will continue to function primarily as de facto casket retailers, dependent on high mark-ups on the line of caskets they sell and dependent on the continued demand for caskets, preferably expensive ones. This is inconsistent with the discernible trend in the number of consumers who prefer cremation. Even if they also desire a funeral service, it is not very sensible for them to opt for an elaborate casket.

It is important to emphasize that even if third-party casket providers such as casket stores do charge lower prices for caskets than funeral homes charge for the same caskets, this does not necessarily imply that consumers in general are being overcharged by funeral homes for caskets, because funeral homes have traditionally relied upon casket margins to cover a part of their costs of providing funeral services for which they undercharge.

To compete on a price basis with comparable goods sold by casket stores, funeral homes would have to sell caskets at normal mark-ups and establish prices for their services more in line with costs. Since these costs vary widely among mortuaries, the effect of such a change would be to create wide disparities in the quoted prices of their services. Of course this situation could be exploited by rivals who have not taken this step, threatening the long-run survival of inefficient firms.

More rational pricing throughout the industry would have other beneficial effects as well. One result of present practices has been to provide a large incentive for funeral directors to sell complete funerals, and to discourage consumer choice which departs from traditional funeral services with the body present, requiring a casket. This appears to have placed a major obstacle in the way of widespread acceptance by funeral directors of cremation as an acceptable path to final disposition — whether it be scattering, inurnment followed by burial, entombment, or preservation in a columbarium. If funeral service charges for personnel and facilities more adequately reflected their costs, this incentive would not be as strong. In a similar way, innovative business practices, such as the wider use of rental caskets, might be initiated by more mortuaries. All of these effects tend to imply greater concern for consumer welfare than we see under present practices.

Rental Caskets

Fine caskets with preservative features are appropriate for funeral services which conclude with burial or entombment. For funeral services prior to cremation, a fine casket may be desired, but it is less appropriate to the process of cremation itself, inasmuch as the casket is burned along with the body. Hence a line of combustible caskets has been designed by several casket companies, as illustrated in a previous section.

In connection with direct cremations and immediate burials offered by a funeral home, the FTC rules specify that a range of prices shall be quoted to consumers for each type of service, together with such information as a separate price for direct cremation where the purchaser provides the container, a separate price for immediate burial where the purchaser provides the casket, and other detailed price information (see Appendix).

As an alternative, the option of renting a casket for use in a ceremony preceding cremation is offered by some mortuaries. An example of a rental casket is shown in the photo on page 163. This seems to serve the purpose of providing a wider choice of caskets for use during funeral services, while recognizing that the destruction of the casket in the process of cremation is a factor tending to affect the willingness of consumers to spend on expensive caskets. From the consumer's standpoint, the rental of a casket presents the opportunity to

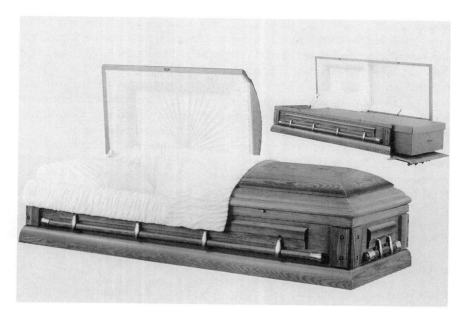

A rental casket. Courtesy of the York Group, Inc.

use a fine casket during ceremonies without having to purchase it. From the standpoint of the mortuary, the decision to offer a line of rental caskets may encourage the use of ceremonies in connection with cremation, since viewing, visitation, and funeral services are enhanced by the use of a casket of higher quality and different styles than those which a combustible container provides.

Because, as a rule, mortuary services tend to be underpriced, the rental charges for caskets must be set at a level that will compensate for the accompanying underpriced services. This entails an inclusion in the rental charge of an amount of profit equal to that earned on the sale of a casket of equal quality. Consideration may, of course, be given to the role that the use of rental caskets plays in attracting business and encouraging the selection of funeral services by those who might otherwise forgo them.

In any event, the availability of rental caskets represents an addition to the options provided to consumers by mortuaries and indicates greater concern for consumer welfare.

Children and Indigent Decedents

Some final remarks are necessary to complete the foregoing description of mortuary operations. As noted, the discussion has generally focused on total adult cases, ignoring several categories of services performed by mortuaries — including partial-adult cases that do not involve complete mortuary services and those involving the shipment of remains among firms, cases involving children, and so-called welfare cases, or those involving indigents. None of these is the mainstay of a mortuary, but as a form of public accommodation each may be handled at times. Under price itemization requirements, shipping costs are added to the costs of any other items provided in connection with less-than-complete services rendered when bodies are shipped from one mortuary to another facility. Two topics remain: children and indigent decedents.

Since the funerals of children constitute only 2 percent of all funerals, based on casket sales figures, it is clear that the number of children's funerals conducted annually by the typical funeral home is not large. Nevertheless, the way in which these funerals are handled is a matter of disproportionate significance. Services for children may bind a family to a funeral home for years to come. Funeral homes may thus not seek to cover fully their cost in spite of the fact that the service required may be the same for children as for adults. But because of the difference in the size of the casket, which is the significant factor in pricing, prices are substantially lower for children than for adults.

There appears to be less sensitivity attached to the death of indigent members of a community. Large cities usually have some procedures and reserve funds for the purpose of providing death care to the indigent, often involving burial in a municipal cemetery or cremation. In communities where there are no procedures and inadequate funds for the purpose, death care may be provided by local funeral homes or cemeteries without charge or at charges less than customary for the services rendered, some of which may never be collected.

9. *Final Disposition*

Cemeteries as Sites of Final Disposition

Ceremonies commonly associated with a death are not a necessary component of death care. The fact that ceremonies are customarily desired by survivors, however, accounts for the role of the funeral director as the primary provider of death care goods and services. The funeral home is expected to serve as a proper place for holding the funeral ceremonies. In order to prepare for these, the funeral home is called soon after a death to collect the body and prepare it for the ceremonies to follow. If no ceremonies are desired, the role of the funeral director is limited to the set of activities involved in preparing for final disposition of the body. In cases where the body is to be disposed of by cremation, little or no preparation may be required, and the mortuary may provide merely for transportation of the body in an appropriate container. For earth burial or mausoleum entombment in a cemetery, a casket is ordinarily required and supplied by the funeral home which handles the body.

In most cases, of course, visitation occurs and a funeral service is held at a funeral home or place of worship prior to final disposition of the body. Following the funeral service, it is customary for the funeral director to transport the body to the cemetery or crematory and to oversee the graveside or committal services, if any. In so doing, the funeral director interacts with the cemetery or crematory personnel, who have the responsibility for opening and closing the grave or tomb, cremating the remains, or providing other merchandise or services relating to the final disposition.

For most consumers, "the funeral" connotes the whole process which begins with visitation at the funeral home and ends when final disposition is complete. "Funeral expenses" and "final expenses" are two terms used interchangeably to denote the costs of this complete process, perhaps also including a marker, monument, or urn.

It is nevertheless the case that consumers have tended to view the purchase of a funeral service as a transaction to be conducted by the survivors at the time of need, whereas they have tended to regard the purchase of cemetery property as a transaction to be entered into before need.

There are several possible explanations for this difference in views. For one thing, cemetery property is a tangible thing which may be viewed as an investment in real estate. Services, on the other hand, have only recently tended to be viewed as something to be acquired in advance. Second, the common desire of related parties to be interred together in a family plot requires prepurchases to be made. Third, the members of religious or fraternal groups have long shared a belief in the importance of common burial grounds, leading them to create such facilities for their members or to obtain allocations of space for their use within commercial facilities. Finally, commercial cemeteries have used pre-need sales programs to expand their sales and to reach consumers prior to the time of need. In sharp contrast, funeral homes have tended to ignore pre-need sales and concentrate on at-need selling of mortuary services, the purchase of which is usually covered to some extent by life insurance proceeds.

Cemeteries as Permanent Facilities

Superficially, the business of a cemetery is simple. It buys land, subdivides it into small lots, and sells them at a profit. In these respects, as well as in those involving zoning, permits, and infrastructure construction, the establishment of a cemetery represents a venture in real estate development. For the developer of a cemetery, however, the duration of the venture ordinarily extends over a far longer period of time than is associated with most types of real estate development. This is because the size of the unit of sale — the individual lot — is so small in relation to the size of the property as a whole. Even the development of cemeteries of modest size results in an inventory representing volume to be sold over many years. Thus cemeteries must create a continuing sales program extending over a very long period.

What is sold by a cemetery in the form of a gravesite or mausoleum crypt is not, of course, the real estate itself in the usual sense, but a right of interment. Adler (1972) asks whether this is "a real or a personal right." He then points out that there is confusion over this point. "Most authorities categorize a right of interment as an easement or a license. Generally an easement is considered real property, while a license is personalty." He indicates further that court cases are in hopeless conflict on this point (p. 9). Following interment cemetery property is unique in that legally it cannot be sold, mortgaged, or seized for debt. From the standpoint of the seller, laws generally prohibit the promotion of cemetery property as something to be purchased for the purpose of speculation. In any event, the product of a cemetery is not merely the property or right it sells initially; the cemetery product, if it is to meet the expectations of consumers, must include continuing maintenance and security to ensure perpetual care. To provide assurance of the ability of a cemetery to deliver this feature of the product, its operation as a commercial enterprise entails a corporate form of ownership and the creation of perpetual care trust funds dedicated to the indefinite maintenance of the facility. Even though funeral homes and other types of death care providers may cease to operate when their owners die or retire or their businesses fail, cemeteries must continue indefinitely. In a technical sense, this requirement of permanent existence makes a commercial cemetery a unique business making unusual demands on its owners. For all practical purposes, a cemetery cannot relocate or abandon its facilities. It is expected to exist as a permanent "city of the dead," undisturbed by changes in the area surrounding it and unaffected by changes in business and economic conditions which affect other business.

It is necessary to consider some implications of these considerations for the operators of cemeteries as commercial enterprises.

Origins of Heritage Cemeteries

The asset composition of firms in most industries is subject to considerable variation. In contrast to this usual state of affairs, all firms in the cemetery business have substantially the same composition of assets because their most important asset, land, cannot be leased. It must be owned outright in order for it to be developed for present or eventual sale to lot-holders. Moreover, the amount of land owned by a cemetery when it is developed must exceed by a wide margin the current demand for cemetery lots. To some extent, this overdevelopment is a necessary result of future planning at the time when a cemetery begins development because adjacent land for expansion may be unavailable at a later date.

These considerations lead to a distinctive feature of cemeteries which has tended to determine their fates: the major products (individual units) they provide require them to own, in advance, large tracts of land suitable for use and development as a cemetery for years to come. The investment required for this has served to limit the number of new cemeteries built over the years. Also, for public health reasons, zoning ordinances now require that new cemeteries be located at some distance from the center of town. Tracts of land feasible for cemetery development have usually been available only in undeveloped or barely developed areas on the outskirts of cities and towns long before suburban expansion made the cost of such a volume of real estate too great for the return it was expected to yield over an unspecified period of time.

Despite this fact, in the United States people always have expected cemeteries to remain forever "permanent resting places" for those interred there and all those yet to be. Hence, cemeteries have stayed put, while the communities from which they were once remote have reached and in many cases surrounded them. Well-designed and well-maintained facilities of this type have often become landmark properties characterized by their distinctive appearance in their communities. With high volume and large remaining capacity, these have come to be known as the "premier" or "heritage" facilities in their market areas. The customer base of such facilities derives from the family ties of those in the community whose ancestors or other significant relations are interred in the cemetery.

The premier establishments compete with one another and with lesser establishments in their market areas on the basis of the prices they charge as well as on the basis of nonprice factors which differentiate them as distinctive properties. The value consumers attach to these heritage death care facilities, and therefore the prices they are able to charge, rests to some extent on the fact that there is no other facility exactly like them. In other words each is by its very existence unique in character and placement, even though each meets competition from a number of rival establishments of differing degrees of distinction.

Although every cemetery is unique in some respects by virtue of its setting, not all cemeteries formed in the past have acquired a heritage status. Even in the case of many that have, their status is largely due to events transpiring since their inception, which have positioned them fortuitously. Most of the properties which have become over time the envy of some in the industry were once remote tracts of vacant land located in sparsely populated areas, attractive to few. Even Forest Lawn was "little more than an overgrown hill" (Sloane, 1991, p. 178). The decision made at the time to invest the funds necessary to acquire such properties for cemetery use entailed considerable risk. For example, a cemetery, as a dedicated facility, is the epitome of the single-use asset devoted to a special purpose for the duration of its existence. Furthermore, investment in a new cemetery must necessarily be on a scale which far exceeds the current demand, leading to excess capacity which must be carried and maintained by the business over an unspecified time. A factor offsetting some of the risk, however, is that the future demand for the outputs of cemeteries as a class of business is highly predictable, based on demographic characteristics of the population they serve. What makes the risks worth taking to developers is that cemetery developments promise substantial potential returns resulting from the purchase of land by the acre which can subsequently be sold by the foot. This had a natural appeal to the early real estate developers, who often backed the promotion of new cemeteries and memorial gardens or parks.

Cemetery Innovation

Commercial cemeteries evolved as privately operated alternatives to municipal, church, and family graveyards. In so-called "rural" cemeteries dating from the mid–nineteenth century that were located near large urban areas, lots were sold for monumented gravesites and private mausoleums. These were followed by the development of lawn parks and, later, of memorial parks which require flush markers in order to reduce maintenance costs (see the photo on page 169). Community mausoleums consisting of multiple crypts were an early extension of the cemetery product line which has persisted (see the photo on page 169). More recently, a number of cemeteries and memorial parks have entered into the operation of crematories and in some cases mortuaries.

It may seem at first glance that a crematory is quite different from a

Top: A monumented cemetery; *bottom:* a memorial garden, including a community mausoleum in the background. Courtesy of Loudon Park Cemetery in Baltimore, Maryland, and St. Bernard Memorial Gardens in Chalmette, Louisiana.

Examples of crypts in a community mausoleum. Courtesy of Lake Lawn Park in New Orleans.

cemetery as a kind of business, but on closer analysis it is clear that they are to some extent in the same business. Neither the cemetery nor the crematory "disposes" of the human body in a physical sense (even though cremation is considered legally to be a form of final disposition). Clearly, a cemetery, the site of earth burial or entombment, is in the business of providing a common area within which bodily remains are placed in small individual sites where they decompose over many years.

A crematory is the site where the process of cremation occurs, causing the rapid reduction of remains. Like the process of burial or entombment, cremation decomposes the body, but it does so in a rapid and violent manner, leaving in a very short time a smaller volume of remains consisting of ashes, bone, and other matter. Further processing of the cremated remains to pulverize the bone and other fragments results in matter known as "cremains." These may be returned to the family for scattering or safekeeping, but they also may be buried or entombed in a cemetery or placed within a columbarium on cemetery grounds. Many cemeteries have constructed columbariums where urns containing cremains may be interred permanently and memorialized.

In a technical sense the outputs of cemeteries may be described as various forms of final disposition chosen by consumers: (1) earth burial of a casket containing the bodily remains, (2) crypt entombment of a casket containing the bodily remains within an individual or family tomb, community mausoleum, or other structure, (3) earth burial of an urn/package containing cremains; (4) crypt or niche entombment in a cemetery structure of an urn or package containing cremains, and (5) formal scattering of cremated remains in a garden on cemetery grounds maintained for this purpose.

From the standpoint of cemeteries as providers of these forms of final disposition, each of these alternatives entails different costs. These costs result from investments in land and sometimes facilities which are then subdivided into sections containing small parcels sold as individual or family gravesites, crypts, or niches. After such investments are made, allocations of specific amounts to particular sections or parcels are arbitrary, because the investment in them is sunk and cannot be undone. Before investments are made, however, allocations are relevant to the feasibility of the project. That is, the development of any section or structure within a cemetery will depend on the expectations by owners that the investment will be justified by the net revenues it generates over its lifetime.

In estimating the net revenues (total revenues minus operating and maintenance costs and selling expenses) expected to flow from a development project, the production and sale of added burial space, crypts, or niches are not treated as undifferentiated forms of final disposition. Instead, those products are highly differentiated on the basis of such factors as location, embellishments, and other qualities known to enable a cemetery to serve some of its customers at higher prices and others at lower prices. In this way, a cemetery may gain larger total revenues than would be possible if a single price were to be charged for an undifferentiated cemetery product. Thus a cemetery finds itself in a situation parallel to that of a mortuary, as described in Chapter 8; in the case of cemeteries, different sections of a cemetery, mausoleum, or columbarium serve the same purpose that different caskets serve for mortuaries. For a cemetery, it is profit-maximizing behavior to differentiate its product line to capture as much consumer surplus as is consistent with the costs of differentiating the output.

Cemetery Prices

Cemeteries have sometimes been called "cities of the dead." They commonly are divided into different "neighborhoods" comprising the sections, gardens, or other distinctive areas within them. These areas have features distinguishing them one from the other, making them more or less attractive to consumers. The prices charged by cemeteries will tend to reflect the values consumers place on the distinctive features of a cemetery generally (its location, heritage, and the like), as well as on the distinctive features of its various sections. These two factors underlie the pricing practices of cemeteries, insofar as they are memorial sites of final disposition for bodies or cremains. Sloane (1991) provides a historical example of this when he comments:

One memorial-park owner experimented in the early 1950s with a small feature section, nothing more than a circle surrounding a small birdbath worth less than $500. He priced this section's lots differentially, with the highest priced lots closest to the birdbath, the lowest farthest away. The highest priced lots sold first. After that, this memorial park's sections were all differentiated circles surrounding increasingly sophisticated features. This practice was typical of the pricing structure in most memorial parks {p. 187].

For established cemeteries, as for existing residential and commercial real estate, it is obvious that cost loses its significance in the pricing process and cost-plus-markup formulas are irrelevant. Selling prices are determined by conditions in the market area from time to time, subject to the influence of expectations about future conditions of supply and demand. In general, "select" places will fetch higher prices than nonselect ones. Proximity to the graves or tombs of famous occupants of cemeteries may increase the demand for adjacent or nearby spaces. The headline of a newspaper article reads: "Fans Pay Big Bucks to Spend Eternity with Stars." According to the article, "some of the most-sought sites surround Marilyn Monroe's wall crypt at Westwood Memorial Cemetery outside Los Angeles." The exact premium her presence adds to the section of the cemetery near her crypt is unclear from the article and perhaps impossible to calculate, but it is pointed out that "Gravesites at Westwood begin at $15,000 and spaces near Monroe's crypt cost many times that" (Slud, *Times-Picayune*, August 14, 1994). Clearly, the prices of cemetery space are subject to the influence of location and numerous other factors operating in real estate markets generally.

Improvements, embellishments, and so on are made by cemeteries rationally, just as they are by potential sellers of residential property, when the cost is expected to produce an increase in revenues sufficient to justify the cash outlay. Improvements of properties may or may not be made, but maintenance is necessary, and the costs of maintenance must be incurred in order to maintain the value of real property. Nevertheless, the costs of maintenance may sometimes be avoided or deferred, either because of financial constraints or because of judgments that these costs are unlikely to be recouped in the future. The consequence of this is neglect and decline, a condition seen in some cemeteries. To avoid this, the use of perpetual care funds has been adopted by cemeteries as a legal or commercial necessity, and a portion of the prices charged by cemeteries provide these funds. The adequacy of such funds is a common concern of consumers, and thus an actual or potential basis of competition among cemeteries.

Cemetery Merchandise and Services

Cemeteries engage in the sale of property rights and also in the sale of merchandise and services in connection with the use and maintenance of cemetery property. In general, the cemeterian's role as a retailer of merchandise entails the use of pricing formulas which mark up wholesale costs of merchandise based on competitive conditions and the influence of prices on consumer demand. The former obviously are affected by the ability of a cemetery to "tie" the sale of merchandise to the sale of cemetery property rights and to restrict the use of merchandise provided by independent suppliers (funeral homes, monument dealerships, and others). The same considerations surround the cemetery's sale of services which actually or potentially are available from funeral homes, monument dealers, or independent providers.

With regard to cemeteries as the site of final disposition, services such as opening and closing the grave, setting the marker or monument, and others must be provided within the cemetery, but the services themselves may be provided by others. Arrangements for those services required in connection with interment are sometimes made when cemetery property rights are purchased at-need; more often, however, the purchase of cemetery property rights occurs before need. The services required at-need are charged to consumers when they are provided — at the time of final disposition.

In cemeteries which are small or inactive, these services must be acquired from outside sources, but they usually are provided from within by commercial cemeteries. In some cases, cemeteries have attempted to reserve the exclusive right to sell monuments and markers, but federal courts have held that it is an unfair competitive practice to tie grave sales to memorial purchases. On its face, this practice is similar to tying the purchase of a casket to the purchase of funeral services from a mortuary, a practice which the Federal Trade Commission has taken steps to prohibit. For the same reason, the FTC considered the need for an antitying prohibition in the case of cemeteries when it reviewed the Funeral Rule that applies to funeral homes.

The FTC review cites a 1981 case in which the court held that "with the exception of an inspection fee based on actual labor charges," it is an unfair competitive practice for cemeteries to impose fees which impede monument dealers from installing memorials in their facilities. In 1986 the American Cemetery Association and the Monument Builders of North America agreed upon "Recommended Installation Guidelines" that conform with this ruling. The FTC review did not find sufficient evidence to indicate that a significant number of cemeteries prevent third parties "from installing monuments in their cemeteries, charge excessive inspection fees, or charge discriminatory installation fees" (U.S. FTC, June 1990, pp. 118–20).

As a matter of sound industry practice, it would seem defensible for cemeteries to impose an inspection fee on third-party installers of monuments based on the actual labor costs they incur in conjunction with precautionary measures taken to reduce risk of error and ensure quality control — measures including title search, verification of precise location, inspection of monument setting according to expected standards, etc. Moreover, it would seem defensible also to extend this right of inspection fees to cases involving independent grave openings and closings provided by unrelated third parties, who may not be liable for errors that might be committed by them through lack of sufficient knowledge. It should be noted that cemeteries are liable for errors in burial placement and therefore must exercise control over their risk of liability in all cases, including cases in which they have not performed or overseen the burial or installation. Precautionary measures necessarily entail expense, and it is unreasonable, if not unjust, to ask a cemetery to incur the expense associated with allowing outsiders to conduct openings and closings or other proprietary activities on its grounds without allowing it to recover the related costs.

From Burial to Cremation

Both burial and cremation are ancient forms of death care which have served as functionally fit means of disposing of dead bodies. In ancient times cremation was the general practice, except in Egypt, China, and parts of Judea; among nomadic peoples it had the distinct advantage of not entailing the necessity to care for graves (Hendin, 1973, p. 224). In modern times the preference for burial or cremation has tended to reflect cultural and religious factors and the conditions under which different societies live. The tradition of a Judeo-Christian burial on which the American practice was established may be traced to the biblical accounts of the "burial" of Jesus. As given by Matthew and John, these accounts seem to depart from the practice of a hasty, minimal affair consistent with death by crucifixion "to one involving a clean white cloth and a new tomb (Matthew), and finally to an honorable entombment with a mass of fragrant spices (John)" (Steinfels, *New York Times*, April 2, 1994).

As part of a review of *The Death of the Messiah* (1993) by the Rev. Raymond E. Brown, Steinfels points out that in recent years these latter accounts have been questioned by biblical scholars, including one whose thesis is that "No one buried Jesus, or at best the Roman soldiers, respecting Jewish piety, threw his body in a shallow grave where it might have been eaten by dogs." According to Steinfels, this scholar "views the growing reverence of the Gospel's burial accounts ... as desperate imagination. It reflects the revulsion of Jesus's early followers to the brutal likelihood of his non-burial." The Rev. Brown's analysis contradicts such views and concludes instead: "That Jesus was buried is a historical certainty." This assertion does not settle such disputes, of course, but it is a source of support for the Christian belief in the biblical accounts to the effect that "He was crucified under Pontius Pilate, died and was buried." Commenting on the significance of the Rev. Brown's study, Steinfels concludes that "believers are apt to approach the short phrase 'and was buried' with a new sense of its importance."

This remains to be seen, but it is clear that adherence to burial as a means of final disposition has been eroding in some areas of the United States for many years. The first modern American cremation is reported to have occurred in South Carolina in 1792, but the first crematory was built in Pennsylvania in 1876. That facility was intended only for the cremation of the bodies of the builder and his friends, but by the turn of the century there were 24 crematories operating in 15 states, mostly located in cemeteries (Hendin, p. 226). Even so, the practice of cremation did not become popular among Americans during the first half of the twentieth century, and in 1960 it was performed in connection with fewer than 3.6 percent of deaths.

Following relaxation of religious and cultural restrictions, cremation has become more appealing to a larger and steadily increasing percentage of the population. This growing acceptance of the practice follows closely the rising number of crematories available throughout the country, especially in certain areas. The number has grown from 250 in 1970 to more than 1,000 today, roughly half of which represent additions to cemeteries, with the rest operated by funeral homes and related enterprises.

Crematories as Businesses

There are some important similarities and differences between the processes of burial and cremation as partially substitutable forms of final disposition discussed more fully in Chapter 6. They are similar in the sense that both are a means of disposing of the dead body by decomposition. They are different in that cremation reduces the time it takes for the decomposition to occur from many years to less than an hour. This is accomplished by burning the dead body at very high temperatures in what amounts to an incinerator for human remains, a modern version of which is depicted here in the photo on page 176. Improvements in the technical design of cremation equipment have increased the efficiency of modern crematories dramatically. The first facility in Pennsylvania required "four hours to cremate the body, and over forty-eight hours to preheat and cool down the crematory. Today, a gas-fired crematory cremates a body within one-half hour, requires virtually no preheating, and needs an hour of cooling between cremations" (Sloane, 1991, p. 228).

From the business perspective, the economics of cremation have been studied to the greatest extent in Britain, where cremation is provided as a local public service by more than 160 public crematories. These facilities have developed along with numerous private crematories as "the demand for cremation services has increased dramatically in the last forty years to the point where over 60 percent of deceased persons are now cremated. There is every reason to expect this demand to continue to rise" (Knapp, 1982, p. 447); hence the need for an examination of the economic characteristics of the supplying agencies.

In many respects, the conditions surrounding the operation of the British facilities studied differ widely from the American conditions. Nevertheless, the conclusions of the study are noted here as a basis for a consideration of some presumptions which underlie the operation of crematories in the United States. By applying statistical cost analysis to data obtained only from public crematories, the study found as expected that the average operating costs of such facilities is dependent on such factors as "the geographic location of the crematorium, the age and intensity of use of its major capital equipment, and upon

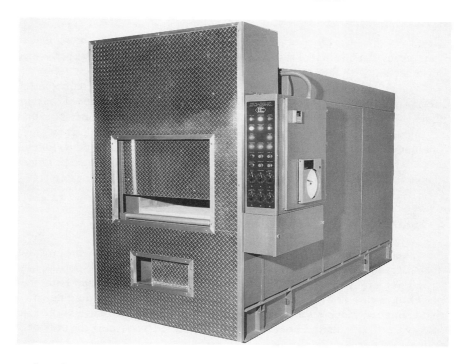

A modern crematory. Courtesy of Industrial Equipment and Engineering Co.

the particular range of services offered" (Knapp, 1982, p. 452). Summarizing, the author of the study concludes:

> The general finding is one of significant, though not dramatic, economies of scale in the operation of British crematoria up to a fairly large scale, followed thereafter by gradual diseconomies of scale.
>
> Studies of economic aspects of local public services are generally severely hampered by data constraints. It is thus unusually fortunate to have a national collection of fairly detailed data for individual production units from which valid and reliable output and quality of service indicators can be constructed.
>
> Whilst the actual shape of the average operating cost curve is dependent in part upon a number of factors (the geographical location of the crematorium, the age and intensity of use of its major capital equipment, and upon the particular range of services offered), the general finding is one of significant, though not dramatic, economies of scale in the operation of British crematoria up to a fairly large scale, followed thereafter by gradual diseconomies of scale. These economies at lower levels of activity can probably be attributed to input specialization, economies of massed resources and of large scale purchasing, and economies of administration. ... [It] is difficult to rationalize "pure" diseconomies of scale in the operation of the cremation service. As the scale of operation increases, management coordination becomes more difficult, staff morale may deteriorate, and the traditional

elements of X-inefficiency may creep in. Few cremation authorities have yet reached the cost-minimizing level of service provision and there would thus appear to be strong justification for the cooperation of local authorities in the provision of this increasingly important service in large crematoria. It is important to remember, however, that the customer of the service may prefer small, intimate settings to larger and more impersonal ones [Knapp, 1982, p. 452].

At the risk of oversimplifying these results of a careful study, it should be noted that they appear to confirm the common sense view that crematories are most efficiently operated on a large scale and in conjunction with related death care activities with which their operation is effectively coordinated. In the United States, this provides a rationale for the development of crematories by cemeteries within which they are operated to offer another process of decomposing the body which consumers may choose.

The critical factor driving the substitution of cremation for burial by consumers has been the addition of crematories to existing cemeteries whose core business is the development and sale of burial space. The effect of this has been to enable some cemeteries to replace lost sales of burial space with the sale of crematory services and, in some cases, with the sale of columbarium niches in which cremains are interred for perpetual care. Superficially, this may appear to result in a net reduction in the revenues and income of a cemetery, inasmuch as cremation is typically less expensive than burial. If the crematory only served customers who otherwise would have chosen the cemetery, this might be true. But it is likely that such a facility also attracts those who would otherwise have been buried elsewhere. Furthermore, promotion by a cemetery of cremation followed by memorialization of the cremains via burial or inurnment and niche interment may result in average revenues that are equivalent to those resulting from traditional interment or entombment.

This contrasts with the effects of this trend on the operations of funeral homes because a much larger percentage of cremations than burials do not include funeral services and the casket selected for use in services followed by cremation is often less elaborate. Nevertheless, the impact of cremation on the revenues of funeral homes has been lessened by the fact that crematories do not ordinarily promote and provide their services directly to consumers without the involvement of a funeral home. "To guard against public health problems and the misuse of the crematory by criminals, most states prohibit a cremation without the involvement of a licensed funeral director" (Sloane, 1991, p. 228). In effect, this requires consumers to arrange for cremation through a funeral home which is called at the time of need, providing funeral homes with an opportunity to promote the value of funeral services regardless of the form of final disposition selected. Alternatively, some licensed funeral directors operate crematories or offer mortuary services that do not entail any funeral services in connection with a crematory. These so-called "direct disposal" services have so far been confined mostly to large cities in areas where cremation rates are high.

The Cremated Remains

In effect the process of cremation involves incineration of the dead body in equipment designed to perform this process efficiently. The operation of this equipment results in the reduction of the remains into a smaller quantity of matter which is approximately one cubic foot in size and weighs up to eight pounds. The photo below shows the cremated remains immediately following incineration. This incinerated matter is commonly referred to as "ashes," but it actually consists of a mixture of noncombustible materials that are human (skeletal matter) and nonhuman (matter such as metal). The nonhuman material is removed by various means from the human matter which remains. This human matter includes bone fragments of sufficient size and shape to be recognized as such; hence it is standard procedure to grind these fragments into unidentifiable form and uniform consistency through mechanical pulverization or the use of a mallet (see the photo on page 179). Whatever comes out of this process constitutes the "cremains," which as physical matter require some further disposition. The human origins of this matter will influence attitudes regarding which forms of final disposition are appropriate.

Cremated remains before pulverization into cremains for scattering, inurnment and niche interment, or other forms of final disposition.

A machine for pulverizing cremated remains. Courtesy of Industrial Equipment and Engineering Co.

Just as the body has significance after death, so may the cremains. As discussed more fully in Chapter 4, although cremation is considered legally in most states to be a form of "final disposition," it is clear from the photo on page 178 that it is a "pre-final" stage in the process of final disposition. In actuality the process of cremation does not finally dispose of human remains, it rapidly decomposes the body, reducing it to a small package of physical matter requiring further disposition. As a legal matter, however, most states make an explicit distinction between bodily remains and cremains, in that laws prohibit family ownership of bodily remains but allow family ownership of cremains. Accordingly, families have an expanded variety of final disposition options from which to choose after cremation, unless a certain option has been pre-planned prior to death. As previously discussed, such forms may be formal or informal scattering, burial/entombment/niche interment of an urn or other container of cremains, or even permanent possession of the urn or other container of cremains, usually decorative, for memorial safekeeping or display in the home or another location.

For some, scattering the cremains at sea, directly on the ground, or on the ground from the air, is a practice which appeals to their sense of the natural order of things. For others, burial of the cremains in a family plot, entombment in a family tomb, or niche interment in a columbarium is the preferred form of final disposition, allowing for formal means of memorialization. For others, keeping a decorative urn or other container of cremains in a place of honor, whether on the mantle or elsewhere, is the preferred choice. For still others, wearing a small portion of the cremains in a piece of jewelry is the preferred choice. If desired, the cremains may be divided and shared. Manifestly, the acceptability of these options depends on the attitude of the survivors toward cremains.

In general, however, because of the significance of the cremains, they are properly considered to be a very sensitive artifact of the physical body which once represented the human being who is now dead. They are expected to be handled with due respect and care for their contents. Legal actions alleging "callous disposal" or even knowledge of such, have been successfully litigated in the courts.

Attitudes Toward Cremains

In spite of their being human remains, cremains differ from bodily remains in their essential sanitary nature and their portability. This has led to their peculiar status as compared with that of bodily remains. Cemeteries have historically been designed to accommodate the final disposition of bodily remains; but in an adaptation they have designed facilities to accommodate cremains, such as niches in mausoleums and columbariums. The mere availability of these options does not of itself convince consumers that cremains contained in an urn or other receptacle require further final disposition and memorialization through traditional means provided by cemeteries as "final resting places" for human remains. The difficulty for cemeteries which offer these options lies in the need to convince consumers that cremains require formal final disposition and memorialization, just as bodily remains do. Contributing to their difficulty is the fact that cremations are often arranged by funeral directors, who may simply return the cremains to customers in a box following cremation or who may formally perform the act of scattering the cremains, often with ceremony, for the consumer. If they do not sell urns, they have no incentive to mention them to consumers. Many of their customers therefore may be unaware of opportunities to inurn the cremains for burial or entombment followed by further memorialization of the deceased.

Cremation is ordinarily arranged by funeral directors who stand to profit from selling urns, but they do not profit directly from further final disposition of cremains in a cemetery. Indeed, they may lose by this in "zero-sum" terms (see Chapter 6). Economically, their best interests may be served by allowing a family to remain ignorant of such options. It is wiser to direct the attention of consumers to such services as formal scattering, which profit funeral homes when they are performed by funeral directors. Some states, in fact, require or countenance that the scattering of the cremains be performed by a funeral director. In zero-sum terms, it would be foolish for funeral directors to encourage the choice of any option other than one which they themselves provide, such as placement of cremains in an urn purchased from the funeral home, designed for placement in the customer's home or elsewhere.

On the other hand, cemeteries have an economic incentive to promote the option of burying or entombing inurned cremains. But because funeral directors have lacked a strong incentive to sell further disposition and memorialization of cremains to consumers, many of those who purchase cremation do not purchase further death care. Indications are that less than half of the annual number of cremations lead to final disposition in a cemetery, with or without some form of memorialization. Sometimes the cremains are never retrieved from the funeral home (U.S. FTC, July 1990, p. 145). This clearly signifies a difference in the attitudes of consumers toward cremains versus bodily remains. What this implies is that cremation is not only a threat to traditional attitudes toward the funeral service, but also toward the desirability of memorialization. Sloane attempts to explain the development of a relaxed attitude of consumers toward cremains in the following way:

> Death has become an intensely private matter, which is a reversal of the public expression of death in the last century. Cremation, with its mechanical disposition witnessed by none of the family, incorporates the desire for privacy and efficiency. Cremation is the final disposition, which means that the survivors are free to choose the ritual of burial if they wish. This freedom of choice has led to the popular folk story of Father or Mother placing Grandmother's cremains in the car at Christmas for the trip home. The family can reclaim control over the burial of the dead through cremation [p. 229].

This reclamation of control by the family is made possible by the portability of cremains coupled with the legal right of survivors to possess them in most states. Yet one wonders how many families really want to reclaim control over human remains, even as sanitized cremains in a decorative vessel, by treating them as household objects. No doubt, the failure of different types of death care providers to promote death care as a complete process, or even to understand it as such, has contributed to a relaxation of traditional attitudes about the value of a permanent place of final disposition accompanied by complementary memorialization, even when cremation has been chosen. Given the degree to which consumers historically have shared an urge to memorialize the dead, it does not seem far-fetched to suppose that there is a similar desire on the part of those who choose cremation. It is likely that this desire has not been addressed adequately by the sales methods of cemeteries, perhaps because they are attuned to the sale of burial space which traditionally, and naturally, entails memorialization.

The Impact of Cremation on Funeral Homes

Two factors appear to have played a significant role in the development of cremation as a form of death care in the United States. One is the historical fact that it was introduced and became established initially as a logical, inexpensive alternative to traditional earth burial. It was often advocated as an alternative to the funeral as a whole rather than as a means of final disposition within a complete process of death care. Viewed as an alternative form of death care as a whole, the choice of cremation directly affects the need and desire for prior funeral services and subsequent memorialization. In effect, the act of cremation is viewed as the complete process. Even when cremation is viewed as an alternative to burial, within a complete death care process, its choice may also affect directly the desire for commemorative funeral services and appropriate memorialization.

This is due to the degree of complementarity between different types of death care goods and services. In particular, burial and entombment are forms of final disposition which are consistent with the use of elaborate caskets that preserve and protect the dead body to some extent.

In this respect, these forms of final disposition are highly complementary with funeral services that incorporate the display of the corpse in a casket during visitation and funeral services. Cremation, on the other hand, is a form of final disposition that involves complete destruction of any container that is used in the process. This is inconsistent with the use of expensive wooden caskets that are burned along with the body. It is certainly inconsistent with the use of metal caskets with preservative features, which resist incineration. It is understandable, therefore, that a trend toward the practice of cremation has been viewed by some as a threat to the basic function of funeral homes as providers of commemorative funeral services with complementary caskets.

It is for this reason that cremation, even when incorporated into a package of complete death care, has been opposed by funeral directors and their associations, but such opposition seems destined to fail. A much more effective strategy might be for funeral directors to take the position that cremation is an entirely acceptable alternative to burial or entombment in the death care process, which need not adversely affect spending on the mortuary services stage of the process. Along with such a position, it would be necessary to defend the value of traditional funeral services, which it is the primary business of funeral homes to provide. This seems to be the direction taken by some funeral directors as the practice of cremation has spread to their markets. Their adaptation to this trend has taken the form of efforts to add high-margin merchandise which complements cremation as a choice of final disposition by their customers, such as urns, designer sculptures, and mourning jewelry containing cremains. This compensates to a large extent for the loss of profits resulting from the sale of lower-end caskets which complement cremation. As a strategy, it may enable funeral homes to adapt to the degree of cremation practiced in other countries such as England and Australia.

Up to this point, however, a significant part of the problem faced by American funeral homes attempting to adapt to the growing preference for cremation has been their adherence to a casket-pricing formula. This has resulted in the systematic underpricing of their services, causing them to depend excessively on the sale of caskets in order to cover their costs of providing services as well as merchandise. Since the choice of cremation affects the willingness of consumers to spend on caskets, the pricing practices of funeral homes have been incompatible with the more frequent choice of cremation as a form of part of the final disposition stage in the death care process. In effect, the pricing practices of funeral homes today are still predicated on the preference of past customers for burial in a cemetery.

Accommodation of the effects of the substitution of cremation for burial by more of their customers will require alteration in the pricing practices of funeral homes, so that the costs of delivering services are covered by the prices charged for those services rather than by the excessive contribution margins built into the prices charged for caskets. This change of tactics would also clear the way for the greater use of rental caskets in funeral services involving cremation, a development which would reduce the cost of services to consumers.

This point, which was made in the last chapter, bears repeating: as long as funeral homes rely on the sale of caskets as their primary source of revenues from which to cover the costs of providing insufficiently priced facilities and services, their ability to adapt to the growth of cremation and its impact on the casket selected, as well as to the growth of casket availability through third parties, is limited.

The Impact of Cremation on Cemeteries

For cemeteries, even those which operate crematories, substitution of cremation for burial or entombment has repercussions for the memorialization part of the death care process. When chosen by consumers, cremation does not automatically result in a grave or tomb as a natural site of complementary memorialization, whether in the form of a monument or a marker. For some reason, the cremains do not appear to evoke the need or impulse to memorialize that is associated with ground burial and entombment. Furthermore, the legal treatment of cremation as a form of final disposition entirely reinforces the popular conception that nothing is required after the act of cremation to effect actually final disposition of the cremains. Such laws fail to recognize the necessity for further disposition of the cremains to lay them to rest once and for all.

Nevertheless, the shift in the American's attitude about the matter is a fact, and this is described aptly by Sloane (1991) as follows:

> Interestingly, most Americans are not shocked by the failure of many survivors to memorialize the cremated dead. Few Americans complain that a heritage is being lost or state that the dead deserve permanent remembrance. Nineteenth-century Americans created rural cemeteries to ensure that their dead would be permanently interred and remembered. Twentieth-century practitioners of cremation believe that the dead can be memorialized in other ways or live in the hearts and memories of those who knew them [p. 229].

The impact of this fact on the operations of cemeteries has been to require them to develop opportunities for those who cremate to memorialize the cremains in appropriate ways, burial or niche interment in a columbarium. Hence cemeteries have tended to add such facilities along with crematories as the practice of cremation has spread. One example of a columbarium is depicted here in the photo on page 185.

The challenge to cemeteries and their sales forces is to market this memorialization process in more of the cases of cremation that they handle, which is likely to be a growing percentage of the total volume of deaths in the future. To meet the challenge, cemeteries and crematories must overcome a casual attitude that has developed toward the truly final disposition of cremains, based at least partly on the legal position that cremation constitutes final disposition of the remains. The lax attitude of consumers toward cremains undoubtedly is encouraged by this legal (mis)conception.

Vertical Facilities

Given the ability of cemeteries to promote permanent memorialization of the cremains in a columbarium, the continued substitution of cremation for burial by consumers provides cemeteries with a measure of increased flexibility, in that it reduces the limits on their capacity imposed by the land they occupy. This trend has also fostered the development of community mausoleums within cemeteries because those structures allow many more interments per acre of land than do traditional burial plots and family tombs. In terms of efficient usage of space per unit, the columbarium greatly exceeds even the community mausoleum. "An urn of ashes, when buried, fills only a sixteen inch square. Thus eight urns can be placed in the space taken up by one body buried in the currently traditional mode. Thousands of urns can be placed in a single, small memorial chapel" (Hendin, 1973, p. 224). The implications of space use have been calculated by Stephen Saltzman of the Chicago Corporation and are presented in Table 9.1 on page 186.

The space-saving advantages of vertical facilities in the form of community mausoleums for the interment of bodily remains and columbariums for the interment of cremains are evident. These space-saving features are the chief means cemeteries use to address concerns about the amount of land required for traditional earth burial. In this respect, they have reduced the pressure to make changes in traditional burial practices themselves, such as up-right interment of caskets and multiple interments, which consumers may resist. The development of vertical facilities and their acceptance by consumers allows existing cemeteries, including those approaching capacity, to expand vertically, enabling them to continue to serve future generations in many cases. New cemeteries may likewise economize on land use by emphasizing vertical facilities. Such facilities traditionally have been located in cemeteries, but there is no inherent reason why they may not be located in high-rise facilities which are

Inurned cremains displayed in columbarium niches, Lake Lawn Park Mausoleum. Courtesy of Lake Lawn Park in New Orleans.

more accessible to some areas than land-intensive cemeteries. It is possible to imagine entirely new forms of cemeteries which are largely vertical facilities or include vertical interment, multiple interments, and other innovations in the future.

Regulation of Final Disposition

As a permanent part of the community, cemeteries are similar to public parks, the existence of which enhances environmental quality. On the other

Table 9.1. Comparison of Interment Densities

Interment Method	Interment Density (number per acre)
Casketed Burials, Single Density	1,000–1,250
Casketed Burials, Lawn Crypts, Double Depth	2,000–2,500
Casketed Entombments, Community Mausoleums, Per Single Story	5,000–10,000
Cremated Remains, Burials	6,000–7,500
Cremated Remains, Niche Interment Mausoleums and Columbariums	30,000–60,000

Source: The Chicago Corporation.

hand, the association of cemeteries with death and their operating features as establishments attracting traffic, vandals, and visitors are sources of concern for some members of the communities in which they are located or in which an attempt is made to locate them. Efforts by cemeteries to expand into the operation of mausoleums, crematories, and mortuaries are also matters of occasional concern. Zoning regulation therefore is a major form of social control to which they have been subjected, primarily at the local level. Public health concerns were once at the center of regulatory efforts surrounding cemeteries, but improved methods of burial and entombment have alleviated such concerns. More recent regulation has shifted the focus of attention to the protection of consumers and the environment, including such problems as ground water contamination and the ventilation of community mausoleums.

The nature of crematories as incinerators has attracted the attention also of the Environmental Protection Agency of the federal government. Under the

Clean Air Act of 1990, the agency weighed a proposal to classify crematories as biomedical waste incinerators. If adopted, the proposal would have required extensive and costly retrofitting of crematories, forcing many of them out of business. On reflection, following meetings with representatives of the industry, the EPA agreed that human remains are not biomedical wastes — at least not for now. Crematories remain classified as "other solid waste" incinerators which will not be regulated before 2005, if ever (Cronin, *American Cemetery*, December 1993).

Partly as a result of the prominence of the funeral director as the primary death care provider, the marketing practices of cemeteries have generally escaped the attention of federal regulation designed to protect consumers. Another reason for this is that funeral homes are virtually always commercial businesses, whereas a large number of cemeteries are noncommercial operations. Except to a limited extent, cemeteries have not sold both merchandise and services, thereby raising concerns about bundling. On the other hand, commercial cemeteries and memorial parks have adopted aggressive pre-need sales techniques, the use of which may be expected to result in occasional complaints from consumers.

It is somewhat surprising, therefore, that in its review of the Funeral Rule, the FTC staff noted that it had not received many complaints concerning unfair or deceptive acts or practices by cemeteries or other providers not subject to the rule. It also noted that "an AARP review of 238 funeral-related complaints received by the FTC between May, 1984 and January, 1988, disclosed that 20 percent related to cemeteries, or approximately one complaint per month.... The mishandling of burial arrangements was the most frequently cited basis for complaints.... In response to an AARP solicitation for cemetery complaints from its 30 million members only 55 complaints were received" (U.S. FTC, July 1990, p. 131).

Following its review, the FTC staff recommended that the Funeral Rule not be extended to cemeteries for the following reasons:

> (1) Operators of those businesses generally itemize and disclose prices for both outer burial containers and caskets, the principal goods sold by them. (2) The services provided by cemeteries do not include a wide variety of different services and goods which are packaged or bundled into a single funeral at a stated price. The bundling issue is the primary unfair and deceptive act or practice addressed by the Funeral Rule. (3) The overwhelming number of complaints against cemeteries are not attributable to bundling, lack of price disclosure, or misrepresentation. They relate instead to gravesite maintenance and the refund of the purchase price or resale of cemetery lots [U.S. FTC, 1990, p. 142].

Furthermore, the FTC staff did not believe that alleged discrimination by some cemeteries against monument dealers was sufficiently widespread to warrant the inclusion of cemeteries under the Funeral Rule. Nevertheless, they remain subject to applicable state and federal laws and to regulation by cemetery boards in most states. Areas of cemetery operation which have been or may be the subject of regulatory initiatives include uninvited sales solicitation, repurchasing of unused interment rights, and determination of the percentages of pre-need sales revenues required to be set aside in merchandise trust funds or perpetual care funds. Furthermore, the Internal Revenue Service has not yet resolved the issue of the appropriate point of taxation of cemetery property rights sold on an installment basis. Adjusting to changes in the latter rules would affect cemetery operations, sales practices, and financial performance.

Vandalism

As accessible open spaces in urban and suburban communities, cemeteries have been more vulnerable to the risk of vandalism than most businesses. Their often asserted sacredness has not spared them from intrusions by those bent on committing various acts of vandalism ranging from littering to the desecration of memorials to assaults on legitimate visitors to burial sites. Incidents of these kinds have been reported by cemeteries throughout the United States. Examples of the damage done to durable memorials are depicted on page 189. In one case the head and one hand of a vandalized statue lie at its base; in the other, several discarded paint cans litter the scene of a splattered monument.

Curl (1993) notes that "In Britain, vandalism, arson, and lack of maintenance have reduced some of the great cemeteries to horrifying wildernesses where graves are desecrated, chapels are burned, and destruction of the most disgusting kind is widespread." He adds: "No truly great society desecrates the abodes of its dead, so the phenomenon of present times should be seen in a most serious light" (p. 360). In the United States, stricter laws have been proposed, and passed in some areas, to deal with the problem. Moreover, since vandalism occurs in every state, the need for federal legislation has been suggested. Meanwhile, the problem continues, causing suffering for the survivors of those whose memorials are affected and imposing financial burdens on cemeteries in the form of costly repairs, extra maintenance, and added security measures.

The National Cemetery System

The National Cemetery System comprises 113 cemeteries located throughout the United States. These facilities are operated by the Veterans Administration. In addition, the U.S. Army operates Arlington National Cemetery in Washington, D.C., and the American Battle Monuments Commission is responsible for 24 overseas military cemeteries and 18 separate monuments, 14 of which are abroad. Since the 1970s the federal government has cooperated with some states to develop a system of state-operated veterans cemeteries designed to supplement the national system (Sloane, 1991, p. 232).

According to Sloane, the national cemeteries were established "to inter soldiers who had died on Civil War battlefields. This represented an emergency

Examples of cemetery vandalism: *Left:* the head and one hand of a vandalized statue lie at its base; *right:* discarded paint cans litter the scene of a marble monument splattered by vandals. **Courtesy of Kates-Boylston Publications, Inc.**

measure, "but the right of burial was gradually extended, initially to "honorably discharged soldiers in a destitute condition." Eventually, the requirement of destitution was removed, and starting in 1890 spouses were permitted to be buried together with the veteran. Later all married children and unmarried adult daughters were added to the list. Sloane notes, however, that the "impact on other burial places was negligible ... as long as Americans retained their loyalty to local cemeteries, the number of national cemeteries was limited, and the number of veterans remained relatively low in proportion to that of the remaining population" (p. 232).

Recent experience shows that the national cemeteries attract only 10 percent of eligible veterans (Snyder and O'Dell, 1993, p. 150). Private cemeteries are more conveniently located, and they cater for the business of veterans by creating special sections for them and even providing free graves as a promotional practice. Beyond this, the U.S. government has itself encouraged the preferences of veterans for burial in local cemeteries by providing free markers adapted to the requirements of private cemeteries and memorial parks. Nevertheless, veterans groups have lobbied for expansion of the national cemetery system, based on projections that the space remaining in most of them will be exhausted by 2020. The objective of those groups is an expansion of the system until there is a cemetery located "within one hundred miles of each veteran, because the number of veterans who will choose to be buried in a national cemetery plummets when it is farther than that distance" (Sloane, 1991, p. 233).

Expansion or Subsidization

To expand the national cemetery system is one way to improve the conditions under which the right of burial is made available to veterans. An alternative is to subsidize the burial of veterans in private cemeteries. Compared with expansion of the national cemeteries, a system of subsidization would have the effect of making the right to burial available to all veterans equally in local communities, where they seem to prefer to be buried. This seems preferable to the present system in which some receive free burial, while others receive little or no assistance with burial expenses because they opt for a private cemetery. To attract veterans with families, it is necessary for the national cemeteries to permit the burial of certain survivors of veterans because of the common desire of related persons to be interred together. The use of a subsidy extending only to the veteran would reduce the number of burials for which the government is obliged to provide either space or a subsidy. This, presumably, would be a cost advantage of a subsidy program, compared to expansion of the present system. This advantage would depend, of course, on the level of the subsidy to be provided to all veterans, compared to that now provided to the few who currently take advantage of the national system.

Apart from the costs involved, the fundamental question here is whether the government belongs in the cemetery business at all. Although many cemeteries are owned by a number of state and local governments, they are operated at public expense primarily for the destitute. This was the original intent of the national cemetery system, but that is no longer its limited objective, or at least it is not the objective of those who oversee its operation. Through enlarging the system's scope over the years, complimentary burial now is available to all veterans and certain members of their families, regardless of need. Yet only those who live near the few open facilities are the actual beneficiaries of the system as it presently operates. Even extensive expansion of the system would be unlikely to serve the needs of every eligible veteran, many of whom have established attachments to private cemeteries. A fairer way to recognize the patriotic contributions of all veterans would appear to be a flat subsidy, or a means-tested scale of benefits, payable to all veterans directly upon death, to defray the expenses of burial, mausoleum, or columbarium space in private cemeteries of their choice. This would replace or augment the current reimbursement system which provides limited burial benefits for pension recipients. A similar subsidy might also replace the present "gravestone" program of the veterans administration. This would permit veterans or their survivors to select a memorial in conformity with the form of final disposition chosen and with the memorials of family members interred near them in private cemeteries.

Subsidy programs of the sort suggested here would appear to represent a uniform death care program for veterans conforming to the manner in which the military has provided mortuary services for those who have died on active duty. Currently, when a member of the military service dies while on active duty, a basic monetary benefit is provided for mortuary services, transportation to a national cemetery, or for burial in a private cemetery. Provided a veteran is not buried in a national cemetery, a modest plot allowance also is available for those who were discharged from active duty because of disability or died while receiving a pension or died while in a VA facility. In some cases a cash allowance is also available to veterans in lieu of a government headstone or marker (Snyder and O'Dell, 1993, p. 152). Thus, subsidization is used presently by the government to provide death care benefits for veterans in various ways. What seems to be needed is a further rationalization of the present system of subsidization, gradually reducing the role of government as a direct participant in the death care economy.

10. *Memorialization*

The Memorialization Process

To memorialize is to commemorate the memory of someone or something. The function of memorialization is to stimulate others to recall or to remember the life of a deceased person or some aspect thereof.

For a time, immediately following death, the memory of a deceased person is vivid because it is recent. At a funeral with the body present, it is acute. Even at a memorial service without the body present, it is evoked by the shared recollections of the participants. In these respects the social activities in which people engage after a death involve a large measure of memorialization, or remembrance of the deceased. To some extent, therefore, the process of memorialization is integrated with the processes of mortuary services and final disposition for the limited duration of those activities. Once the funeral or memorial service is over and final disposition of the remains has occurred, the memory of the deceased is prone to fade, however. In time, without the aid of memorial products, everyone is forgotten. Only through memorialization is the memory of anyone prolonged beyond the lifetimes of those who remember them based on experience.

Many people desire to preserve the memory of their own existence or that of others beyond this natural biological limit. To some extent this occurs for famous people or notorious ones and for some ordinary people in works which record their lives or deeds in books or films or works of art, including architecture.

For most of us, of course, there are no such exceptional memorials. It is up to us or our survivors to memorialize our lives. By custom, this is done in ways which are varied and subject to the influence of changing tastes and technologies.

In modern times the most prevalent form of memorialization has been the erection of some form of monument at the site of final disposition, commonly a cemetery. The epitome of this is the classic version of the tombstone on which is carved the name, dates of birth and death, perhaps the relationship of the deceased to some others, and in some cases an epitaph. The form and substance of such monuments and markers have undergone a process of coevolution with the process of final disposition, but their memorialization function is essentially unchanged.

The Impact of National Cemeteries

Although the cemetery is the natural site of both final disposition and memorialization, these two parts of the death care process were traditionally provided by different types of establishments, the cemetery and the marble shop. In part this was because most early cemeteries were noncommercial enterprises whose role was limited to providing a final resting place; to provide a monument or marker was the business of others. Under such conditions the two different types of death care providers coexisted and interacted as necessary. As a rule, early American cemeteries did not prescribe the form of monuments permitted to be erected within their grounds. Variety in the style of the monuments chosen by plot-owners was a source of distinction among individuals and families interred in cemeteries (Sloane, 1991, p. 187). Variations in these monuments still provide an historical record of the socioeconomic distinctions among the previous inhabitants of many communities throughout the United States. This contrasts sharply with the simplicity and uniformity of the monuments and markers used to identify the graves of those interred in modern cemeteries and memorial parks, reflecting a trend in memorialization practices which has significantly affected the economic features of the memorialization process.

Historians of American cemeteries attribute the standardization of monuments in modern cemeteries to the impact of the original nineteenth century design of a system of national cemeteries which adopted the practice of requiring a "general" headstone. "Only in Arlington and some other cemeteries, and only for a short time, were individuals allowed to put up privately purchased monuments." Commenting on the impact of this government decision to mark graves with simple markers, Sloane observes that "Although Americans admired the simple sentiment of the national cemeteries, most did not emulate them.... Not until the twentieth century would some Americans accept a limitation on their right to erect elaborate family monuments" (p. 115). This acceptance coincided with the emergence of simple designs for large commercial cemeteries based on the use of identical flush markers that integrated the memorialization and final disposition processes in the total concept of the memorial park as an alternative to traditional monumented cemeteries.

Monument Dealers

This trend was fraught with consequences for the businesses of monument dealers who sold monuments and markers to cemetery lot-holders. Most of these dealerships were small businesses run by self-employed monument men or stone-cutters. Often clustered around cemeteries, they typically varied their offerings to appeal to the economic status and tastes of the customers of those cemeteries. Their products ranged from granite and marble grave markers through family monuments to private mausoleums of many different sizes and designs. As the final death care expenditure, and the only one that could be postponed, the demand for these products was far more subject to the influence of economic conditions than was the demand for products of funeral homes and cemeteries. During the depression years of the 1930s, monument dealers were more adversely affected than either funeral homes or cemeteries, although the latter were also squeezed by reduced revenues and by high per-grave mainte-nance costs (Sloane, 1991, p. 203). In an effort to control such costs, most ceme-teries were subsequently designed and developed as memorial parks which pro-hibited monuments and provided their customers with a lot and a flush marker for each grave as a package deal. They also developed community mausoleums which reduced demand for the sort of private mausoleum previously sold and erected within cemeteries by monument dealers.

As a result of the growth of memorial parks and community mausoleums, the role of monument dealers in the death care economy was substantially reduced. In effect, their fate was sealed by the business practices of memorial parks which tied the sale of markers to the sale of burial space and crypts, effectively excluding monument dealers from the market they had traditionally served. As might be expected, the trade associations of monument dealers and their suppliers resisted the entry of cemeteries into their business, but the strongly complementary nature of final disposition and memorialization prod-ucts favored the common ownership of the businesses providing these products to consumers. In other words, final disposition and memorialization are so closely linked in the concept of the memorial park that the two may properly be regarded as a single product which can be most efficiently provided to con-sumers by a single firm. Even though several court decisions have held that con-sumers are entitled to shop for monuments and markers from third-party providers and installers, the right of cemeteries to charge various fees in con-nection with work performed on their premises by third parties discourages the use of the latter by consumers (U.S. FTC, July 1990, p. 133).

Sloane points out that the development of memorial parks also affected quarries and foundries that had previously supplied stone and metal to monu-ment makers and dealerships whose sales declined as a result of this change. Nev-ertheless, some of them were able to replace such lost sales by selling to ceme-teries which sold markers directly to their customers. Judging from the advertisements in trade publications directed at cemeteries, there continues to be an active wholesale trade in memorialization products. Moreover, the demand for monuments continues to be strong for memorial dealers who cater to the cus-tomers of special monuments and private mausoleums, especially in monumented ethnic, religious, and rural cemeteries. Sloane writes that in recent years shifts in tastes and disposal have increased the demand for larger, more expensive cemetery lots that include monument space (1991, pp. 226–27). Meanwhile, a struggle continues between cemeteries and monument dealers over who will provide and install monuments and markers (U.S. FTC, June 1990, p. 116).

Criticism of Memorialization

It is an interesting commentary on the critics of American death care that the practices they have tended to criticize are among the oldest forms of human behavior. For example, the practice of erecting monuments in memory of deceased persons has given the world the pyramids, the Taj Mahal, the Jefferson Memorial, Grant's Tomb, and countless other examples of enduring tributes to persons who have lived and inevitably died, sometimes hundreds or thousands of years before. A sampling of these may be seen in *A Celebration of Death* (1993) by James S. Curl, who· provides a compelling argument for the significance of human memorialization. At present, however, he notes a growing neglect of memorials, which he explains in the following terms:

> The neglected cemeteries, poorly designed crematoria, and abysmal tombstone designs of the present insult life itself, for death is an inevitable consequence of birth. By treating the disposal of the dead as though the problem were one of refuse-collection, society devalues life. The architectural memorials of great cultures are works that, by their Sublime qualities, express something of the infinite. Such architecture transcends the prosaic. Creativity and vigor characterize a true celebration of death. We could learn much from the funerary architecture of the past if we are to give new significance to a celebration of life in our own time [p. 367].

Earlier, Curl observes:

> A celebration of death has proved a rich field for designers, and has left a record of the prevalent taste of society. The current attitudes towards death and graveyards perhaps reflect other aspects of how society sees the old and the infirm. This is an age when youth is worshipped, the cult of youth having almost become a religion itself. Old age, like death or illness, has no place in such a cult, so there will be no architectural expression of death [p. 361].

Apart from such considerations, there have been those who at various times in this century have criticized monument-building as a waste of money which could better be used for other purposes, such as helping the poor. One finds this critical theme reflected in contemporaneous accounts of the building of some public monuments and memorials, such as the following:

> As this is being written, a public controversy is going on in Washington on the advisability of cutting down the cherry trees to build a costly and useless memorial to Thomas Jefferson. The writer does not predict how this fight is going to come out. There seems, however, little possibility that the memorial will take the form of a housing project. Housing projects, which are fitted to our conception of what the poor can "afford," are not considered sufficiently ornamental to perpetuate the names of great men [Arnold, 1937, p. 321].

This is a one-sided way of framing such an issue, and it is clearly not representative of the way in which we typically frame our decisions to spend on different categories of things, whether as societies or consumers. We do not regard hamburgers as substitutes for movies; we desire both and we allocate some of our budgets to each category of goods. In this case, and the "costly and useless" Jefferson Memorial was constructed instead of a housing project bearing his name. As a result, the "useless" memorial has been "used" by millions of visitors whose enjoyment of the experience has justified its cost and will continue to do so into the foreseeable future.

No similar debate about useful versus useless forms of memorialization erupted over the erection of national monuments such as the Vietnam Veterans Memorial and the proposed Korean War Veterans Memorial in Washington, D.C. What is more, it was recently announced that the Franklin Delano Roosevelt Memorial beside the tidal basin in Washington will be constructed on a far grander scale than the slab of stone the size of a desk he himself envisaged. The actual memorial "will sit on a seven-and-a-half acre site and will comprise four outdoor rooms, each representing one of the president's terms. There will be a statue of him and a bust of Eleanor Roosevelt." The purpose of this memorial, according to U.S. Interior Secretary Bruce Babbitt, is to provide "a place where our children and generations to come can visit, that will bring history alive, that will capture the greatness of his deeds, the inspiration of his words," at a cost of $10 million raised in contributions and $42 million appropriated by Congress" (Brozan, *New York Times*, October 14, 1994). This action confirms modern acceptance of the continued importance of memorialization as an integral part of American life.

In such cases, however, where the use of public monies are involved, there is perhaps room for debate over whether to build a monument to great men and women or housing projects for poor ones, or either. When it comes to private decisions about the memorialization of a family member in one way or another, there is nothing to debate. No public monies are involved, and it is strictly up to families to decide this question or to the deceased, who may arrange for memorialization in advance of death. Within the bounds of legal propriety, such decisions are the business of nobody else. Social criticism of the practice is so much hot air.

As for the effects of durable memorials such as monuments, one of the most important ones is the historical record they provide. This would appear to be of both personal and social value. Unfortunately, it is often the case that the historical record endures long after those to whom it is personally relevant, except as an anonymous artifact of history. Without the benefit of perpetual care, the monuments erected over the years in many cemeteries have fallen into disrepair and, worse, have become the objects of vandalism and desecration. Not even the nation's public monuments such as Grant's Tomb have been exempt from these signs of the times. What seems to be called for on the part of the public is wide support for legislation to impose harsher penalties for those convicted of crimes committed against cemetery property.

The insecurity and neglect of memorials erected in poorly maintained cemeteries would seem to offer an opportunity to cemetery operators to promote the sale of final disposition and memorialization products which entail permanent security and perpetual care features as part of a marketing strategy.

The American Way of Memorialization

Oddly enough, or perhaps not so oddly, Mitford was not especially critical of the memorialization component of American death care. She actually had very little to say about the practice other than to recount the role assigned to man's "memorial impulse" by Dr. Hubert Eaton, the creator of Forest Lawn. Underlying the concept of Forest Lawn was Eaton's belief that a memorial impulse or instinct was inherent in human nature, as demonstrated by the extent to which evidence of memorialization is found in various societies throughout history.

The design or redesign of Forest Lawn under Eaton's supervision was an attempt on his part to redirect the memorial impulse in ways which were more suitable under modern conditions of life than the forms provided by earlier monumented cemeteries. The fundamental importance of appealing to the memorial impulse of consumers is emphasized in the sales philosophy espoused by Eaton. To draw attention to this, Mitford quoted Eaton's sales motto: "Accentuate the spiritual!" She further quoted Eaton to this effect: "It is the salesman's duty to measure the force of the Memorial Impulse in his client and to persuade him to live up to that noble urge in accordance with his means.... Most important of all, every salesman should understand that if properly inspired the Memorial Impulse will do more for him than he ever did for himself, but let your financial desire be tempered by the Memorial Impulse" (1963, p. 127).

While Mitford appeared to belittle the sincerity of the Eaton philosophy as being exploitation, the universal evidence for the existence of a memorial impulse made it difficult if not impossible for her to attack the practice of memorialization as an oddity of "the American way of death." If anything, the memorial park as conceived by Eaton and emulated by other facilities located throughout the United States seems to represent a development which allowed for the most logical and efficient expression of the impulse in connection with burial under modern conditions. In this sense it represented the evolved state of the cemetery in America. The resulting memorial park merged or integrated the final disposition and memorialization components of death care into one combined process performed by the cemetery. The addition of mortuaries at memorial parks further merged or integrated the mortuary services component with final disposition-memorialization to form facilities capable of providing complete death care, for which purpose the cemetery was the logical and natural site.

The Economic Impact of Memorial Parks

The effects of the formation of cemetery-mortuary combinations have been noted above and will later be discussed at length. The point to which attention will be drawn here is the extent to which the development of memorial parks, community mausoleums, and columbariums may have altered the ability of their customers to express the memorial impulse. By limiting the variety of memorial products to uniform markers and plaques which facilitate landscaping and maintenance, the memorial park concept appears to have greatly reduced the opportunity of consumers to express the individuality and distinctiveness of the person who is the object of memorialization.

Some have referred to this effect as the "democratization" of death care (Sloane, 1991, p. 187). It would perhaps be more accurate to describe it as an example of the application of the concept of egalitarianism to the memorialization part of the death care process as a whole. With the choice of memorials limited to a single type of flush marker or plaque, everyone became equally recognized at death. The sections of a memorial park and the mausoleums and columbariums contained within it may be distinctive in themselves, but the memorialization product itself is reduced to uniformity and conformity. The aesthetic and economic appeal of the new forms of final disposition contributed to the gradual "creative destruction" of the old forms of final disposition and their complementary forms of memorialization. The economic impact was doubtless to shift some consumer expenditure from memorialization products themselves to the combined final disposition–memorial product provided by the memorial park. This in itself did not necessarily result in a reduction in consumer expenditures on these two components of death care taken together, and it is unclear whether it resulted in any net change in combined revenues for the providers.

This raises the question of whether the memorial park concept was a strategic success which contained within it a tactical flaw in the form of the restrictions it placed on the opportunities for individuals and families to construct distinctive memorials. By blunting the degree of distinctions possible in the memorials designed for graves, crypts, and niches, the memorial park may have seriously affected the desire of consumers to spend on varied memorial products. Clearly, the spending by consumers on private durable memorials was adversely affected by the design of memorial parks. It is important to note, however, that the memorial park strategy expanded the scope of the cemetery operator by making the cemetery design itself into the memorial product. In effect, this strategy allowed the cemetery as the provider of final disposition options to usurp the role of the monument dealer. Even if spending on memorials was reduced as a result of the development of memorial parks, the strategy benefited their developers in the sense that they became the memorial provider. What is more, total spending by the average consumer on memorial park products may not have been reduced by comparison with their spending on space in a monumented cemetery and on a distinctive memorial.

Mitford took note of another possibility in her statement that "The Memorial Impulse can also be channeled to remedy what was perhaps a tactical error in the early days of the [memorial park], insistence upon the use of small, uniform bronze grave markers" (1963, p. 127). According to this interpretation, the strength of the memorial impulse was apparently expected to support the creation of an extensive variety of memorial products for which the cemetery was the natural and ideal site for both purchase and placement. Community mausoleums, crematories, scattering gardens, urn gardens, columbariums, and even mortuaries were natural additions to the designs of many memorial parks, extending their scope far beyond the limits of land-intensive monumented cemeteries. This expansion of scope was at the heart of the concept of the cemetery as a "comemoral" of the sort envisaged by Eaton. In the future such comemoral facilities may serve as providers of new forms of memorialization and commemorative activities within their communities, some of which will be mentioned at a later stage.

If the memorial impulse is as strong as this concept suggests, it is possible that large numbers of consumers might be attracted to death care "malls" in the same way that they are attracted to modern shopping malls which offer goods and services of all kinds in settings that incorporate entertainment, food courts, seminars, and other amenities. Medical malls of this type have recently emerged in the health care sector.

Financial Memorials

In Chapter 6 the varieties of memorialization were enumerated. It is not necessary to consider all of them in much detail. Beyond monuments, which are commonly provided by death care establishments, several other kinds of memorials deserve special attention. Perishable memorials such as flowers are the output of other industries, and financial memorials take the form of a variety of donations, contributions, and other activities undertaken on behalf of and in memory of deceased parties. The extent of these activities is a sign of the desire to memorialize in ways which are not necessarily associated with the event of death or with the delivery of death care as a commercially provided set of goods and services.

No attempt will be made here to explore the effect of financial memorialization as an economic activity. We simply note that in some cases, large gifts perpetuate the names of deceased persons on universities, colleges, graduate professional schools, hospitals, museums, libraries, parks, scholarships, fellowships, and professorships. On a lesser scale, many contribute to charities or other organizations, endow a park bench, plant a tree, lay a brick, or do similar things in memory of others.

Sometimes these gestures are made at the time of death, but they may be made at any time, even during one's own lifetime. In the latter case, they are referred to as "living memorials." They are interesting here less in their own right than as substitutes for the two other classes of memorialization identified above. Not only are they substitutes for durable and perishable memorials, they have the distinct advantage of being tax deductible for the person who contributes to qualified organizations in memory of others. Even so, their role in the memorialization process appears to be one which is not a close substitute for more traditional memorials.

Perishable Memorials

The major types of perishable memorialization are flowers, both real and artificial, sympathy cards, and related paraphernalia. As noted, these are examples of products used in the death care process, but they are the products of other industries. For the most part these products are sent to surviving families as expressions of sympathy and as tributes to the deceased. While flowers are ordinarily sent to the funeral home, where they are displayed during visitation and services, they are subsequently transported to the cemetery for use on and around the grave or crypt. From time to time flowers are also brought to cemeteries to decorate graves or crypts or niches.

Most flowers are purchased from independent florists, who deliver floral arrangements to the funeral homes designated by their customers. There are also some death care firms which operate related flower shops, especially at combined facilities. This has advantages for the customers of those establishments and presumably allows providers to integrate the promotion and sale of flowers into the complete death care process for use in funeral services and as cemetery tributes. Appreciating the beauty of floral tributes may be a source of comfort for the survivors. Hillard opined that "The instinctive and universal taste of mankind selects flowers for the expression of its finest sympathies, their beauty and fleetingness serving to make them the most fitting symbols of those delicate sentiments for which language seems almost too gross a medium."

It may be difficult to imagine that the practice of sending floral tributes for use during funeral services could become the subject of criticism, but criticism has been directed at the cost and "waste" represented by spending on flowers. This is analogous to the argument cited above for the view that the Jefferson Memorial is an example of a "costly and useless" public monument, the money for which might have better been spent on a housing project. Unlike public spending on a memorial to a great man, flowers involve private spending on floral tributes to ordinary ones. Both types of spending are a means of aesthetic expression. As such, they are incommensurate with spending on biological necessities or social problems. They are different in kind, and it is fallacious to compare them as if one precludes the other in the sense that they are mutually exclusive. In affluent societies public and private spending on goods and services that satisfy a variety of needs occurs simultaneously. The choices we make do not ordinarily involve choosing between monuments, housing projects, food and flowers. As a society and as individuals, we allow for all.

At the private level, the sending of flowers for use during a funeral is a personal gesture of respect for the deceased and of sympathy for the survivors. It is difficult to understand why anyone would object to such a benign practice or regard it as "wasteful." It is in keeping with the use of flowers as decorations and tributes on other special occasions, and it is hardly wasteful if it serves a desirable purpose for those inclined to express their sentiments in this way.

Families may request in death notices that flowers be omitted or that donations be made instead to a favorite charity or a designated one. Frequently the family of a person who has died of a particular disease may desire to forgo flowers in order to express support for organizations which are devoted to finding a cure for that disease or to providing support for those who suffer from it. It may seem to such families that it is reasonable for them to include in the death notice a request that "contributions to Organization X are preferred in lieu of flowers." While understandable on an emotional level, few of us are likely to believe that by omitting flowers at funerals and contributing the sums saved to charity we are likely to have a cure for cancer or heart disease sooner than we otherwise would. If we truly believed this, we would never spend on any of the amenities of life without feeling that we have deprived the world of the cures for all its woes and social ills.

The issue of omitting flowers at funerals is important not only for florists but also for other death care providers as well. Insofar as a desire to commemorate underlies most death care other than basic mortuary services and final disposition, the omission of flowers at funerals may be perceived as a step in the direction of omitting other nonessential elements of the complete process. Mitford cited evidence to the effect that funeral directors have long sensed this. As she pointed out, the handling of flowers is a costly task for funeral homes, but funeral directors have strongly supported the efforts of florists to promote the use of flower arrangements at funerals and to resist those who advocate their omission (1963, pp. 87–88).

Death Care as Memorialization

It is virtually impossible to separate memorialization from funeral services and final disposition. Funeral services are essentially commemorative in nature, and the place of final disposition is the natural site of durable memorials under modern conditions. These multiple facets of memorialization, which underlie virtually all postdeath activities, were vividly brought to light by Dr. Eaton's focus on the memorial impulse. While fully recognizing his point, it is perhaps unfortunate that this description may leave the impression that memorialization is entirely emotional or impulsive, rather than intellectual and rational. It seems important to recognize that the process of memorialization is entirely consistent with the rational desire to provide a history of the family for future generations. The historical role of the cemetery in the community has often been recognized, but it does not appear to have been exploited effectively by the promotion of cemeteries as archives, where family histories and records are kept safely in perpetuity along with remains.

Perhaps this expansion of the traditional role of the cemetery is what Eaton envisaged when he foresaw the centralization of the memorial activities of a community, including even the activities associated with the administration of financial memorials, within the grounds of cemeteries. To describe this expanded concept of the cemetery of the future, Eaton coined the word "comemoral" by combining the traditional notions of "commemorative" and "memorial." Although these cemeteries of the future have not been fully realized as yet, the conception of the cemetery as the natural and ideal site for mortuary services, final disposition, and memorialization has indeed been realized at a growing number of facilities located throughout the country.

Clearly, the concept of the "comemoral" was ahead of its time. This may be part of the reason Eaton's idea was not followed up by others for so many years and has never achieved the scale that he envisioned. Few practical examples of complete comemoral facilities exists, although Forest Lawn in Los Angeles, Rose Hills in Whittier, Restland in Dallas, and Lake Lawn Metairie in New Orleans are contenders for such status.

One of the greatest impediments to the implementation of the comemoral concept can be traced to the original development and subsequent persistence of a death care infrastructure consisting of separate and distinct facilities which are incapable of providing complete death care. This has tended to create conditions under which the producer of one or two parts of the complete process has often been unconcerned about promoting and marketing the other part or parts, but this is a shortsighted view. The decision by consumers to omit flowers from funeral services is not the concern of florists only. The decision by some consumers to substitute memorial services for traditional funeral services is not the concern of funeral directors only. The decision of consumers to scatter cremated remains or to keep them at home is not the concern of cemeteries only. All of these decisions and others like them affect the way in which death care is perceived by consumers and conceived as a product by providers.

When providers and their respective trade organizations are concerned only with the promotion and sale of their own parts of the complete process, it is easy to lose sight of the importance of the process as an integrated whole. For example, cremation was introduced and advocated as a substitute for complete death care rather than as a substitute for one component of the complete process. Although some providers are now engaged in attempts to reverse this conception, it is clear that the most effective way to insure that death care is promoted and sold as a complete process is for all parts of the process to be provided by a single firm or collection of firms operated together.

Combined facilities with a funeral home located at the site of a cemetery which serves as a source of permanent memorialization are concrete representations or symbols of the complete death care process. Their presence in a community reinforces the complementary nature of the integral parts of the process in the eyes of consumers and potential consumers. More commonly, however, the consumer is confronted with stand-alone facilities which are symbols of the fragmentation of the process into distinct, separate, and perhaps avoidable goods and services provided by different establishments.

The adoption of the term "death care" would emphasize the fact that the process as a whole is the sum of its three component parts (mortuary services, final disposition, memorialization), and it would tend to raise the consciousness of the consuming public regarding the incompleteness of one of these parts without the others. The operators of establishments capable of providing only one or two of the three components may thus be reluctant to adopt a usage which draws attention to their limitations. On the other hand, the operators of combined facilities and clusters of stand-alone facilities may be expected to endorse such usage as a means of enhancing their advantages as providers of complete "death care." In time it is possible that the wider adoption of the term will occur, first as a technical term, then gradually in the vernacular of the trades, and finally as a popular term.

One of the effects of the analysis in this book is to shift the focus of attention from the separate parts of the death care process and the different types of death care providers to the death care process as a whole. This shift in views highlights the components of death care as parts of the larger process which is a complex product that is most efficiently produced and effectively sold to consumers as a whole by a single provider. The widespread development of combined facilities provides extensive evidence for this, and the strategy of clustering existing facilities appears to be a less efficient organizational means of achieving the same effect by emphasizing the sale of complete death care. Much of the analysis throughout the rest of this book will present the case for such developments in the death care economy.

Before proceeding to a presentation of that case, however, the discussion of memorialization would be incomplete if it did not consider some further, nontraditional forms of memorials. If we are correct in believing that memorialization is entailed in most death care, it behooves death care providers to develop new products which appeal to the desire of consumers to memorialize their own death or that of others. Consideration will be given to several ways in which this has been done on a limited scale.

Death Portraits

Photographs have long played a role in the process of memorialization. Family albums serve as an archive of sorts in which the images of family members are preserved. These images contained in photographs are visual links between generations. Except to a limited extent, the practice of photographing the dead body does not occur at modern funerals, although it was once a common practice at death. It is instructive to consider the rise and fall of death photography for the light it sheds on the interplay of taste and technology in this area of consumer behavior.

Death, quite naturally, has been an inspiration for artists, and art has long been a medium of memorialization of the dead. Memorials often take the form of works of art, and in recent years artists have shown a revived interest in death as a subject matter of their work. This includes writers, painters, and film makers, as well as photographers. Vicki Goldberg, a photography critic for the *New York Times* (May 23, 1993), discussed this trend in an article entitled "Death Is Resurrected as an Art Form."

Taking her cue from the publication of a history of photographs of the dead entitled *Looking at Death* (1993) by Barbara Norfleet, a curator of photographs at Harvard, Goldberg recounts a brief history of the role photographers have played at death in this country:

> For most of this century art photographers shied away from the subject, yet during the medium's first 60 years the camera regularly made portraits of the newly deceased. These were extremely popular. Eighteenth and 19th-century painters like William Sidney Mount occasionally painted them, but only the rich could afford paintings. Photography gave the middle class the same opportunities as the wealthy to have permanent records of their features, alive or dead.
>
> Death offered a good living. Daguerrotypists' ads exhorted customers to "Secure the Shadow 'Ere the Substance Fade." In 1854, one daguerreotype gallery was put on the market with the claim that "pictures of deceased persons alone will pay all expenses."
>
> These photographs were displayed on mantelpieces, worn in lockets and sent to friends. In this century such images were banished from view and replaced by pictures of dead relatives taken while they were still alive. Yet Ms. Norfleet makes clear that commercial studio photographers continued to do a brisk business in death portraits through World War II; the pictures were no longer put out on the mantel but tucked away in albums. James Van Der Zee, the Harlem photographer, took pictures of the dead into the 1940's, often with heavenly figures fluttering tenderly above.

Describing the sweep of death photography through time, Goldberg states:

> In the 19th century, death was frequent, omnipresent and in its way ordinary. Because hospitals were notoriously unsafe, death occurred at home, and funerals were held there too, in the front parlor, which was only renamed the "living room" late in the century when funeral "parlors" took over. In Paris, the door to the morgue was always open, and people strolling by could, and did, stop in to see the display of corpses. The century romanticized what it could not avoid: Keats said he was "half in love with easeful death," and tubercular heroines in operas remained beautiful and died splendidly between a cough and a high C.
>
> Death came sooner then. Ms. Norfleet notes that infant mortality rates were so high that babies sometimes were not named before they were 1 year old. Pictures of dead children were common; one photograph in *Looking at Death* shows a dead baby girl cradled in the arm of her dead older brother.

Celebrities of the time could count on being photographed shortly after breathing their last. Jesse James and other outlaws were shown in their coffins as evidence that they were truly gone, Lincoln in his as a matter of reverence. The French portraitist Nadar photographed Victor Hugo on his death bed. This notion of preserving the great persists with a twist or two: Lenin and Mao embalmed as museum exhibits; "slab shots"—on the autopsy table—of stars like Steve McQueen and John Lennon on the front pages of the tabloids.

As the 19th century progressed, death slowly receded from view. Antiseptic practices and the understanding of infectious disease so improved the cleanliness and safety of hospitals that before the end of the century people considered them the proper place for treatment, and death began to leave home. Then the funeral establishment took the body off the family's hands. Death, no longer so familiar, and no longer expected to happen until late in life, was suddenly a taboo subject.

So naturally it was intensely fascinating. Photography found novel ways to satisfy a heightened curiosity: in effect, by first making death portraits affordable, and then shifting the terms towards violence.

Goldberg devotes much of her attention to the public fascination with images of death in the media and films. Her article is illustrated by the photograph shown here in the photo on page 206, which is among those included in *Looking at Death.*

Clearly, there is something striking about the image represented by the photograph. One imagines that it is the sort of artifact which might be highly valued by the family, if not immediately after death, then in later years and by subsequent generations. Yet demand for such photographs waned and eventually disappeared, and one has to suspect this occurred because such photography did not fit in well with the way in which funerals have evolved during the second half of the twentieth century. In particular, the tendency to take death out of the household, to medicalize, and to isolate it, diminished the value of mementos which depicted it starkly.

As a form of memorialization, however, there is something to be said for depicting the life of a person rather than their death. Images of living individuals would seem to have more appeal for consumers than images of deceased bodies. Is it possible to create a demand for the latter kind of photographs?

Probably not, for several reasons. In the first place, people now can make their own still photographs, or even videotapes at funerals as they see fit. In the second place, a tendency to focus on the death of a person by photographing the body afterwards is perhaps indicative of a past age, whereas the tendency now is to focus on the life of a person who has died. An example of this new age approach is the montage of film clips from the past lives of famous personages, which are shown repeatedly on television after their deaths. This modern tendency provides new opportunities for the promotion of memorial merchandise and services based on existing and emerging technologies.

A death photograph, circa 1925. Courtesy of the Caulfield and Shook Collection of the University of Louisville Photographic Archives.

Video memorials

With the invention and commercialization of home videotape recorders and players, the use of videotapes now supplements the use of still photographs in the lives of many families. Like photographs, the videotapes of living persons provide a record which may be used to remember relatives or others following death. The existence of videotape players in more than three out of four American homes has enabled some funeral homes to offer videotapes of funeral services to out-of-town relatives or those unable to attend services due to illness. Beyond this use, however, the widespread availability of videotape players has created a large potential market for video memorials which pay tribute to the life of a deceased family member in much the same way that famous people have often been the subject of televised remembrances broadcast following their deaths. The televised tributes to the life of Jacqueline Kennedy Onassis following her death are recent examples.

Even when the funeral is a private affair, as in the case of Jacqueline Onassis, these televised memorials provide the viewing public with a retrospective look at the key events and significant occasions in the lives of such people at the time of their deaths.

Advances in technology have now made it possible to introduce such videotaped memorials into the funeral services of average people. The concept of such "tribute programs" as a death care product offered by or through funeral homes was developed by National Music Service Company (NAMSCO) of Spokane, Washington, a leading provider of recorded music for funeral homes and mausoleums. Merrill Womach, the president of NAMSCO, conceived the idea of such recorded remembrances after the assassination of President John F. Kennedy in 1963, which was followed by many televised retrospectives of his life. Womach speculated that this form of memorialization used for presidents and other famous people might appeal to ordinary persons. Later, during the 1980s, the development of rapid mail services allowed memorabilia such as snapshots and perhaps tape recordings of the deceased person to be collected and forwarded to the studios of National Music Service for the production of a video memorial. Such personal material is incorporated with stock footage of nature or other scenes and music selected by the family into the finished product. According to Womach, the video memorials are meant to celebrate the life of a person rather than merely marking the fact that a

JUST A FEW of the visuals from a TRIBUTE PROGRAM

A Tribute Program will help you remember all the love between the laughter and the tears.

Scenes from a video memorial. Courtesy of National Music Service Co.

death has occurred. A montage of clips from a brochure used to promote Womach's video memorials is shown at right.

Following the overnight production of such memorial tributes, the videotape is sent back to the funeral home in time for it to be shown during visitation or as a part of the formal funeral service. Afterwards, the videotape becomes a permanent memorial record of the life of the deceased party for use by survivors in the grieving process and as a means by which later generations may see and remember earlier ones. Thousands of these video memorials have been produced since they were first introduced by NAMSCO in 1989, and they are now offered by funeral homes throughout the United States. The idea has met with some appeal, and it seems an ideal addition to the product line of funeral homes.

Moreover, it would appear to offer the potential for cemeteries to become repositories of video memorials, oral histories, and other memorabilia commemorating the lives of those interred or entombed there. The sale of such products on a pre-need basis will allow biographic materials to be accumulated in advance of need so that higher quality video tributes are produced, further enhancing their attractiveness to consumers.

Impact of Cremation on Memorialization

The fact that cremains themselves constitute a memorial of sorts has tended to allow consumers to satisfy the memorialize impulse in ways never before possible. Thus it becomes possible to imagine scattering the cremains over land or sea as memorialization without containment. It remains possible to contain the cremains in an urn or other container for burial or entombment followed by formal memorialization. It is possible to contain them in decorative urn or other container for display at home or elsewhere, as in a shrine. It is possible to contain a part of the cremains within jewelry or sculpture. It is possible for family members to divide cremains memorializing their shares in different ways.

This greater variety of memorialization options which complement cremation signifies changing consumer attitudes and desires for various types of final disposition and memorial products. Many of these products need not be provided by cemeteries or memorial dealers; they may be provided by funeral homes as well. This signifies the need for adaptation on the part of death care providers, which promises to alter the existing structure of the death care economy, its industries, firms, and establishments.

Pet Memorialization

The memorial impulse is not limited to a desire to memorialize human beings who have died. There is also a widespread desire to memorialize pets following their death. This has stimulated the growth of pet cemeteries and crematories during recent decades. Most of these facilities provide for durable monuments, but financial memorials also are used in connection with the death of pets. As a case in point, the Companion Animals Require Excellence (CARE) Fund was created in 1989 by the Animal Health Center at the College of Veterinary Medicine of Mississippi State University. It allows pet owners to memorialize pets through tax deductible donations to a fund used to finance continued improvements in veterinary medical teaching, research, and service.

Cyberspace Memorials

A high-tech alternative to traditional forms of memorialization for both humans and pets has recently emerged on the Internet computer network. In what has been described as "virtual memorial gardens" on the World Wide Web, remembrance material incorporating text, image and sound files may be stored and retrieved for generations to come (Irwin, *Times-Picayune*, July 27, 1995). Like the technology on which it is based, this electronic means of memorialization is still in its infancy, but it would seem to anticipate the eventual development and commercialization of cyberspace "sites" of memorialization very unlike traditional cemetery sites that link memorials with final disposition. Cyberspace is a global network through which information of all kinds is broadly accessible on demand to a potentially unlimited worldwide community. Memorial sites on this network represent another area for commercial development by alternative providers of online services. These electronic memorial sites may either complement or compete with cemeteries as sites of traditional forms of memorialization.

11. *The Buying and Selling of Death Care*

Post-Death Arrangements

Hitherto the importance of the dead body has been cited as a phenomenon which underlies the death care process. Whatever common sense explanations exist for this phenomenon or whatever more sophisticated ones may be provided by anthropologists, psychologists, theologians, or other technical specialists, it is a matter of fact for which the evidence is extensive. The symbolic value of the body is exemplified by the strenuous efforts devoted to the reclamation of remains in connection with war deaths and casualties of natural disasters. The desecration of human bodies evokes horror. For centuries the dissection of cadavers was forbidden by ecclesiastical laws, and even today most Americans are uncomfortable with activities which involve tampering with human remains. Under most circumstances it is unlawful to do so; only licensed funeral directors, mortuary technicians, beauticians, and other authorized personnel may handle remains as a commercial matter. In every state, interment requires a permit, as do cremation and disinterment.

One clear sign of widespread sensitivity toward the body following death is the low rate at which autopsies are performed in the United States. "The national rate is now about 13 percent," according to Dr. Nuland (1994, p. 79). Part of the reason for this low rate is the reluctance of families to grant permission for autopsies in spite of their importance for the purpose of establishing the exact cause(s) of death.

Historically, the next of kin was legally entitled to possession of the body "in the same condition in which it was at the time of death" (Hendin, 1973, p. 61). Practical justification for this view was apparently based on the social role of the family as providers of death care. Under modern conditions, however, the common law view is in some respects anachronistic. In particular, it is sometimes at odds with the desire of many people to make arrangements prior to death for the disposition of their bodies, to donate organs, or to pre-arrange their own death care. Such desires have resulted in the enactment of statutes which specifically recognize that individuals have the legal authority to dispose of their own bodies, or parts of them, as they see fit. Under those statutes it is possible uniformly to donate one's body to medical science by will or by a document signed in the presence of two witnesses. In such cases, the next of kin must comply with the wishes of the deceased according to the laws in effect in most states (U.S. FTC, 1978, p. 156).

Death Care Law

No similar uniformity exists in state laws pertaining to the pre-arrangement and pre-funding of death care by individuals prior to their death. In general, however, there is a modicum of law relating to dead bodies which is consistently applied. At the root of this body of law is an appreciation of the fundamental premise that a dead human body is not considered to be property per se. "It cannot be bought, sold or transferred; nor can it be left by will (except where statutes specifically permit it); nor does the body descend to the heirs of the deceased" (Greenberg, 1976, p. 93). Stueve (1984) refers to the peculiar legal status of the dead body as a "quasi-property" (p. 15).

This particular legal point is not itself an issue here. Our concern is with the effect of the legal status of the body on the manner in which death care is bought and sold.

In this respect it appears that a person has the right to give away his body, or parts thereof, after death for use in appropriate ways. Failing this, the right and duty to dispose of the body falls on the next of kin. Stueve enumerates the order in which this duty vests, as follows:

> As a general rule on the death of a husband or wife the surviving spouse has the paramount duty of disposal, and this right is subject only to the statutes bearing generally on the disposal of the dead and the expressed wishes of the decedent....
>
> As a general rule, where there is no surviving spouse, the right and duty of disposal passes to the next of kin. Next of kin being the relations by blood or consanguinity to the deceased.
>
> As among the next of kin, the right of disposal is usually held by those closest in relation to the decedent. Priority would be as follows: children of legal age, parents, brothers and sisters, more distant kind. Of course, this rule is subject to a number of variable factors which may influence a court to create exceptions.
>
> Factors such as living under the same roof, financial support or a special intimacy between the decedent and a relative may justify a court in awarding the right of disposal to that relative even though there are next of kin with a higher priority of relations. Likewise, a next of kin present at the time or place, or both, of death may have the power to act in the absence of any contrary indications from other next of kin.
>
> Where variable factors are present, as is true in most cases, the parties, of course may, by agreement, act in concert either expressly or impliedly [pp. 31–32].

Greenberg elaborates further:

> First, the duty and right falls upon the surviving spouse. If the deceased was unmarried, then upon the nearest kin of sufficient age and possessed of enough money to defray the expenses. If no kin, upon the coroner or person having the authority to handle such bodies when an inquest is held. If no inquest, then to the person in charge of the poor. If all these persons above enumerated refuse to act, then the duty falls upon the tenant of the premises where the death occurred, and if no tenant on the premises, then upon the owner. In death at sea, the duty falls upon the master of the vessel or the owner if the vessel has no master [p. 96].

Executors and administrators of the estates of decedents are not among the parties mentioned because they may not be appointed until after the funeral. An executor named in a will may give instructions regarding death care arrangements and expenses, but such instructions may not be followed against the wishes of the surviving spouse or next of kin (Stueve, 1984, p. 33). Apparently only the next of kin possesses the legal right to arrange death care for the deceased. This raises the question of whose desires prevail when the wishes of the next of kin differ from those of the decedent. As Greenberg notes, this question is yet to be answered from a legal point of view. Presumably the next of kin prevails, but ordinarily survivors are inclined to honor the wishes of the deceased person. Thus, the conditions under which death care is pre-planned have tended to produce relatively few incidents of conflicts of authority, none of which need concern us here. In certain cases, however, complications may arise at death which require family members to depart from pre-arranged services. Following death, survivors may also desire to upgrade the funerals chosen by decedents themselves, and this may be encouraged by the practices of funeral directors.

Death Care Transactions

Because death care goods and services are delivered following death, either they must be sold in advance, like life insurance, while the individual is still alive, or they must be sold to survivors after death has occurred. It is important to consider the different methods of selling death care traditionally favored by each type of death care establishment. Attention will be devoted to sales by funeral homes, which use mostly at-need methods, and sales by cemeteries, which use mostly pre-need methods.

As discussed previously, the marketing practices of funeral homes are subject to regulation by the Federal Trade Commission; cemeteries are excluded from such regulation. Both types of establishments are subject to other federal and state legislation and regulation which explicitly recognize that the sale of death care goods and services arises from two types of transactions:

> (1) *At-need sales.* These are made to survivors at the time of death. For all practical purposes, this includes those cases in which so-called pre-arranged

funerals are planned and filed with a funeral home, but not paid for by the decedent prior to death. In both cases the actual purchase and sale of goods and services occur at the time of need when survivors are presumably required to make arrangements and to pay for them under the pressure of time and the stress of bereavement and possible financial duress.

(2) *Pre-need sales.* These are made to consumers at any time they wish to make arrangements for funeral services, final disposition, and memorialization in advance of need, without the stress associated with the event of death. The term "pre-need" is interpreted to entail both pre-arrangement and pre-funding, regardless of the method used to achieve the latter. The phrase "pre-need sales" expresses the vantage point of death care providers; the term "pre-planning" expresses the vantage point of consumers. They are used interchangeably throughout this chapter.

Much of what is said here applies to both funeral homes and cemeteries, but there are differences in the extent to which each emphasizes one method of selling over the other. Commercial cemeteries have tended to develop and promote the purchase of their products on a pre-need basis. A recent survey by the American Cemetery Association found that 99 percent of their members sold some cemetery property in that manner; 82 percent reported that a majority of their sales were made before need (U.S. FTC, June 1990, p. 117). In contrast, funeral directors traditionally have favored at-need selling, for reasons that have already been mentioned. According to trade sources, the percentage of funeral home calls that involve some form of pre-arrangement now exceeds 30 percent; it is expected to reach 40 percent by the end of this century. A major force behind this growth is the emphasis which the regional and national companies and cemetery-mortuary combination establishments place on pre-need selling in order to build their backlogs and to secure their market shares by tying customers to their facilities and locking them into traditional funerals to the extent possible.

Advantages of Pre-Planning

It is widely recognized that there are a number of advantages for consumers who pre-plan funerals as well as final disposition and memorialization. Most of these advantages relate to the more relaxed conditions existing at a time when there is no crisis, grief, or other emotional distress and when no purchase is required to be made. Under such circumstances consumers are better able to weigh alternatives, to comparison shop if desired, and to take their time before making decisions which many find difficult and disturbing. By contrast, when a death has occurred or is imminent, the party responsible for making arrangements may be under various kinds and degrees of distress, to the point of requiring medication in some cases. Yet they face an urgent need to make final binding decisions involving significant expenditures with little time for reflection. It has been claimed at times that this state of distress and financial strain suffered by survivors immediately after a death is exploited by some funeral directors.

It is difficult to deny that the possibility of exploitation exists when decisions are made under the conditions faced by death care consumers at the time of need. Indeed, there is a strong possibility that consumers may make bad decisions under such circumstances, even absent any tendency for funeral directors to exploit the situation. Without impugning the integrity of funeral directors generally, it is difficult to argue with the proposition that the at-need consumer is not in a position to make a careful and informed choice among alternatives involving death care goods and services, which include a large variety of caskets in numerous styles with different features that are hard to understand and to compare.

Pre-planning, on the other hand, affords consumers the opportunity to become more fully informed about available options in death care goods and services and allows them to make decisions in their own time. Unfortunately, consumers have been reluctant to take such steps without the encouragement of a pre-need sales effort on the part of providers. Cemeteries have often adopted such an emphasis, but funeral homes have not. By adhering to at-need selling practices, funeral homes have virtually invited regulation designed to protect the consumer from exploitation in the at-need sales process. A review of the proceedings leading up to the formulation and promulgation of the Funeral Rule and the major provisions of the rule suggests that it was intended to address some of the difficulties faced by at-need consumers. The federal trade rules relating to funeral homes require the quotation and itemization of prices, and they forbid funeral directors to engage in certain trade practices. In spite of these forms of protection, however, the at-need consumer faces the difficult problem of making unfamiliar decisions under conditions of emotional distress and perhaps financial duress.

It has been said that the sales techniques employed by funeral directors, such as their casket presentation methods in the selection room, are designed to exploit the vulnerability of their customers by encouraging them in subtle ways to purchase more expensive merchandise. Ordinarily, this is what salesmen in most businesses are expected to do. Yet, because of the conditions surrounding funeral transactions, the methods used by funeral homes to sell merchandise and services, such as the casket pricing practices discussed at length in Chapter 8, are especially controversial in nature. Many of those methods are long-established practices which are exceedingly difficult to change for the industry as a whole. Because of those practices, funeral homes depend on their sale of caskets and other merchandise to subsidize the costs of providing services. The effect of this has been to direct their sales efforts away from funeral services as such and toward merchandise. As a result the performance of funeral homes as businesses has been tied to their success as merchandisers rather than as service providers (see Doody, 1994), and the perpetuation of such pricing practices has tended to exacerbate the difficulties of at-need consumers.

The basic choice with which consumers are confronted at-need is the choice among an extensive array of casket-price alternatives. If they have not previously done so, they must also choose between earth burial, mausoleum entombment, and cremation. At the cemetery they must choose among varied sections, gardens, or other differentiated spaces. If cremation is chosen, they must select a means of scattering or safekeeping the cremated remains. They may have to choose among alternative niche locations in a columbarium. In the case of burial in a monumented cemetery, they must select among countless differentiated monument designs. In some markets consumers may avail themselves of the services of direct disposal firms, discount providers of curtailed services, and casket stores.

The existence of this wide variety of death care goods and services provided by different establishments over a wide range of prices adds to the difficulties of making death care decisions at the time of need. Only if precautions are taken under such conditions will the extensive freedom of choice made available to death care consumers not be offset in many cases by the increased complexity of the decision-making process.

One such precaution available to consumers is for them to rely on others to guide them at the time of need. The person relied upon may be a family friend, a clergyman, or a lawyer, but not uncommonly it is the funeral director himself on whom consumers depend to advise them, trusting to his professional reputation to ensure the propriety of the advice given.

A more effective approach would obviously be for consumers to arrange funerals in advance of need. There are psychological barriers to such advance planning on the part of some people, however, and the procedure is not without its practical difficulties in a mobile society. Even so, as noted above, it is a common practice for consumers to purchase cemetery property in advance of need, and a growing number of consumers have pre-arranged their funerals, whether or not they have actually pre-funded them. In any case the opportunity to do both is generally available to consumers who so choose, and the promotion of the practice by death care providers is a trend resulting from consolidation in the death care sector. This appears to be in the interest of consumers.

Consumer Welfare

In effect, the pre-planning of funeral services, which involves both pre-arrangement and pre-funding, transforms the deceased party into the consumer who makes the selections otherwise made by survivors at-need. This may seem preferable since it results in the selection of death care goods and services which satisfy the desires of the deceased, rather than those of his or her family.

Yet there are important distinctions between death care products and those which we ourselves consume as living beings. One of these is found in the ceremonial and memorialization components of death care, which are consumed or used strictly by the survivors rather than the deceased person. Even the mortuary services must be considered to be performed for the benefit of the survivors. The satisfactions derived from the goods and services accrue to the survivors whose participation and remembrance they are meant to inspire. The argument can be made that their inspiration is likely to be increased if they are the ones who make the arrangements and select the casket or urn, decide on the nature and extent of the services, and choose the memorial. It is commonly thought that the process of arranging the funeral and selecting the memorial helps also to relieve at least some of the grief experienced by survivors. In these respects it may be desirable to leave the purchase of death care products, or some parts of it, to survivors.

By the same token, the individual who pre-plans his own death care in whole or in part may derive satisfaction from knowing that he has provided for the last necessities of life, from selecting the personal style of death care he wishes to receive, and from some assurance that his wishes are likely to prevail. Who better is entitled to select the death care for any particular individual? In spite of the legal rights of next of kin to dictate such matters following death, the opportunity to pre-arrange and to pre-fund the death care of his choice prior to death is at least available to the individual himself, thus making his will known. Experience suggests that it is extraordinary for the survivors to change the death care goods and services pre-selected and entirely pre-funded by the deceased. It would clearly be unseemly for survivors to downgrade the pre-planned services, although it is possible that they may wish to upgrade them at their own expense, a practice which providers may encourage.

For pre-arranged death care which is not pre-funded and for at-need arrangements paid for by survivors, the actual consumers are entitled to select the goods and services they desire. In short, the death care consumer is the one who backs up his choices by paying for the chosen goods and services. Survivors may endeavor to respect the wishes of deceased persons who have made unfunded pre-arrangements or have simply expressed the occasional wish to be disposed of or remembered in one way as opposed to another, but they retain the freedom to act otherwise. The key then to ensuring that the wishes of an individual are honored is for the individual to provide for the purchase of the items desired in advance. This is what individuals ordinarily do in the case of cemetery property and related memorialization, but they have been less inclined to pre-purchase funeral services in the same way. As a result, a portion of the death care of many people has typically been selected by them, the other portion by their survivors. This seems odd, but, as was suggested above, it may be explained in part by a popular reluctance to buy "services," as opposed to tangible property, in advance of their delivery. In a mobile society, few know where they will be when they die; better to leave the selection of a funeral home until later or even to survivors after the event. Thus one hears, "It's my family who'll attend the funeral service, not I, and they, not I, should be the ones to decide what the services will be." Or, "Why should I buy cemetery property in advance? Who knows where I'll be when I die?"

To address such concerns, there are lot exchange and crypt exchange programs which allow cemetery property to be swapped between participating establishments in different areas on an equivalent-value basis. Nevertheless, such attitudes as those expressed above are a hindrance to consumers who might otherwise wish to provide in advance for the complete death care package of their choice. There are also the psychological barriers most people have which prevent them from discussing or planning their own death, even with those who are closest to them or with death care specialists. In spite of such barriers, some of us do manage to make a will, and most buy cemetery property in anticipation of our own deaths. Why then leave to survivors — especially a bereaved husband or wife — the unpleasant task of making funeral arrangements for us under difficult circumstances?

It is not uncommon for consumers to purchase medical, dental, legal, and other services in advance of need through insurance and other pre-payment plans available from the respective providers of such professional services. For death care providers to offer the opportunity to pre-arrange and to pre-fund a complete package of death care goods and services fits within this modern approach to satisfying consumer demand for advance provision for future needs, such as illness, disability, and retirement.

Restrictions Placed on Pre-Need Sales

In spite of the advantages of pre-planning for consumers, there are various disadvantages to small funeral homes of organizing and promoting the pre-need sale of funeral services. The operators of many small establishments have therefore tended to regard pre-need sales as a practice favoring larger firms, clusters, and combined establishments. Accordingly, they have at times used their influence to impose statutory and regulatory obstacles to pre-need selling by funeral homes. For example, they have tended to support legal requirements that 100 percent of pre-need sales proceeds be placed in trust funds, thus preventing the use of any pre-need sales revenues to cover selling costs and other expenses. They also have supported a prohibition on the sale of pre-need funeral plans by anyone other than licensed funeral directors. Finally, they have supported prohibitions on the initiation of contacts with consumers for the purpose of selling pre-need funeral arrangements. These so-called "non-solicitation" laws are intended to limit the ability of pre-need sales organizations to use methods already subject to specific consumer protection (U.S. FTC, July 1990, pp. 156–57).

No legitimate basis seems to exist for the adoption of such broad restrictions on the sale of pre-need death care. Their potentially anticompetitive elements are evident, and the Pre-Arrangement Association of America has called for the FTC to "prohibit funeral providers from engaging in a course of conduct that would tend to prevent or restrain: (1) price advertising, (2) at-need or pre-need sales by any person or entity, (3) operations of a memorial society, or any arrangement between a society or any other group of persons and a funeral provider for funeral goods and services, and (4) operations of a joint cemetery-mortuary operation, or any other arrangement between a cemetery, crematory or funeral provider for the sale of funeral goods and services" (U.S. FTC, July

1990, pp. 161–62). Nevertheless, the FTC staff declined to adopt any such pro-visions in its 1990 review of the Funeral Rule. Thus a patchwork of state statutes and regulations continues to restrict unnecessarily the pre-need sale of some forms of death care.

Pre-Need Funding

For legal and business reasons, the methods by which companies are required to fund pre-need sales vary from state to state, affecting their sales and account-ing practices. According to company reports, it is generally recognized that sales involving the future delivery of death care goods and services or the future upkeep of property after it is sold require death care providers to ensure the availability of funds at future times when goods and services sold under pre-need agree-ments must be delivered. The ways in which this is done vary, but pre-funded funeral plans are generally financed through trust or escrow arrangements estab-lished by providers, or through insurance, depending on the regulatory require-ments of each jurisdiction in which an establishment operates. According to analysts at the Chicago Corporation, the backlogs of funerals funded by each of the different methods may be estimated as shown in Table 11.1 on page 221. Funding by insurance typically involves the use of a single premium policy which identifies the funeral home as the beneficiary. In the case of trust- or escrow-funded plans, all or a portion of the payments for pre-planned funerals must be placed in trust funds or escrow accounts established by the provider. When a pre-planned funeral is funded through a trust or escrow account, a percentage of the sale price, which may be paid in installments, can generally be retained by the provider to defray expenses related to the sale, and the remainder is placed in a trust fund or escrow account. The percentage of the sale price placed in trust funds or in escrow accounts varies among different jurisdictions.

For accounting purposes, providers do not ordinarily recognize revenue from the sale of pre-planned funerals until delivery of the related goods and services. Nor does it appear to be appropriate for a provider to recognize as rev-enue on a current basis any dividends and interest earned or net capital gains realized from trust escrow accounts until delivery occurs under them. Any accu-mulated income in those accounts may be needed later to cover the related costs of delivering the goods and services required to be provided. Only upon deliv-ery is it possible to determine whether and how much income has been earned on such business. Yet some providers recognize such income unless state regu-lations provide that it reverts to the customer on cancellation of pre-planned funeral service contracts. In any event, principal and earnings are withdrawn only as funeral services are delivered or contracts are canceled, except in juris-dictions that permit earnings to be withdrawn currently.

For cemeteries, pre-need sales involve two classes of goods which are treated differently in terms of the financial arrangements they entail. One of these is the pre-arranged sale of rights to cemetery property: lots, lawn crypts, community mausoleum spaces, and columbarium niches that are usually financed by providers through the use of installment sales contracts. The terms of these typically run from one to seven years and are accounted for on the books of the provider as installment sales. As with other forms of installment sale contracts potentially involving repossession, it may seem to be appropriate for cemeteries to delay recognition of any revenues or earnings from such sales until a substantial portion of the purchase price (say 20 percent) has been received.

This is consistent with the generally accepted method of accounting for the installment sale of real estate, but burial rights are not entirely analogous to real estate. Both involve the use of land, but for very different purposes. The motives behind the purchase of a grave are different in kind from those that motivate real estate purchases generally. The amount involved is also ordinarily much smaller than that involved in real estate ventures. The amounts involved in purchasing a typical grave or a crypt are much less than those required for the purchase of an automobile, for example; they are closer to amounts paid for durable consumer goods, like personal computers, which are also commonly purchased in installments.

In accordance with the accrual concept under conventional accounting, the revenues and income from purchases of automobiles or durable goods are recognized during the period in which they occur, with appropriate allowances being made for a reasonable level of bad debts based on the experience of the firm. This practice is followed even though the purchasers take possession of household appliances and automobiles. Since purchasers of cemetery property do not take possession of the cemetery lots and mausoleum crypts prior to payment in full, their repossession is less subject to complications faced in connection with other installment sales operations. Under such circumstances it would appear that the sale of such property is sufficient evidence to justify recognition in an accounting sense, based on the prevailing rationale which has been expressed as follows: "The general approach is that if a sale has been completed, it should be recognized; if bad debts are expected, they should be recorded as separate estimates of uncollectibles. Although collection expenses, repossession expenses, and bad debts are an unavoidable part of installment sales activities, the incurrence of these costs and the collectibility of the receivables are reasonably predictable" (Kieso and Weigandt, 1995, p. 955).

The pre-need sale of cemetery merchandise, such as monuments, memorials, and burial vaults, is analogous to funeral merchandise sold on a pre-need basis. Thus, pre-arranged cemetery merchandise trust funds and escrow accounts are used to provide funding for the future delivery of the pre-arranged merchandise sold by cemeteries in some jurisdictions. A portion (ranging from 50 percent to 100 percent) of the sale price received is placed in trust funds or escrow accounts. For accounting purposes, providers recognize as revenue on a current basis the dividends and interest earned and net capital gains realized by pre-arranged merchandise trust funds or escrow accounts. At the same time, the liability for the estimated costs to deliver cemetery merchandise is adjusted through a charge to earnings to reflect merchandise cost increases. Principal and earnings are withdrawn only as the merchandise is delivered or contacts are canceled.

In connection with at-need and pre-need sales, cemeteries may be obliged to provide for the maintenance of their grounds under general or specific perpetual care contracts or applicable legislation, the provisions of which typically require the cemetery operator to place a portion — say 10 percent — of the proceeds from cemetery property sales into perpetual care trust or endowment funds. The income from these funds is used for maintenance of those cemeteries, but principal, including in some jurisdictions realized and unrealized capital gains, must generally be held in perpetuity, although its future adequacy is not guaranteed.

Pre-Need Marketing Strategies

Regardless of the methods of funding used, pre-need marketing methods replace or supplement the influence of various factors on the basis of which funeral homes and cemeteries are selected at the time of need. Forced to choose under such conditions, survivors are pre-disposed to select an establishment whose name comes to mind based on their past experience with it or due to its general reputation in the community. Without such pressure, however, consumers may be open to offers from other establishments which stimulate their interest in pre-planning through some form of advertising or direct sales technique. It is possible, therefore, for a firm which reaches out to potential customers through effective pre-need sales techniques to capture business that might eventually go to a more passive firm chosen by survivors at the time of need. Pre-need selling thus may diminish the significance of reputation and prior experience as factors in the consumer's choice of establishment. This is clearly indicated by the fact that new funeral homes operated in conjunction with cemeteries have effectively penetrated the market for funeral services in areas dominated by well-known, stand-alone establishments with which many families have long-standing relationships. To break these relationships, the pre-need sales organization of the cemetery is used to promote the sale of funeral services to the existing customers of the cemetery. In selling to new prospects, the funeral home trades on the name and reputation of the cemetery and the advantages of combined operations from the standpoint of consumers. Even if the sales effort fails to produce a pre-need sale of funeral services, it serves to promote the existence of the combined establishment for future at-need sales.

It is clear that the advantages of pre-need purchasing apply to funeral services and memorialization as well as to final disposition, which is generally pre-marketed by the sales organizations of cemeteries. It is a small step, but a potentially highly effective one, for those organizations to sell funeral services together with cemetery and memorial products as a package of "complete death care." In fact this is the pre-need marketing strategy employed by cemetery-mortuary combinations and clusters of funeral homes operated together with a cemetery.

Table 11.1
Estimated Aggregate Backlog of
Pre-funded Funerals (Millions)

Pre-Funding Method	Estimated Number of Funerals
Insurance	3.0–4.0
Trust/Escrow Accounts	6.0–7.0
Total	9.0–11.0

Source: The Chicago Corporation, 1994.

Stand-alone establishments of either type are not generally equipped to sell a complete package of death goods and services in this integrated manner. Their pre-need sales efforts are limited to promoting and selling the partial forms of death care they provide. This may stimulate consumers to pre-purchase less than complete death care (e.g., cemetery property only). To pre-plan for the complete process, consumers must deal with stand-alone funeral homes and cemeteries separately, their alternatives must be discussed separately with the salespeople of each establishment, and their funds must be allocated to each separately through purchases made in separate transactions. This inconvenience is avoided when consumers deal with clusters of several funeral homes which include a cemetery or with a combination establishment. The appeal of the latter may be enhanced by the prospective convenience which the unification of facilities provides when the goods and services are delivered to survivors and friends at the time of need. Thus the availability of all facilities in a single location has been promoted in the pre-need marketing programs of integrated providers.

Importance of the Sales Effort

For various reasons the methods used extensively by firms to sell other types of goods and services may not be equally effective in stimulating the demand for death care products before need. In spite of their importance to consumers, death care goods and services are not the kinds of things they tend to buy as a complete package on their own initiative before they are needed. The tendency to buy them on impulse appears only at a time of another's death when awareness of need for the product is heightened dramatically. Death care goods and services must be sold, therefore, by an effective sales force of well-trained salespeople. The development and use of such organizations by cemeteries has been an effective technique, but its application to the pre-need sales of funeral services has been slow in coming.

It is clear that there are significant differences between the operations of funeral homes and cemeteries. In particular, the smaller scale of many of the former makes it much more difficult for their operations to support an effective sales organization whose benefits offset its costs, and the limited market served by most of them is an obstacle to the success of their pre-need sales efforts. They may attempt to increase their scale by forming a local cluster of several funeral homes or by entering into joint marketing arrangements with one another, but as providers of a single component of the total death care package, the scope of their line of products and services is limited in spite of their scale. This has the effect of restricting the average value of their sales, which may restrict the average sales compensation and motivation for their salespeople. This is true even for the sales effort of large stand-alone funeral homes or clusters of funeral homes which do not include cemeteries. It is also true of stand-alone cemeteries which do not include mortuaries. For such establishments, the pressure on their salespeople to urge consumers to select higher priced funeral services or cemetery property is greater because they sell only one component of death care. Because the salespeople of combined establishments and clusters have more to sell, their average sale is naturally higher than that of salespeople of stand-alone firms of either type. By selling complete death care through one sales organization, combined establishments and clusters which include cemeteries are more effective and efficient than stand-alone establishments, other things being equal.

With the development of these more effective forms of selling complete death care, it is inevitable that more consumers will purchase pre-planned funeral services in the future, along with cemetery and memorial products which traditionally have been sold pre-need. This is likely to have two beneficial results for consumers. One is an increased sense of security in the knowledge that the mortuary services, final disposition, and memorialization of one's choice have been fully provided for in advance. The other is the satisfaction that one has made a balanced allocation of total pre-need expenditures among the three components of death care, in the proportions desired. The first part represents the security feature, and the second part represents the balance feature.

The security feature depends on the continuity of the provider and the sufficiency of the funds set aside in trust or through life insurance to cover the future costs of delivering the goods and services called for. As a common feature of pre-need sales contracts, the latter has been the subject of regulation by the states, but the former must be assessed by consumers themselves. In making such assessments, it is reasonable to suppose that consumers rely upon the reputation of the seller. For cemetery property and services, the expectation of continuity is enhanced by the permanence of the facilities, which extends by association to the facilities of a mortuary located in and operated in conjunction with a cemetery. This is an advantage which may be featured in the sales presentations of cemetery-mortuary combinations.

The balance feature depends on the consumer's ability to strike a desired balance among the amounts allocated to each component of the total death care package desired, with the three components considered and purchased simultaneously. Consumer satisfaction seems much more likely to result from a single transaction involving a provider capable of offering and delivering the complete set of death care goods and services desired at a package price in what might be termed a "zero-sum exchange." In practice, this zero-sum sale, whether made pre-need or at-need, could be made only by an agent of a combination mortuary-crematory-cemetery-memorialization establishment or by a cluster of funeral homes which includes a cemetery and crematory and a memorial dealer or by a multipartite combination establishment. The advantage of the zero-sum exchange would provide key selling features to the sales organizations of these multi-establishment firms.

It is fair to suppose that the pre-need sales efforts of stand-alone funeral homes are not only likely to be less effective and efficient than those of clusters and combinations, they also are likely to serve consumers less well by comparison, in purely economic terms. To correct this deficiency, these single establishments, would need either (1) to form or to join a cluster which includes a cemetery and memorial dealer or a combination establishment or (2) to enter into some form of joint marketing venture which would merge the sales effort of a funeral home with that of a cemetery or combination. It is probable that the tendency for stand-alone firms to affiliate with regional or national chains which include both funeral homes and cemeteries has probably been encouraged by considerations of this kind.

Pre-Need Risks

A final important consideration involved in buying or selling death care has to do with the effect of shifting the risk of future price increases from the consumer to the provider. Along with the various reasons for pre-need purchases discussed above, this factor may play some role in influencing consumer attitudes toward the desirability of pre-planning from time to time. Consumers know from experience that prices — especially of land and services — show a tendency to rise over the years. It is thus reasonable to expect that prices will be higher in the future, including the price of death care goods and services. By purchasing in advance of need, consumers may expect to lock in the death care of their choice at present prices, an expectation which providers of those services may reasonably attempt to satisfy in their promotion of pre-need sales.

The seller assumes most or all the risks of rising costs entailed in delivering pre-planned funeral services and related merchandise at the time of death, which may be years after they were prepurchased and pre-funded. The legal and contractual requirements surrounding the funding of pre-need sales merchandise and services are intended to ensure the ability of providers to deliver such merchandise and services in the future. There is no guarantee of this, of course, so a measure of risk-management is inherent in reputable contracts involving the future delivery of goods and services of all types.

Under such conditions in some sectors of the economy, sellers may hedge their positions with offsetting "futures" contracts, but this is not feasible in the conditions under which funeral homes engage in the sale of pre-funded funerals. In recognition of this situation and to ensure the use of their merchandise in the case of pre-planned funerals, several casket companies have devised programs which guarantee the wholesale prices of their caskets at present levels. One example is the price guarantee program of the Batesville Casket Co. and the Forethought Group, a pre-need insurance provider, both of which are units of Hillenbrand Industries. The program, styled "Total Casket Protection," guarantees the wholesale prices of caskets until the merchandise is delivered under pre-need contracts that both use Forethought insurance as a source of funding and specify Batesville caskets. According to the two companies, the plan provides 100 percent protection for funeral homes, thus increasing the protection of consumers.

For established cemeteries (as distinguished from those still under development which pose special risks), the problems faced in connection with the pre-need sale of merchandise (e.g. burial vaults) are similar to those faced by funeral homes. On the other hand, the pre-need sale of burial rights is different in kind, owing to the nature of existing cemetery property. The special risk associated with cemeteries affecting their attractiveness to both at-need and pre-need purchasers is the adequacy of their perpetual care funds. As noted, the capital of these cannot, as a contractual or legal matter, be encroached. The income from the corpus of the capital is available for general maintenance, but future inflation can erode the capacity of the fund to generate income sufficient to cover the costs of cemetery maintenance.

As a competitive matter, therefore, the adequacy of the perpetual care fund of a cemetery is a factor which may significantly affect not only its attractiveness to consumers, but also its very viability as a commercial or noncommercial operation. One of the largest such funds is that of Mount Auburn Cemetery, which was established in Cambridge, Massachusetts, in 1831. Its endowment exceeds $50 million, an amount expected to be sufficient to care indefinitely for the 174-acre facility in spite of the fact that the cemetery will cease to be an active facility around the turn of the century, based on its master plan (*American Cemetery*, March 1993).

Unfortunately, there are far more cases of cemeteries with inadequate perpetual care funds. Their plight is chronicled at length by Sloane (1991), who associates it with the "isolation of death" in the twentieth century. Curl (1993) deplores the neglect of cemeteries and memorials in contemporary society, attributing it to a "cult of youth." The vandalism of cemeteries and the problems of cemetery security are frequent topics of cemetery trade associations and publications. As discussed in Chapter 9, changes in local and state laws relating to cemetery vandalism, and perhaps enactment of a federal law, have been advocated by cemetery and civic groups. But the problem remains. This sad state of affairs affords a serious opportunity to the operators of cemeteries, who are in a position to take advantage of it, to promote their ability to deliver perpetual care as an important feature of final disposition and memorialization desired by many consumers. One way to do this is to advertise or to otherwise promote the security features of cemeteries as well as their financial strength, which is a factor favoring cemeteries owned and operated by national companies and regional chains.

For consumers, however, there is also a simple way to begin to assess the care cemeteries deliver. Sloane (1991) suggests it when he urges:

> Take a walk in a cemetery during the first week in June. Are there flowers on the graves? Do American flags fly over the graves of veterans? Is the grass mowed and are the bushes clipped? Are there fresh mounds of dirt, a yard of new sod, or other signs of new graves? Americans tend to think of the cemetery as a static institution, one that has existed, and will exist, forever. But the cemetery is dynamic. Cemeteries, like farms, cities, suburbs, theaters, businesses, and people, are born, live, and die. Anyone who has ever walked through the high grass and broken stones of a country graveyard or urban cemetery knows this [pp. 241–42].

It would serve a useful purpose if more consumers took Sloane's suggestion. If they would only take the time to acquaint themselves with the death care providers and establishments in their communities, they could look for the signs Sloane mentions and ask questions about products and prices. Is there a mausoleum, and is it built to last? Is the cemetery still dynamic, and is this made possible through adequate perpetual care funds? Is there a funeral home located within the grounds or adjacent to them, and are tours of this facility offered? Who are the people who will be in charge of arrangements at the time of need? What is the reputation of the establishments and their owners? Who, indeed, are the "owners?" If Americans are truly ignorant of their death care options as has been claimed, there is no better antidote for their ignorance than gaining knowledge about what is available now and is likely to be available in the future. Fortunately, this knowledge is within the reach of all.

Unresolved Issues

No matter how attractive or accessible death care facilities may be, few people have actually been inclined to seek out cemeteries and funeral homes for the purpose of arranging for death care in advance of need. Among the younger members of the population, this is understandable in the light of average life expectancies at early ages and the high priorities attached by young consumers to other needs. As individuals age life expectancy decreases, but it remains relatively lengthy even for middle-age groups. Few of the healthy members of such age groups may be stimulated to approach cemeteries and funeral homes on their own. Even the elderly, and the terminally ill, do not necessarily wish to pre-arrange their own death care, either in part or in full. If and when they do, they are more likely to purchase cemetery property in advance than to pre-plan their own funeral services.

Perhaps this is a matter of deliberate choice on the part of consumers, but it seems more likely to have something to do with the different ways in which death care goods and services have traditionally been marketed by cemeteries and funeral homes. As commercial real estate developers, cemeterians have generally been more aggressive promoters of their properties, the development of which has often depended financially on their pre-need sales programs. Funeral directors, on the other hand, have tended to operate on a scale and in a manner which has led them to favor at-need sales practices. Although most of them now provide opportunities for consumers to pre-arrange and to pre-fund funeral services, the commitment of any funeral directors to a pre-need sales effort has often been half-hearted.

It may seem possible to promote effectively the pre-arrangement and pre-funding of funeral services by similar sales techniques based on direct-to-consumer methods used successfully in cemetery sales programs. This is what funeral homes have usually sought to do whenever they have developed a pre-need sales program of their own, especially when a cemetery has been included among a cluster of funeral homes. Expanding their product line, cemetery-mortuary combinations have generally added funeral services to lines sold by their existing cemetery sales forces. In all of these cases, the tendency has been for the pre-need sale of funeral services to piggyback on firmly established concepts of an existing marketing strategy for cemetery sales. Yet funeral services are inherently different from cemetery products, and the most effective techniques of selling the one may not fully apply to the other. This would seem to have occurred to those involved in the process of selling death care, especially when the process entails the marketing of all three elements of death care through a common sales force. Nevertheless, there appears to have been little if any serious exploration of the appropriate emphasis to be placed on various elements of the marketing mix — direct selling, advertising, and market research — in order to facilitate the sale of varied death care products and services to consumers.

From all appearances there is considerable variation in the sales methods used by different firms, and even within different regional divisions of the same large firms in some cases, in terms of the emphasis placed on the salesperson's knowledge of death care products and markets, the sales presentation, talking points, and closing techniques. Methods of selection of salespersons, the nature and extent of their training, types of compensation and bonus plans, forms and degrees of supervision, and other aspects of sales organizations differ widely throughout the death care industries. Accordingly, no generally accepted standards of performance have been devised for the effective marketing of death care goods and services on a pre-need basis. The stigmatized or polluted nature of such products and traditional limitations on the means of promoting them have historically limited the attractiveness of pre-need selling as an occupation.

The result is that firms have sometimes faced recruitment problems and high turnover among sales personnel. New methods of attracting and developing creditable salespersons with a view to selling a total line of products and reaching out to younger markets seem to be important ingredients of the successful exploitation of clusters and combinations of complete death care facilities.

To inform this process appears to require more attention to marketing research aimed at understanding death care products, markets, and consumer behavior than has been undertaken by death care providers in the past. In particular, there appears to be a need for the development and testing of methods for selling to pre-need consumers of funeral services in a manner which is as effective as the at-need methods traditionally employed by funeral directors. Such methods are unlikely to be suggested from sources outside of the death care field. True, there is no lack of books on marketing and salesmanship generally, including direct selling, integrity selling, relationship marketing, niche marketing, aftermarketing, and so on — all of which are important features of the marketing strategies of many death care providers. Nevertheless, none of the marketing strategies and sales techniques they espouse are specifically designed to take into account the distinctive features and sensitive nature of death care goods and services.

What seems to be needed in the death care economy is a thorough treatment of the role of the sales process in the marketing of death care goods and services to consumers under modern conditions. Such a treatment would take into account the full implications of the differences in the types of sales, pre-need and at-need, and selling establishments — cemeteries, funeral homes, memorial dealers, and clusters and combinations thereof. It would explore the implications of these differences for the relationship between the sales and operations of establishments of each type. It would take into account the differences in goods and services which those establishments provide and the markets and submarkets in which they operate. It would explicitly consider the implications of differences in the ages, incomes, and other characteristics of the consumers who comprise those markets and submarkets. Further, it might also address more fully such unresolved issues and questions as may relate to any possible future expansion of the product lines of funeral homes and cemeteries. In addition, it might assess realistically the potential vulnerability of those establishments to possible future expansions of the product lines of firms in other industries, such as financial services.

Although some funeral directors have operated related businesses, such as insurance agencies or companies, ambulance or limousine services, and others, there has been no systematic general tendency for them to expand their scope in these directions. In some respects it seems correct to say that the nature of funeral directing as an occupation has tended to limit severely the expansion of the activities of its practitioners. This may explain the reluctance of funeral directors to embrace the role of providers of practical assistance to survivors in a much larger sense than the marginal expansion of their role entailed in their efforts to be recognized as "grief therapists" who engage in providing psychological support to their bereaved customers. By assuming such a limited role, they appear to have left the door open for others to gather momentum in the larger role of providing practical support to survivors. While funeral directors play some modest role in assisting survivors with filing claims for life insurance and other death benefits, they have not expanded this side of their business to assist survivors with the multitude of legal and financial burdens that often accompany dying and death in modern society, especially the death of a spouse.

Survivor Support Services

Beyond the need to arrange funeral services and to adjust to the loss of a family member, survivors often must make important decisions about pensions, insurance, Social Security, mortgages, taxes, and investments, among other important matters. Yet there are few sources of guidance about such matters to which survivors can turn, and death care providers have not aspired to become such a source — perhaps because of the nature of the legal and financial assistance it entails. Yet according to the *Wall Street Journal*, financial services firms have recently entered the field of specifically providing such counseling services for persons with terminal illnesses and for survivors following death. At some large companies, the provision of survivor support services has developed as a fringe benefit for employees. A contract provider of such counseling services in the form of a "survivor support" program is Ayco Corp., a subsidiary of American Express. Similar programs are made available to the employees of some of the client companies of major accounting firms (Schultz, *Wall Street Journal*, September 16, 1994).

Many financial planning firms also provide informal survivor support services outside of an employment program. The American Association of Retired Persons operates a "Widowed Persons Service" that refers interested members to local AARP-sponsored support programs in their areas. In contrast to the formal Ayco program, however, the AARP system relies on referrals to outside providers of counseling services. The Ayco program is a direct provider of survivor support services through its own counselors who "can start at the beginning, helping with funeral arrangements, ... [or can] help employees or their survivors file medical claims, untangle conflicts with hospitals, handle estate decisions, and apply for Social Security and other benefits. They also reassess life insurance needs, which may have changed, and help develop a new estate plan" (Schultz, *Wall Street Journal*, September 16, 1994).

It is difficult to avoid the impression that funeral directors may have missed a significant opportunity to expand the scope of their role by providing fee-based counseling services of the kind just described to their customers. Instead of aspiring to the role of "grief therapists" for which they appear to have been unable to charge for their services, they would perhaps have fared better by developing their skills as financial counselors capable of providing survivors with a full range of concrete assistance following a death. The role of the funeral director as financial counselor seems to be a logical extension of his role of providing assistance to customers in connection with filing life insurance and Social Security claims. It also conforms with the financial planning aspect of the sale by funeral homes of pre-arranged funeral services funded by insurance and trust funds.

It is up to those in the field of funeral directing to consider more fully the wisdom of the roles they have attempted to assume to this point. Perhaps there are some of them who have enhanced their revenues and profits indirectly by practicing as grief therapists, but none appears to have discovered how to market grief therapeutic services to benefit them directly. In fact, there appears to be little agreement within the industry about how to market basic mortuary services most effectively. There is much more agreement about how cemetery products are most effectively marketed. What is needed to sort out the unresolved marketing issues is the clear articulation of a coherent strategy for the marketing of death care goods and services of all types by their providers. Clearly, only the providers of those goods and services have the depth of experience and empirical evidence of sales results from alternative approaches to present a convincing case for a particular marketing and sales strategy.

PART V

We must conform to a certain extent to the conventionalities of society, for they are the ripened results of a varied and long experience.

A. A. Hodge

12. *Religious Factors in Death Care*

The Influence of Religion at Death

For most Americans it is difficult if not impossible to disentangle attitudes about the phenomenon of death, whether their own or that of someone close to them, from the religious beliefs they hold. The event of death is poignant: it is the end of a life, and according to the beliefs of many, the beginning of an afterlife. Even for those who hold to no specific religious sentiments, there is something about death, the cessation of life as a human being in the material world, which inspires awe. Death is a great mystery of human life. As an existential phenomenon, it has puzzled philosophers and inspired theologians. Both religion itself and its influence on the secular culture affect many of our ceremonial wants and desires, especially those related to death. From all indications, this has always been so in civilized societies. Thus, according to one thanatologist: "Certainly, belief in a renewal beyond the grave must be almost as old as man himself. Mortuary practices indicating some cult of the dead are coeval with the earliest known civilizations of the Old Stone Age" (Saffron, 1970, p. 313).

Undoubtedly, a dominant influence on the forms of death care provided in this country has been the religion of the deceased and the survivors. When families performed the functions of death care, they usually did so with due regard for the requirements of religious affiliations. As the tasks of caring for the dead were assumed by funeral directors, it was of concern to families that the care provided was not inconsistent with religious doctrines, such as the Roman Catholic liturgical view that "The faithful should be persuaded that arranging for funerals and funeral monuments, they should keep close to the concept of Christian death and eternal life, and should reject any appearance of superstition or pagan symbolism" (McNaspy, 1966, p. 232).

The historical involvement of the clergy and the inclusion of church facilities in funeral services further served to ensure the sanctity of death care practices in the minds of most families. At the same time, it obliged commercial

232

providers of death care to interact with the noncommercial providers of religious services desired by their customers. The economic impact of this somewhat unusual set of circumstances will concern us even though religion itself will not. It is noteworthy, for example, that the prevalence of religious ceremonies at funeral services has eroded somewhat in recent years, as more consumers have chosen to hold memorial services with no religious content or have chosen immediate disposition with no ceremony.

Despite such trends the influence of religion in the event of death remains strong and is likely to continue in the years ahead as the population ages, since older people tend to be more religious than younger ones. In addition, even among younger Americans a large majority expresses some form of religiosity or spirituality, even if rejecting an affiliation with organized religions. Demographically, the proportion of churchgoers among the general population ranges from about 35 percent in the East to 43 percent in the South. Although the rate of growth in membership of "mainline" religions has lagged behind the rate of U.S. population growth during recent years, the impact of this differential has been offset by the growth of some fundamentalist and evangelical denominations among Christians. In addition, there has been a growth in the expression of non–Judeo-Christian religious beliefs in this country as immigration patterns have changed and as Americans have crossed major religious boundaries.

The evidence cited by Naisbitt and Aburdeen suggests that large numbers of Americans are religious "without belonging to a particular religion or church" (1990, p. 275). In support of this view, a Gallup study concludes that "The unchurched today are, by many measures, more religious than they were a decade ago" (cited in Naisbitt and Aburdeen, p. 275). This latent religiosity is most likely to manifest itself at the event of a death. A large proportion of Americans want a funeral service which includes some form of religious rite and some participation by clergy, even if those in charge of making decisions do not adhere to any religious practice ordinarily. To examine the influence of a variety of religious factors on the operations of death care providers, especially funeral homes, is the purpose of this chapter.

The Role of Clergy in the Death Care Process

In previous chapters, discussion has proceeded under the assumption that death care is purchased by consumers in commercial transactions with established providers. In most cases, arrangements for mortuary services and the funeral itself are made immediately after the event of a death, and under such conditions it is not unusual for bereaved family members to be accompanied by friends or clergy. Sometimes these parties become involved in the arrangements process at the funeral home.

There is seldom any precise role which friends are expected to play; nor, apparently, is there a uniform notion of the role of clergy in this process. Indeed, according to Rabbi Jacob Goldberg, writing in *Pastoral Bereavement Counseling*, the training of clergy does not emphasize their intervention following death. He says, "Contrary to what the lay public might expect, the seminaries that educate for the ministry devote little space in their curricula for preparing clergy to face the emotional overtones of their pastoral functions" following death (Goldberg, 1989, p. 24).

This seems odd in light of the traditional connections between death and religion and the commonly accepted involvement of clergy in religious funeral services. Rabbi Goldberg attributes some neglect of the subject to two factors: (1) "grief is a painful subject" and (2) that until recently there was no "systematic self-contained method for helping mourners that could effectively be taught and applied" (p. 24). Consequently, members of the clergy have been obliged to learn from experience the ways in which they may be of assistance following a death. This presumably results in a variety of different approaches taken by clergy. Of his own experience, Rabbi Goldberg relates that "Sometimes I could help in the funeral arrangements; but I found that of greater importance was 'being there'" (p. 26).

Underlying this statement is a tacit assumption, which seems to be justified generally, that the funeral director is expected to be fully acquainted by training and experience with the form and substance of the required elements of the religious services for which consumers express a desire in the processes of death care. In the course of providing services in which members of the clergy participate, an association often develops between particular death care providers and the clergy. Cemeteries may be owned and operated by religious organizations, and commercial cemeteries usually have religious associations. Likewise, funeral homes are often associated with particular religions to which their owners or managers belong and contribute. It is probably no exaggeration to say that many funeral homes appear to be operated under the aegis of the religions with whose clergy they have frequent contacts. It is clearly the case that the perception of a close association is likely to result from the repeated use of a particular funeral home by the members of a local congregation.

Potential Conflicts of Roles

There is some sense in which the relationship between funeral directors and members of the clergy is a natural and inevitable one. It is a common feature of established religions to address the experience and meaning of death, and it is customary for bereaved persons to seek comfort and consolation from their religious beliefs, if any. It is understandable that they customarily desire to arrange funeral services which include religious rites and observances in which the clergy participate. It is one of the duties of the clergy to officiate at such services and to otherwise comfort bereaved members of their congregations. As the party in charge of the funeral arrangements, the funeral director arranges for the participation of clergy in the schedule of services he provides, some of which may involve the use of religious facilities. There is thus a sense in which the role of the funeral director and the role of the clergy are complementary in nature.

At the same time, there is some sense in which the relationship between those who perform these complementary roles may become uneasy. In a chapter entitled "The Nosy Clergy" in *The American Way of Death* (1963), Mitford appears to delight in bringing out the details of the uneasiness which may arise in the relationship. It is likely that she exaggerated the significance of the matter, but the issue seems to deserve a serious airing. Rather than attempt to do this by quoting the opposing positions of religious leaders and funeral directors, we shall mention the points of actual or potential contention between them.

One of these involves the issue of spending by bereaved families on funerals, especially spending on merchandise, namely caskets. Spending on caskets seems to concern the clergy and other critics more than does spending on ceremonies and "services." Witness, for example, the following critical commentary:

> It is not ceremony itself that is coming under judgment in the latter half of the twentieth century. It is that the understandable need for ceremony has led to abuse. When consumers stop to think about it, they realize that the major portion of the large funeral bill is for merchandise. One can argue that the time spent, the personal service provided by the funeral director and his staff, deserves to be paid for. They are, after all, doing the things we do not want to do ourselves. But the rest is coffins, hardware, pillows, mattresses. Soft goods. Hard goods. And sales resistance at the time of death is understandably low, especially if there has been no advance planning [Arvio, 1974, p. 7].

A series of points must be made.

Confusion About Costs

In the first place, the last quoted passage makes it plain there is confusion about the costs of providing traditional death care, particularly funeral services. As we have seen, most of the costs result from the expenses incurred by funeral homes for their facilities and personnel. Merchandise is not the major component of mortuary costs as the above passage seems to suggest, but confusion over this point is understandable because of the tendency for funeral homes to use the prices charged for caskets as a means of covering their fixed costs of providing services. In this respect, the industry has invited the concerns expressed over "excessive" spending by consumers on elaborate merchandise used in funeral services. Given the pricing methods commonly used, it is easy for a member of the clergy or anyone else who accompanies a family to the selection room to succumb to the impression that most of the price of a funeral consists of merchandise costs which are "unnecessary and avoidable." Under such an impression, a rational party is likely to feel obliged to discourage such spending.

The solution to this impression created by the pricing methods used by funeral directors appears to lie in their own hands. It consists of the wider adoption of pricing methods which do not create the impression that funeral services are cheap, but merchandise is expensive. It is likely that more rational pricing methods which reflect the real costs of services and merchandise would reduce the tendency for clergy or others to regard spending on merchandise as a significant element of funeral expenses that is to be discouraged. In turn, this would reduce the vulnerability of funeral directors to the criticism that some of them use devices intended to remove members of the clergy from the selection room (Mitford, 1963, pp. 193–94). As pointed out previously, it would also clear the way for funeral homes to compete directly with casket stores which are an attempt to cash in on the irrational casket pricing systems of funeral homes. In the final analysis, however, changing the method of pricing may do nothing to alter the costs of funeral services, which some may continue to regard as too high or unnecessary or both.

Religious and Socioeconomic Factors

Let it be granted that there is a long history of conflict over questions of spending on goods and services which appear to include some elements of conspicuous consumption. Social events, in particular, whether weddings or funerals or less significant ones, are subject to easy disagreements over what constitutes excessive or wasteful spending. Insofar as the issues raised in this debate involve differences in tastes, they are not strictly of concern here, but the tastes themselves and the factors which influence and alter them, are of concern. These tastes express themselves in terms of demand for particular qualities of goods and services delivered in the segment of the death care process which interests us.

The personal tastes and religious sentiments of consumers affect their consumption of death care goods and services, and it is important to consumers and providers of these products to know the extent to which the religions of their customers encourage simplicity and economy in the choices for death care products. Without pausing here to enumerate the positions of various religious bodies on this proposition, it is probably correct to say that none encourages overspending on funerals, and most or all emphasize the propriety of simplicity and dignity.

There is in all such positions, of course, an element of flexibility which allows for personal choice entailing wide variations in the amounts spent, while conforming to individual interpretations of terms like "simplicity" and "dignity." This appears to be true, for example, in both the Catholic and Protestant religions, among the members of which there is considerable variation in spending according to the influence of such socioeconomic factors as affluence and social status. The existence of such variation accords with the product-lining practices of funeral homes and does not appear to conflict with the tenets of these major religions. Making allowances for differences in practices and rites, the same may be said to apply to the Jewish religion and presumably to others as well.

In any event, the establishments that provide death care to particular religious and ethnic groups are obliged to adapt their operations to accommodate the expectations consumers have of funeral services they will receive, conforming to the requirements of the religions under whose auspices the services are conducted. To fail to do so would threaten the reputation of an establishment as a provider of the death care sanctioned by the religions of its customers. It would seem, therefore, that funeral homes catering to a particular clientele would not be able to depart from traditional observances and rites required by their religious preferences. Subject to this constraint, it may be unreasonable for the methods adopted by funeral homes to allow or even to encourage overspending. Nevertheless, it would appear consistent with their roles as profit-oriented businesses to allow or even to encourage spending in accordance with the preferences and means of their customers. This is standard business practice throughout a free enterprise society in which preferences and means differ widely, resulting in corresponding variations in the styles and prices of many generic products, such as houses and automobiles.

It seems appropriate for death care providers to offer a product line which enables consumers to select the set of services and merchandise which reflects their socioeconomic status as well their religious beliefs. It seems appropriate also for funeral directors to promote the qualities and value of the general and special features of their merchandise which they believe will appeal to their customers. They are, after all, in business.

Equally important, consumers are members of their communities, in which they lead a certain style of life. Death ends a life and it brings an end to the style of life that a person has led, alone and in relationship with others. Since it is the life of the deceased that is to be commemorated, it seems entirely appropriate that funeral services — including the merchandise selected in conjunction with them — do reflect the style and quality of life led by the deceased person. It is entirely reasonable and logical that the event of his or her death should be accompanied by continued recognition through an appropriate commemorative service, appropriate final disposition of the remains, and appropriate memorialization. In all cases the word "appropriate" refers to death care goods and services consistent with the prior style and quality of life led by the deceased person, according to the desires and means of the deceased or the survivors.

A Proposed Solution: Pre-Planning

It is difficult to see how anyone could seriously object to the proposition that seems to result from the previous considerations. In effect, those considerations entail a concept of an appropriate funeral as one which is in keeping with the religious sentiments of the deceased and the socioeconomic status of the party or parties on whom the cost falls. Even where means are limited, it may be questionable for friends or clergy to discourage spending for the kind of funeral that is desired by survivors and may be important to their psychological welfare. The problem to which attention may be drawn by such observers, however, is that the psychological sales techniques use by funeral directors may create pressure on bereaved families to overspend.

It is unnecessary here to fall back on the reasonable defense that this would not be good business practice for a funeral director concerned about receiving payment for his services and maintaining the reputation of his firm. Quite apart from that protection, there is a solution available to consumers at the present time in the form of the opportunity to pre-plan the funeral services of their choice. It would appear that this is an ideal way for consumers to protect themselves from at-need pressure applied by funeral directors and their sales methods. For their part, it would seem that the members of the clergy could perhaps play a role in protecting those in religious circles from such pressures by encouraging the practice of pre-arranging and pre-funding funerals, along with final disposition and memorialization, among their congregations. This would help to relieve some of their concerns about the emotional conditions under which at-need arrangements are made, with or without the clergy in attendance.

Death Care and Aftercare

Whether or not funeral services are pre-arranged and pre-funded, the delivery of death care at the time of need results in the interaction of clergy with funeral directors when religious services are desired. Insofar as the clergy are a group in society directly concerned by their calling with providing comfort and support to bereaved families at the time of death, their role may be described as providers of death care. In this capacity the position they occupy precedes and transcends that of commercial providers with whom they must interact in a complementary manner.

What appears to be important in these somewhat unusual circumstances is the clarity of the roles of clergy and funeral directors. Clarity exists in certain aspects of the relationship between the clergy and funeral directors as things now stand. It is accepted by both, for example, that the funeral director is in charge of the remains, whereas it is the duty of clergy to officiate at various stages in the services which the funeral director "directs." While the job of the funeral director is usually completed with the interment or committal of the body at the cemetery or crematory, the involvement of the family with the clergy may continue. Hence the concern of some members of the clergy with bereavement counseling (see, for example, Goldberg, 1989).

With the expansion of the role of funeral directors into the realm of aftercare, which may involve bereavement counseling and grief therapy, there is an apparent basis for some confusion of roles and conflict between the two different types of death care providers. As a form of service provided by funeral homes without charge, aftercare is not a factor in their economic performance. In some cases it is largely a public relations device. At an earlier point, we excluded it from consideration as an element of death care as the term is used throughout this book. Nevertheless, as a phenomenon in the sector, it is a proper subject of concern. The question may then be asked whether there is any sense in which the delivery of aftercare may become a viable commercial product for death care providers.

For present purposes, we shall consider grief therapy and bereavement counseling which extend beyond the services rendered as a part of the traditional funeral. Without a prototype for the aftercare to be offered, we are limited to a consideration of the nature and extent of the similar services available from providers with whom funeral homes would compete as grief therapists and bereavement counselors. Such services are now provided by psychiatrists, psychologists, social workers, and the clergy. We are lacking any data indicating the effectiveness of the first three, but some information about the effectiveness of the latter is provided by the results of a recent survey of the occurrence of "death and mourning" as a theme in twelve mainline journals devoted to family therapy, as reviewed and analyzed by Eugene Kelly, Jr. (1992).

Among the conclusions reached from the study are the following: "Religion is described as a significant, and in some respects, helpful part of the mourning process for Irish, Black, and Puerto Rican Americans.... However, in only one article are religious (Judeo-Christian) values and rituals clearly described and presented as potentially valuable adjuncts to therapy with families in the grieving process." The author of another article "maintains that families in mourning are increasingly without the support of religious customs, and, therefore, therapeutic procedures based on mental health principles and practices are becoming more important in the mourning process." Another article suggests that religion may be helpful in cases involving the death of a child. Still another concludes that religion offers "a sense of the sacred at the time of death, although this sacredness tends to be undermined by hospital procedures and the insensitivity of some clergy" (p. 191).

With few exceptions, the author of the study concludes that the articles surveyed "present religion as a relatively insignificant factor in either understanding or helping in death and mourning experiences." This result seems surprising and leads the author of the study to conclude the following:

> Yet religion in all forms speaks powerfully to the meaning and experience of death and mourning. Mature religious faith and practice engage persons and communities in an effort to understand, confront, and eventually accept death in a positive way. Despite these profound links between religion and death and mourning, family therapy journal literature generally gives only minor attention to the therapeutic possibilities of religion in treating death and mourning experiences [p. 192].

Evidence of this sort is fragmentary at best, but it nevertheless supports the view that religious counseling in connection with death is not generally regarded as effective. This suggests that there may be room for commercial death care providers to offer aftercare programs which complement or supplement existing efforts by clergy and other therapists. Complementary or supplementary services may be interpreted as a form of competition by some, however, and this may continue to restrain any serious efforts by death care practitioners to offer aftercare as a marketable product. This is especially true because their credentials as therapists are obviously inferior to the established credentials of licensed health care professionals. Nevertheless, even psychiatrists themselves have recognized the peculiarly significant position of the funeral director in relation to the survivors who are affected by grief and bereavement. An outstanding example of this recognition is furnished by Harvard University psychiatrist Thomas P. Hackett in this address to funeral directors:

> If I were to choose a single fault to characterize the funeral director in the last 20 years it is that he has misrepresented himself by placing too much emphasis and training on preparing the body and officiating at the funeral ceremony. You perform a vital service at a time of great distress in the life of a family. It has been pointed out on numerous occasions by renowned social scientists such as Erich Lindemann that your role in the treatment of acute grief or bereavement is a vital function. It is part of your job. Perhaps, as Lindemann thought and as I think, the most important part. Grief is surely mankind's most common painful, deeply felt emotion. No one is spared. In untold numbers the bereaved fail to overcome their sense of loss, and grieving over a period of months becomes pathological. It can result in physical sickness, disability or in mental depression. The process of grieving can be shared and the bereaved can be taught how to cope with his sense of loss and desolation. No one is in a better position to do that than the funeral director who is there from the start [July 1976, p. 21].

It remains true, however, that even though the outcome of the performance of the role of funeral directors may be to relieve grief, the potential conflicts resulting from any attempt by funeral directors to charge for professional grief therapy offered to their customers largely precludes such expansion of their role as death care providers.

Religious Versus Commercial Facilities

There are other elements of funeral services which bring the operation of funeral homes as commercial establishments into actual or potential conflict with the interests of the clergy. One of these is the question of whether the "chapel" of a mortuary is an appropriately sacred place for a religious funeral service at which members of clergy officiate. The necessity of using the sacred facilities of churches removed from the funeral home clearly adds to the cost of providing the funeral. Yet there are still those cases in which it is not considered acceptable for a commercial mortuary facility to be used as the site of certain sacred religious rites.

Questions of "sacredness" are a delicate matter on which we are not inclined to comment. We cannot, however, avoid the business and economic implications of this issue for consumers and providers alike. The question must therefore be raised: Is it possible that issues of this kind are a manifestation of the concern by clergy that their role in the process of death care may become largely that of an actor in the ceremonies conducted by the funeral director who is in charge? This is clearly what Mitford implies when she refers to an Episcopal bishop who insists that "the proper place for a religious funeral service is in church — and not in the 'chapel' of a mortuary." She quotes from an interview with the bishop as follows: "A cause of resentment among ministers, the Bishop said, is the frequent implication that they are being 'hired' as 'props' by the funeral director, who takes it upon himself to indicate to the family an appropriate amount for the minister's honorarium, then acts as go-between by adding this sum to his own bill, collects it from the family, and in due course passes it along to the minister" (Mitford, 1963, pp. 196–97).

In the light of such comments, it is necessary to express the hope that the clergy is generally more concerned with the religious substance of the role they play in the death care process than with the location at which they perform their role and the arrangement for their honorariums. At any rate, just as the development of funeral "homes" and "parlors" brought an end to the practice of holding visitation in residences, more and more funerals are being conducted in mortuary facilities, especially those of combined facilities.

The practice of conveying the body from the mortuary to the church on the way to the cemetery makes some sense when and where funeral homes are separated from cemeteries. But when both facilities are combined, it is difficult to justify the additional time and effort and cost involved in this traditional practice. The inclusion of "chapels" which meet religious criteria, such as the ones shown in the photos on page 242, is the way in which the developers of some combinations have foreseen the impact of those facilities on established death care practices which have strong religious significance. It is an attempt to provide facilities of an appropriate sort for the accommodation of the religious needs of consumers and the clergy who minister to them.

Scheduling and Participation at Funerals

In addition to conflicts involving facilities, the participation of the clergy in death care activities arranged by funeral directors raises other issues which have never been fully resolved among the parties. For example, concern has sometimes been expressed (off the record perhaps) over a lack of consideration shown for demands on the clergy when funeral services are scheduled by funeral directors. This complaint is not limited to the clergy; it is a common problem for cemeteries that they are not part of the arrangements process during which the funeral services are scheduled by funeral directors. The cemetery is simply called and told at what time to expect the arrival of the funeral party for

Examples of chapels: (*top, left*) the chapel at Restland Memorial Park in Dallas, (*top, right*) the Chapel of the Pines at Pine Crest Cemetery in Mobile, Alabama, (*bottom*) the chapel at Lake Lawn Metairie Funeral Home in New Orleans (prepared for a Christian service). Courtesy of those facilities.

graveside committal. By this time the schedule may already have been released to the newspaper for publication. The result is that several funerals scheduled by different funeral homes may arrive at a cemetery at the same time, when each must be accommodated by personnel and equipment.

Such simultaneous demands for the conduct of funerals are unlikely to arise in the case of clergy, but they have other demands on their time. It is clearly desirable for the funeral director to coordinate the scheduling of funeral services with the clergy and the cemetery or crematory. Although there may be instances in which all the participants cannot be accommodated, it would seem to be appropriate for a funeral home to attempt to arrange the services for the convenience of the family and the clergy ahead of the cemetery and the funeral director. At the very least, the funeral director would appear to have an obligation to communicate and to coordinate arrangements with the other parties involved. It is possible, of course, that some funeral directors fail to involve cemeteries and clergy out of fear of their influence on families in the counseling process.

Perhaps most important of all, in connection with the scheduling process and the locations at which services are conducted, is the effect these factors have on the attendance at funeral services — an important source of the economic value of funerals as social events.

In order to encourage the greatest participation at funeral services and to eliminate any justification for nonparticipation (such as time or inconvenience), it would seem to be important for the time and duration of events to be made as convenient as possible for the family and friends who may participate in those services. How can this best be done? It would seem to require that funeral services be held at as few locations as possible, in facilities capable of accommodating large groups, the members of which are able to arrive shortly before services begin and to remain through the graveside or committal stage. It is obvious that this is most likely to occur if the services are conducted in a funeral home located directly in or adjacent to the cemetery in which interment occurs, with ample time allowed beforehand for the clergy to plan and to prepare their message to the family and friends in attendance.

A single location for services is a source of convenience for all who participate in them. When the ceremonies involved in a funeral are prolonged, with the first stage (visitation) held in a funeral home, followed by an automotive procession to a religious facility for the second stage, and a second automotive procession to the cemetery for a third and final stage (graveside or committal), some attrition is observed at various stages (especially during inclement weather). In most funerals, a majority of those who participate do so only in one or two of the three stages of the complete set of services.

Such partial participation has been addressed successfully in recent years in areas where families have been extended the option of holding the first two stages of the funeral at one location, the funeral home, provided that it is equipped with a chapel that is large enough and suitably enough appointed to handle this adequately. The combination of visitation and religious services in one place encourages increased participation in both stages.

It is further reasonable to suppose that when a funeral home and chapel are located in or next to a cemetery in which burial, entombment, or inurnment will take place, the participation in the third stage of services performed at the graveside is increased. It is at this stage that attendance at funerals is often sharply reduced due to the time involved in the procession from a funeral home or church to the cemetery. The location of a funeral home in or adjacent to the cemetery in which graveside services are held clearly increases the likelihood that participants at the earlier stages of a funeral will participate in this last stage.

The time at which services are scheduled is a further factor that may increase or decrease attendance at more than one stage. So is the arrangement for visitation prior to the funeral service. Provided the clergy is available and agreeable, there is no reason why funerals might not be scheduled in late afternoons or evenings in order to make them more convenient to attend.

The practice of holding wakes on evenings prior to the funeral often reduces attendance at the actual funeral service. From an objective point of view, of course, the wake is a social occasion, not a religious one. Nevertheless, it may suffice for people who simply want to express themselves in person to those they know are affected by the death. To encourage attendance at religious rites, it would seem to be in the interest of clergy to support the scheduling of funeral services in a manner which would attract those who might otherwise settle for paying their respects and expressing their condolences at essentially nonreligious or less religious occasions more conveniently scheduled.

Practical Considerations

None of this is to say that families should be discouraged from the use of church facilities, if such is desired or when a funeral home does not possess an appropriate chapel of adequate size. It is simply to point out that there are potential advantages to the clergy which flow from the use of a funeral home as the location of services which facilitate attendance at funerals. The procession from the funeral home to the church is thereby eliminated so that only a procession from the church to the cemetery is required. When the location of the funeral home is also the cemetery site, the procession from the funeral home to the cemetery is eliminated, which saves time. These are practical considerations which need to be weighed against the view that a religious facility is the most appropriate location for funeral services.

Under most conditions the locations of many churches are simply not well suited for daily events. Their parking facilities are inadequate and, moreover, when services are held in churches the processions between funeral home and church and between church and cemetery are awkward and time-consuming affairs. Hours may be spent by all concerned in going first to the funeral home, then to the church, and finally to the cemetery for various parts of the funeral service. Furthermore, many churches operate schools, with schoolyards filled with children at play on most weekdays in the school year; this is inconsistent with the solemnity desired at funerals.

If two or all three parts of the funeral are held in a single location, much time and difficulty can be saved by the participants, and this will encourage attendance at all of the ceremonies and tributes, both religious and social. There is also a practical economic effect of combining stages of funeral services in one or two locations. The cost of the funeral processions and of the personnel involved in coordinating services held in three locations are borne by the funeral home, but inevitably they are passed on to the family which pays for the funeral. The additional time required to separate the location of parts of the funeral service adds to the cost involved because equipment and personnel are tied up for long periods. Scheduling difficulties are also increased due to the variability surrounding the amount of time processions will take.

It is not an uncommon practice for the funeral homes in a metropolitan area to operate a cooperative livery pool, which owns, maintains, and schedules the use of limousines and hearses in funerals conducted by all the firms which are members. In this way such firms may reduce their individual overhead. As a result, however, the firms which rely on a common livery pool place themselves at the mercy of the scheduling of vehicles by the pool. The clergy, the family, and the funeral director in charge of services are compelled to accept a schedule for services requiring a motorcade based on the availability of equipment provided from the pool.

When there is a religious insistence on the use of church facilities requiring one or more motorcades, the effect is to benefit the providers of the livery equipment. When a funeral home with an appropriate chapel is located at a cemetery in which interment is to occur, the necessity and cost of a procession is eliminated or reduced to a fraction of the time required for services which are conducted at different locations.

In the interests of the families and others involved in funeral arrangements, it is important that these practical considerations and accommodations are fully recognized by religious authorities who are in a position to influence the use of such facilities by prohibiting them or describing them as "extreme options." The influence of the positions taken on such matters is obviously important in the case of funerals which include religious services involving the clergy. Statistics are hardly necessary to back up these points, and few are available. Based on the experience of the funeral homes in one large city, however, evidence has been submitted to Catholic church authorities to the effect that once mass was permitted in mortuary chapels by the archdiocese and the use of their chapels was encouraged by funeral directors and clergy alike, it became the choice in over 90 percent of funerals that included a Catholic religious service.

In another example of the effective modification of long-established customs and traditions due to the influence of religion, it may be pointed out that Catholic cemeteries throughout the country have added "interment" or "entombment" chapels in which committal services are held in lieu of traditional graveside services. The advantages of this departure from established practice are numerous, especially during winter months when the ground is frozen, during inclement weather, and at late afternoon or evening services. These advantages have appealed to families, clergy and cemeteries, and the practice has become more widely accepted. The archdiocese of Chicago, for example, has constructed committal chapels with temporary holding crypts in a number of its cemeteries. There is no doubt that the practice will continue to replace graveside services in cemeteries where it is made available.

Cremation and Competition

A further point on which the interaction between death care providers and the clergy is uneasy revolves around issues which influence directly the demand for particular forms of death care, such as cremation and interment. For example, the prohibition or discouragement of cremation among some religious groups is a factor which restricts the business of crematories. On the other hand, acceptance or encouragement of the practice is a source of concern for cemeteries without crematories. It is also a concern for funeral homes because cremation is often associated with some curtailment of funeral services, and even when it is not, the quality of caskets chosen by consumers may be affected. The effects of this choice are exacerbated by the pricing practices used by funeral homes. Whether or not cremation is involved, the acceptance by religious groups and clergy of memorial services without the presence of the body as a substitute for traditional funerals represents a threat to the business of funeral homes. Furthermore, the allowance of donations of the body to medical research, as well as the donation of organs, are other ways in which the operations of death care providers may be adversely affected by religious factors.

Perhaps the greatest potential for contention between clergy and funeral homes exists in those areas where large, well-situated religious cemeteries have the potential to enter into direct competition with commercial establishments by creating mortuaries at the site of those facilities. This has occurred at a large Catholic cemetery in Denver, but such operations seem unlikely to spread, given the questions of commercialization they raise. Alternatively, of course, it is possible that the operators of established funeral homes could enter into more joint ventures with religious or other not-for-profit cemeteries.

A statement published in 1990 by the National Catholic Cemetery Conference (NCCC) expressed concern about these various possibilities. It identified commercialization as a potentially dangerous trend:

> NCCC is concerned with the acquisition fever of the large death care companies. In their zeal to operate Catholic cemeteries, NCCC fears, these firms threaten to dilute and even destroy the sacred responsibility entrusted to Catholic cemeteries; providing a Catholic burial, one of the church's Corporal Works of Mercy.
>
> In a 1990 study on the future of Catholic cemeteries in the United States, "Corporate Invasion of the Sacred Realm" [by death care "conglomerates"] was listed as one of several problems to be confronted.

"These conglomerates are approaching bishops to manage and maintain Catholic cemeteries because they allegedly have 'cemetery experience,'" the report states. "In return, the diocese receives a percentage of plot/crypt sales, or an annual payment for a number of years…. The potential danger to the church is that our Catholic cemeteries could eventually become a 'business only' operation with the sacredness of the human body, the belief in the resurrection, and the Christian virtue of hope significantly reduced or eliminated" [Cronin, *American Cemetery*, December 1993].

Such concerns about commercialization of religious cemeteries, together with the strong ties between the clergy and established stand-alone funeral homes in most areas, diminish the likelihood that even suitable religious cemeteries will ever add funeral homes of their own or allow commercial operators to do so. Such obstacles may serve to limit the development of such facilities to commercial cemeteries and secular not-for-profit associations.

Although concerns about creeping commercialism expressed by those who control religious cemeteries have some validity, there are potential advantages to be achieved by cooperation between religious cemeteries and commercial death care providers. The ownership of cemeteries by religious organizations is a long-established custom in this country, and it conforms with the intimate relationship which exists between death and religion in the belief systems of many Americans. The development of commercial cemeteries in areas served by religious cemeteries has led inevitably to some degree of competition among religious and nonreligious facilities. The success of commercial ownership and operation, driven by the profit motive, has led to the refinement of management and sales techniques by profit-oriented death care companies. Noncommercial cemeteries, whether religious, fraternal, or municipal, have often been able to increase the effectiveness and efficiency of their operations by entering into construction, marketing, and management contracts with commercial firms.

Competition for such contracts would not appear to represent a "corporate invasion of the sacred realm." On the contrary, it allows death care facilities owned by noncommercial organizations with larger missions than the provision of death care to be operated by commercial organizations whose primary mission is to provide death care. Several benefits may result from such arrangements, including the addition of funeral homes to noncommercial cemeteries which lend themselves to the creation of combined operations. As described more fully in later chapters, the addition of mortuaries to commercial cemeteries does not appear to have jeopardized their sanctity, while it does appear to have added security and vitality to their locations. Those effects would seem to benefit the families who use religious and fraternal cemeteries while benefiting also the noncommercial organizations which own them.

13. *Alternative Death Care*

Overview

A common feature of the death care practices of most societies, or segments of diverse societies, is the extent to which they are subject to the influence of cultural traditions and customs, religious sentiments, and superstitions. For this influence, there are various anthropological, sociological, and psychological explanations. From an economic standpoint, this feature is simply a matter of fact, the effect of which is to increase the predictability of the demand for death care goods and services of specific types when life ends.

A death obviously triggers a demand for final disposition of the body. There is also generally a demand for ceremonial services to accommodate the social need of the family and other members of a community to participate jointly in a ritual observance of some major life passage. The funeral ceremony provides the group setting within which the void created by the death of a member is filled or closed in part through a process of collective involvement or communion. The demand for memorialization is an expression of the desire to recognize, to remember, and to commemorate the previous existence of others and of oneself with others.

All of these psychosocial needs underlie the demand for death care goods and services generally. Like goods and services of all kinds, however, the particular array of death care goods and services varies over time as socioeconomic and technological conditions change, resulting in adaptations in customs and traditions. New forms of death care are produced and made available to consumers, such as flat memorials instead of upright monuments, entombment in community mausoleums instead of earth burial, cremation followed by scattering or inurnment and niche interment of cremains, ceremonial funeral services departing from the traditional kind, and memorialization expressed in novel forms, such as memorial services, videotaped tributes, and commemoration in cyberspace.

By alternative death care is meant any form of mortuary services, final disposition or memorialization that does not conform with a long tradition of holding a funeral ceremony with the body present, placing the remains in a grave or a tomb, and identifying the site of interment with a monument or marker.

248

Direct Disposition

An extreme departure from traditional death care as practiced historically in the United States is the immediate disposal of the body after death by cremation or burial. In some areas this service is performed by direct disposition companies which provide only the limited mortuary services legally required with respect to the collection and disposition of a dead body. As required by law, these companies are run by licensed funeral directors who either own or contract with a cemetery or a crematory performing the burial or cremation. The first such operation, the Telophase Society, was founded in 1971 in San Diego, California, but others have since been established in other large metropolitan areas, where they compete with traditional death care providers (U.S. FTC, 1978, p. 82).

The essence of the threat posed to traditional death care businesses by the operation of these immediate disposition companies is that they eliminate many of the costs of maintaining the facilities and providing the goods and services commonly desired from full-service funeral homes, cemeteries, and memorial dealers. This enables immediate disposition firms to make a profit while charging a relatively low price (usually including a membership fee) consistent with the minimally required set of mortuary services they provide. For direct cremations, these include: collecting the dead body, filing the required permits, delivering the body to the crematory, and returning the cremains to the family. In the nature of this process, which is "designed to bypass both the mortuary and cemetery" as well as the memorial dealer, direct disposition does not permit a funeral service with the body present, but those who opt for this method of disposal may hold a memorial service to commemorate the death of the person whose remains have been so handled (U.S. FTC, 1978, p. 82).

It seems likely that the development and promotion of immediate cremation by direct disposition firms has contributed to the increased rate of cremation in their local markets and perhaps beyond. Two factors, however, have limited their influence on a national scale. One is the widespread desire of most families to have a traditional funeral service, and the other is the economics of a direct disposition organization as a profit-making institution. The low prices they are able to charge based on the low cost of the services they provide require that they operate on a large scale, handling a sufficient volume of cases to compensate for their low margin of profit. These factors have served to limit the reach of direct disposition firms beyond large metropolitan areas, reducing their significance as a competitive factor in most death care markets.

Memorial Societies

Prior to the development of profit-oriented firms providing direct disposition services, there had long been those who advocated simplicity and economy in arranging for death care, including cremation and memorial services rather than traditional funerals. In some areas those who shared such views organized so-called "funeral societies" or "memorial societies" to promote their collective interests. Most of these groups have formed consumer cooperatives, often assembled from members of a church, union, university faculty, or other local organization, for the purpose of providing information and assistance concerning arrangements for death care.

The major organization of these local groups is the Continental Association of Funeral and Memorial Societies (CAFMS). The CAFMS is a member of the U.S. Cooperative League, but unlike other consumer cooperative associations, funeral and memorial societies do not themselves provide death care to their members. In some cases they merely serve as clearing houses for information about alternative forms of death care and the establishments which provide it, but in other cases they search out and contract with cooperating providers. The societies themselves do not sell merchandise or services. Staffed by volunteers and financed by membership fees and donations, they distribute death education materials and lobby on behalf of their members as consumers of death care. An FTC staff report summarized their primary role as follows:

> In the funeral marketplace, memorial societies serve two primary functions: as a conduit for information to potential buyers about alternate funeral arrangements and prices and as an active bargaining agent on behalf of a group of buyers (*i.e.* the society's members). Due to various restrictions or the inability to obtain the cooperation of local funeral directors, many memorial societies are confined to the former role of information providers. In this respect, they serve to reduce the search costs and difficulties involved in individual attempts to obtain prices and information on funeral offerings from a variety of funeral homes. Members therefore have access to a greater amount of purchase information than, absent considerable effort, they would otherwise be able to obtain. Those societies which are able to enter agreements with funeral directors can obtain specified services for their members at prices determined in advance. Although the prices charged by funeral homes to memorial society members may be identical to the prices offered to the general public, a member can take advantage of the society's previous shopping efforts and the strong probability that the society has obtained comparatively low prices for services sought. Moreover, the society's group purchasing provides member buyers with additional protection against abusive treatment from the funeral director [U.S. FTC, 1978, pp. 83–84].

Functions of Memorial Societies

As organizations of death care consumers, the nature of funeral and memorial societies does not entail their inclusion as providers of death care. It is rather their function to act as a consumer collective or "buying alliance," which deals with death care providers on behalf of their members. The societies therefore do not replace the role of the funeral home, cemetery, or crematory, although the ways in which such providers transact business with the societies is significantly different than when they deal with consumers directly. We shall be concerned with the economic impact of this, but first it is necessary to establish the limits to which these consumer-based organizations may go. Specifically, the question may be asked whether their function may expand to include providing death care themselves in direct competition with commercial providers.

As a matter of fact, there are a few funeral and memorial societies which operate funeral homes as cooperative organizations. For example, some religious groups have their own burial societies whose members participate directly in the death care process, either under the auspices of the religious community or a participating funeral home. In the Jewish tradition, this is true of the *Chevra Kadisha*, which literally means "Holy Society." The societies are composed of religious community members who are devoted to preparing the dead for burial. A brief description of their ritual follows:

> After the funeral director has arranged for the attending physician to certify the individual's death, and after the body has been transported to the chapel, the *Chevra Kadisha* is called in by the rabbi or the funeral director to attend to the body. A *shomer* (watcher) stays with the body and recites Psalms, while the other members of the *Chevra Kadisha* wash the body and dress it as prescribed by Jewish law [Kolatch, 1985, pp. 179–80].

In addition to such do-it-yourself groups, some have advocated that individuals and families should become directly involved in providing death care for deceased persons. *Caring for Your Own Dead* (Carlson, 1988) is the title of a manual which explains what one needs to know before attempting the task, but it is doubtful that many people are willing to undertake this kind of activity in contemporary American society.

Supporters of the concept of consumer control over the death care process have envisaged, however, the eventual development of consumer-owned facilities devoted to "full service" for consumers of death care and other products. "Full service means full control of the process, no matter the field, in which the consumer is engaged," according to Arvio (1974, p. 58). "With such control comes a sense of controlling prices and quality. Negotiation with owners is one step. To become the owners is the last step on the ladder" (p. 59). Realistically, of course, this is no more likely to happen within the death care economy than it would be in food processing, movie making, pharmaceuticals manufacturing, or any other sector in developed economies.

There is something wistful in such ideas which reflects a longing for a simpler time. Arvio notes, however, that "Memorial societies, by and large, have felt it helpful to locate funeral directors who will cooperate with their members. Because of the traditional secretiveness and suspicion one finds in the funeral fraternity, this is not a matter of thumbing one's way through the Yellow Pages and merely making a phone call. But some memorial societies have been able to develop mutual agreements, with assured price lists made available to members" (p. 43).

Cooperating Death Care Providers

The last statement was written before the promulgation of a federal trade rule which requires funeral homes to provide price lists to all consumers, but that is not to the point. The intention of the memorial society, as a consumer alliance, is to obtain prices from a provider "which compare favorably to rates offered the general public" (Arvio, 1974, p. 43). To accomplish this, the memorial society negotiates a schedule of prices, based on a limited variety of arrangements reflecting the interests of its members. For one society described by Arvio, the variety of services included: "Immediate Cremation," "Immediate Burial," "Cremation with Viewing and Attendance," "Burial with Viewing and Attendance," and "Delivery to Medical School."

Because of the number of members represented by a memorial society, there is an economic incentive for funeral directors to negotiate a price schedule with them which does not necessarily cover the full cost of the variant forms of limited services provided. This incentive lies in the unused capacity of many funeral homes and the price discrimination they practice. The specified mortuary services provided to memorial society members fall into the low end of the range of goods and services delivered as a part of the mix experienced by participating establishments. This allows such establishments to cover variable costs and contribute something to fixed costs. It also may allow a funeral home to benefit from any "trading up" to traditional funerals by the survivors of society members who plan only minimal services for themselves.

Consumer Welfare

Underlying the historical development of memorial societies has been an ideological predisposition toward radical reform of traditional American death care practices. Clearly, the movement has been associated with ideas of consumerism and consumer control. Supporters of the concept of the societies have generally expressed dissatisfaction with the funeral establishment, and with the cost of traditional funerals, especially the merchandise component of it. Again, this is due in no small measure to the irrational pricing methods long used by funeral homes, which results in the appearance that the casket accounts for a large part of the funeral costs and prices.

The adoption of FTC rules regarding pricing and price quotation by funeral homes may have offset some of the momentum behind the formation and growth of memorial societies. What still exists as a factor in the business practices of funeral homes and is a source of support for the movement is the continued reliance of most establishments on at-need sales, which contribute to allegations that psychological pressure is applied in the sales process. As Arvio (1974) explains, in making his case for memorial societies:

> Consumers first feel their frustrations in personal dealings with the Funeral establishment. Then they share those feelings with others. Concern about

high prices, about buying unwanted goods and services, about the sense of pressure leads to the development of memorial societies. Through the act of planning, a consumer who knows what he wants thus becomes freer to exercise, or have exercised on his behalf, his own wishes. A funeral director thus has some restriction or restraints placed on him by the consumer who has planned [p. 59].

Arvio further explains the benefits of planning:

Consumers who have planned their own funerals expect their wishes to be respected, not only by their survivors but by funeral parlors themselves. The search for friendly funeral directors follows. Arrangements are made with one or more who agree to respect the planning arrangements and who may, in fact, spell out the costs and details of low-cost funerals and agree to offer these to memorial society members [p. 59].

With more emphasis on pre-need selling by funeral homes, especially those which are combined establishments or units of clusters operated by regional or national companies, the role of memorial societies may now be served directly by those providers. The memorial society as a grass-roots consumer protection organization seems less necessary than it did under different conditions in the past. Although societies will continue to be served by providers as a source of the contribution they make to their operations, they will be competing with the pre-need sales programs. Consequently the "buying alliances" represented by memorial societies may often be unable to negotiate prices which differ much from the prices at which comparable death care is available to the general public. Even so, it is possible that memorial society members still may benefit from the comparison shopping that the societies have done in an area and the extent to which they have identified the lowest priced services offered by an establishment (U.S. FTC, June 1978, p. 84).

Some funeral homes have responded to the growth of memorial societies by developing a competitive product consisting of a nontraditional memorial service in connection with the choice of cremation by its customers. A funeral home operated together with a crematory and a cemetery in Hollywood, Florida, has recently established a "Cremation Memorial Center" designed to provide an alternative to the traditional funeral home and the memorial society. The operation of the facility is described in *The American Funeral Director* (November 1993):

The Cremation Memorial Center offers everything from a *direct cremation* service without a ceremony, to a *traditional cremation*. Our cremation remembrance services, or receptions, are generally held during one period, unlike a traditional funeral with burial that may utilize our funeral home for two or three days.

A *memorial reception* is a one-to-two hour gathering in either the atrium, garden room, or gallery of the center without a ceremony. A ceremony does not take place during this event. Coffee is provided and a serving table is available for the family to bring in finger foods or it can be catered. A *memorial ceremony* is a gathering that includes a memorial service conducted by a clergy member or other officiant. The urn, or closed casket, can be present if the family wishes. All of the items mentioned in the reception can be a part of this one-to-two hour ceremony.

We also offer a memorial service at another place. The Cremation Memorial Center staff would arrange the service, be present for the ceremony to handle flowers, care for the registration of guests, and clean up at the conclusion. This allows the family to have a gathering at their Moose Lodge, home, or even a park if they wish....

For those families that prefer placement at sea, the cremation memorial center offers a variety of options, including the use of a 61-foot chartered yacht for those families desiring to accompany the cremains.

This is an innovative attempt by a funeral home to redress the momentum of memorial societies by offering a variety of alternatives to the traditional funeral. According to an owner of the facility, its services are moderately priced at less than traditional funerals but more than those arranged through memorial societies. The volume of the facility was 80 cases in its first year, followed by 135 in the second.

Fun Funerals

The memorial services to which reference has been made throughout are examples of do-it-yourself arrangements which depart from the structured ceremonies customarily associated with traditional funerals. Nevertheless, they commonly include a modicum of the decorum usually associated with the occasion. Beyond such less structured forms of ceremonial services, however, there exists another limit of death care which consists of bizarre rites, usually prearranged by the deceased party. These "creative" ceremonies, styled "fun funerals" by the *Wall Street Journal*, are chosen by "a small but growing number of people.... By planning their own send-offs, the forward-looking folks insure a memorable goodbye to loved ones" (Dolan, May 20, 1993).

As an example of this trend, Dolan describes the funeral of a popular Californian politician as taking place in a hotel ballroom in Sacramento where "3000 revelers float among bouquets of balloons and mingle around a trio of bars, an ice sculpture drips over the buffet. A seven piece band, led by a vocalist in a black lace dress, blares out James Brown's 'I Feel Good.' In the midst of the action is the party's host — lying in a flag-draped coffin."

Another example cited is the case of a man dying of AIDS who has planned two different services apparently designed for different audiences: one to be held in the town where he grew up and the other in San Francisco, where he lives. The former will be a traditional religious service, while the latter will feature a videotape of himself. The *Journal* article reports that the man "says he has 'picked some excellent speakers' for the obsequies, handled the catering arrangements and hired a graphic artist to design the invitations. 'I wanted to get on with living, and not keep worrying about dying,' he says."

Also cited is the case of a San Francisco bar owner named Smith who, after learning he had terminal cancer,

> planned a yacht cruise for 100 friends, set to sail the Saturday after his death. Dave Rose, a friend, recalls that Mr. Smith "handed me an invitation, and said, 'I'm having a party. I just don't have the date on it yet.'"
>
> The cruise featured a jazz band and a blues group, plenty of refreshments and a scattering of the deceased's ashes to the playing of "I'll Be Seeing You." Friends have been talking about it ever since.

The article further describes the case of a woman baseball fan who chose to be buried in the uniform of her favorite team in a casket decorated in the team's colors. The music at her service included "Take Me Out to the Ballgame." Her daughter, who at first was afraid of what people might think, later reported that most guests "were really moved."

Other cases described include those handled by a funeral director in Glendale, California, who during thirty years in business: "has met many creative requests, including one from a women who asked to be interred with a portable TV tuned to her favorite soap operas. Friends of a Hell's Angel placed switchblade knives, brass knuckles and marijuana cigarettes beside the biker's body, which was to be cremated."

One couple brought in a parakeet for the funeral director to embalm, "stipulating that the bird be entombed with the spouse who dies first. 'That was about 12 years ago, and we're still diligently holding onto Tweety Bird,' he says."

Another incident described involved a funeral director who "fulfilled a woman's wish to be buried at sea in a hand-carved canoe. Full-body burial isn't legal off California's coast, so he and a colleague 'put her in the back of a U-Haul truck and drove to Oregon,' he says. They then rented a fishing boat, went 15 miles offshore, and pushed the canoe overboard."

The article goes on to describe a variety of creative ideas:

> San Francisco's Ghia Gallery, for instance, has decorated caskets with graffiti and psychedelic art, and it is developing a line of coffins, each carved from an individual tree. Loretto Casket Co. in Tennessee sells coffins emblazoned with the logos of major universities. At a columbarium in San Francisco, people have found their final resting places in tobacco humidors, cameras and cookie jars, while patrons of other vaults have asked to be stored in a favorite hunting decoy or bowling pin. Hunters can arrange to have Iowa-based Canuck's Sportsman's Memorials, Inc. place their ashes into shotgun shells and fire them into the woods.
>
> A venture once proposed by a Florida group to launch cremated remains into space never got off the ground, however.
>
> And some wishes just can't be honored. Kevin Minke, a counselor at the Telophase Society, a San Diego cremation concern, says he has had customers who "say they want their ashes thrown out with the garbage or flushed down the toilet." Both methods are illegal.

Even funeral directors may be drawn to funerals with flair. According to the article, one expressed a desire "to be buried off Canada's Coast in fishing gear. 'I love to fish and I want them to put me out there with the fish'. ... Another has planned a morning cruise for his friends with a menu of pork chops and eggs to accompany a scattering of his ashes. His wife wants her ashes tossed from a hot-air balloon. 'She's always wanted to take one of those balloon trips,' he says, 'but she's afraid of heights.'"

Backlash

If the cases described in the previous section prove anything, it is the truth of the adage "There is no accounting for tastes," even in death. On hearing such tales, one is tempted to pass over them, noting that a disproportionate number seem to be taken from California, where tastes have tended to be more highly varied than in the rest of the country. No doubt the motivation behind such cases is a desire to be creative and humorous to the very end. And why not? To each his own, after all. Isn't there something to be said for demonstrating one's virtuosity and sense of humor at one's own funeral?

Perhaps there are situations, including some of those mentioned above, in which the answer is yes. In general, however, a case can be made for the view that bizarre funerals, even when they are pre-planned by the deceased, are disrespectful, not only to the memory of the deceased but also to the wishes of the survivors and participants who want to show respect for that memory. There is nothing funny about asking people of different sensibilities to participate in bizarre ceremonies which make them uncomfortable at an already difficult time. A source of the value of traditional funerals or even memorial services is that they are familiar means which have proven themselves as forms of ceremonialization which serve the purpose of allowing participants to interact comfortably in the conditions that exist on such occasions. Fun funerals that include bizarre elements interfere with this respectful interaction.

Because of this interference, fun funerals have precipitated some degree of backlash. For example, a deacon in the Catholic archdiocese of San Francisco is quoted in the article mentioned as an example of someone who does not approve of "excessive merrymaking" at funerals. The deacon is quoted as saying "the emphasis 'should be on prayer for the dead, and on ... consolation for those going through the mourning process. I'm not sure if a great big party does a lot to really help'" (Dolan, *Wall Street Journal*, May 20, 1993).

It is not necessary, however, to depend on religious objections concerning this point. The question recently has been decided by no less a secular authority than Miss Manners (Judith Martin), who discussed the matter in a recent newspaper column entitled "What's the Best Kind of Funeral?" in which she suggests that things have gone too far in the direction of "anything goes" celebrations at funeral or memorial services.

As she points out, a source of the value and utility of traditional religious services is that they tend to have been honed over generations to the point where they express their meaning with beauty and dignity. Yet, she admits, such funerals may not be appropriate for everyone.

But neither is a lot of what is going on now appropriate for anyone. Miss Manners has been to "celebrations" at which the chief comfort is that the person being celebrated has blessedly been spared the danger of dying of embarrassment....

Summing up any person's life is also fraught with opportunities to offend, if for no other reason than that people tend to see the same individual in widely different ways, and none of them may resemble what the dead person had in mind.

Miss Manners has noticed an unfortunate tendency lately toward brutal frankness, as if the eulogy were an impartial historical record. The idea should be to put forth as good a case as one can make for the deceased, while still keeping it plausible to the mourners.

Remember the rule about speaking well of the dead? Now that is what the deceased would have wanted [Martin, *Universal Features Syndicate*, March 27, 1994].

The value of this commentary lies in the fact that it expresses the observations of a popular columnist on the problems involved in the trend away from traditional funeral services to memorial services to "creative" services at which anything goes and no rules apply. There is room in death care, of course, for variety which makes funeral services more meaningful affairs. But to depart far from established guidelines is to invite some degree of social uncertainty and discomfort, according to Miss Manners. If the past is any guide, furthermore, there are limits to the creativity which most people will accept in these areas of life which most have always considered too important to treat lightly. The object of the concern expressed by Miss Manners was the tendency toward excessively "creative" funerals, but she did not address a form of death care which is even more bizarre — freezing bodies permanently.

Cryonic Death Care

Cooling boards and corpse coolers have long been used by morgues and mortuaries for short-term preservation of the body, prior to embalming or final disposition. Cold retards the decomposition process, and complete freezing of the body prevents the onset of rigor mortis until the body is thawed. Medical uses of cooling or freezing commonly include the preservation of blood, tissues, organs, and semen (animal and human). Based on the demonstrated success of preserving human bodies at low temperatures, the cryonic movement is founded on the assumption that medical science will eventually be able to undo the damage of the freezing process. Successfully thawed out, the dead person "is restored to life, cured of his disease and rejuvenated. The man lives on until he dies of another disease or old age; then he is again frozen and the entire cycle repeated" (Hendin, 1973, p. 198).

The process of preservation in anticipation of future resurrection involves freezing the recently dead body by placing it in a container resembling a thermos bottle, cooled by liquid nitrogen, which has a constant temperature of

-321°F. The process is advocated by cryonics societies which provide presuspension counseling and guidance, but presumably it entails some participation by a licensed funeral director and the suspended body is stored in a funeral home, cemetery, or elsewhere.

Technically, the organizations which provide the services required for cryonic suspension of dead bodies are a part of the death care economy. Economically, however, they are an insignificant part. For present purposes, they are interesting primarily for what they indicate about the extent to which people will go to deny the finality of death and its consequences, the decomposition of the body. One hesitates to include cryogenic suspension under the category of final disposition since the kind of death care provided is not intended to be final. It is perhaps best described as a temporary disposition. It can be viewed as an energy-intensive stage of the traditional cooling of bodies to prevent their rapid deterioration following death. Thus it appears to be an extended form of mortuary services rendered in connection with death which is not regarded as a final event.

No matter how scientific or secular this form of death care may seem, it has a spiritual quality like most other forms: it hopes against hope for life after death, not in heaven, but right here on earth in a miraculously and repetitively repaired body. Others resist the end of life and physical existence with less tenacity. Who is right? That is not the question; the question is: Who is willing to back up his hope with a sufficient endowment to maintain the required temperature? The answer seems to be: not many.

Alternative Forms of Final Disposition

So far the discussion has focused on alternative funerals, usually followed by one of three modes of disposing of dead bodies: burial, entombment, and cremation followed by further final disposition. As a matter of taste and social convention, these have tended to be the only alternatives which suit contemporary American sentiments and circumstances. Other forms of final disposition, such as collective ("pit") burial, water burial, exposure to the elements, animal consumption, and cannibalism, do not conform with widespread and deep-seated views of the decent and dignified treatment of human remains. Until recently neither did cremation. Strong advocacy and commercial availability were necessary to establish a foothold for that practice, but it is unlikely that any of the methods mentioned above are likely to attract advocates. Few, we think, are likely to be moved by critics of American death care who have advocated processing human remains into fertilizer as a means of dealing with food shortages in various parts of the world.

As a matter of fact, it is an interesting commentary on the stability of death care practices that burial itself has been subject to so few modifications over the years. Most of these have involved the tendency to use more protective caskets and vaults for the buried body as opposed to wooden coffins which decay, returning the decomposed remains back to the earth, literally. Traditional adherence to the single use of graves of standard length and depth, with no further disturbance of the remains, has prevailed in spite of criticism of the rate at which such conventional burials use up scarce land. It would seem that various measures which conserve land use such as multiple interment, vertical interment, deep burial, and the like, would have attracted advocates and commercial experimentation. Nevertheless, they have not. Even if it is claimed that such innovations have not been economically desirable for those in the industry to exploit, it is odd that they have not been advocated by others.

As Curl (1993) observes, the use of ossuaries, or "charnel houses" where bones or ashes of the dead are kept, has long been acceptable in Europe and in other parts of the world. It is practiced also in southern Louisiana, where it was transplanted from France. Variations of the practice are advocated by Curl as alternatives to cremation, which he believes has some objectionable features:

> Cremation now accounts for the disposal of the majority of the dead in Britain. The amount of energy taken to destroy a human body is very considerable, for it takes about an hour and a quarter in a furnace at high temperatures to do so. It would be much less extravagant in terms of energy, and more ecologically apt, to bury in the mediaeval fashion in shallow graves without coffins, and to re-use the ground after a decent passage of time. Francis Seymour Haden, in his letters to *The Times* in 1975, said that cremation was "a wild project" and that to "drive into vapour the bodies of the 3,000 people who die weekly in Greater London alone, at a needless cost," was an "infinite waste." Certainly it would seem that he was right, and that a less destructive and more rational return to ecological methods would be more reasonable: the bones could eventually be stored in catacombs, and possibilities for awe-inspiring designs are endless [p. 361].

Continuing, Curl cites examples of European practices which might be adopted elsewhere as alternatives to cremation and traditional burial and entombment:

> The catacombs of Paris, and the great charnel houses of Europe are examples to us, for often the Paris cemeteries have graves for a limited tenure. When the lease is up, the bones are stored in the large underground catacombs and charnel houses, so the ground is always used. The great galleries of Italian cemeteries would suffer the fate of the catacombs of Brompton and other British cemeteries unless the income for a place of burial were ensured. Italy still builds huge galleries with *loculi* in her cemeteries, and these spaces are leased at realistic figures to make the upkeep of the buildings possible. In Spain and Portugal tombs similar to those in New Orleans are common, arranged in banks or galleries. Even niches in the columbaria at Père-Lachaise are let for very short periods, so the space can always be had there, and prices can be adjusted with rising costs. The system of ensuring that realistic sums are paid to ensure that cemeteries are maintained prevails throughout Europe. The Roman Catholic countries naturally maintain their graveyards, and vandalism in Italy, Spain, and France is practically unknown compared with the state of affairs in Britain. In Scandinavia,

Holland, and Germany a less urban type of burial ground is usual, and planting plays a more important part in the design. Vandalism and maintenance seem to raise fewer problems in those countries as well [pp. 361–62].

In another passage Curl refers to the objectionable features of cremation and points out that technological modifications of the process have been attempted:

> Cremation appealed to rational reformers who were worried about hygiene and about the amount of land being used for cemeteries. From the last century, cremation has been quickly established as a major mode of disposal. There are indications, however, that cremation has brought its own problems. This mode of disposal is currently very expensive, and likely to become more so with rising costs of fuel. Experiments are being conducted in America to reduce the mass of human bodies without using the crude method of burning. A corpse can be cooled and solidified by using liquid nitrogen, after which it can be pulverized in an automatic crusher so that it is reduced in size by "freeze frying" [sic] which removes all body fluids. The remains can then be stored in an urn or casket. This method is likely to be expensive, however, and so a rational means of disposal involving burial at sea (which would provide food for fish), or shallow earth burial might well be sought [p. 359].

The development of these new means of disposal remains in the experimental stage, and their acceptance by the public is far from assured. Yet the resemblance to cremation would appear to favor their eventual acceptability as an alternative to that practice. Modifications in the traditional practices of burial and entombment of dead bodies in a single grave or tomb of conventional dimensions, without subsequent disturbance, may pose greater obstacles to wide acceptance.

In Europe, where limited-tenure burial and ossuaries have been used, they have generally been imposed on the public by fiat. Under freedom of choice, there appears to be a strong preference on the part of the public for perpetual interment — for a final resting place that is indeed final. Yet there is something about the "recycling" of graves and tombs which may appeal to ecologically conscious consumers. The same concerns that led to the development or imposition of reuse in other countries may now provide a basis for the promotion of that practice in this one.

Recycling of Graves

An example of the need for innovation in burial practices as land resources become strained is provided by recent events in the United Kingdom. Reference was made above to the rapid rise in the cremation rate in England during the postwar period. Nevertheless, the annual number of burials has tended to overtake the remaining supply of available burial space in many areas of England, including the city of London. Symptomatic of the general problem is the City of London Cemetery, where more than half a million bodies have been buried since 1856, making it the largest municipal cemetery in Europe. According to the *New York Times* the cemetery is now expected to run out of space for new burials in less than three years, with no new facilities currently planned to take its place. Other large cemeteries in London have only enough space to last through the end of the century. Meanwhile, the demand for burial space is expected to grow due to the aging of the population, which includes various segments who resist cremation for reasons of cultural or personal preference (Schmidt, *New York Times*, September 20, 1994).

To address this pressing problem, legislation endorsed by the British cemetery industry has been proposed which would allow graves to be recycled by permitting new burials atop old ones. In the past the reuse of graves by family members has previously been permitted at municipal death care facilities like the City of London Cemetery, but the proposed legislation would extend the prevailing practice to allow reuse of graves by unrelated parties:

> Under the proposal, a cemetery could reuse a grave only after 75 years had passed, and then only if it was unable to locate any surviving family members. For those graves, the cemetery would be allowed to exhume the remains, rebury them at a greater depth and place the casket of the new tenant on top.
> Unless the headstone had special architectural significance, the old grave marker would be removed, although the cemetery would keep a register of original burials [Schmidt, *New York Times*, September 20, 1994].

Noting the impact of such changes on the established conception of the grave as a "private place" and a permanent one, Schmidt reports a range of views regarding the proposed legislation:

> "We have got to rethink the idea of perpetuity, so far as the grave is concerned," said Bruce Hall, an Australian consultant working with British cemetery managers. "Putting new burials on top of old burials makes better economic sense for the family and the cemetery, and it is good land use planning too."
> The notion of the grave as a limited tenancy agreement, rather than a final resting place, not only plays havoc with a lot of funeral oratory, but it is provoking negative reaction as well.
> "It would be a sacrilege if they started disturbing graves," protested Mary Powell, a member of the local government council in Islington, a London district with one of the cemeteries in question, where several members of her family are buried. She said the whole notion smacked of "putting profit before people's feelings" [*New York Times*, September 20, 1994].

One wonders what is meant by the latter comment since 90 percent of the cemeteries in England are municipal facilities owned and operated by local governments, not commercial firms. As the account in the *New York Times* points out, the British Parliament would have to pass legislation delegating to municipalities the necessary authority to permit recycling of graves, "and there are doubts that the current Conservative Government would support such a proposal." Still, "more than a century after overcrowding first caused London's cemeteries to push into the suburbs, Britain is running out of graveyard space. With the cost of land even outside the city prohibitively high, the Government is being forced to rethink the economics of death and burial."

Supposedly, burial at sea and "woodland burials," whatever they may be, are under consideration. As a sign of the dimensions of the problems, the *New York Times* reports that "In an editorial last month, *The Guardian*, a London newspaper, endorsed the idea of recycling graves, arguing that Britain 'now faces a fresh need for a thoughtful and socially responsible debate on the disposal of the dead'" (Schmidt, *New York Times*, September 20, 1994].

Impact of the Remains

A final example of an alternative form of final disposition cum memorialization is provided by the project of a group of funeral directors who proposed to launch cremains into space, allowing them to orbit forever at approximately 1,900 miles above the earth. In an account of the proposal, the *New York Times* quoted a Florida funeral director involved with the project: "Celestis is a post-cremation service. ... We further reduce and encapsulate them [the cremains], identify each by name, Social Security number and a religious symbol and place them into the payloader" (January 25, 1985).

This sounds humorous, but the reason for relating it here is serious. It vividly illustrates the distinctions drawn earlier between bodily and cremated remains. Physically, legally, and psychologically the intact dead body is a burden because of its large volume and septic nature. These qualities strictly limit the set of options available for final disposition and complementary memorialization. The smaller volume and antiseptic nature of cremains greatly expands the potential set of alternative options for final disposition and memorialization available to consumers. For example, the portability and acceptable divisibility of the cremains allows a minute portion of them to be incorporated within items of jewelry which may be worn as shrines.

Such alternative forms of final disposition and memorialization are novel, but the desires for the fundamental functions they perform on behalf of bereaved survivors are the same as always. These constant human desires express themselves as demand for death care goods and services which vary through time. This persistent demand within a society supports and sustains the structure of the death care economy within it, a structure that continually adapts itself in ways designed to provide the particular goods and services desired by consumers at any particular time. The extant structure of the American death care economy is examined in the next chapter.

PART VI

There is one thing more powerful than all the armies in the world; and that is an idea whose time has come.

*Closing entry in Victor Hugo's diary
on the night he died, 1885*

14. *The Structure of the Death Care Economy*

Structure and Change

By the structure of the death care economy is meant the organization of facilities for the production and distribution of death care goods and services in a society. This structure consists of many elements: the number and locations of death care establishments of different types, sizes, and ages; the characteristics of the firms which own and operate such establishments, including their legal forms (proprietorships, partnerships, private and public corporations); the variety of inputs used by establishments to produce the variety of outputs they provide; the number of the actual and potential customers of establishments in a geographic area; and the lines of demarcation between the boundaries of their markets whether geographic, demographic, or other.

The arrangement of all these elements of structure and infrastructure, taken together at a particular point in time, presents a static view of the structure at that time. A series of such static views, taken at various points in time (a "time series"), provides a dynamic view of changes occurring in the structure over time. Such structural changes may be discerned as evidence of past trends and developments in an economic sector. Typically, an analysis of these is used as a basis for the consideration of possible future changes and their implications in an economic sector. This chapter attempts to provide such an analysis for the death care sector of the economy.

Structure and Stability

In dynamic societies the structures of many sectors of the economy undergo continual and often dramatic changes. Virtually all manufacturing industries and most service industries of the U.S. economy have experienced a series of structural shifts throughout the twentieth century and especially in the postwar era. Almost no sector has escaped the effects of continued technological, demographic, economic, social, cultural, and other changes in the organization

264

of the economic activities occurring within it. One has only to think of developments in the retail sector or in the restaurant and computer industries to be reminded of the swiftness of structural changes that challenge producers and confront consumers under modern conditions.

Yet, in spite of what may appear to be a constant onslaught of change in the variety of goods and services available and in the manner of their production and distribution, the patterns of consumption have exhibited remarkable stability when viewed in terms of the general categories of consumption. While the character and quality of specific goods and services produced and consumed have changed dynamically, the fundamental categories of consumer expenditures, based on human wants and needs in general, have remained relatively constant for generations. Proof of this lies in the virtually identical list of categories used to classify consumer expenditures in 1935 (Lough, 1935, p. 92) and today in the *National Income and Product Accounts of the United States: 1995*:

1935	1995
Food and soft drinks	Food, beverages, and tobacco
Alcoholic Beverages	
Tobacco	
Clothing	Clothing, accessories, and jewelry
Women's Clothing	
Men's Clothing	
Personal appearance	Personal care
Transportation	Transportation
Home Maintenance	Housing
Housing, Furnishings, Supplies,	Household operations
Fuel and Light, Household services	
Sickness and Death	Medical care
	Personal business
	Life insurance expenses, Legal services, funeral and burial expenses
Recreation	Recreation
Social-Cultural Activities	Education and research
Withholdings (Taxes and Savings)	Religious and welfare activities

Allowing for minor discrepancies in descriptive terminology (for example, "Sickness and Death" in 1935 versus "Medical care" in 1995), there has been virtually no change in the major categories of consumer expenditure. What has changed so noticeably in our lifetimes is not the fundamental nature of goods and services demanded by consumers, based on needs and wants of human beings, but the specific nature of goods and services available to consumers for the satisfaction of those needs and wants. The driving force behind the changes in specific items produced and consumed is the technological progress which has driven the development of so many new goods and services, as well as new ways and means for organizing many industries economically. To what extent do these facts pertain to the industries of the death care sector?

As one of the fundamental categories of consumer goods and services, death care was recognized as a unique category in the early classification of consumer expenditures. Even before such classification systems were devised, however, the event of human death has always presented every generation of human beings with at least one fundamental need: the need to dispose of the dead body. Nothing has altered this basic necessity. Our fullest understanding of the meaning and significance of death may have developed in different ways, and the conditions under which we live may have changed, requiring us to adapt our behavior in order to meet our needs in the event of death, in the ways of our time. But the physical need to dispose of the body following the event of death is fundamental. Moreover, it is a pressing need experienced in a social context which virtually forces the living to confront and to deal with the inevitable consequences of human mortality at various points in their lives.

Advances in science and technology have not altered this fundamental need, even if they have altered the technical means of disposal, but even here the effect has been slight. The strength of socially and culturally reinforced beliefs in the propriety of traditional means of disposal — burial, entombment, and cremation followed by further disposal — has been sufficient to retard the development of any really novel means of disposal. In a similar way, the strength of socially and culturally reinforced beliefs about the propriety of traditional funeral services incorporating rites and ceremonies has served to retard the development of novel ways of providing the place and means for enacting the rituals of grievous ceremony after the event of death. These two strong undercurrents of stability in society from ancient through modern times have played a dominant role in moderating the pace and degree of change in the structure of the death care economy.

The implications of stability in the means of disposal will be considered first. Until relatively recently, consumer preference for either burial or entombment, both of which were provided by monumented cemeteries or memorial parks, was fostered. The structural changes in the organization and operation of cemeteries, resulting in the development of memorial gardens and parks with standardized markers, had a negative impact on the operations of independent monument dealers and changed the landscape but not the function of American cemeteries.

Recent growth in the demand for cremation came about largely as a result of the addition of crematories to cemeteries and mortuaries, a development which has changed the existing structure at the margin in those areas and markets where it has occurred. The effect of the operation of these added facilities would have been limited if cremation had been accepted by consumers as a mere pre-final stage in the final disposition process. But cremation was advocated instead as an alternative to complete death care. As a result of acceptance of this view, the spread of crematories affected the demand for goods and services used in every stage of the process, such as traditional funerals (caskets), cemetery products, and durable memorials. The structural impact of this distinctly American view of cremation has affected production of the outputs of cemeteries, mortuaries, memorial dealers, and casket manufacturers. The attempt to alter this view so that cremation is seen as a mere pre-final stage in the final disposition part of the death care process has the potential for altering the structure yet again, but in the reverse direction.

Another source of stability in the structure of the death care economy has been the constant demand for traditional funeral services maintained in part by the growth in population during the years since cremation became more acceptable in the United States. Adherence by consumers to traditional funerals with the body present has brought funeral homes a steady source of demand for the basic products (goods and services) they are equipped to provide and on which their economic survival depends. Pricing flexibility has generally allowed most funeral homes to compensate for the effects of unfavorable demographic factors in their markets as well as for a growing demand for alternative services on the part of some customers, especially those opting for cremation. Most funeral homes have tended to survive for generations as stable businesses serving their markets in the community, often operating out of the same facility. The average mortuary establishment is more than 40 years old, and funeral homes more than 100 years old are not unusual (Hopke, vol. 2, 1990, p. 250). Modern memorial parks date from early in this century, and many cemeteries are well over a century old. This element of structure in the death care economy has been highly stable, with changes occurring at the margins as a few establishments exit the sector and a few new ones are added each year. Given the permanence of cemeteries and the economic stability of funeral homes, the structure of the economy they comprise has been highly stable.

To understand the current structure, it is useful to consider the conditions under which these types of death care establishments emerged as providers of goods and services desired by consumers in connection with the event of death in our society.

Structural Evolution and Adaptation

In the early days of the American colonies and states, funerals were performed by the families of deceased persons, often using caskets obtained from local cabinet makers and hearses provided by local livery stables. As communities grew, the opportunity arose for the creation of a separate type of business to provide death-related merchandise and services to families who desired to purchase death care. This led to the development in the late nineteenth century of funeral homes operated by funeral directors or undertakers, as they were then known. The services provided by such establishments ended with the final disposition of bodies in family burial grounds, church, or municipal cemeteries. The family then arranged for a marble shop to erect an appropriate monument, if desired. Most funerals thus involved a family in a series of arrangements made with several separate providers of death care.

As many communities experienced growth, the traditional separation of death care providers into three different types of businesses persisted for several reasons discussed at various points. One of these was the specialized nature of the occupations of the owners of each type of business, which restricted the scope of their business activities to only one component of death care, thus limiting the capital investment required and affording economy. Funeral homes owned by funeral directors did not have to invest in land for a cemetery or the equipment required by a stone cutter. In some cases they practiced their trade from their homes, which accounts for the terms "funeral home" and "funeral parlor."

For the convenience of their clientele, it was necessary for funeral homes to be located within the communities they served. Early family, church, and municipal burial grounds were also located within local communities, but these were eventually superseded by large cemeteries and memorial parks owned at first by not-for-profit associations and later by commercial operators. The latter might have included funeral directors, but generally they did not — presumably because of the directors' specialized occupations and the costs of entering into the cemetery business. The initial investment required for establishing a new cemetery or memorial park at a suitable location was often sizeable. To justify such an investment as a commercial matter, a cemetery was required to operate on a larger scale than a funeral home was, usually by serving as the site of final disposition for the cases handled by several of the funeral homes in a given area. Ownership of that cemetery by one of those funeral homes might well have affected the cemetery's ability to attract the cases referred by rival funeral homes. This was an obstacle to the common ownership of funeral homes and cemeteries. A similar kind of obstacle prevented cemeterians from entering into the operation of funeral homes. In some instances these obstacles became codified in the laws of some states.

Obviously, the structure of the death care economy has been influenced by such obstacles to integrated ownership and operation, which have served to limit the size and scope of most death care establishments. This has ensured a high degree of fragmentation of the infrastructure of the death care economy. The perpetuation of this fragmentation has historically served to keep many units of the death care sector small and weak, resulting in a structural web involving interrelationships and interdependencies among different types of death care providers and related enterprises. As an adaptation to this fragmentation, strategic alliances were forged among various elements within and without the structure of the death care sector in order to serve separate interests in mutually beneficial ways. One of these adaptations was the formation of separate trade associations as official bodies dedicated to the pursuit of the special interests of their members. These trade groups have served to sustain a level of fragmentation that virtually precludes the possibility for unified structure. As a result, the trade associations have become an integral part of the infrastructure of the death care economy.

This structural arrangement persists in many areas, maintained by inertia and by active support of the status quo, but in other areas a series of developments in the structural elements has established the model for structural changes. These developments are the result of efforts to consolidate and integrate death care providers. Ironically, it is the very fragmentation of the sector's infrastructure which has served to set the stage for the eventual restructuring of the death care economy, forging a different set of alliances and threatening to replace trade associations as the mechanisms of linkage within each group of the different types of providers.

Economically, a fragmented structure is subject to the criticism that it fails to exploit economies of scale and of scope. The pursuit of greater profits resulting from the exploitation of these economies is an irresistible force driving the evolution of new structure in the death care sector now, just as it has driven the structural evolution of other sectors of the U.S. economy in the past. Historically, this evolution has often begun with the consolidation and integration of the operating units within an economic sector. This is also how it has begun in the death care sector, forming the basis for the inevitable evolution of a new organizational structure for the death care economy.

Economies of Scale and Scope

The limited scope of most death care providers has confined them to the production and sale of less than complete death care. A full breakdown of establishments in terms of their different degrees of completeness as death care providers is presented in Chapter 16. Suffice it to say here that the vast majority of establishments are incomplete providers to some extent. The size or volume of their specialized operations has been limited also by the extent of the market or submarket served by each. Historically, growth in the size of particular establishments has been largely influenced by expansion and contraction in the population of the market or submarket served. As population growth occurred in many urban and suburban areas during much of this century, some small funeral homes grew into large ones. The volume of cases handled by new and established cemeteries also increased. But because many of these were memorial gardens and parks with flush markers, rather than monuments, the demand for the latter form of memorials did not increase to the same extent.

With the passage of time, the volume of cases handled by well-located and successfully operated funeral homes and cemeteries has established their reputations as prime facilities in their markets, allowing them to achieve "heritage" status. Because of the large volume of such establishments, they are able to achieve some benefits of operating on a larger scale, spreading their fixed costs over more cases or interments. For cemeteries this entails achieving an optimal volume of interments that fully utilizes their operating personnel and equipment, supports the administrative structure, and allows for the most effective sales program. For funeral homes it means attaining an optimal level of volume consistent with the full employment of service and administrative personnel and the use of facilities and equipment at a rate which allows for the randomness of demand for their services. Because of this latter factor, however, it is likely that most funeral homes, even those with heritage status, do not handle an optimal number of cases as long they are single establishments. Furthermore, it is unlikely that most stand-alone funeral homes will ever achieve an optimal level of operations because of the limited size of the markets they serve.

For greatest efficiency in the death care economy, perhaps each metropolitan area should have only one or a few large funeral homes and one or a few large cemeteries. Moreover, to achieve the full benefits of a "complementary combination," the operations of these large funeral homes should probably be combined with those of the large cemeteries to create large "death care facilities" providing all of the death care required in a community. On efficiency grounds alone, the same might be said of the way in which most other local industries "should" be organized. It would be far more efficient, based on economies of scale, to have only one of these types of establishments in each county, or even each state, to which bodies could be sent for disposal. This is what is done in countries like China, where efficiency considerations are the official basis for centrally organizing the country's industrial system. Thus, for a population exceeding 1.2 billion people, all of the country's death care needs are provided by the state via only 1,376 funeral homes, crematories, and public cemeteries, employing 30,000 people. In Beijing, with a population of 12 million and 100,000 deaths in 1992, there were only 12 death care facilities of all types — two of them in Beijing proper and the rest on the outskirts of the city. Some of the crematories operated 24 hours a day. The form of final disposition to which one is entitled in China is determined largely by where one lives. In urban areas it is limited to cremation, presumably with the cremated remains given to the family for further disposition while in the country it is limited to earth burial (*The American Funeral Director*, November 1993). This probably is a more effective means of organizing the death care providers of a country based solely on efficiency considerations, but this would hardly provide the variety of choice desired by the members of a diverse society. In the United States and other free societies, desire for choice has led to domination of the death care economy by small neighborhood firms.

Overcapacity in Perspective

One of the consequences of this feature of the death care economy is that critics and industry participants alike have tended to agree that there are too many funeral homes in the United States. After all, there are more than 22,000 establishments, many of which handle fewer than 100 cases annually. Superficially, this sounds like an excessive number of low-volume establishments, but it is not inconsistent with the number of other public and private entities throughout the United States which render fundamental services on a local basis, such as libraries, nursing homes, post offices, public secondary schools, florists, and so on, according to the latest available figures presented in the *Statistical Abstract of the United States, 1994.*

Even though this proliferation of establishments is economically inefficient, it serves a social need to invest in an infrastructure which provides goods and services considered fundamental at the local level of virtually every community. This need, together with the preference of consumers for distinctive local funeral homes has inevitably resulted in inefficiencies resulting from overcapacity and unused capacity in the American death care sector due to the large number of noncompetitive small operators. It is important to note, however, that even though these small units are noncompetitive, there are inherent limits to what they can charge, as discussed in Chapter 8. Thus, in a structural adaptation designed to accommodate the requirement for these products to be provided to consumers in spite of inefficiencies, death care providers have employed some features of the operation of their establishments in order to reduce the cost of their unused capacity as small operators. This has been possible because many funeral homes are so small that they have no employees or they utilize mostly part-time employees and independent contractors such as trade embalmers. Also in some cases they are not burdened with inventories because casket showrooms are maintained in their areas by casket manufacturers. As a consequence of these conditions, the unused capacity of funeral homes has largely involved the idleness of funeral directors and their facilities and equipment. Several factors serve directly or indirectly to mitigate the effect of this idleness. For example, funeral directors may be actively engaged between funerals in such activities as after-service calls, maintenance, sales, and other business functions. Funeral directors and cemeterians may also engage in public services and civic activities which are quasi-business in nature. In this respect they are not idle, even when they are not conducting a funeral or opening and closing a grave. In some cases they also operate other related or unrelated businesses (such as an insurance agency). Sometimes they are employed in other occupations in their communities. Such instinctive adaptation has allowed basically inefficient operations to survive in large numbers.

In a similar way, the facilities of a firm are also used in some cases for purposes other than funeral services. When these activities are related to the basic purpose of the facilities, as when funeral homes add memorial products to the merchandise sold, this is said to extend the scope of the business, which may involve "economies of scope." Commercial cemeteries have been particularly active in expanding their scope over the years by adding memorial products to their traditional line of products and services sold both at-need and pre-need. The addition of mortuary services is simply the latest expansion of their scope. Forest Lawn is the premier example of this, but smaller, less spectacular, and more representative cases are now not uncommon.

Stand-alone funeral homes have not expanded their scope in this way, but they have added pre-need sales efforts to their basic business in some cases. They have also utilized their facilities and time for community-based activities, death education, and aftercare programs. Limousines and other equipment are sometimes rented or loaned for other purposes. Furthermore, in some areas small competing mortuaries have achieved some of the economies of larger-scale operation by participating in cooperative buying arrangements and livery pools. All of these considerations operate to reduce the extent to which the personnel and facilities of death care providers are unemployed in delivering services in between the periodic occurrence of deaths requiring their occasional use. Even insofar as they are idle, however, it will be clear that they are not unlike other facilities which a society maintains for occasional use, when and as needed, such as churches, fire houses, police stations, clubhouses, municipal buildings, public parks, auditoriums, sports stadiums, and so on. We do not ordinarily consider the existence of these types of facilities and their respective personnel to represent waste or overcapacity because there are periods during which their full capacity is unused or underused. We regard them as the infrastructure of our society, and this includes the infrastructure of the death care economy. It is necessary to weigh the cost of maintaining this infrastructure against the desires of those who pay for them to have their services available at all times, whether or not they are in use.

In some respects the facilities of cemeteries are like museums in which historical artifacts are carefully maintained. Funeral homes with chapels are places where religious rites are performed. Even those that do not have chapels are places of reverence and solemnity. Memorial studios are similar to art galleries. It is pointless to attempt to determine how many such establishments a community needs on efficiency grounds alone. The appropriate number is the number that survives the tests of time by attracting sufficient numbers of customers.

Unlike not-for-profit museums and religious organizations, virtually all funeral homes and many cemeteries are operated as commercial businesses engaged in various forms of competition in their market areas and even between the different segments of the market in an area. An area with a number of establishments of various sizes and degrees of unused capacity may receive higher quality service than it would with only one or a few high-volume establishments. This, along with the increased locational convenience of multiple facilities in a single area, may be viewed as the return on investment from the unused capacity of multiple death care facilities and personnel.

There is an additional advantage to the consumers in an area served by many different establishments. In a diverse society, consumers differ in tastes as well as in the locations of their homes. The existence of a variety of different establishments located throughout a metropolitan area is a form of organization that has developed to provide the different qualities of death care desired by consumers. These qualities relate not only to the technical elements of the forms of death care provided, but also to consumer perceptions of factors such as the character of the facilities operated by a provider, the convenience of their location, the socioeconomic orientation implied by these factors and by the family names of the owner-operators, and of an establishment's general reputation in the community.

Market Structures

Given a diversity of markets and submarkets within an area, the array of providers may range from high-volume heritage establishments to low-volume ethnic establishments to discount providers of limited funeral services to "no-frills" direct disposition companies providing limited mortuary services at low prices, and so on. The variety of establishments required to cater to consumers with different tastes and locational preferences thus results in some duplication of death care establishments and personnel, especially among funeral homes. This hierarchy of death care establishments is similar to the hierarchy of establishments that exists in a variety of retail industries providing local markets with lodging, dining, apparel, and so on. Few of these things are made available to consumers as undifferentiated basic commodities, and neither is death care.

The death care product includes a highly differentiated set of goods and services to which consumers respond. As a form of personal services which vary in their basic nature from one ethnic group to another, from one religion to another, and in other particulars, it is clear that those qualities and characteristics inherent in the aura and practices of an establishment may exert an influence on the choices of consumers seeking to be served in ways that make them most comfortable at a time of distress. The socioeconomic orientation of a funeral home, as indicated by its history, location, and reputation, may be an important factor in this selection by consumers. Similar factors may influence this selection of a cemetery as the site of the "final resting place" for family members. In other words, the individual distinctiveness of death care establishments and providers is a major competitive factor.

Such competition among differentiated suppliers of similar goods and services is described as "monopolistic competition," implying that distinctive suppliers are monopolists in two respects: (1) the death care they provide is not a perfect substitute to that obtainable from other providers and (2) no provider is capable of delivering death care that is a perfect substitute for that of any other provider. In explication of this, Chamberlin points out that product differentiation may be based "upon certain characteristics of the product itself, such as exclusive patented features; trade-marks; trade names; peculiarities of the package or container, if any; or singularity in quality, design, colour or style" (Chamberlin, 1947, p. 56). Quoting Chamberlin, Ryan, 1965, adds:

> Differentiation of the products may also arise because the productive services that any firm uses are not perfect substitutes for those being used by any other firm: thus, in retail trade, there may be differences between one firm and another in "the convenience of the seller's location, the general tone or character of his establishment, his way of doing business, his reputation for fair dealing, courtesy, efficiency, and all the personal links which attach his customers either to himself or to those employed by him. In so far as these and other intangible factors vary from seller to seller, the 'product' in each case is different, for buyers take them into account, more or less, and may be regarded as purchasing them along with the commodity itself" [Ryan, pp. 300–301].

Under such market conditions, death care providers are in a position to behave in some respects as a monopolistic supplier of a product. Under monopolistic competition, however, the pricing freedom of a death care provider is restricted by the existence of other providers of various classes of death care goods and services. In many retail businesses, this may be an important distinction, but it is less so for death care providers because their outputs are usually technical substitutes rather than economic ones. That is, the reputations of a mortuary for serving a particular segment of the market may essentially set it apart from the other firms with which it coexists in an area, but with which it does not effectively compete. Thus in a single geographic area served by, for example, five different funeral homes, the degree of competition between any two of them may vary greatly. A may compete actively with D but hardly at all with B, C, and E. Clearly this depends on how the different establishments are viewed by consumers, on where they are located in relation to one another, and on other factors which affect whether consumers view them as "substitutable," not only technologically but also economically (Ryan, 1965, p. 303).

These considerations suggest that traditional descriptions of market structure do not apply with the usual force to death care goods and services. In particular, a firm may be a monopoly provider to a market segment within a geographic area served by numerous firms. Yet, despite this monopoly status, the owner of that establishment may have less control over prices than is possessed by three or four other firms which compete with one another on mostly nonprice grounds. Even an isolated firm which exists as a virtual monopoly provider in a nonmetropolitan area may have limited pricing power. These unusual features are due to the fact that the operations of a mortuary are geared to serve its community, the members of which vary in affluence, requiring that an establishment offer a product line that varies over a range of prices for merchandise (i.e., caskets) even when essentially the same basic funeral services are required to be provided in conformity with the customs of the community served.

Regardless then of differences in market structure, there are limits within which a given firm may set its prices. Firms must be concerned with both the prices they charge and their costs. This is true even in markets where prices are not an important concern of consumers when they choose a funeral home. Prices become a consideration once consumers have chosen a particular establishment and are confronted with a set of goods and services to choose among, and these often vary widely in price. There are limits to what consumers can or will pay for death care, so providers such as mortuaries must respect those limits for good business reasons as well as ethical ones. These limits are imposed by the resources of the consumers, by their desire for value, and by their decision to allocate only a certain sum for a certain purpose. Neither the size of an establishment nor the number of establishments in an area will alter these market factors. In order for their businesses to survive and grow, the prices charged for goods and services by funeral homes and cemeteries must meet the needs of their customers without excessively straining their means.

Death care providers must thus control their costs and pay attention to their price structures even if there is little or no price competition in the markets they serve. Because their pricing flexibility is limited to some extent, any failure on their part to control costs leads inevitably to pressure on their profit margins and reduces the return on investment they are able to achieve. In competitive industries, this would lead to pressure on the low-volume, high-cost producers of a good or service. In the death care economy, it has allowed for small distinctive facilities to provide opportunities for their most efficient operation as units of a local, regional, or national chain.

Multiunit Operations

The rationale for multiunit operation is rooted in the economics of death care providers and markets. Market segmentation, the absence of price competition in most markets, and consumer preferences for small or distinctive facilities all contribute to the persistence of a number of firms in many area. The unused services of the owner-operators of some of these firms have provided the opportunity for them to become multiunit operators by branching out to the suburbs or acquiring additional establishments in the same area, often following the death or retirement of other owner-operators. Thus a pattern of multiunit operation has characterized the organization of funeral homes and cemeteries in many areas of the country large enough to support a number of establishments.

Under this concept, operating economies resulting from more fully utilizing personnel and equipment are obtained, while goods and services continue to be delivered at the local level in the distinctive types of facilities preferred by consumers. Direct calls to each of the multiple units can be handled by a central office operating twenty-four hours a day. Subject to regulatory requirements, centralized embalming and preparation rooms may economize on facilities that are functionally required at each distinctive location. Central pools of limousines, hearses, and other equipment can be maintained for use at different locations as needed. Casket inventories can be centrally stored and controlled. Centralized accounting, purchasing, and other administrative activities might also be used to achieve some of the advantages of scale associated with a larger single facility. The broader potential customer base may also allow a multiunit firm to support a pre-need sales program which may be a important factor in retaining customers who are committed to traditional funerals in the years ahead. Because of their larger operations, the more specialized managements of these firms are better able to adjust their prices and control their costs as conditions in their markets indicate the need for them to do so.

As a result, a number of multiunit operations have tended to emerge in the death care economy, leading to a gradual restructuring of the sector into firms which operate multiple units in the same area, including a relatively small number of regional and national firms. Nevertheless, the sector continues to be dominated by a very large number of small, family-owned firms.

Degree of Consolidation

As enumerated in the latest Census of service industries (1992), there were more than 22,000 establishments classified under the heading, "Funeral service and crematories" (SIC 726). Approximately 9,500 of these were establishments without paid employees. The remaining 15,647 establishments employed 88,328 people and had receipts of more than $7.1 billion. These 15,647 establishments were owned by 12,423 firms. The bulk of these 12,423 firms (10,654 of them) operated single establishments, but there were 1,769 multiunit firms.

Of these multiunit firms, 279 were "one-establishment" multiunit firms, meaning that they were firms operating only one funeral home but also operating at least one other establishment of another type. The remaining 1,490 multiunit firms were classified according to the number of establishments operated as follows:

	Firms	Establishments
2 establishments	1003	2006
3 or 4 establishments	382	1231
5 to 9 establishments	85	504
10 or more establishments	20	973

Accordingly, 1,490 firms, consisting of two or more units, operated 4,714 establishments. Inclusive of these, the 15,647 establishments with payrolls included 979 which were not operated the entire year. The remaining 14,668 establishments were broken down by the size of their annual receipts, including cash advances, as set out in Table 14.1. This breakdown is indicative of the domination of the death care economy by small establishments, only 1,270 of which had annual receipts of more than $1,000,000 in 1992. Reflecting the presence of a number of multi-establishment firms, a somewhat larger number of firms have receipts in excess of $1,000,000, as shown in Table 14.2 (page 278). Nevertheless, it remains the case that the degree of concentration resulting from consolidation in the death care industries is small, based on the percentage of total establishments operated by multiunit firms. Given a tendency for the large firms to operate establishments whose receipts exceed the average for their industries, the percentage of total revenues generated by the largest death care firms is much greater than the percentage of establishments they represent.

Furthermore, due in part to variations in the severity of legal barriers from state to state, the process of consolidation has tended to be more concentrated in some areas of the country than in others. In confirmation of this, an analysis performed by Steven Saltzman and Gregory Capelli of the Chicago Corporation, using data obtained from the National Funeral Directors Association, provides a clear indication of the limited extent to which consolidation has advanced so far in many areas. Their analysis, the results of which are shown in Figure 14.1 (page 279), indicates that only a small percentage of funeral homes

Table 14.1
Size of Annual Receipts of Establishments with Payrolls Classified as Funeral Service and Crematories (SIC 726)

Annual Receipts	Number of Establishments
$10,000,000 or more	7
5,000,000 to 9,999,999	16
2,500,000 to 4,999,999	92
1,000,000 to 2,499,999	1155
500,000 to 999,999	3272
250,000 to 499,999	5102
100,000 to 249,999	3850
50,000 to 99,999	787
25,000 to 49,999	264
10,000 to 24,999	90
Less than $10,000	33
Includes establishments operated entire year	14668
Excludes establishments not operated entire year	979

Source: U.S. Census of service industries, 1992.

are owned by the seven large death care companies(two of which have since been acquired by SCI or Loewen) in the 48 contiguous states and the District of Columbia. For the country as a whole, only 7 percent of a total of 22,542 establishments are owned by those firms. The number drops to 5 percent if California, Texas, and Florida are omitted. In those three states, the seven large companies owned 23 percent of the total number of funeral homes, representing 30 percent in Florida, 23 percent in California and 18 percent in Texas. Yet these figures greatly overstate the degree of consolidation in the country as a whole.

This analysis suggests that after 30 years of consolidation activity, the movement is still in its infancy. While many establishments in a relatively few states have now been consolidated, there remain many areas of the country in which the consolidation of funeral homes is a new phenomenon. Furthermore, the degree of consolidation among cemeteries is not as great as funeral homes. Thus there remain a number of independently owned facilities which represent potential acquisition targets for consolidation into clusters or sites for the development of cemetery-mortuary combinations. It is important to consider the extent to which establishments of each type may be considered desirable acquisition candidates by consolidators. As a background, it is instructive to examine the implications of a set of data and estimates developed from U.S. Census Bureau data by Saltzman and Capelli. As presented in Table 14.3 (page 280),

Table 14.2
Size of Annual Receipts of Firms with Payrolls
Classified as Funeral Service and Crematories (SIC 726)

Annual Receipts	Number of Firms
$10,000,000 or more	18
5,000,000 to 9,999,999	35
2,500,000 to 4,999,999	143
1,000,000 to 2,499,999	1104
500,000 to 999,999	2731
250,000 to 499,999	4089
100,000 to 249,999	2762
Less than $10,000	679
Includes firms operated entire year	11561
Excludes firms not operated entire year	862

Source: U.S. Census of service industries, 1992.

data for 1987 and projections for 1992 provide a graphic indication of the distribution of funeral homes by size, expressed in terms of the annual number of cases handled. What these data and estimates show is the heavy concentration of business handled by funeral homes performing from 50 to 200 cases per year. A careful reading of these data and estimates shows that the size distribution of establishments is gradually shifting in the direction of larger establishments and away from smaller establishments. Less than 5,000 establishments fall into the class which handle an average of 200 or more cases per year. Approximately 10,000 establishments handle in excess of 100 cases per year. Roughly one-fourth of these have already been consolidated, and another one-fourth may be disqualified as consolidation candidates on grounds other than annual volume (e.g., local market conditions, the unwillingness of owners to sell, and so on). This leaves about 5,000 establishments suitable for consolidation. The eventual acquisition of these establishments by chain companies would result in a degree of consolidation equal to one-third of all funeral homes, representing perhaps one-half of industry revenues.

Acquirable Firms

Within the trade it appears to be conventional wisdom that the largest death care companies, whether public or private, regard funeral homes with annual call volume of 200 or more as attractive acquisition candidates. The number of such establishments is limited, however, and there is some disagreement as to the level

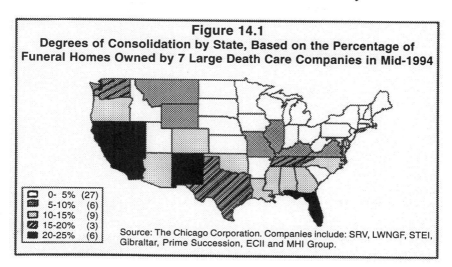

Figure 14.1
Degrees of Consolidation by State, Based on the Percentage of Funeral Homes Owned by 7 Large Death Care Companies in Mid-1994

0- 5%	(27)	
5-10%	(6)	
10-15%	(9)	
15-20%	(3)	
20-25%	(6)	

Source: The Chicago Corporation. Companies include: SRV, LWNGF, STEI, Gibraltar, Prime Succession, ECII and MHI Group.

of attractiveness of those establishment with an annual volume below 200 cases. At a meeting of the Casket and Funeral Supply Association of America in 1993, a panel of executives from the three largest public companies and the largest private one agreed that the attractiveness of any establishment depends on factors in addition to call volume alone. A representative from SCI pointed out that "a funeral home doing 200 calls a year 'standing alone in the middle of nowhere' is not as desirable as one doing 100 calls that fits into a company's strategic plan for a particular market area" (*The American Funeral Director*, November 1993).

An officer of the Stewart firm who participated in the panel provided figures purporting to indicate the numbers of "desirable" acquisition candidates, based on two ranges. According to the criteria used by Stewart, there were 3,270 firms responding to between 100 to 149 calls annually and 1,755 responding to between 150 and 199.

Perhaps the most informative response was provided by the Loewen representative, who indicated that revenues, not call volume, is the key to the attractiveness of an establishment. According to this executive, funeral homes with revenues in the $300,000 to $400,000 range (excluding cash advances) are acquirable, while those with smaller revenues are likely to appeal primarily to an acquiror that is in the process of building a cluster in the surrounding market area. Based on census data presented earlier in Table 14.1, this confirms that there are 5,000 or so "acquirable funeral firms" (representing a somewhat larger number of establishments) still unaffiliated with a national or regional chain. The most attractive of these are undoubtedly the much smaller number of establishments that have experienced persistent growth in their case loads in recent years.

The focus of the large firms on the acquisition of funeral homes is indicated by the failure of executives of those companies to address the question of the remaining number of cemeteries which are subject to acquisition. In a

Table 14.3
Number and Percent of Funeral Homes
with Payrolls, Ranked by Average Call
Volume, 1987 and 1992 (Estimates)

1987		
Average Calls	Number of Funeral Homes	Percentage of Funeral Homes
2,427	6	0.04%
1,156	53	0.36%
477	645	4.39%
231	2,331	15.86%
121	4,589	31.22%
59	4,797	32.63%
26	1,422	9.67%
13	615	4.18%
7	216	1.47%
2	27	0.18%

1992		
Average Calls	Number of Funeral Homes	Percentage of Funeral Homes
2,000	12	0.08%
1,000	117	0.80%
400	1,140	7.77%
200	2,933	20.00%
110	5,133	35.00%
55	4,033	27.50%
28	880	6.00%
12	29	2.00%
6	110	0.75%
2	15	0.10%

Source: U.S. Census Bureau data and the Chicago Corporation estimates.

general way, the factors which affect the attractiveness of cemeteries include trends in the annual volume of interments, the unused space and undeveloped acreage, the location and heritage of the facility, and the demographic features of the surrounding community. As an educated guess, this means that perhaps 1,000 or so acquirable facilities remain, the most attractive of which are the 300 to 400 which are suitable locations for the establishment of new funeral homes.

Assuming that many of the most desirable funeral homes and cemeteries will affiliate eventually with a consolidator, some of the remaining firms will face a variety of conditions under which their survival may become increasingly difficult. In the long run, judging from the survival patterns of firms in other industries which have undergone consolidation, it is reasonable to expect that a large number of unconsolidated establishments will eventually cease to operate as independent firms. In the case of cemeteries, the consequences are likely to create problems for the communities in which they are located.

Impact on Small Establishments

So far the success of chain operators has not necessarily come at the expense of small independent operators in the field, perhaps because the strategy of consolidation employed by the chain companies has involved the acquisition of existing establishments rather than the development of new ones which compete with existing establishments. As a rule, the consolidators have not altered the methods of competition which prevail in the markets they have entered. In most areas these methods do not include active competition by the acquired units for the customers of rival establishments, whether independently owned or units of other chains. This is true in spite of the fact that the unused capacity of chain units, even when they are organized into a cluster, would appear to lead chain operators to adopt more competitive practices, such as pre-need selling, which may have the effect of increasing their volume at the expense of other establishments.

With the greater resources available to chain companies, it is possible that each of them may eventually seek to increase the market share of their units by more aggressive methods. But without a "brand name" identification for the chain units, their promotional advantages are limited. The areas in which their operations have the greatest marketing advantages over independent funeral homes are clearly those in which their clusters include cemeteries or combined establishments. The existing pre-need sales programs of these units represent the most effective channels through which pre-need funeral services may be sold along with cemetery property as a means of increasing the market share of the related mortuaries.

It appears, therefore, that the continued consolidation of the death care industries does not pose an immediate threat to the large number of small independent firms in the sector. This contrasts sharply with the experience of most other industries which were once characterized by the existence of mostly small establishments, but are now dominated by the units of large chains. One of the common features of those cases is that price competition and mass marketing methods have often played a much larger role than they play among funeral homes. Chains of supermarkets, discount stores, building material stores, and movie theaters have forced many independently owned and operated businesses of those types out of business.

The consolidators may wish this were true of independent death care establishments, but considerations other than prices are very important in determining which funeral homes consumers choose. The majority of families select a particular funeral home because of their past experience with it or because of such factors as its location or its established reputation in their communities. This aspect of consumer behavior sustains established firms in spite of the relative inefficiency of their operations when compared with the units of chains. Under such circumstances the operators of small funeral homes may be able to compete effectively with chain operators largely on a nonprice basis. These considerations, together with the certainty of a gradual increase in the number of deaths occurring annually in the United States, do not auger a drastic reduction in the number of small concerns in the death care industries.

It is likely, of course, that more small establishments in the sector will be operated as units of local, regional, and national death care companies. The desire of the latter companies to continue to consolidate the death care sector, backed by the resources available to them, will undoubtedly succeed in overcoming the reluctance of some family owners to surrender their independence by selling their establishments to the chains. As businesses and regulatory complexities continue to multiply, including the spread of price competition and pre-need selling to more areas, the owners of more independent funeral homes are likely to consider the sale of their firms. The personal circumstances of some funeral directors (advancing age, family size, and the varied interests of younger family members, impending retirement, succession planning, estate tax considerations, and so on) may also lead more of them to consider affiliation with a chain at some point. A strategic focus on succession planning issues has tended to characterize the acquisition programs of the chains, but external factors such as interest rates, stock prices, and capital gains tax rates influence the pace of acquisition activity in the death care sector. As in other sectors of the economy, these latter factors affect the multiples of earnings before interest and taxes which acquirors are willing to pay for independent firms and thus the amounts which their family owners receive (after taxes) if and when they sell.

In light of all these considerations affecting the structure of the death care economy, we next consider two processes exerting pressure for structural change in the sector: the consolidation of establishments into chains owned by large firms and the integration of the operations of funeral homes and cemeteries. Chapter 15 will examine the consolidation process, and chapters 16 and 17 will examine the integration process.

15. *Consolidation in the Death Care Economy*

Death Care Chains

The consolidation of establishments in an economic sector leads to the ownership of a number of them by large corporations which exercise varying degrees of centralized control over their operations. Consolidated operation is an element of the structure of many industries, but it is characteristic of the retail industries, which consist of many units operated as parts of large chains. Such chains vary in size from local multiunit firms which own a few establishments in a given area to regional firms to national and international companies which own and operate thousands of units. In some cases the units are more or less uniform entities which offer standardized goods and services to consumers under a broadly recognized brand name. In other cases the units of chains are distinctive establishments owned and operated by a common parent company. So far the large chains which have emerged in the death care sector have tended to be of the latter type, although some local firms have operated distinctive facilities under a common name.

Chains of death care establishments may be composed of funeral homes or cemeteries or both, and the large chains have tended to operate establishments of both kinds in different proportions. The consolidation process has thus involved some integration of industries in the death care sector by firms which own and operate establishments of several different types. This has usually resulted from the consolidation of existing funeral homes and cemeteries which retain their established local identities and names.

It follows that the term "chain," as it pertains to the death care sector in the United States at the present time, is not used here to describe a string of identical or uniform outlets comparable to fast-food restaurants or motels, to which the term is typically applied. It is used rather to mean a dispersed group of distinctive facilities owned and operated by a common parent firm. Thus a death care chain shares some features of media chains and certain hotel chains, including premier hotel chains. Multiple death care establishments which are part of a chain may operate under separate names and with separate identities

283

in a single market area and in multiple markets. The differentiation of their units is a strategy by the parent firm to cater to multiple segments of the market into which the consumers of an area are divided, based on such factors as socioeconomic status, religion, and ethnicity. Some death care firms have also extended into multiple geographic markets, becoming regional, national, and even international chains.

An Early Chain of Cemeteries

An early attempt to promote the development of a chain of distinctive death care facilities involved the case of Memory Gardens Association (MGA), begun in the late 1930s by Edward L. "Doc" Williams, a midwestern real estate developer. "Williams assembled well-trained sales people from the real-estate and insurance businesses, taught them a sophisticated direct sales technique, and loosely managed the individual operations" (Sloane, 1991, p. 186). These consisted of new cemeteries designed to exploit the efficiencies of memorial parks, featuring flush markers that were easy to maintain and garden-style sections embellished in ways which appealed to different segments of the community. The MGA eventually managed over 125 memorial gardens throughout America, most of which were located near the growing cities of the Midwest and South (Sloane, p. 186).

Williams exploited the "local" character of each new memorial garden he developed, emphasizing the local name of the facility and the names of local persons associated with it. This set the standard for later death care consolidators who have followed the same policy even to this day. Sloane comments on the tactical advantage of this strategy:

> Interestingly, when Memory Gardens Association or other speculative memorial-park operations decided to open a new memorial park in an area, they recognized and profited from the local character of the burial place. Often, a group of local business people and civic leaders could originally announce a new memorial park. Only later, when various town and city boards approved the project, or only after the memorial park went into operation, would a manager arrive from the home operation. Local business people and civic leaders were lured into participation through offers of a share in the profits, and in many cases through excellent sales pitches that lead [sic] them to believe that they were doing a public service [p. 236].

According to Sloane, the cemetery empire developed by Williams "demonstrated that consolidation offered tremendous opportunities to cemeteries and memorial park operators ... but it collapsed amid various court cases and personal rivalries" (pp. 235–36). Following the collapse of MGA in the 1940s, no further attempt at organizing a national chain of cemeteries occurred until the 1960s, although there were areas in which multiunit operations consisting of funeral homes, cemeteries, or both were formed locally. By adding units in other areas some of those operations have become regional and national death care chains.

The Modern Consolidation Movement

In other industries, entrepreneurs have often formed chains by building new facilities in one market after the other. This was the approach used by companies that created chains of stores named for the consolidator, like A&P supermarkets, Sears, Wal-Mart, and other retail businesses. A similar strategy has been the basis for the development of a number of independently owned multiunit death care branch operations at the local level. This approach of building new facilities was used also by MGA in the development of its chain of memorial gardens, but its use as a modern consolidation strategy in the death care sector has been virtually precluded by the particular difficulties of entering local death care markets. These difficulties were summarized in the initial prospectus of Equity Corporation International:

> The death care industry [*sic*] is characterized by significant barriers to the establishment of a new funeral home or cemetery in an existing market, the most formidable of which typically is local heritage and tradition. Heritage and tradition afford an established funeral home or cemetery a local franchise and provides the opportunity for repeat business. This is true particularly in small towns where there are few market participants. Other barriers to entry include local zoning restrictions, substantial capital requirements, increasing regulatory burdens and scarcity of cemetery land in certain urban areas. In addition, established firms' backlog of pre-need, pre-funded funerals or pre-sold cemetery and mausoleum spaces also makes it difficult for new entrants to gain a foothold in the marketplace [October 19, 1994].

As used in this passage, the word "heritage" implies a high degree of customer loyalty which virtually guarantees repeat business through generations of families. In spite of various barriers to entry into local death care markets, well-established local ("heritage") funeral homes have been able to expand by adding branches, essentially to serve customers who have moved to the suburbs, thus developing local multiunit operations under their own name and management. Furthermore, well-established local (heritage) cemeteries have been able to add funeral homes to their facilities, because of customer loyalty based on previous interments and pre-purchases of cemetery property, combined with the value placed on convenience by many consumers. Such factors enable a combined facility to overcome the traditional loyalty of consumers to established funeral homes in their geographic area.

These techniques have also been employed by regional and national companies to some extent, but most of them have been built through the process of acquiring established local operations and combining them into a chain of dozens or even hundreds of funeral homes and cemeteries. Although the founder of the largest such firm once told *Business Week* that his objective was to become the True-Value hardware of the funeral service industry, the actual process of consolidation observed in the death care sector has differed in important respects from the True-Value/Holiday Inn/McDonald's models of the nationally recognized provider of standardized goods and services whose establishments adhere to uniform standards relied upon by consumers everywhere in the world.

In fact, there has been no attempt by any of the big death care firms to establish a uniform national identity or image of standardized quality and service anywhere that could capitalize on consumer fears of being abused by small, local death care providers. On the contrary, all of the national death care firms have sought meticulously to maintain the distinctive local identities of the different establishments they have acquired, even when those establishments are located in the same area. The economic motive behind this approach has been to achieve the advantage conferred by customer loyalty to the acquired local establishment, whose name and reputation as a local business is a source of its attraction to consumers. Thus the consolidators have had little impact on the face of the death care economy at the level of the individual establishment. In fact, the appearance of continuity in family ownership and operation is nourished by the advertising programs of the chains and by their policies of retaining some former owners as managers.

Virtually all of the changes wrought by consolidation have thus taken place behind a facade of an unchanging sector of the U.S. economy. During the earliest phase of the consolidation movement, dating from the 1960s, the major benefits of consolidated operation were derived from improved management techniques imposed on the units of the regional and national firms. One of the effects was to purge the acquired funeral homes or cemeteries of the often unsophisticated sales and operating techniques practiced by their independent owners/managers. Another effect was to achieve the efficiencies of purchasing and financing on a larger and more efficient scale than was possible for small multiunit firms.

The Cluster Phase

In what might be described as the "cluster phase" of the consolidation movement dating from the 1970s and 1980s, the strategies of the regional and national death care firms began to incorporate a so-called cluster approach into their acquisition strategies. Under this approach more of their acquisitions were geared to the development of a rational set or "cluster" of multiple facilities in many of the market areas in which they established operations. The goal of such a strategy was to reduce operating costs in the cluster area by such means as centralized embalming at a single location, shared equipment, and common personnel. This is illustrated in Figure 15.1 by a diagram of a typical cluster similar to one pictured in the 1993 annual report of SCI. In some cases the local clusters resulting from the pursuit of such a strategy have included a cemetery jointly operated in conjunction with a group of funeral homes which cater to different segments of the market, whether ethnic, religious, or otherwise.

From a purely economic point of view, clusters formed in this way represent local multiunit operations which are not as efficient as the operations of

Figure 15.1

A Cluster of Death Care Facilities

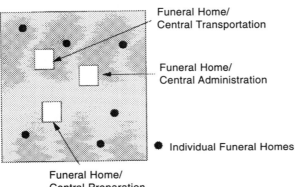

Funeral Home/
Central Transportation

Funeral Home/
Central Administration

● Individual Funeral Homes

Funeral Home/
Central Preparation

single establishments of equivalent volume (due to the costs associated with investment in multiple facilities). Nevertheless, in the case of funeral homes, market segments or "niches" in most areas are not capable of supporting a single establishment large enough for efficient operation based on the full exploitation of economies of scale. Active cemeteries whose volume consists of portions of the output of several local funeral homes are better able to achieve economies of scale as a single establishment by catering for several segments of the population within a given market area. It is conceivable, therefore, that a consolidator of cemeteries might realize economies while operating only one establishment in each market or submarket. Due to the segmentation of most funeral service markets, however, it has been a common practice for the consolidators of funeral homes to realize economies by operating multiple establishments in each market, usually consisting of a cluster of several establishments serving different submarkets. These economies are above and beyond the basic advantages associated with selling and financing on a large scale.

Underlying the cluster strategy employed by the consolidators of funeral homes in particular is the view that the operating costs of local multi-establishment operations consisting of jointly operated facilities are less than those of low-volume, single-unit establishments which coexist with clusters. What is not clear is whether any such advantages or benefits of scale provide the units of a cluster with any real competitive advantages over their local rivals in the sense of obtaining more business through lower prices. It is possible that the economies associated with consolidation resulting from clusters merely increase the profits of the consolidators. Due to the lack of aggressive price competition among funeral homes in most areas, the operation of clusters may be more profitable than the operation of similar noncluster establishments, but the volume of the latter may be largely unaffected by this fact. Perhaps this is why few, if any, funeral homes which compete with the units of clusters have failed, and the prices at which such firms are acquired by consolidators are not noticeably different from those paid for establishments which do not compete with clusters.

Causes of Consolidation

It is difficult to explain the consolidation of death care providers strictly in terms of the inherent operating advantages of large chains over multiunit operations owned locally. Clearly, the added advantages resulting from the leverage conferred by regional and national ownership of chains (such as buying power, negotiating power, centralized purchasing, administering, and financing) do not appear to be as significant as those associated with the development of local multiunit operations. Clusters and combinations of local establishments are able to achieve operational advantages by utilizing their facilities and personnel more fully on the local level. Hence it is understandable that the consolidation of death care providers has tended to evolve into a strategy of consolidating clusters of local facilities.

In the death care economy, the cluster approach has tended to be adopted in order for consolidators to achieve the economic advantages of local multiunit operation along with whatever advantages accrue in general from operating as large scale companies. From the standpoint of consumers, the distinctive features of the separate local units of the chains continue to inspire their loyalty and repeat business. Except in markets characterized by price competition therefore, there is no reason to suppose that the lower costs of clustered units are passed on to consumers in the form of lower prices. Instead the cost savings derived from the advantages of the consolidated operation of clusters of establishments translates primarily into greater earning power for each cluster compared to the total earning power of the separate establishments before consolidation. The effect of this consolidation is an increase in the value of the organized cluster above the sum of the values of the separate establishments from which it was formed. This factor has been a chief motive behind the continued consolidation of death care providers based on the addition of units to existing clusters.

The operating leverage of clusters results from the operation of several establishments together in a common area. As the distance between establishments becomes greater, the unique advantage of cluster operation becomes smaller. Thus small stand-alone operations in nonmetropolitan areas offer few operating advantages even when they are units of chains. Nevertheless, since they serve markets in which they may be one of few available providers, their ability to adjust margins has made them attractive candidates even though they are not capable of operating as a unit of a cluster. This has been a motive behind the acquisition strategies of some death care chains. A third motive has been to acquire large, well-established cemeteries in which to build new funeral homes to be operated as combined establishments. A fourth motive has been to create a new chain to be sold at a profit, due to enhanced organizational value, to one of the large national companies.

These economic motives account for the continued growth of chains to include a larger and larger number of units. Theoretically, this process could continue until all the establishments in the death care sector were controlled by one company that might be called U.S. Death Care, Inc. In practice of course, there are limits beyond which the process becomes unfeasible. Some of these have to do with the practical difficulties of financing the acquisition of more and more units, of consolidating their heterogeneous operations into a rational network of local clusters, and of administering a larger and larger organization of widely dispersed units. In any relevant market, there are limits imposed also by antitrust laws on the extent to which any one firm may dominate the market for a particular product or service. Finally, a very important limit to the extent of possible consolidation among death care providers is the determination of many owner-operators of funeral homes and cemeteries to remain independent regardless of the prices being offered by the consolidators. Even though units of chains and of clusters operated by chains may be more efficient than independently owned and operated establishments, they may have little effect on the volume and profitability of the independent operators. Furthermore, even when they do, the family owners of the latter may still resist selling out.

Various factors affect the inclination of families to sell, including the age(s) of the owner(s) and concerns about succession planning, especially if they lack a second or third generation of family members committed to working in a stigmatized occupation thrust upon them by birth. All of the national companies have appealed to the interests of such owners and their families by using acquisition strategies based on succession planning. Even so, the family owners of many successful firms have been reluctant to sell out because they know they own a valuable franchise and they have reservations about turning it over to the control of a chain.

The competition to acquire the most attractive facilities in an area has been especially fierce because of the desire of the chains to establish a foothold or to expand a cluster in key markets. Market conditions frequently oblige acquirers to compete against one another on issues other than the prices they are willing to pay. These issues include the value of their corporate image, their reputation for management depth and financial strength, opportunities for family members to advance through management ranks, the commitment to maintain the establishment's name and reputation in its community, and the promise of continuity on the part of the acquiring firm.

In the process which results in acquisitions, there is often some reluctance on the part of the sellers, but there is also an urgency on the part of some chain operators. The intensity and pace of the drive to acquire cannot be explained entirely by economic forces. The emergence of this kind of behavior can be observed throughout history wherever territorial expansion has been at issue.

Examples include dynastic alliances for acquiring territory, colonization, and military aggression. Naturally, this is beyond our scope and concern. Nevertheless, the fact that the struggle for strategic alliance and dominance in the death care sector has reached this point of involving such a basic psychosocial level of competition reveals that there are immensely powerful forces at work and that this is a time of strategic shifts in economic power which will set the course of the future for years to come. What economic forces have given rise to this kind of struggle in the death care sector?

A Model for Consolidation

Death care firms are basically retail businesses that are now undergoing a process that has previously been seen in many other retail businesses. From the vantage point of the 1960s, the decade during which consolidation in the death care economy began, Gentry and Taff (1966) looked back on the history of consolidation in the retail industries. They described the following set of economic forces behind the formation of retail chains:

> Chains are able to buy in large quantities and thus effect certain savings in that respect. They are able to take advantage of a division of labor in that they are often large enough to justify the hiring of specialists. Buyers who specialize in certain merchandise categories and management specialists in areas such as advertising and personnel administration may be employed. This is in contrast to the small independent store where we often find one man responsible for many different tasks. The chains have also been comparatively progressive in their management. They utilize marketing research in selecting store sites and in planning store layout. They may be able to acquire capital more readily and thus be able to adopt new innovations ahead of the small independent. The corporate chain also faces certain limitations. It is generally thought of as an impersonal store and less able to offer the type of service desired by some customers. The corporate form of ownership often means that the store is owned by interests outside the market in which it operates. Some customers tend to voice prejudice against absentee ownership in contrast to local ownership. Public hostility toward chains was evidenced in the 1920's and 1930's and this even led to the passage of discriminatory taxation in some states. During this period, the independents were struggling to combat the development of chain stores, and it is probable that hostility was a by-product of this struggle. In recent years, there seems to be little resentment directed toward the chain as a method of retailing [p. 334].

Against the backdrop of this historical model, it is possible to understand the continued consolidation of the death care sector of the economy. The consolidation process, which may take decades to accomplish, is illustrated by the history of SCI. As an early consolidator, much of its history is a matter of public record, and it is likely that its experience over many years has informed the later consolidators. It appears, for example, that the lessons learned from SCI have enabled the two other major public companies to avoid similar mismanagement in the implementation of their consolidation strategies. This appears to be especially true of the strategy of Stewart, which has focused from the very beginning on developing clusters and combinations of facilities in order to exploit the economies of integrated as well as consolidated operations. The basic advantages of consolidation both nationally and internationally will be considered in the rest of this chapter.

Purchasing Power

Because of the relatively small size of most independently owned funeral homes and cemeteries, they are not able to buy in large quantities on better terms, as does a large chain. A large organization of small establishments may also benefit from more advantageous terms it is able to obtain in connection with selling and distributing its products.

In some industries, consolidated firms have sometimes vertically integrated themselves backwards by acquiring their suppliers. For an important economic reason, such a strategy of vertical integration is counterindicated in the case of consolidated death care providers. This is because a major advantage of consolidation in their case is the power it gives a large firm to "squeeze" its suppliers. Since caskets, vaults, embalming fluids, grave liners and markers, and equipment (e.g., hearses, flower cars, etc.) are highly specific to funeral homes and cemeteries, the manufacturers of these goods are entirely dependent on death care providers for their sales. It is therefore possible for those with large buying power to exploit the dependency of their suppliers in order to negotiate the most favorable terms. In some respects therefore, the consolidation movement may be a greater threat to such dependent suppliers than it is to the operators of small, unconsolidated funeral homes and cemeteries.

Notwithstanding the strength of the case against vertical integration by consolidated death care firms, it is interesting to note that SCI did in fact attempt to integrate backwards by acquiring a manufacturer of caskets and other funeral supplies. In 1988 it also acquired a leading manufacturer of bronze markers for cemeteries. In a subsequent reversal of this strategy, these manufacturing subsidiaries were later divested, probably because vertical integration entailed some loss of both purchasing advantages and potential markets. Customer loss might have occurred due to the reluctance of establishments competing with units of SCI to purchase supplies from an SCI subsidiary.

Management and Development

While the small, family-owned establishment is generally regarded as the optimal unit for delivering death care goods and services to consumers, the proprietors of small firms who function as funeral directors/embalmers/cosmeticians/sales counselors/bookkeepers/owners/managers are unlikely to be equally effective in each of the roles they play. Few single-unit firms attract sufficient volume to allow family members and other employees to specialize in particular functions involved in the operation of funeral homes or cemeteries. Efficiencies from specialization in management are usually not achieved until a critical mass results from bringing many units together into a local, regional, or national chain. Even the local multiunit death care providers and the regional chains may not achieve sufficient size to justify the highest managerial compensation required to attract the most talented managers. Only the large regional and national companies can afford such compensation, by spreading its costs over the large volume of services and interments they perform. Even so, the quality of their management may suffer from the negative effects of lingering nepotism brought to the national companies through terms of employment negotiated during the acquisition process.

Another feature of large firms has to do with their ability to engage in research and development. The heavy expense of this is prohibitive for small single-unit firms and even for multiunit ones operated at the local or regional level. Characteristically, large death care firms do not engage in product or market research and development, but since they are required to fund aggressive acquisition programs, some do engage in extensive analysis of demographic trends. Thus in a wide-ranging interview with the *Wall Street Transcript* (June 6, 1992), SCI's chairman Waltrip discussed SCI's capacity for such analysis as a strong point of the firm.

> What we do has to do with morbidity and mortality reports, with births and deaths and shifts of population. We have all of that in our big computer, and I guess we know as much about that type of movement in America as anybody. So I really don't know how we could improve on that too much. We've been very efficient in positioning ourselves in these areas where the number of deaths is going to increase over the next decade.

Critics may call this ambulance chasing on a grand scale, but it is difficult to quarrel with it as a business strategy. Beyond carefully analyzing demographic trends, however, even the largest death care companies have been slow to adopt a progressive approach toward research and development. Indeed within the death care economy, there seems to be a remarkable lack of interest, as well as the kind of imaginative thinking usually spurred by such interest, about new products and services which might be developed and marketed effectively, such as financial support services for the bereaved, which are already being marketed effectively to survivors by companies outside of the death care sector. Some further comments Waltrip made to the *Wall Street Transcript* illustrate this point: "It's hard to think of any products and services that we're not offering at the present time. Being that this is a predominantly service-type business, I think we're doing most everything that we'll be doing in the future. Over the next few years, more and more of it."

To some extent those on the cemetery side of death care have felt more anxiety about this simple prescription of providing more of the same. Rather than to create new products through research, however, cemeteries have tended to develop and to market aggressively various novel alternatives to earth burial, including garden mausoleum crypts, cremation followed by inurnment and memorialization, and columbariums, and so on. Among the consolidators, Stewart has been a leader in this process because of its origins as a cemetery operator and developer of community mausoleums, both of which involve extensive pre-need marketing and sales.

Allocative Efficiency

As heirs to their locations, the businesses of independent funeral homes or cemeteries are tied to their local areas. Their fortunes are linked to the demographic changes occurring around them, over which they have virtually no control. Their expansion through branching has been limited to the confines of their geographic areas. By contrast, expansion of the national companies, based on demographic analysis of the kind used by SCI, has enabled them to allocate resources more efficiently. Thus the national companies may be regarded as "sector funds" holding "portfolios" that are diversified in different ways (geographically and industrially) according to the strategies pursued by their managements.

The units held in the portfolios presumably are selected by virtue of their superior prospects for profitability (as in non-metropolitan markets where competition is weak and adherence to traditional funerals is strong) or for growth (as in the growing metropolitan markets here and abroad). This is what distinguishes the consolidated companies from one another, as will be discussed fully in Chapter 18.

In the consolidation process, the national companies have tended to pursue the most attractive establishments in the most attractive areas within which to operate, based on demographic and other factors affecting long-term prospects. As consolidation has proceeded in key areas, many choice establishments have been acquired by a consolidator. Waltrip makes this point about SCI:

> There will never be another company like Service Corporation International. It was formed at a time when there was a definite need for consolidation within this particular industry. The number of businesses it acquired that are now part of our corporate family is just not available any more within the confines of North America where we operate. Therefore, there's just not any way a company could come in and duplicate what we've put together. The names and reputations of these particular funeral firms are the most prestigious in the world, and to go back and try to duplicate that would be impossible [*Wall Street Transcript*, June 6, 1992].

While there is some truth in this statement, it is also true that funeral homes and cemeteries are not exempt from the operation of outside forces. A subsequent statement by Waltrip bears this out:

I do expect to see shifts geographically in our revenue sources going forward. That has to do with the demographics regarding shifting of population. In some areas of the country, that's a lot more serious than in others.
For instance, in a town like New York, a community or borough can change
in a year to something completely different than it was. We try to anticipate that and be there ready when it happens.

There is no explanation of how the company does this, but at times SCI
has tended to readjust its portfolios as a result of changing conditions and strategies. An example was the spin-off in 1990 of a large number of funeral homes
previously acquired by SCI. The spin-off resulted in the emergence in 1994 of
a publicly traded company, Equity Corporation International (ECI), in which
SCI retained an equity interest. According to ECI's prospectus, the reason for
this transaction was "to acquire from SCI 71 funeral homes and 3 cemeteries that
SCI had determined no longer fit within its strategic plan to concentrate on clusters of funeral homes and cemeteries in metropolitan areas. The funeral homes
and cemeteries acquired from SCI were predominately located in non-metropolitan areas."

Such transactions are unusual. For the most part, the portfolio adjust-
ments by the national companies have involved the addition of units, either in
new areas or those in which they currently operate. As mentioned, acquisitions
of established funeral homes and cemeteries are presumably guided by the relative attractiveness of the return on investment represented by available acquisition candidates. Also, the headquarters' staffs of the national companies are
presumably in a position to direct the development of new facilities and the
expansion of existing ones in a more rational manner, effecting a better allocation of available resources among areas and different types of facilities. On the
other hand, it is possible that because of the large upfront costs associated with
the development of new death care facilities, the managements of the public
companies have generally preferred to pursue mature operations.

Investor Ownership

As family-owned businesses with stable operating characteristics and cash
flows, single-unit establishments have moderate financing needs seldom requiring more than occasional bank borrowing. Even multiunit operations resulting
from the building of branches by established funeral homes have generally been
financed by mortgages backed by new and existing facilities. The limited nature
of these needs for capital has not generally required such firms to resort to capital obtained from the investing public.

Consolidation involving the acquisition of a large number of established
businesses is a more expensive proposition, especially when the prices of those
businesses involve large premiums over the value of the assets acquired. Mort-
gage financing is insufficient for this purpose, and active acquisition programs
outstrip the ability of any firm to generate adequate funds from operations. To

support an extensive acquisition program therefore, it is necessary for consolidators to borrow heavily. Initially most of this borrowing is arranged through banks and insurance companies, but eventually the need for capital outstrips the supply available from private sources. Accordingly, at some point a company with an active acquisitions strategy is forced to resort to the public securities markets. Loewen, SCI, Stewart, and ECI have all followed this route to their present status as investor-owned death care companies; so have several other national and regional companies, some of which have subsequently been acquired by the leading ones.

The feasibility of raising capital to finance business growth through a process of consolidation depends on conditions in the debt and equity markets and on the prospects for profiting from the effects of the consolidation. Both of these factors vary over time, as shown by the history of the treatment of the stock of SCI and some earlier consolidators. For some time the performance of the stocks of the leading death care companies has benefited from generally favorable conditions in the stock market and a generally favorable outlook for death care providers because of the continual aging of the U.S. population.

Investors have been as attracted to the investment promise of consolidation in the death care sector as they were to the promise of returns through earlier consolidations in other industries. This has led to the active involvement of the investment banking community as underwriters of the securities of attractive consolidators. Thus the death care companies, in spite of the nature of their business, have been especially attractive to investment bankers because their consolidation strategies entail a continuous series of debt-financed acquisitions followed by a need to raise new equity capital by selling more stock. This provides repeat business for the underwriters.

Under the influence of all the forces described above, the consolidation of the death care economy by national and regional companies has gained momentum. At this point the investor-owned companies account for a continually growing share of aggregate industry revenues in the death care sector. When added to the revenues of several dozen regional chains, the market share of the consolidators in the sector is even greater. As more independent funeral homes and cemeteries are acquired by these firms, it is inevitable that the combined market share of the consolidators will continue to expand for decades. This will represent a major shift in the economic structure of the death care economy away from the traditional pattern of family-owned and -operated establishments.

Consolidation and Debt

A final feature of the economics of consolidation bears description in terms of its potential advantages and associated risks. The incidental and direct costs of raising and servicing funds may be less for large than for small firms. The public debt and equity markets are accessible only to large firms. In order to finance the consolidation of large numbers of funeral homes and cemeteries, the major firms have tapped these sources repeatedly, periodically building up large levels of debt which are kept in acceptable limits by occasional new issues of stock. There is always risk associated with this strategy of using debt heavily to finance rapid expansion through acquisitions.

Consolidators in other industries, such as supermarkets and department stores, have suffered the consequences of relying too heavily on debt. A mitigating factor which undoubtedly reduces the risk for death care firms is the highly stable sales revenues and cash flows of their operating units. This feature of the operations of funeral homes and cemeteries has enabled them to establish very low failure rates as businesses, and it translates into an even greater power of survival for the consolidated firms. Their reserves are larger, providing them with more room to maneuver, to take advantage of opportunities, and to allow for errors in what they do. At the same time, their very size and the magnitude of the decisions they make, such as a decision to integrate backwards into manufacturing or to pursue consolidation to the point of acquiring foreign operations, entail new forms of risk unlike those directly involved with operating a funeral home or cemetery.

Also in contrast to the circumstances under which small privately held funeral homes and cemeteries have traditionally operated, the public ownership and financing of the large national firms obligates them to publish extensive information about their operations, finances, and management, especially the compensation of the latter. To attract sufficient debt and equity capital on favorable terms, the publicly owned companies have sought to portray their financial performance and prospects in the best possible light. This is understandable as a commercial proposition, but it is potentially a source of renewed and even intensified criticism of the profitability and prices of funeral homes and cemeteries, especially from organized interest groups such as the American Association of Retired Persons. Whether such criticism is deserved is not the point. Nor is there much of a threat that consumer expenditures will be affected by such criticism, because this has not happened in the past. The real threat is that various levels of government will again be attracted to investigate and perhaps eventually to regulate the industries in the sector to a greater degree.

But there is a further risk associated with the public ownership of death care companies which may well eventually affect the quality of service provided to consumers by the funeral homes and cemeteries owned by the public companies, as compared to the family-owned and -operated firms and the local or regional chains. The publicly owned companies, to attract the financial support of individual and institutional investors, have committed themselves to providing a rate of return which meets investor expectations year after year without fail. In the efforts of managements to deliver the expected return by becoming more and more efficient and profitable, the temptation may be for the units of the investor-owned chain companies to become impersonal processors of funerals rather than providers of family-to-family services. Chain operation and investor ownership are still in their infancy, but as the public chains continue to grow and to face continued pressure to produce short-run financial results as investor-owned companies, there is always the danger that their units will cease to offer the personal attention and care that owner-operated establishments are uniquely suited to provide.

The investor-owned companies seem to be aware of this danger and have tended to address it by retaining some or all of the family members of acquired firms in the capacity of managers of those units. It is not necessarily the case, however, that such family employees are a satisfactory substitute for family ownership. Neither is it clear that this basis of management selection is an appropriate means of staffing the managerial ranks of results-oriented, investor-owned companies. The consolidation of other industries like department stores and newspapers by investor-owned companies has often involved new methods of operation to which it was difficult for previous family owners to adapt. It may prove to be similarly difficult for the previous owners of family-owned death care establishments to adapt to the methods of operation imposed on them by the managers of the units of an investor-owned company subject to the performance demands of outside investors. So far it appears that the greater part of the performance required of these companies has been satisfied by the pace of their acquisition activities. But in the long run, it will have to be satisfied by the growing profitability of their operations. When this happens, it will represent the first real test of the suitability of investor-ownership to the industries of the death care sector.

At times in the past, there have been signs of SCI's dissatisfaction with some of the obligations that arise from the status of investor ownership. Earlier in its history as a public company, it weighed a proposal to take the company private again. According to press reports in the 1970s, an independent committee of the board of directors was appointed to consider a proposal under which the company would have been acquired by a corporation to be owned by certain SCI officers and investors. But since that time, the company has generally fared better, based largely on its success as an acquirer (Smith and Schoen, May 1978).

Risks and Advantages

In addition to the economic consequences of the continued consolidation of death care providers, there is also the legal issue of whether this process has proceeded too far in any relevant market from an antitrust standpoint. In this connection the concern is with the impact of the cluster strategy which entails acquiring multiple units in a single geographic market area rather than internally building volume. Antitrust laws generally forbid excessive concentration in a "relevant" market area under the prevailing "rule of reason" approach. This means that a company must have willfully acquired a monopoly position as distinguished from having grown into it as a consequence of a superior product, business strategy, or historical accident. A cemetery-mortuary combination that achieves dominance in a local market based on the latter factors would not appear to be at risk, but a cluster formed through repeated acquisitions in a given market might violate antitrust laws, depending on how the relevant market is defined. Successive acquisitions have sometimes led the Federal Trade Commission to order divestitures in an attempt to preserve competitive conditions in a market area. This is one of a number of risks that sometimes offset the advantages of large-scale operation in any economic sector. There are others as well.

Small firms historically have dominated the death care trades for several reasons. The principal inputs used to produce death care are the technical skills and personal knowledge of those who run cemeteries and funeral homes. The principal output of the latter at least is personal service rendered to families which have experienced the loss of a member. The highest form of personal service has been the "family-to-family" style on which funeral directors and cemeterians have long prided themselves. Consumers have responded to this tradition by demonstrating strong loyalty to local family-run establishments. Although the consolidated firms continue to cultivate an image of their establishments as family-run (perhaps even family-owned) providers of personal service to their customers, this image is essentially a guise. Some former owners may still be associated with units of consolidated firms, but they are actually employees of those firms rather than owner-managers of a true family business.

It may be too early in the consolidation process for the customers of funeral homes to notice much change in the quality and value of the services provided with this transition, but it is a notorious fact that in other industries (banks and supermarkets, for example) the quality and value of personal service at formerly autonomous establishments have declined as a result of consolidation. For many consumers such establishments have become impersonal parts of large organizations to which it is hard to relate personally or to maintain a strong sense of loyalty. Such impersonalization does not pose serious problems for death care chains if they want to be seen as efficient providers after the fashion of fast-food restaurants, discount retailers, and other dispensers of uniform products who compete on the basis of price, convenience, and limited service. To this point, however, this has not been the case among most death care providers. Their strategy so far has been to maintain the image and distinctive features of family-to-family establishments, operated more economically within a consolidated structure. The difficulties of succeeding at this are chronicled in articles written about the consolidation of distinctive hotels, which have not always fared well as units of chains. In an article entitled "Can the Savoy Cut Costs and Be the Savoy?" a *Wall Street Journal* reporter recently wrote: "Profits can be frustratingly elusive in the luxury trade, where standards must be maintained regardless of economic conditions and empty rooms" (Guyon, *Wall Street Journal*, July 12, 1994). Nevertheless, it must be remarked that in the "luxury" death care sector, Frank E. Campbell has operated successfully in New York City for many years, even while owned by SCI (whose name has been kept in low profile), and Stewart has tended to specialize in the operation of heritage properties (while promoting the names of the establishments rather than that of the corporate parent).

Difficulties Peculiar to the Sector

Small establishments dependent on a given neighborhood clientele are exposed to the risk of changing local conditions. A chain is able to hedge against this risk by operating establishments in a variety of different local markets. Offsetting this, differences in the local characteristics of customers and competition call for different methods of operations at the units of consolidated firms. It follows that some advantages of consolidation in other industries, such as the economies associated with operating and promoting identical facilities for producing a standardized line of "branded" products, are incompatible with the conditions under which funeral homes and cemeteries operate. On the contrary, their facilities are often unique and their product-lining strategies depend on customer tastes which vary over different regions and even in the same area based on ethnic, religious, and socioeconomic differences. This makes it difficult for chain operators to compare and to control such things as maintenance costs and sales prices, which are a critical part of the success of, say, fast-food chains and discount stores.

By comparison with such firms, the operations of consolidated death care providers are less subject to centralized control and more sensitive to the quality of operational management at their units and the divisions of their units. There is thus a serious risk that they may become more centralized as they grow into larger and larger chains of greater heterogeneity. Even the centralized recruitment and training of employees which produces service personnel would appear to interfere with the distinctly local flavor of funeral homes and cemeteries in their markets. This raises questions about the effectiveness of the centralized training facilities developed by chains in an attempt to exploit their scale as a large employer.

Beyond Consolidation: Globalization

Faced with natural limits in domestic markets, a common pattern of expansion by firms in a number of industries has been to embark on a strategy of entering new markets abroad, often by acquiring existing firms currently operating in those markets. The SCI entered the Canadian market early in its history, and Loewen expanded from Canada into the United States. For various reasons, however, none of the leading firms ventured far beyond North America in any significant way until 1993, when SCI acquired a major consolidator of funeral homes in Australia. This followed a period of experimentation with operating there which began in 1989 (McMillen, *The American Funeral Director*, January 1995).

A year later SCI's acquisition of Great Southern Corp., a large operator of funeral homes and crematories in the United Kingdom, brought out the issue of cultural differences which are likely to accompany the globalization of death care companies. Aside from the usual conflicts which characterize unwelcome takeover attempts, an official of Great Southern raised the question of whether SCI appreciated fully the cultural differences between British and American death care consumers and providers, such as a much stronger preference in England for cremation and a corresponding use of much less elaborate caskets than in the United States. In addition, the methods of marketing funerals and cremation differ in significant respects in the two countries. In a statement opposing a takeover by SCI, the deputy chairman and chief executive officer of Great Southern emphasized that death care "is a very culturally different affair" in Britain than in America. He also stated: "I certainly wouldn't have the arrogance to believe I could run a successful American business without having to assimilate the cultural differences."

The president of SCI downplayed Great Southern's resistance to his company's hostile takeover bid: "[We] are in every kind of ethnic market there is.... The cultural differences between New York and California, between Hispanic and Jewish or Korean and Cuban are far greater than any between the U.S. and the U.K." (Guyon, *Wall Street Journal*, July 12, 1994). He refused to comment on the difference in sales methods claimed by the Great Southern spokesman, but it is certain that the issue of cultural differences is one that will be raised again and again as the globalization of death care companies proceeds. The argument that U.S. companies operate in a multicultural society is not an entirely satisfactory basis for claiming sufficient experience to enter the death care market in foreign countries.

Given the added risks of operating abroad, it would seem that a substantial case for the benefits of international consolidation must be presented in support of such efforts by SCI or others who undertake them. In many other industries, there may be various kinds of gains that accrue from the products and production techniques, but they do not seem to apply to the international expansion of death care firms because of the distinctly local character of death care customs and practices. The chairman of SCI has cited the counterseasonal features of operations in the southern hemisphere, but this seems an insubstantial basis for a global strategy. As Milgrom and Roberts (1992) point out, internationalization requires firms to develop

> enough flexibility in procedures to accommodate local patterns of business relations, labor-market practices, and government regulation. Additional demands are placed on the organization by the need to develop means to coordinate information flows, make decisions, and implement plans across national borders and time zones, to surmount linguistic and cultural differences, and to take advantage of the particular skills and resources that are most prevalent in each region [p. 590].

Still, this is the age of international business, and the largest death care firms already operate internationally. This expansion is likely to continue, and it is possible that in the future there will be an expansion of foreign firms, other than Loewen, into the U.S. market. In any event, there is no doubt that the large North American death care chains will expand further into the Americas, Australia, Europe, and beyond. The SCI has pursued opportunities in Australia and Great Britain; Stewart has expanded into Australia and Mexico. Among the attractions of foreign expansion is the opportunity to diversify globally, focusing on countries with favorable demographic trends and cultures in which traditional death care is highly valued. Expansion into developing areas and economies may yield the additional benefit of increases in the demand for high-quality death care goods and services as the general level of income rises.

An example is provided by recent events in China, where it has been reported that lavish forms of death care are sought after by growing numbers of affluent Chinese. This yearning for opulent death care has led to entrepreneurial attempts to provide the desired goods and services. In a Communist country, however, some of these attempts have "prompted federal authorities to outlaw the latest funereal offender: A cemetery known as Ghost Capital, where the dearly beloved can rest in 'palaces' with names and decor borrowed from folklore and the legends of the nether world" (Schmetzer, September 10, 1994). This and other developments in Chinese death care are described by Schmetzer:

> Ghost Capital in the city of Hengyang, Hunan province, was to have been inaugurated last week on Devil's Day, when paper money is burned and food is left at graves to fortify the departed for the coming cold weather. The cemetery's owners already had sold $4 entrance tickets to tourists before authorities closed it down for its "scenes from hell." ... But Hunan officials don't mind the "Refrigerated Crystal Coffin Factory" in nearby Anyang, where transparent five-sided caskets facilitate viewing of the dear departed for weeks before burial or cremation. Each refrigerated coffin also boasts a humidifier and generator in case of blackouts, not uncommon in China.
>
> The coffins also break into funeral music if approached by mourners. China's Electronic Business News reported this month that the see-through product, now on sale in eight provinces, "has already won the trust of consumers."

Such reports indicate an appetite for death care in foreign markets which American firms may seek to enter. Of course, there are also risks of operating abroad, even when the operations of foreign establishments are similar to domestic ones. Cultures differ, as do the conditions under which businesses operate in different parts of the world. Foreign operations are remote from their U.S. headquarters and corporate staffs, they are managed and staffed by foreign nationals, and the customers of foreign establishments are influenced by different customs and habits. Other risks of operating abroad involve the possibility of political instability, economic policy changes, inflation, and fluctuation in the rate of exchange between foreign currencies and the dollar, including devaluations (Chambers, 1986, p. 129), an example of which recently occurred in Mexico.

A strategy of international expansion by the North American death care firms is thus subject to risks which affect the comparative merits of foreign versus domestic investments. Judgments about these risks undoubtedly explain in part the reluctance of the national companies to expand internationally. It is noticeable that their first steps in this direction were a long time in coming and were limited to very familiar areas. Based on the apparent success of those first steps, more rapid expansion into international markets may be expected in the immediate future. It is possible also that one of the regional or national companies may provide an attractive opportunity for a foreign company to acquire a foothold in the death care economy of the United States, just as some foreign companies have done in other American industries.

Finally, it must be pointed out that the internationalization of some firms will affect all firms, as Milgrom and Roberts (1992) make clear:

> Even firms that decide to stick to serving their local or national markets are affected by the growing internationalization of business because their competitors or the lowest cost supplier may be from other parts of the globe. This means that the ability to operate in global markets is of very general value. It also means that there are strong forces driving firms to adopt the strategic and organizational adaptations that help them to operate in international markets. Just what these adaptations may be is not yet clear: These are relatively new management problems, and international firms are experimenting with many kinds of solutions [p. 590].

Under conditions prevailing in the death care economy, the effects of the internationalization of some firms may be muted by the local character of death care markets. In some markets, the experience gained from operating in foreign markets may enhance the competitive effectiveness of operations. But in most markets, it is unlikely that the operation of domestic establishments will be affected to any significant degree by the international reach of the parent companies of rival establishments in the same local area. Of course, the international scope of the large companies may shift some of their attention to foreign markets and reduce the rate of their domestic acquisition activity, thereby affecting acquisition prices in this country.

16. *Complementary Combinations of Death Care Providers*

Integration as Opposed to Consolidation

Forces favoring the continued consolidation of the death care economy will inevitably lead to the operation of more and more establishments together in clusters, some of which will include cemeteries and combined facilities. The economic case for combined facilities represents an additional force tending to encourage the development of funeral homes at the site of a greater number of cemeteries, whether they are independently owned, owned by the chain companies, or perhaps even owned by religious and other noncommercial organizations. The effects of these integrated operations on the death care sector are to be distinguished from the effects of mere consolidation considered in Chapter 15. In the first place, there are various operating advantages of integrated establishments which arise from the better coordination of the different stages in the death care process. These improve on the performance of such establishments but they do not necessarily affect the volume of other establishments with which they compete on a nonprice basis. In the second place, the integration of the operations of funeral homes and cemeteries, and especially the physical integration of their facilities, not only creates operating advantages, it also provides integrated establishments with a distinct marketing advantage not available to stand-alone establishments or clusters of stand-alone establishments which do not include a cemetery.

In effect, the economies of integrated operation represent the advantages of scale and scope associated with a local cluster, but without the disadvantages incurred by multiple locations. A "combination" can be described as a highly compressed cluster of different facilities operated together in one place as a unit. There are now hundreds of such facilities throughout the United States. State-of-the-art operations of this sort are full-service facilities capable of providing complete death care to consumers at one convenient location. The location is necessarily the site of an existing cemetery or memorial park to which have been added a crematory, a mortuary, a community mausoleum, a columbarium, a memorial outlet, and a flower shop. Death care goods and services are sold to consumers, especially the existing customers of the cemetery, using modern sales techniques which emphasize the pre-need purchase of a complete package of death care from one established provider.

The spread of combined operations, more so than the consolidation movement, is a factor that appears to threaten the independent establishments and even the stand-alone units of the clusters with which combinations compete. The availability of a funeral home at the site of a cemetery increases its attractiveness to the existing and future customers of the cemetery who might otherwise be inclined to use a stand-alone funeral home in the area. This inherent attractiveness of a funeral home attached to a cemetery may be exploited through the pre-need sales program of the cemetery. Unlike the benign process of consolidation, therefore, the effect of a process of combining a funeral home with a cemetery, especially a heritage one, may be to threaten the long-term survival of nearby stand-alone facilities. Like the effect of the development of supermarkets on the independent operators of stand-alone grocery stores, bakeries, and butcher shops, cemetery-mortuary combinations have the potential to use their marketing edge to gain market share at the expense of the stand-alone establishments with which they compete. There is thus a need to examine the development and operation of combinations as a force affecting the death care economy along with the consolidation movement.

Background

At one time not so very long ago, the concept of cemetery-mortuary combinations capable of providing complete death care to consumers was at odds with the tradition favoring a separation of the operations of funeral homes from those of cemeteries. As a historical artifact, this traditional separation of death care providers into two complementary types was justified by virtue of the convenience it provided when cemeteries (especially the larger, newer ones) were often less conveniently located than were many established funeral homes in relation to most mature residential neighborhoods. Economically, such separation probably implied some operating inefficiencies, but such was the cost of providing the kinds of death care goods and services desired by consumers from a divided death care sector.

Once established, this fragmented structure persisted in the face of changes which rendered it increasingly obsolete in growing metropolitan areas. Communities spread out, surrounding many suburban cemeteries and memorial parks, gradually making their locations more accessible and convenient than those of most older, urban funeral homes. In recognition of this obvious trend, some of the latter establishments relocated or branched out to the suburbs, but the separation of their operations from cemeteries was largely retained. On the one hand, this "stand-alone" strategy allowed a funeral home to cater to potential customers with preferences for many different cemeteries. On the other hand, it created the opportunity for commercial cemeteries to expand the scope of their operations by adding mortuaries. This opportunity differed from that represented by new stand-alone funeral homes for several reasons.

Advantages of Complementary Combinations

In the first place, an existing cemetery is already in the business of providing death care goods and services to the community in which it operates. By becoming a combined facility, it is merely adding to the array of goods and services it provides. This has the inherent appeal to consumers of having all the services required at death, from first call through memorialization, provided by one source at a single location. For services resulting in burial or entombment, this location must be a cemetery. Even when cremation is involved, crematories are normally located within cemeteries. Regardless of the form of final disposition desired, therefore, the union of funeral home, crematory, burial space, and memorialization goods and services together is a natural one, and this totality can exist only in a cemetery.

By exploiting the advantage of convenience, a new combination facility is likely to experience a much more rapid growth than is typical for new stand-alone funeral homes. Thus, the lengthy amount of time normally required to reach a break-even level of volume, a traditional barrier to entry into competition with existing funeral homes, is shortened for funeral homes built in cemeteries with established reputations and existing customer bases and sales organizations.

Moreover, the initial investment outlay required for cemeteries as they enter into the funeral service field does not involve the purchase of land. Additional investments required in other operating assets (e.g., equipment) also may be less than they would be for a comparable stand-alone facility. As a result, lower operating costs may be expected to result from the economies of scope associated with the joint operation of physically integrated facilities providing a wider variety of goods and services. Especially important in this regard are the savings in time made possible through unification of facilities engaged in providing a complete set of death care goods and services to consumers.

Technically, a measure of these economies of scope is

$$s = \frac{TC(Q_c) + TC(Q_m) - TC(Q_c,Q_m),}{TC(Q_c,Q_m)}$$

where $TC(Q_c)$ is the total cost of operating the cemetery by itself, $TC(Q_m)$ is the total cost of operating the mortuary by itself, and $TC(Q_c,Q_m)$ is the total cost of operating the cemetery-mortuary combination (Petersen and Lewis, 1994, p. 205). Given the necessary data on operating costs, the extent of the economies of scope associated with the joint operation of combined facilities is calculated as a percentage reduction in the total costs of operating other facilities together, instead of separately. A firm that takes advantages of economies of scope can operate at lower costs than other firms which do not, other things being equal. In a free market economy, entrepreneurs may be expected to seek to capture these economies of scope and, under competitive conditions, to pass them on to consumers (Petersen and Lewis, 1994, p. 205).

There are also miscellaneous advantages of combined operations. For example, we have mentioned the importance of a cemetery's existing customer base as a source of demand for its related funeral home. An additional consideration is that the location of a funeral home within a cemetery may increase the attractiveness and sales of cemetery goods and services to funeral home customers. These special interrelationships tend to enhance the profitability of both operations. The net effect of these factors is that higher rates of return on investment (or, alternatively, lower prices) are possible for funeral homes that are combined with cemeteries than for stand-alone funeral homes of comparable size and volume.

Further, because operating costs are lower for combinations, they can maintain profit margins while aggressively promoting the sale of pre-planned funeral services, in spite of the tendency for pre-need expenditures to average less than those at-need. Moreover, with respect to the pre-need sales operation at a combination, the higher values of the complete set of goods and services it offers for sale may be expected to increase the motivation, efficiency, and effectiveness of its sales force. More to sell, more to make, as they say.

The Legacy of Forest Lawn

The concept of such physically integrated facilities for providing death care actually is not new. It was pioneered by the late Hubert Eaton, who was the first to add a mortuary to the facilities at Forest Lawn Memorial Park of Glendale (Los Angeles), California, in 1933. According to Sloane's history of American cemeteries, "Eaton's decisions to expand the services offered by the memorial park was [sic] a major innovation in the history of the cemetery." He goes on to explain:

> A death in a nineteenth-century city usually meant work for a nurse (washing and preparing the body), a carpenter (making the coffin), a funeral director (supervising the funeral), a grave digger, a florist, and a stone carver (carving the marker or monument). The "full-service" memorial park threatened every link in the chain of service because it prepared the body, sold the casket and vault, arranged the funeral and grave or crypt, sold the flowers, and dictated that a customer place on the grave a bronze marker or statuary purchased through the management [1991, p. 176].

It was noted in Chapter 10, that Eaton coined the synthetic word "comemoral" to encompass his comprehensive view of a cemetery as a facility which is at the center of commemorative and memorial activities within a community. As a composite term, however, "comemoral" fails to include the role of the mortuary as a provider of technical mortuary services within the comprehensive facility.

To include this necessary aspect of the comprehensive facility into a single term, the word "morterial"— formed from the words *mortuary*, *cemetery*, and *memorial*— is suggested as an alternative to describe the comprehensive, complete death care establishment. Such a term might sound odd at first, but this is true of any composite term created to describe a new product or commercial establishment. In the absence of acceptance of this term, however, we hesitate to use "morterial" to refer to the "complete death care establishment." To refer to facilities of varying degrees of completeness in earlier chapters, we used the terms "cemetery-mortuary combination" frequently, "combined operations" often, and "combined establishment" occasionally, and we will continue to use these terms hereafter to refer to such facilities, whether they are "fully complete," "core complete," or "incomplete" death care establishments in a technical sense.

In Chapter 7 the number of combined establishments in the United States was reported to range from 900 to 1,450, based on industry estimates. The uncertainty about how many such facilities exist is due to confusion over the meaning of the term "combined establishment." To remove any uncertainty here the term "combined establishment" is defined as a facility capable of providing at least "core complete" death care. Technically, a "fully complete death care establishment," or "morterial," consists of a unified, physically integrated set of complementary facilities capable of providing fully complete death care: mortuary services, pre-final disposition, final disposition, and memorialization, all in a single location (a cemetery) owned in common. A "core complete" establishment must include a mortuary, a cemetery, and a memorial outlet, operated together in a single location which may or may not be owned in common. Any establishment which lacks one of these core elements is an incomplete death care establishment, even if it provides more than one element of the complete death care process.

To be complete, combined establishments must include the substitutable and complementary outputs of a mortuary, a cemetery, and a memorial outlet. Complete establishments may or may not include a flower shop providing floral goods and services to participants within the death care sector even though it does not fall within the sector.

A fictional version of a comemoral or morterial establishment was lampooned as a colossal American joke by British novelist Evelyn Waugh in his book *The Loved One*. Forest Lawn itself, and Eaton's vision that produced it, were targets for Mitford's criticism of American death care as a fraud perpetrated on the American public. Nevertheless, in America the ultimate test of an innovative business development is how well it sells. In this respect the development of Forest Lawn into the first complete death care establishment was a spectacular success. It established the model for memorial parks throughout the United States to emulate, as suburbanization created conditions in their areas which promised similar results.

This process occurred slowly but surely in several major metropolitan areas in the U.S. during the postwar years. Eventually the trend gathered momentum, and more and more cemeteries undertook the investment required to develop a mortuary on their premises. The prospects for success fueled an aggressive trend, in spite of the large investment it involved, frequent opposition from nearby funeral homes, and the often onerous state regulatory and local zoning requirements placed in its path.

On the model of Forest Lawn, most combined operations have arisen piecemeal from an established cemetery or memorial park whose suburban location has gradually become attractive for additional facilities, beginning with community mausoleums, then a crematory and columbarium, and finally a mortuary, including a flower shop. Existing customers of the cemetery thus have been offered additional goods and services which in turn have attracted new customers. With more to sell, the sales force of the cemetery achieved a larger average sale and a higher commission. Moreover, consumers themselves, when offered funeral services in addition to the customary line of goods and services sold by the sales force of a cemetery, could purchase a full package of death care products from such salespersons, often in advance of need, the way cemetery property has traditionally been sold. Unlike the mere consolidation of funeral homes and cemeteries, this posed a direct threat to the future business of so-called "stand-alone" funeral homes. And the threat was great, for the latter had relied traditionally upon the at-need sale of funeral services and had never developed aggressive pre-need sales organizations consisting of highly trained salespersons backed up by effective advertising and direct selling techniques.

As mentioned above, several of the national death care companies have been among the leading developers of funeral homes in the cemeteries they own. The most aggressive among them has been Stewart, which began as a cemetery operator and developed into a public company based at least in part on an expressed strategy of developing combined operations. On the other hand, it is a sign of the historical division within the death care sector that SCI, created by a funeral director, did not combine its cemetery and funeral home divisions until 1992, thirty years after it was organized. The second largest death care company, Loewen Group, also the creation of a funeral director, has not historically pursued a strategy of developing combinations within its cemeteries.

Consumer Welfare

The effects of the evolution of cemetery-mortuary combinations can be evaluated in two economic dimensions: (1) its impact on the welfare of consumers and (2) its impact on the performance of the death care sector of the economy. We begin with the former.

Obviously, the historical separation of death care providers into three or more types of establishments has meant that consumers at the time of death have had to contend with the problem of dealing with a variety of firms engaged in providing related goods and services. The difficulties of doing this and the potential confusion that it creates are exacerbated by the fact that consumers usually are forced to deal with the different establishments under difficult circumstances, which requires them to coordinate multiple decisions in a short period of time.

Alternatively, the decisions of consumers may be spread over long periods of time. Some of the decisions required may be entered into in advance of need, some at-need, and some even after the funeral and final disposition are over. Such disjointed decision making, involving transactions with several different firms, has its costs, and in terms of the analysis presented in Chapter 4 of this book, it seems likely to result in a less-than-optimal allocation of funds among the three components of death care. The integrated death care provider reduces the transaction costs incurred by consumers as they engage in the process of making death care choices. Whether their choices are made at-need or in advance of need, the fact that they occur together in a single transaction with an integrated establishment enables consumers to make an optimal allocation of funds among the three components of death care.

The single location of combined facilities contributes to attendance at funeral services, and it eliminates or substantially reduces the length of time required for funeral processions, as well as the need for a police escort. These time-saving and cost-reducing elements of funerals conducted at combined facilities represent potential advantages for consumers, but there are also value-enhancing features of an aesthetic nature which may contribute to consumer welfare, directly or indirectly. The serene environment of a cemetery seems more suitable as a background for the dignified services desired by most families than does the urban or suburban environment surrounding many stand-alone funeral homes or churches.

There is a another point bearing on consumer welfare, to which attention should be drawn. Several historians have noticed a modern tendency for the American public to avoid cemeteries, rarely visiting them and setting them apart from the life of the communities. One historian has called attention to "the isolation of the American cemetery" (Sloane, 1991, pp. 157–58).

Whatever the reasons, the effect has been for many cemeteries to become isolated places, divorced from the rest of society, often neglected and sometimes vandalized. This can only be interpreted as detrimental to the welfare of the real consumers — the survivors who visit the graves of deceased relatives, or even those who do not, but whose interest extends to the security of burial grounds. In this general sense it may be said that the combination of a funeral home with a cemetery brings vitality to the cemetery by tying the success of the funeral home to the continued maintenance and security of the cemetery. This, in turn, enhances the attractiveness of the mortuary.

The value-enhancing consequences of these mutually beneficial aspects of combined facilities may be expected to increase the welfare of consumers, and their benefits are likely to be used to advantage by combined operations in competitive situations.

Sector Performance

There is little doubt that from an economic standpoint the development of integrated death care establishments represents a rationalization of the fragmented way in which death care products and services have traditionally been delivered to consumers. The economic basis of this correction is rooted in the cospecialization of resources (assets and skills) employed in the production of the highly complementary components of complete death care. Maximizing organizational value requires using cospecialized assets together in the production of complementary outputs such as funeral services and burial. This implies a strong tendency for such assets to be owned by the same person or organization (Milgrom and Roberts, 1992, pp. 312–13).

Despite the case for this proposition, it expresses a tendency only. In actual practice a variety of factors affect the organization of industries and the way in which their organization evolves. One significant economic factor is the increased investment required to bring cospecialized assets under common ownership. A lack of available capital undoubtedly accounts for why so few urban funeral homes have attempted to integrate themselves into cemetery-mortuary combinations by acquiring or developing cemetery properties in the suburbs to which they could relocate or establish branches. An insufficiency of capital may also explain why it took so long for so many cemeteries and memorial parks to emulate Forest Lawn's successful attempt to develop combined operations in the 1930s. In the case of cemeteries, there was the further fact that many of them relied upon funeral homes as a source of at-need business. Funeral homes were in a position to black-ball cemeterians who considered adding a mortuary. Fearing this, cemeterians were slow to expand their scope.

For most cemeteries it was necessary also to wait for suburban development to make their locations on the outskirts of urban areas readily accessible for visitation and funeral services. Until this evolution occurred, the more convenient locations of stand-alone funeral homes, as compared with cemeteries and memorial parks, favored a continuation of the traditional separation of death care providers into funeral homes and cemeteries owned and operated by different persons or families.

The different occupational specializations of the owner/managers of each type of business was a further obstacle in the path of the "cemetery man" entering into direct competition with the "funeral directors," possibly provoking them to retaliate by directing customers to other cemeteries. Even though they had occasionally engaged in turf wars over such issues as the sale of vaults and other products, cemeterians who dared to establish a mortuary could expect strong resistance from funeral directors and their state and local associations. Eventually, of course, the prospects of high returns from beginning combined operations emboldened some cemeterians to make the investment in spite of possible conflicts with, and retaliation by, funeral directors. Their success then stimulated those in other areas, and the movement gathered momentum, to which the activity of several of the well-capitalized national companies has contributed.

As a result of this momentum, combined operations are now legal in most states, although obstacles remain in the form of state licensing requirements and local zoning ordinances which vary widely from place to place. One effect of these is to limit the extent to which complete death care establishments are available to consumers in some markets; another effect is to retard the entry of more cemeteries into the operation of integrated facilities. The economic value of combined operations has nevertheless been demonstrated in a large number of cases subject to vastly different local conditions.

Many local death care markets are characterized by some degree of monopolistic competition in the market for mortuary services or final disposition. There are also many cases of establishments which serve small towns or "niche" markets in large metropolitan areas that are virtually monopolists in the mortuary services or final disposition markets. When there is only one establishment of each type serving a market, they represent "successive" monopolies. The combined operation of those establishments eliminates the successive monopolies and produces a single integrated firm created from two separate firms having monopoly power in their separate markets. This arrangement has been shown to be socially preferable to "double" monopolies. The term "second best" is used to describe such arrangements. The term "first best" would entail competition at both levels, that is, there would be multiple establishments of each type, some of which might also be combinations. A textbook illustration of this is a case involving successive monopolies engaged in the production of motor boats and outboard motors by separate firms, each of which is a monopolist. By merging the two firms, the successive monopolies are eliminated, and the profit maximizing behavior of the combined firm can be shown to lead to lower prices for consumers. By comparison with the maintenance of the separate firms, "both the firms and consumers gain from the merger!" (Viscusi, Vernon, Harrington, 1992, pp. 222–24).

Such technical explanations require certain conditions and assumptions to be met, but in general and intuitively, a related case can be made in financial terms. If the combined facility involves a smaller total investment and some operating efficiencies by comparison with two separate facilities, then the revenues required from a given volume of cases may be less while providing an equivalent target rate of return. This implies lower prices for a combined facility. Furthermore, mature combined establishments tend to be higher volume operations than stand-alone funeral homes (due to the diverse customer bases of the cemeteries in which funeral homes are located); the higher volume of cemetery-mortuary combinations suggests that they are able to earn an equivalent target rate of return while operating on lower margins than is feasible in comparable stand-alone establishments with lower volume. This is clear from the basic financial nature of the rate of return on investment in assets (R.O.A.) of any type, namely:

R.O.A. = Profit Margin x Asset Turnover
R.O.A. = (Income/Revenues) x (Revenues/Assets)

Insofar as operating costs are lower when a mortuary is operated together with a cemetery, the combination is capable of providing a given target rate of return on assets while earning lower margins (based on lower mark-ups on merchandise costs) than for comparable stand-alone facilities. But that is not all. Insofar as the advantages conferred by combined operation result in higher revenues or lower investment in assets at a combined establishment, its turnover rate will be higher than for a comparable stand-alone establishment. At higher levels of turnover, lower margins (mark-ups) are necessary to provide a given rate of return on assets. Nor is that all. Insofar as similar advantages accrue to a cemetery that is operated together with a mortuary, the same is true for its operations. Other things being equal, therefore, the joint impact of these factors is that combined facilities are capable of higher rates of return on assets than comparable facilities operated separately. That is to say, combined establishments are capable of earning the same rate of return as comparable stand-alone establishments while charging lower prices than the latter. Even when the stand-alone facilities are operated as a part of a cluster, comparable combined establishments are potentially better equipped to compete with them and to out-perform them financially.

Market Impact

In terms of industrial performance, it appears that physically integrated death care providers are able to achieve economies of scope by expanding the variety of goods and services they offer to consumers. Insofar as these derive from the advantages of selling an expanded line of products through an existing sales organization, they are not unlike the economies that might be achieved by a local cluster of funeral homes that includes a cemetery. From a marketing standpoint, however, the combination establishment has the additional advantage of promoting to consumers the benefits of having complete death care provided at one convenient location. The combination also has significant advantages over a cluster in other respects. It saves the time of consumers by consolidating all services, products, and activities in one place, which is necessarily the site of a cemetery. To the extent that the attractiveness to consumers of a full-service provider leads to an increase in business at one or more of its component facilities, an integrated operation gains the benefits of economies of scale, which are associated with achieving fuller utilization of complementary equipment, facilities, and personnel. If costs are lowered as a result, as seems likely, the profits of integrated operations are likely to be higher than for clusters of equivalent volume, even if prices to the consumer are equal or lower.

If the prices charged by combinations are lower than those charged by cluster units or stand-alone firms with which they compete, the competitive advantages of combined operations are greater still. Insofar as these advantages of integrated establishments enable them to gain market share at the expense of unintegrated rivals, the profits of the latter are likely to decline over time, or their prices are likely to rise, or both. In the latter case, of course, the effect of raising prices is to drive one's customers toward the maximum end of their demand, as discussed in Chapter 8. Even if there is little price competition in a market, this is a risky strategy to adopt. It may well invite more customers to opt for caskets near the lower end of the line offered by a funeral home, or even for an alternative to the complete funeral. This, in turn, may result in customer dissatisfaction, which may lead to a loss of future business, possibly to the integrated establishment.

In any event, the mere availability of a mortuary in a cemetery seems likely to encourage the latter's customer base to use its mortuary also. Yet the probability that cemetery customers will switch to the mortuary on the same premises is a function of the strength of their attachment to existing stand-alone funeral homes. This attachment is a function of the reputations of the respective stand-alone funeral homes and the experiences of their customers with them. In some cases there may also be some deterrent (exclusionary) effect in the particular reputations of both mortuaries and cemeteries, but as a rule the large commercial cemeteries are designed and operated in ways which enable them to include a variety of groups which it is in their interest to attract. One effect of this has been that when cemeteries have entered into the operation of mortuaries, they have been able to promote the availability of a mortuary to the divers groups represented within the cemetery customer base. This has broadened the size of their potential market for mortuary services, enabling them to attract customers from most local mortuary rivals whose customers use the cemetery. The exception to this is those customers who return to the rival firms which appeal to them because of the deterrent (exclusionary) effect of their reputation. The customer base of such establishments may be less subject to erosion due to customer switching to combined facilities entering their market areas.

In light of the competitive advantages of combined operations, it is important to compare the development of combinations to the development of clusters. As a practical matter, the two strategies have tended to be employed together by the consolidators of the death care sector. Nevertheless, it is possible to draw some conclusions from a consideration of some basic differences between the two approaches.

Combinations vs. Clusters

For a long time the advantages of combined operations went unexploited by those in the cemetery field, despite the ripening of conditions in a number of areas. Combined operations first began at Forest Lawn in 1933 and at Restland of Dallas in 1957, but these were notable exceptions to the traditional separation between cemeteries and funeral homes. It was only a matter of time, however, until the success of these early combinations led to similar developments in most states where they were not prohibited by law. In many areas with varied local conditions, a growing number of independent cemeteries have now developed funeral homes on their properties. Some of these have done so in cooperation with established funeral homes, although the latter have tended to adhere to a stand-alone strategy, perhaps with multiple locations.

For their part, most of the large death care companies have historically owned and operated both cemeteries and funeral homes, while emphasizing the acquisition of the latter because of their generally higher profit margins. Often their acquisitions have involved unrelated stand-alone facilities spread over a sufficiently broad set of markets to justify a regional, national, or even international designation. In some cases the acquirees have been multiunit operations, and in others several acquisitions have occurred in the same market area, resulting in the development of clusters of separate facilities located near one another and operated together. Such a strategy may enable a chain company to achieve operational economies in local markets while appearing to grow more rapidly as acquisitions occur than a strategy of internal growth through the development of combined facilities, from the ground up so to speak. But this strategy is not without its drawbacks.

To begin with, the upfront funds required to add a mortuary to an existing cemetery, including the investment required, start-up costs, and the costs of carrying the facility from start-up to break-even, are smaller than the funds required to purchase a mature stand-alone funeral home of equal capacity. But the purchase of an existing establishment offers an immediate return to an acquiror because the margins and cash flows of the acquiror are not burdened with the costs of operating a new facility at low levels of utilization during its developmental and promotional stages. As a combination matures, however, the growth in its volume is likely to proceed at a rapid pace as a result of its appeal to consumers and its promotion by the pre-need sales force of the cemetery. The result is that a mature mortuary developed within or adjacent to a cemetery is likely to represent a much smaller investment than would a mature stand-alone facility of comparable size and volume. In other words, building volume through the development of a new combined facility is less costly than acquiring an equivalent case load by purchasing a mature establishment.

Direct investment in new facilities which then exploit the reputation of the cemetery avoids the necessity to pay for the established goodwill of an existing funeral home. Nevertheless, for public companies which are under pressure to improve upon financial performance year after year, the prospect of initially lower margins, earnings, and cash flows is an inhibiting factor tending to encourage those firms to acquire existing operations rather than to develop new ones. In the long run, the effect of this form of short-run thinking is to reduce the potential growth rate and rate of return on investment on those firms which adopt it. What is more, by inhibiting the development of new combinations, the effect of such a strategy of acquiring mature firms over the development of new combined establishments is to reduce the potential welfare of consumers who might well opt for the convenience of the new facilities. This effect may be permanent if the development of a local cluster, including the cemetery, reduces the incentive for it to be developed as a combination facility.

In local markets, a clustering strategy employed by death care chains tends to reduce competition and consumer choice, whereas the addition of mortuaries to cemeteries increases choice and competition. For the chain companies, the advantage of the latter strategy is that it effectively captures the growth to maturity of new facilities, enhancing long-term performance when compared to a strategy based on the purchase of mature funeral homes, often at premium prices. The cost of acquiring mature establishments would appear to exceed the cost of developing combinations. Further, the economic benefits of clusters, even when they include a stand-alone cemetery, are not as great as those of combinations resulting in integrated unified facilities, which save considerable amounts of time by virtue of their single location. Moreover, clustered facilities do not provide consumers with the convenient, time-saving features of combinations. Consequently, clusters would appear to be open to the threat of potential competition from cemeteries which establish their own funeral homes. Clusters do not of themselves address this threat to their stand-alone units, although the greater combined resources of a multiunit operation may be better able to absorb a loss of cases to a combination in their area.

Perhaps these considerations have not been lost on the death care chains, because all of them do indeed operate a number of combined facilities and have others under development. Nevertheless, in the aggregate only a small percentage of the properties owned by them at present are combined facilities, and most of these were the original creations of individual cemetery operators. Furthermore, when their strategies are examined more closely, only one of the national companies — Stewart Enterprises — appears to have adopted a growth strategy based specifically (but not exclusively) on the development of combinations. This may have something to do with the fact that the evolution of Stewart into an investor-owned chain company began in 1979 with the establishment of Lake Lawn Metairie Funeral Home on the premises of Metairie Cemetery, New Orleans. Much later, this commitment to a combination strategy was confirmed officially in documents Stewart filed as a public company with the Securities and Exchange Commission. These stated in part: "Because combined operations and clusters of individual funeral homes typically produce higher profit margins and cash flow than individual cemetery operations, the Company seeks primarily to acquire combined operations, premier cemeteries on or adjacent to which it can build and operate a funeral home, or individual funeral homes and cemeteries that form the basis of or strengthen a cluster of deathcare facilities."

A Case Study

The competitive advantages of combined operations over stand-alone funeral homes and clusters will be illustrated by a concrete case of the development and successful operation of an actual combination establishment.

Although it might be useful to present a variety of such cases, space permits us to present only one representative case. For this purpose we do not select Forest Lawn because of the special circumstances surrounding its origins as the first facility of its kind. For similar reasons we do not select Restland of Dallas (1957) or any other case of a very early combination. The history of each of these is interesting in its own right, but the long existence of those facilities diminishes their illustrative value. The conditions under which they were developed are unlike those which commonly exist today, and both cases benefited from long periods of rapid population growth in their geographic areas.

Lake Lawn Metairie Funeral Home (LLMFH for short) is a more representative case of the successful development and operation of a cemetery-mortuary combination in a mature market area with little or no population growth. Furthermore, as it happens, this facility is a combination we have followed from its inception in 1978. Accordingly, we have been able to observe the growth path of the facility over its entire life to this point. In addition, we prepared an earlier study of the success of LLMFH and its impact on the market in which it operates, using data provided by Stewart. With the further assistance of the company, these data have been brought up to date for use in the figures to be presented throughout.

In Chapter 17 these data will be examined along with evidence of the repercussions of the presence of LLMFH on other funeral homes in its market area. Before proceeding, however, it is important to point out that the establishment of LLMFH by an individual cemetery operator provoked legal opposition in the area — a reaction which has occurred in other areas also, not always with the same results.

Legal Opposition to LLMFH

In the case of LLMFH, the legal opposition took the form of three simultaneous lawsuits initiated by plot owners who objected to the establishment of the funeral home for several reasons. Each of these plot owners was related in some way to the owner-operators of local stand-alone funeral homes, but we leave that aside and consider the merits of the case. The three lawsuits, which were consolidated by the court, may be summarized in terms of their essential features, as described in court documents.

It was the contention of the plaintiffs in the case that Metairie Cemetery was "a dedicated cemetery for the burial of human remains" and that the use of the property for the operation of a funeral home was "contrary to cemetery purposes." It was contended further that any use of cemetery property by a funeral home constituted a "violation of plaintiffs' contractual rights" and was "also a violation of local zoning ordinances." One plaintiff contended that he had purchased his burial plot "under the representations made to him that the entire cemetery was dedicated exclusively for burial of the dead" (*Cressy*, 1980, pp. 1–2). In rebuttal, lawyers for Stewart and its partner in the venture contended that the operation of the funeral home on the premises "neither violates any vested rights of plaintiffs nor any zoning ordinances of the City of New Orleans," and they argued further that the operation of a funeral home in Metairie Cemetery "is consistent with the use of the property for cemetery purposes" (p. 2).

The court concluded that the sole issue for determination in the case was whether the construction and commercial operation of a funeral home, with administrative offices and a flower shop located therein, was "permissible use of Metairie Cemetery, consistent with cemetery purposes" (p. 2).

Court Findings

After examining various elements of the history of the property on which Metairie Cemetery is located, the court concluded: "It is clear that the entire cemetery property was indeed dedicated to be used for cemetery purposes. The intent was manifested by the owner, and there has been continuous use, for cemetery purposes, since 1872" (*Cressy*, 1980, p. 5). Nevertheless, the court held that dedication for cemetery purposes did not "limit the use of the property exclusively for the burial of dead bodies," as plaintiffs contended:

> There was no evidence presented in the form of a written instrument, which would support plaintiffs or which would indicate that specific restrictions were applicable and prevented any use of the property other than for burial of the dead. The evidence presented revealed that, contrary to plaintiffs' contention that representations were made that the entire cemetery has been dedicated for the burial of the dead, over the years there has been constructed on the cemetery property an information office, a chapel building, an administration office, a storage area, a sexton's house, a flower shop, and a crematory, all of which are incident to cemetery purposes but not exclusively for burial of dead bodies.
>
> No one would dispute the fact that cemeteries are destined to survive all other works of mortal man, and that they are decidedly among the permanent records which humans can leave for posterity. Accordingly, landscape and memorial art should be balanced and coordinated [so] that there will be an ideal fusion of God's art and that of man's. But regardless of the sacredness of a cemetery, there must be a certain amount of commercialism attached to it since it is a business and is subject to rules and regulations of the corporation owning it as well as laws of the State and municipality wherein it is located [*Cressy*, 1980, p. 5].

With respect to the rights of lot owners, the court affirmed that the cemetery had the right to use property not yet sold to an individual for "cemetery purposes, including interment of the dead or for anything" involved in the operation of a cemetery, a mausoleum and a crematory and, "without limitation, the interring of, and preparing for interment, dead human bodies, or for anything considered necessary, incidental or convenient in relation thereto" (*Cressy*, p. 6).

On the particular interests of the three plot-owners who filed suit, the court commented as follows:

> It is equally as interesting to note that the plots of all three plaintiffs are located a considerable distance from and out of sight of the funeral home. Yet no plot owners adjoining the funeral home site or within vision thereof have protested either the construction thereof or the operation of the facility, despite extensive advertisement between October 29 and November 3, 1977, publicly announcing the development of the funeral home in Metairie cemetery [*Cressy*, 1980, p. 7].

A clear distinction was drawn by the court between the Metairie case and an earlier case (1940) involving a misuse of cemetery property:

> The case of Humphreys vs. Bennett Oil Corporation, 195 La. 531, 297 So. 222 cited by plaintiffs has no application to the case at bar. The Humphreys case was a suit to collect damages for mental anguish and suffering caused by the desecration of a cemetery and the graves therein through the erection of drilling equipment on the cemetery property, a purpose inconsistent with the use for which it was dedicated [*Cressy*, p. 8].

Considering all the evidence presented, the court concluded that the construction and operation of Lake Lawn Metairie Funeral Home in Metairie Cemetery was "a use of the property consistent with cemetery purposes." Moreover, the court added: "The structure itself has beautified the cemetery, thus immortalizing reverence and sentiment, which should exercise an elevating influence on the entire community" (*Cressy*, p. 8). The structure is depicted on page 319 as it appears today.

Rivalry via Legal Channels

The legal reasoning adopted in this case followed closely that applied in *Wing v. Forest Lawn Cemetery Association* (1940). In that case the California Supreme Court held that a funeral home may be constructed and operated on cemetery property as long as it does not interfere with the access of lot holders to their lots.

Commenting on the importance of the Metairie case, Lapin (1981) notes that the rulings in other state courts have differed from those in the courts of Louisiana and California:

> There is, however, authority to the contrary in Georgia where *Greenwood Cemetery, Inc. v. MacNeil,* 213 Ga. 141, 97 S.e.2d 121 (1957), was tried, and courts in the state of Kansas have followed the *Greenwood* line of authority. It is the belief of the author, however, that the *Wing* line of cases is more fully reasoned and more consistent with desirable public policy in the interests of the consumer. The *Metairie* case is therefore significant, since it follows the line of cases most advantageous for the industry.
>
> This subject is likely to be litigated in other jurisdictions as the trend

Lake Lawn Metairie Funeral Home. Courtesy of Stewart Enterprises.

toward establishing funeral homes on cemetery property continues. Future cases with results similar to those in *Cressy v. Metairie Cemetery Ass'n* will help accelerate this trend [Lapin, 1981, p. 7].

To forestall this trend, the funeral directors in a number of states have attempted to establish legislative or regulatory obstacles in the way of complementary combinations. For example, as described in a recent article in *The American Funeral Director*, the Wisconsin Funeral Directors Association (WFDA) lobbied successfully for an amendment to a 1989 state law which itself prohibited cemetery-mortuary combinations.

The amended law would continue the previous prohibition and also forbid ownership of stand-alone funeral homes and cemeteries by the same company. This would limit the access of chain companies to the Wisconsin market. The WFDA claimed victory in this case, but SCI responded by buying a fourth cemetery in the state and filing a lawsuit against the agency responsible for enforcing the new legislation.

According to a report in *The American Funeral Director*, SCI's lawsuit seeks a "declaratory relief judgment" that asks the enforcement agency to interpret the amended law. The SCI explained its decision to pursue the lawsuit in the following statement made to *The American Funeral Director* (June 1994):

Like any successful business, SCI believes in America's free enterprise system. We believe that an open, competitive environment encourages all business to stay alert, and vibrant, and attuned to the needs of the public, since the value of any business concept is ultimately decided by consumers. We believe that public interest is better served by using the legislative process only to maintain a business environment in which all can compete.

In 1989, a very broad law was passed in Wisconsin. It prohibited funeral home and cemetery combinations, and further prohibited common ownership funeral home and cemetery businesses within the state. Hypothetically, an individual could circumvent this law by running a funeral home business in his or her own name and setting up a cemetery business in the name of a spouse or child. Companies like SCI do not have that option, so we compete by setting up separate companies to operate our funeral businesses. Shortly after the common ownership law was passed, the legality of SCI's operating position was challenged. After a thorough review, the legality of that operating position was confirmed by Wisconsin's Attorney General.

We do not believe that any recent modifications of the 1989 law have had any effect on the legality of SCI's operations within the state. We do believe, however, that the law is somewhat ambiguous and susceptible to varying interpretations in the future. Rather than continuing to operate under this uncertainty, we have filed a declaratory relief action in Wisconsin, for the court to interpret the law.

What is it about cemetery-mortuary combinations that leads funeral directors to mobilize against them in states like Wisconsin? They clearly are based on solid economic advantages arising from the joint operation of physically integrated facilities. They follow established patterns of the pursuit of such advantages by businesses in other industries. They are legal in the large majority of states, based on the kind of clear legal reasoning shown in the Louisiana and California cases mentioned above. In short, the combined operation appears to be a truly good idea for both consumers and providers of death care. So why are some funeral directors in Wisconsin and a few other states so adamantly opposed to cemetery-mortuary combinations? Through examining the history of Lake Lawn Metairie Funeral Home in the next chapter, perhaps the answer will be revealed.

17. Economic Impact of Complementary Combinations

Recapitulation

This is the second of two chapters devoted to an examination of some aspects of the performance of cemetery-mortuary combinations in the death care economy. In the previous chapter, an attempt was made to demonstrate the relative superiority of combinations over stand-alone funeral homes or clusters of stand-alone facilities in a single market area.

Among the many advantages of combinations, the most critical one is the competitive advantage which allows a combination to penetrate the funeral services market with relative ease. To demonstrate this in the context of a large metropolitan area, consideration is given here to the growth experienced by Lake Lawn Metairie Funeral Home (LLMFH) from its inception through 1993, a fifteen-year period. As described in Chapter 16, that establishment is located on the contiguous grounds of Metairie Cemetery (MC) and Lake Lawn Park (LLP), two jointly owned and operated cemeteries to which several community mausoleums and a crematory have been added over the years.

Since it began operation in 1979, the volume of the funeral home has grown dramatically to near-capacity at the present time. Based on such success, Stewart Enterprises has recently completed construction of All Faiths Funeral Home located on property leased from, and adjacent to, Greenwood Cemetery, a large, not-for-profit, fraternal burial ground near LLMFH and in the vicinity of six or more church or fraternal cemeteries in the area. In the face of this further expansion in an otherwise mature market, it is interesting to consider the effects of LLMFH's success on the competing stand-alone funeral homes in the area.

Case History

When first proposed by Stewart in 1977, the pending entry of a local cemetery operator into the funeral service market attracted the immediate attention of the owners of the local funeral homes with which the new combined facility would compete. In fact, at some point following the initial announcement, there developed negotiations leading to a decision by Jacob Schoen & Son, Inc., one of the oldest and largest local funeral home operators, to participate in the ownership and operation of the new facility. Many factors may have contributed to the decision of the family which owned the funeral firm, but it seems reasonable to assume that the decision was influenced by a perception that the new facility posed a serious threat to its future business, especially at its largest funeral home, where a significant number of cases involved interments in Metairie Cemetery and Lake Lawn Park.

The new combination facility thus became a joint venture between a leading funeral home and a leading cemetery operator in the metropolitan area. To facilitate its entry into the funeral service market, it might have helped for the combined facility to incorporate the name of the participating funeral home. This did not occur, however, because of fears that it would accelerate the loss of cases at the firm's stand-alone locations. Unable to capitalize on the name and reputation of the participating funeral home, the combined facility became known instead as Lake Lawn Metairie Funeral Home based on the names of Metairie Cemetery and Lake Lawn Park. Although we identify the facility by name, it is not our purpose to promote this particular facility; it is rather to examine the practical effectiveness of a combined operation as a successful phenomenon together with its remarkable impact on its market area — events which increasingly are facts of life in the death care economy.

In the 1970s, of course, a cemetery-mortuary combination was still a novel idea untried in the New Orleans area. Perhaps the most indicative early sign of its potential, however, was that LLMFH's entry into the market led to the three simultaneous lawsuits backed by competing funeral home interests that were discussed in the previous chapter. Interestingly, although these lawsuits failed, the publicity surrounding the litigation probably served to accomplish two unintended results: (1) to inform the existing customers of MC and LLP of the availability of a funeral home at their location, and (2) to promote the convenience and attractiveness of a full-service facility in one location, features which were not previously available to consumers in the area. In any case the combined facility went forward as a joint venture, which was eventually dissolved upon the sale of the participating funeral service company by the family. Subject to previously agreed upon terms in the joint venture, the company which owned the cemetery then became the sole owner of LLMFH, which is now a mature facility handling in excess of 1,250 cases annually.

Graphic Results

Since we first began to study combined operations in 1977, we were given the opportunity to review the original projections for LLMFH. In the beginning we were skeptical about the ability of the facility to deliver the rapid growth in volume of funerals projected over a planning horizon of ten years. Yet, as we

have followed figures compiled from death notices published in the area's newspaper over the years, the actual growth we have observed has been convincing.
Rather than base our analysis on these newspaper notices, however, we were
able to obtain from the chairman of Stewart Enterprises the official figures on
LLMFH's performance. The data are presented here in figures 17.1 through 17.5.

Figure 17.1

**Total Funeral Calls of LLMFH,
1979–1993**

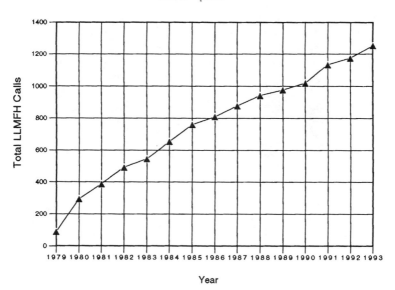

As shown in Figure 17.1, the annual number of cases (calls) handled by
LLMFH has grown from 88 in 1979 to 1,250 in 1993. This is undeniably an
impressive record of growth, almost unheard of for a new entrant into the funeral
service field. As a case in point, it provides compelling evidence for the competitive advantages of cemetery-mortuary combinations postulated above.

In further confirmation of those advantages, Figure 17.2 (next page) presents the cumulative backlog of pre-planned funerals at LLMFH for each year
during the six-year period from 1988 through 1993. As may be seen, the backlog grew rapidly to around its 1993 level over the facility's early years. At this
stage of maturity, the upward drift in the figure suggests that pre-need sales
continue to exceed a growing number of pre-planned services delivered each
year. The 1993 backlog amounted to roughly six times the facility's annual volume. This figure, which far exceeds the national average backlog for funeral
homes, must have benefited to some extent from the advantages of selling

Figure 17.2
Historical Backlog of
Pre-planned Funerals at LLMFH

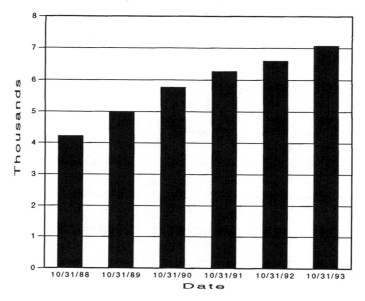

pre-planned funerals through the cemetery's existing sales organization. Obviously, the costs of acquiring this large backlog of funerals have been reduced because it was produced jointly with the sale of cemetery goods and services.

Figure 17.3
Total Funeral Calls at LLMFH (1979–1993)
and Total Interments at LLP and MC (1963–1993)

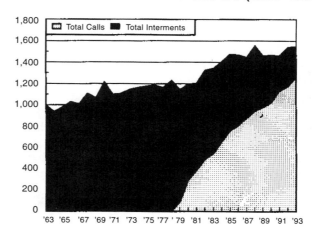

In Figure 17.3 a series representing the annual number of interments in LLP and MC since 1963 is superimposed on the annual number of calls at LLMFH since its inception. This is done to illustrate the shot in the arm experienced by the cemetery as a result of the addition of the funeral home. That also was postulated above, and it implies that the combined operation gains a competitive advantage over the stand-alone cemeteries with which it competes.

Figure 17.4
Percent of Interments in MC
and LLP That Used LLMFH

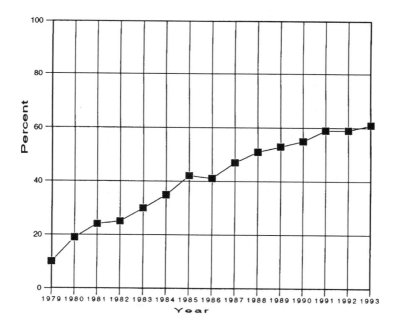

Figure 17.4 is a presentation of the percentage of the annual interments at MC and LLP which used LLMFH. It will be noted that this percentage has increased from 10.2 percent in 1979 to 58.9 percent in 1991 and is still rising. In other words, since its inception the funeral home has continued to capture the customer base of the cemetery, as predicted in the analysis presented above. Based on the experience of fully mature combinations, this rate may eventually reach as high as 80 percent, but there are too few such facilities to regard this as a reliable expectation.

A final set of data, presented on page 326 as Figure 17.5, shows the percentage of the annual number of cases handled by LLMFH which result in interments in MC or LLP. As will be seen, this figure has remained relatively stable over the years at a level in the 70 percent range. This provides further evidence for the view that consumers are strongly attracted to the convenience of a

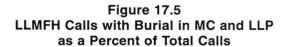

Figure 17.5
LLMFH Calls with Burial in MC and LLP
as a Percent of Total Calls

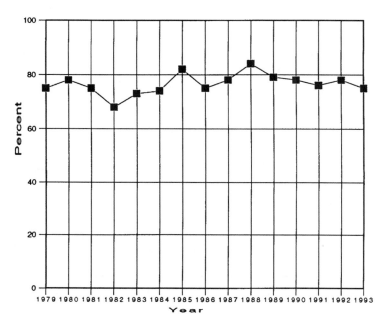

combined facility. Conversely, it also suggests that LLMFH has continued to draw around one-quarter of its growing case load on its own merits as a provider of funeral services unrelated to its status as a combination.

Taken together, figures 17.4 and 17.5 are indicative of the large extent to which a combined facility may be expected to obtain the benefits of joint operation because it is clear that a majority of the interments at the cemetery now involve cases handled by LLMFH, and roughly three-quarters of the cases handled by the funeral home result in final disposition in the cemetery.

In Summary

Data relating to the financial performance of LLMFH are not separately disclosed by Stewart Enterprises. Although rough estimates of the success of the facility in financial terms may be derived from the figures provided on its case load, any attempt to make such estimates here would be a digression. It would involve the use of averages based on the company's funeral service segment revenues, operating expenses, and profit margins available in its annual report. But such averages reflect the results of the company's mix of clusters of stand-alone funeral homes and cemeteries as well as its combined operations. Figures of that sort do not permit any inferences about the prices, costs, or profits of a particular facility. The operating efficiencies postulated above for combinations must remain in the nature of plausible hypotheses.

As to the miscellaneous advantages of combined operations discussed above, the data presented appear to be consistent with the view that the sales and profits of a cemetery are benefited by the presence of an affiliated funeral home, and vice versa. Similarly, the data presented on the growth of the backlog of pre-arranged funerals at LLMFH and the boost it provided to interments in the cemetery would seem to confirm the mutual benefits of a combination on the sales effort. Admittedly, these relationships are not more closely analyzed, but clearly the data presented in figures 17.1 through 17.5 demonstrate convincingly the effectiveness of a facility like LLMFH at penetrating an existing market by exploiting the competitive advantages of combinations.

Implications

It goes without saying that results as impressive as those of LLMFH may not be forthcoming in every case. No two cemeteries are alike; in terms of their locations, sizes, reputations, and many other factors, they are different operations, subject to different conditions prevailing in their local market areas. Obviously, in evaluating the prospects of any cemetery as a site for a related funeral home, all these particulars must be taken into account. Any one or more of them may affect in varying degrees its feasibility as a potential combination.

Where feasible, however, the potential of combined operations has been proven by the number of such facilities established in the last twenty years. According to industry observers, most or all of these have performed well by effectively penetrating their markets. Apparently, there are some aspects of the present case which are applicable to many cemeteries, namely, those competitive advantages discussed above. Perhaps the most important of these is the existing customer base of a cemetery as a source of potential demand for the services of its related funeral home, but its reputation for providing death care and its sales organization and methods are also important contributors to its success.

With respect to the success of LLMFH in particular, it is important to emphasize that the cemetery in which it is located is what has previously been described as a "premier" or "heritage" cemetery. At such a facility, the annual number of interments represents a not insignificant share of the local market, a factor which undoubtedly contributed to the rapid success and growth in volume experienced by LLMFH at the expense of the existing stand-alone funeral homes in the area. With LLMFH now approaching capacity (for its initial size), it is likely that steps will soon be taken to expand that facility. In addition, as noted above, Stewart recently established a new funeral home adjacent to a large, not-for-profit fraternal facility located a short distance from LLMFH in a neighborhood that contains no less than six other active church or fraternal cemeteries. This second facility thus represents a new form of combined operation with a twist, so to speak, involving a partnership of sorts with cemeteries not owned by Stewart. This is an extension of the strategy of adding funeral homes to cemeteries owned by the company.

It remains to be seen whether a second combined operation in the same neighborhood can duplicate the success of LLMFH. Clearly, the company is counting on tapping the existing customer bases of the adjacent cemetery and the other ones nearby while exploiting the competitive strengths it demonstrated in the previous case. Minor differences aside, it seems likely that the outcome will be similar. But we can be sure that the existence of a second combination of the sort proposed can only add to the loss of cases suffered so far by some of the existing stand-alone funeral homes in the area as a result of LLMFH. To examine the extent of the losses experienced by such firms, and their responses to them, will be the purpose of the rest of this chapter.

Impact on the Market

In what follows, we do not identify the stand-alone firms involved as we do not wish the conclusions to be taken as anything else than the product of plausible observations based on some general knowledge of the conditions under which funeral homes operate. One of these conditions common to mature market areas is the relatively stable number of deaths occurring each year as life expectancy improves and the population ages simultaneously. This is true in the area under consideration here, for example, where the annual number of deaths per year is today approximately the same as before LLMFH entered the market more than a decade ago. Since then, however, the number of cases it handles each year has grown steadily from zero to 1,250-plus as the attractions to consumers of its combined facilities have proved sufficient to overcome strong traditional loyalties to existing stand-alone funeral homes in the area. It follows that the case loads of those competing establishments must have dropped considerably, impacting them all to some extent and perhaps even threatening the survival of some.

Other things being equal, the repercussions of a continuing loss of cases for the affected stand-alone funeral homes would necessarily be a lower level of profits. That, in turn, would imply a loss in the values of their funeral homes as profit-making businesses. Other things do not remain equal, of course, as existing firms initially anticipate and later experience the impact of new competition, pressuring them to respond. In this case the greatest pressure was forecast to be experienced by several local funeral homes, many whose customers were also the actual or potential customers of MC or LLP. The LLMFH posed less of a threat, or none at all, to nearby mortuaries whose customers were mostly tied to cemeteries other than MC or LLP or were likely to select other cemeteries based on such factors as location, prices, ethnic orientation, and so on.

Social and Business Relationships

As expected, the success of LLMFH led to various responses on the part of the affected stand-alone funeral homes in the area. Those responses are discussed here within the context of a general consideration of the methods by which rival establishments and firms may attempt to compete with one another. In this case, all of the firms affected by LLMFH were long-established firms owned or managed by families with strong reputations as funeral directors. As is typical of the field, the owners and managers of these firms were active participants in social and service organizations in the area. Each served, more or less well-defined segments of the local market as a whole. All of them performed services which involved interment in Metairie Cemetery, Lake Lawn Park, or other cemeteries in the area owned by Stewart Enterprises. Although they sometimes were in a position to steer some customers away from Stewart-owned cemeteries as a form of retaliation for the entry of LLMFH into their market, it appears that any such action had little or no adverse impact on the volume of business at MC and LLP (see Figure 17.3). Nevertheless, it is only reasonable to suppose that it did occur and has occurred, perhaps with more noticeable effects, in other cases where cemeteries have added a mortuary in direct competition with the established funeral directors in the area who were in a position to "steer" their customers away from the cemetery in question. This sounds like a shady practice, but to abstain from it would be to risk losing future generations of business to the funeral home of the combined facility by default.

Legal Maneuvering

The operations of both cemeteries and funeral homes are subject to laws that vary considerably from state to state, and at various times the relationship between these two primary providers of death care has been the subject of legal maneuvering on both sides, with varying degrees of success, producing a patchwork of different laws and regulations applicable to each. In most states, however, cemeteries are now allowed to operate a related funeral home. At the same time, there are still some states or municipalities in which cemeteries are prohibited from doing so in spite of the difficulties of justifying such a ban under the conditions of free enterprise to which most of us supposedly subscribe.

Even in areas where combinations are not prohibited, the operators of funeral homes have sometimes attempted to use state or local laws and regulations to restrict or to impede the freedom of cemeteries to enter into competition with them. In the case of LLMFH these attempts were futile.

Cooperation

The goods and services of cemeteries and funeral homes are complementary in nature, and the two types of establishments are closely linked in the public mind. Combinations and clusters which include a cemetery have linked their operations as well. But where the two businesses are separately owned and operated, their points of contact have often resulted in animosity and conflict — historically over sales practices and more recently over the development of cemetery-mortuary combinations. While most funeral home owners have viewed the latter as a threat, a few have taken the opportunity to participate with a cemetery in the operation of a combined facility. Through partnerships or joint ventures of this kind, a funeral home relocates or establishes a branch in or adjacent to the cemetery, gaining access to its customer base and pre-need sales organization. The cemetery obtains the benefits of the reputation and following of the funeral home which participates in the project. This could be especially important to the growth in volume of the combination in the early years of its operation before the effects of its pre-need sales program begin to pay off.

As discussed in a previous section, after LLMFH was proposed by Stewart Enterprises, it subsequently became a joint venture between that company and a leading funeral home operator in the area. As a partner, the latter stood to make up for the cases it lost to the combination. To avoid accelerating such losses, however, it did not allow its name to be used in connection with the combined operation. It is therefore difficult to say what, if anything, other than financial support, the cemetery gained from the partnership. Eventually the joint venture was dissolved when the participating funeral service firm was sold by the family. Full ownership of the combination then reverted to the owner of the cemetery in which it is located. In other cases, however, cooperation between a cemetery and a funeral home in the operation of a combination has endured, and it may provide the basis of a potential trend toward more combinations owned jointly by independent cemeteries and local funeral homes affiliated or unaffiliated with the chain companies. Nevertheless, cooperation represents an option which may not be available in many cases, and even if it is, the opportunity is limited to only one of the funeral homes likely to be affected by a proposed combination. The fate of most stand-alone firms is to attempt to coexist with new competition from such a facility. This is what has occurred as affected funeral homes have responded to LLMFH's presence in their market area by one or more of the strategies discussed in the following sections.

Cost Reduction

When stand-alone funeral homes experience a loss of cases due to the competitive presence of a combined facility, their average cost per case rises. In most industries this would signal a need to reduce costs, but a large proportion of the costs of funeral homes is fixed. This feature of their operations limits their ability to adopt a cost-cutting strategy without affecting quality, which in the delivery of funeral services includes the capacity to be of service on demand. In addition, most funeral homes, like other businesses, experienced higher operating and regulatory costs during the decade of the 1980s while the initial loss of cases to LLMFH was occurring. They may also have experienced some shifting away from traditional funerals toward lower-priced alternatives involving cremation. It seems unlikely, therefore, that under such conditions the benefits of any cost reductions undertaken by the most affected firms could have been commensurate with their loss of revenues, implying higher prices or lower profits or both, unless other means of improving efficiency like consolidation were also pursued.

Consolidation

Unable to reduce costs much on their own, firms experiencing or expecting a declining case load may attempt to achieve greater operating efficiencies by joining a regional or national chain organization. The benefits of this derive in part from the ability of chains to create clusters of funeral homes or cemeteries or both within the same geographic area, with resulting operating economies. This is precisely what occurred in the case under consideration here, and with a vengeance. Since LLMFH began operation in 1979, most of the affected funeral homes — consisting of eight firms operating at fifteen stand-alone locations — have been sold by their previous owners to Security Industrial Companies, a privately owned burial insurance company based in the state of Louisiana. That company also acquired a large cemetery in the metropolitan area, creating a complete cluster of facilities which it sold to Loewen in 1995. Another local firm operating two stand-alone funeral homes in the metropolitan area was sold to Loewen in 1994.

We do not know to what extent, if any, the competitive threat posed by LLMFH influenced the owners of all these firms to sell when they did. We do know, however, that several of the firms handled a large number of cases that involved burial, entombment, or cremation at LLP or MC, where LLMFH is located. We also know that most of the firms were long-established, family-owned and operated firms which had previously never been sold. One such sale might not justify any inference, but a pattern of sales would seem to suggest that these firms encountered some difficulties in continuing to operate on their own in a more competitive marketplace. The benefits of operating as part of a chain may better enable them to overcome these difficulties without resorting to substantially higher prices in order to maintain customary levels of profits.

Increased Advertising

In some industries the appearance of new competition in a local market might lead rival firms to reduce prices in order to retain customers and attract new ones. But for various reasons, funeral homes do not ordinarily compete on the basis of prices. Faced with the prospect or actuality of a loss of cases, they are more likely to seek other ways of reinforcing consumer loyalty and attracting new business. One of the traditional ways of doing this is to engage in advertising whereby the name and heritage of a funeral home is kept in front of consumers — in newspapers, on radio and television, or on billboards. According to local observers, some of the stand-alone firms affected by LLMFH have increased their advertising, but we do not know to what extent this increase was due to competition from LLMFH or to what extent it has succeeded in overcoming the attractions of a combined facility that also advertises heavily and employs direct selling methods practiced by a major sales force trained to sell a complete package of death care products.

Some of the advertising copy used by the local cluster of stand-alone funeral homes has pointed out to consumers that they are not obliged to use a funeral home simply because it is located within or adjacent to a cemetery of their choice. But it is the convenience of doing so which appeals to the customers of such cemeteries. In their minds this factor may overcome even long-standing ties to a stand-alone funeral home. Nevertheless, the owners of stand-alone establishments may have little choice but to attempt to increase their advertising as a means of reinforcing their heritage or other attractions. Whatever positive effects may be expected to flow from such a competitive strategy, it is certain to add to the costs of the firms which adopt it as part of an overall strategy. Unless the advertising is so effective as to do even more than simply retain a case load, the average cost per case will rise as a result, suggesting a decrease in profit unless other costs are cut or prices are raised, or both.

Promotion of Pre-Planning

In order to finance their development and to avoid competing directly with funeral homes at the time of death, cemeteries long ago began to sell death care goods and services in advance of need. As a result, many of them developed strong pre-need sales organizations which employ marketing techniques such as canvassing and telemarketing aggressively. This strategy has been the key to the long-term growth of many cemeteries whose annual pre-need sales often exceed at-need by a wide margin. But in sharp contrast, the opposite is true of funeral homes whose owners have hesitated to adopt pre-need sales methods for various reasons. As a result, most funeral homes do not have strong sales organizations equal to those of cemeteries. When the latter have established funeral homes, they naturally have sought to integrate the sale of pre-need funeral services into their existing sales apparatus. Integrated selling presumably gives combinations an advantage over stand-alone funeral homes which attempt to develop a pre-need orientation. Nevertheless, some of the advertising campaigns undertaken by the rivals of LLMFH have emphasized pre-planning in an apparent attempt to tie future business — involving traditional funerals — to their firms and to earn additional income from selling insurance used to fund pre-planned services.

Again, we cannot attribute this to the competition from LLMFH. It probably has more to do with the fact that a burial insurance company initially acquired so many funeral homes in the area, as mentioned above. The situation may thus be a special case. In general, there are several reasons why a strategy of promoting pre-planning may be uneconomic for a typical stand-alone funeral home trying to compete against a combination:

1. In addition to the costs of promoting and administering a pre-need business, which may or may not be offset by the sale of insurance, further pressure on profits occur if pre-planned services are substituted for at-need in a firm's case load. At least this is so to the extent that pre-need expenditures for traditional funerals tend to average less than those arranged at-need. If so, this implies lower profits, at least in the long run, for firms which seek to compete with a combined facility by promoting pre-planning. The same does not apply, however, for combinations, whose operating costs are likely to be lower than for comparable stand-alone firms, allowing profit margins to be maintained on the pre-need sales of the former.

2. Pre-planned funerals may lock consumers into traditional funerals, but they are not a reliable means of tying future business to a particular funeral home. Unlike pre-sold cemetery property, the insurance sold to fund pre-need funeral services is easily transferable to competing funeral homes. What is more, such transfers are likely to be actively encouraged in the advertising campaigns of combinations such as LLMFH.

3. Many consumers already know that pre-planned funerals are available from most funeral homes. Promotion of the practice, to the extent that it involves advertising the generic benefits of advance planning, may simply serve to heighten the awareness of consumers about its importance. This actually may redound to the advantage of the stronger marketing force which typically belongs to the integrated sales organization of a combined operation.

Despite these considerations, stand-alone firms faced with increased competition from combinations may be forced to promote pre-need sales in an effort to minimize the continued erosion of their case loads. Where clustering has taken place in a market, as in the present case, the greater resources of the cluster may contribute to the effort, but the above three considerations raise doubts about the ability of the cluster to maintain the case loads of its units by promoting pre-planning. If those doubts are correct, the affected units or the cluster as a whole eventually will be obliged to raise prices or to accept lower profits or both as cases are lost to a combination.

Higher Prices

It may seem that the easiest way for existing stand-alone funeral homes to cope with a loss of cases to a combined facility would be simply to increase their prices. A sufficiently higher average price per case perhaps would help to cover higher average costs per case sufficiently to maintain profits. Since the loss of cases to LLMFH was spread over several firms with high volumes, the price increases required may not have been large enough to affect their acceptability to customers. Excessive price increases required to compensate for a heavy loss of cases might not be acceptable and might adversely affect a firm's reputation in the market. Even moderate increases may alter an establishment's stable pattern of sales by causing some customers to trade down in a given line of goods and services or even to choose a less traditional funeral.

It is thus incorrect to assume that higher prices will automatically enable a funeral home to maintain profits as its case load falls. This casts doubt on the effectiveness of simply raising prices as a means of adapting to increased competition from a combination. If the price structure of the latter reflects lower costs resulting from its operating economies, price comparisons become increasingly unfavorable to existing stand-alone firms as their prices rise. And while price competition and advertising are still unusual in most mortuary services markets, funeral homes are now required to quote prices under federal regulations so that comparisons can be made if consumers are inclined to make them.

Reduced Profits

Whether or not one or a combination of the above strategies, was utilized, it is likely that part of the impact of LLMFH has been absorbed by an erosion of profits at some firms in its market area. A reduction in profits is consistent with a smaller volume of business, but it is inconsistent with the customary stability of funeral homes as businesses. A moderate reduction may be acceptable to the owner-managers of firms who are not compensated solely from profits. As investments, however, the value of any business depends mostly on profit levels and trends. If the profit potential of a stand-alone funeral home is adversely affected by a combination, its investment value will decline by an amount approximately equal to the present value of the reduction of future cash flows attributable to the increased competition over time.

It is not clear whether LLMFH has trimmed the values of rival establishments in the New Orleans market. In the case of several recent acquisitions, it appears not to have done so, but it is difficult to judge from only a few cases. Too many idiosyncratic factors affect negotiations resulting in a particular transaction. Also, it may be that competition among chains in pursuing acquisitions has helped to support valuations, even in markets in which combinations exist or are planned. This is especially so where acquirers stand to benefit from operating a cluster of facilities in a particular market. In general terms, however, the competitive advantages of combinations would seem to affect adversely the expected profit streams — and therefore the projected cash flows — of affected firms. In simple present value terms, this can only lead eventually to lower calculated business values on which transactions are based. This assumes, of course, that the competitive advantages of combinations are recognized by acquirors and acquirees as they negotiate purchases and sales. It is not entirely clear that such is the case.

Summary and Implications

If this assessment is correct, the market in New Orleans has managed to absorb the impact of more than a decade and a half of competition from LLMFH by a combination of strategic responses aimed at stemming a continuing loss of cases and adapting to a lower level of volume. Unfortunately for the stand-alone firms involved, none of the available strategies seems to be without its complications, and most appear to entail some necessity to raise prices in order to maintain customary levels of profit. Given the ability and willingness of affected firms to take such action, it may well be that some firms have been able to maintain their customary profit levels in spite of the cases lost to LLMFH so far. This, however, seems unlikely to have been possible for the firms most affected.

The question now becomes whether firms already subject to the impact of LLMFH will be able to absorb the impact of another combined facility located, for all practical purposes, in a second cemetery in the area and near several others. Further loss of volume by competing firms will lead almost certainly to further pressure on them to increase prices or to accept still lower profits. Further consolidation may occur; also aggressive advertising, some promoting pre-arrangement, will probably continue to characterize the market.

In the long run, which may be even longer than usual in an economic sector characterized by strong, even intergenerational, loyalty to individual establishments, the profits of the firms most affected eventually will suffer, leading to lower values for some funeral homes in this area and in other markets where cemeteries establish their own mortuaries as a means of increasing their revenues and exploiting their pre-need sales organizations. Market areas differ widely, of course, and in the one under consideration here, the loss of cases was spread over several large existing multiunit establishments, limiting the effect on any one of those firms. In other mature markets, especially smaller ones served by fewer firms, the impact per firm may be greater. This is true, for example, in a number of markets where funeral homes are currently planned in cemeteries owned by the large chain operators. In some areas the impact of a combination may be greater because it comes on top of unfavorable demographic trends or a gradual shift away from traditional funerals. Even in growing markets, the competitive advantages of combinations must be viewed as a potential threat to the traditional stability and longevity of existing funeral homes. They too may have to consider using strategies such as those discussed above, or still more innovative and effective ones, to cope with the inherent attractiveness to consumers of combined operations whose services are promoted and marketed aggressively.

Any attempt to explore all the options available to independent stand-alone funeral homes is beyond the scope of the present case study. One option bears mentioning, however, because it was a factor in the case presented above. Some of the affected firms were participants in a cooperative livery pool, and such pooling arrangements have become a growing trend in other industries in which small firms have begun to share resources (e.g., equipment, facilities, and personnel) as a means of adjusting to difficult economic conditions and increased competition from units of chains. This is only one example of the directions in which funeral homes may go as they rethink their traditional ways of doing business in order to mitigate the impact of combinations and clusters on their operations.

The evolution of these new forms of competition appears to require that independently owned stand-alone firms coevolve if they are to coexist as alternative providers of death care. Expansion of the niche-building in which funeral homes have traditionally engaged may be the basis for holding or even increasing their market presence. Franchising has not been tried in the death care industries, but it would appear to have some application. From time to time, one hears of radical departures from traditional business practices by some funeral directors (Levine, *Forbes*, May 11, 1992), and other industries provide examples of strategies (e.g., joint marketing or purchasing arrangements) which may be appropriated by funeral homes.

Although the latter have been slow to adopt new methods of operation and competition in the past, wider adoption of such methods is likely to occur as more of them are forced to meet the competition posed by the spread of cemetery-mortuary combinations and clusters of facilities in a local area. In the case presented here, the largely defensive tactics employed by rival firms do not appear to have done much to offset the competitive strengths of a well-positioned combination. It would nevertheless be unwise for any cemetery to base a decision to establish a combined facility on the assumption that funeral homes in general are too inflexible and tradition-bound to compete against combinations aggressively. In particular, clusters of stand-alone establishments operated by the national chains may represent stronger competition for a combination than the locally owned cluster formed in the present case. Generally speaking, though, the competitive position of a combination is superior to that of a cluster of separated establishments in an area.

As a final point, it should be mentioned that the above analysis has concerned itself with the impact of a combined facility on the existing stand-alone funeral homes in an area, regardless of who owns and operates the combined facility. It will be recalled that the facility discussed here began operation as a joint venture between a leading cemetery and a leading stand-alone funeral home, and this has occurred in other cases as well. Different roads may lead to the same destination, which appears to be a growing number of combined facilities providing complete death care to consumers. Whether these facilities are the creations of cemeteries alone or partnerships between cemeteries and established funeral homes is up to those in the two traditionally separate segments of the sector. In any event, the practical result is the integration of the operations of various types of death care providers which breaks down the traditional boundaries separating them.

In a similar way, one of the important long-run effects of the development of chain companies has been to impose cooperation on the cemeteries and funeral homes which belong to their organizations. In the process, of course, they have sometimes encountered dissension between those different units or divisions. Differences in the socialization, experience, and orientation of those who move into the management structure of an integrated firm may limit its capacity to develop a unified outlook and strategy. Through the creation of appropriate structures and policies, the regional and national death care companies are, however, in a better position to impose order on the members of their industries than are the trade associations. They may thus be a force for unification of the death care economy as a whole, especially where their strategies involve the development of clusters and combinations which unite funeral homes and cemeteries as operating units. By the same token, the existence of large religious and fraternal cemeteries in some areas would appear to form the basis of a potential trend for noncommercial cemeteries to join forces with local funeral homes or the regional and national chains with the resources and experience required for such projects.

The net effect of these trends is likely to be a gradual but continual blurring of the lines that historically have separated cemeteries from funeral homes. The ultimate outcome may be that in more market areas the two types of establishments will lose their separate identities in a larger concept of death care provided by "morterials." Taking a backward look, it is clear that the development of unified facilities focused on providing complete death care has proven to be a major force for change in the structure of local death care markets. In terms of its ultimate impact in those markets which lend themselves to it, it may turn out to be far more important than the advent of investor-owned chains and federal regulation or the inroads made by cremation and alternative services.

Creative Destruction

The LLMFH combination appears to represent a case of what has been described as a process of "creative destruction" in which a better way of doing business upsets traditional ways. In some industries this process has been driven by what Porter (1990) describes as an "imperative to de-integrate" on the part of most service providers (p. 244). This refers to the increased ability or necessity for such firms to systematize their service delivery processes. Porter remarks:

> The firm is able to replicate services consistently and efficiently at many locations because it creates standardized facilities, methodology, and procedures to guide the behavior of employees, and automates individual service delivery tasks. The ability to systematize service delivery is partly a function of the tendency toward more *narrow specialization* in the services provided in an individual establishment. Instead of garages, for example, we now have quick oil change centers, muffler shops, transmission centers, and a number of other specialized car care establishments [p. 245].

This has occurred also in the death care economy to a limited extent. Firms providing direct dispositions or graveside services only and even casket stores have emerged in some markets. Yet the dominant trends in the death care sector have been in the direction of integrating the functions involved in providing a broader spectrum of death care to consumers. This is because the interest of modern consumers in convenience and value, which has driven the "de-integration" of other industries, has tended to promote the integration of establishments, firms, and industries within the death care sector.

What is to be feared in the future is a declining interest on the part of consumers in one or more parts of the complete death care process. This would set the stage for more "de-integrated" providers of specific services, such as immediate dispositions (cremations or burials) or curtailed services (e.g., graveside services only) performed by standardized units operated or franchised by a chain, perhaps under a common name.

Meanwhile, the persistence of demand for complete death care by consumers has favored the dominance of integration as a trend in the sector. This process has been and will continue to be disruptive to the status quo among death care providers. For many of them, this disruption will pose a threat; for others it will present opportunities to create a more effective death care delivery system serving the interests of consumers and providers alike.

PART VII

The young may die, but the old must!

Henry Wadsworth Longfellow

18. *Leading Death Care Companies*

The Big Three

Along with a growing number of regional chains, several large investor-owned death care companies have become a fact of life in the death care economy. The three largest such firms, SCI, Loewen, and Stewart, have some features in common, but they are primarily the unique creations of the founders and management teams who have overseen the growth of each company into its present position in the death care sector. The tangible results of their efforts are reflected in the historical record of the development of each company as a dominant force in the consolidation and pending globalization of the death care economy. By comparing various features of their records, it is possible to identify some basic similarities as well as significant differences among the three companies. Further indications of how the companies operate are provided by several sources: the annual reports, prospectuses, and proxy statements of the companies, reports of securities analysts, published interviews with the senior officials of each company, and the like.

By its nature much of this type of material becomes dated as time passes, and it expresses the views of management and analysts which must be considered as opinion. Such material and any conclusions drawn from it are presented in this chapter in an effort to capture a variety of views about the leading companies in the death care sector and to incorporate these into the larger context of the subject on which this book is focused. This chapter is basically an attempt to use all available material to inform the descriptions of and distinctions among the major companies based on the ways in which they have tended to operate in the past. For current information on the companies mentioned or others, the reader is referred to the companies themselves, to the financial press, and to brokerage firms.

In addition to the three firms featured in this chapter, a fourth company was created in 1990 when Equity Corporation International (ECI) was divested by SCI. In 1994 ECI then became a public company, but due to its limited history it is not included among the firms discussed in the present chapter. There

On this and the next two pages are the founders of the international death care companies. Above: Robert L. Waltrip, chairman and founder of Service Corporation. (Photographs courtesy of the three companies.)

also exists a handful of large privately held death care chains which have not yet been absorbed by the largest companies. Information about these private firms is not publicly available, and they are not discussed here. Neither are the public and private companies that are large suppliers to the death care sector, such as Hillenbrand Industries (caskets and urns) and Matthews International Corporation (memorials).

Different Origins

All three of the leading North American death care firms are the outcomes of successful attempts by their founders to introduce the advantages of public ownership and consolidated operation to the highly fragmented death care sector. Starting with a family funeral home, SCI's chairman and CEO Robert L. Waltrip pioneered this approach in the 1960s. Early success on his part attracted financial supporters and led to the formation of Southern Capital and Investment

Frank B. Stewart, Jr., chairman and founder of Stewart Enterprises.

Co. in 1962. More than thirty years and almost two thousand funeral homes and cemeteries later, his vision has resulted in a company which is not huge by the standards of some industries, but it is a huge provider of death care. On Wall Street the market value of SCI's stock approached $4 billion at the end of 1995, firmly establishing it as the largest death care company in the world.

Following in Waltrip's footsteps, Loewen president and CEO Raymond L. Loewen has created a death care empire which is the second largest in North America. From a Canadian base, Loewen extended into the U.S. market, where most of its funeral homes are now located. The company also operates a growing number of cemeteries, but has not historically focused on such facilities. Like Waltrip, Loewen started out as a funeral director in a family business, and it is toward that side of death care that the chains built by both men have tended to be more heavily weighted.

Stewart differs from SCI and Loewen in that it originated as an operator of cemeteries rather than funeral homes. This is significant because commercial cemeteries have generally been more progressive businesses than funeral homes have been. For example, commercial cemeteries have tended to stimulate changes in consumer preferences over the years by introducing new products.

Raymond L. Loewen, chairman and founder of the Loewen Group.

Through the construction and promotion of community mausoleums, crematories and columbariums, they have provided consumers with attractive alternatives to earth burial. They have aggressively marketed new products through the development of sales organizations built on a strong commitment to pre-need selling. Finally, some cemeteries have become fully integrated death care facilities by building funeral homes in or adjacent to their properties. As a result, they have become complete death care providers with a distinctive competition edge over stand-alone establishments of either type.

These tactics are illustrated by the history of Stewart, which began as a family-owned cemetery business in 1910. In the 1970s, as head of the firm which owned five New Orleans cemeteries, Stewart chairman Frank B. Stewart, Jr., correctly foresaw the opportunity which certain cemeteries provided for placing new funeral homes on their premises. He monitored the success of a few forerunners like Forest Lawn of Los Angeles and Restland of Dallas and concluded that so-called "heritage" cemeteries — those steeped in tradition and consisting of crypts and plots owned by thousands of prominent families —

represented an ideal base from which to market the complete range of options provided by total death care facilities now known as combined operations. He correctly assumed that once those options were made available by cemeteries, public acceptance of the concept of combined operations could be accelerated by effective pre-need selling through the existing sales organizations of the cemeteries. He saw that a strategic sales effort could be directed at the existing customer base of the cemetery and backed-up by advertising campaigns aimed at promoting the advantages of having all death care products provided at a single convenient location.

In less than two decades during which Stewart has pursued this strategy as a death care provider, his family firm has been turned into the most fully integrated of the large public companies, based on the percentage of combined facilities operated. Along the way, however, Stewart has had to contend with myriad competitively inspired legal restrictions and obstacles to unified death care operations, many of which were erected to restrict competition (for example, laws which still forbid or restrict cemetery-mortuary combinations in a number of states). In an interview published in *The Southern Funeral Director* (May 1992), Stewart characteristically extolled the virtues of combinations as entities uniquely capable of providing "seamless" death care to consumers at one convenient location. He also criticized any remaining resistance to combined operations from old-line funeral directors. So far his own company has managed to overcome such resistance to become the third largest firm in the sector by emphasizing combined operations more heavily than either SCI or Loewen. In contrast to those firms, Stewart's mix of facilities is more evenly balanced between funeral homes and cemeteries.

Key Events

By far the most important key event in Stewart's history which set in motion its evolution into a national death care firm was the development of Lake Lawn Metairie Funeral Home in Metairie Cemetery in New Orleans in 1979. This followed the 1969 acquisition of Metairie Cemetery — a heritage facility adjacent to Lake Lawn Park and Mausoleum property in New Orleans. The role of Lake Lawn Metairie Funeral Home in the development of Stewart as an integrated death care firm was presented in an earlier chapter.

Early events in the history of the other two leading companies seem to have played a critical role in their development as well. It is not possible to provide a lengthy examination of these events, but a brief outline of ones occurring during the formative years may be instructive. For SCI a key event was described contemporaneously in a *Barron's* article (Edmands, April 2, 1971). It involved SCI's purchase in 1971 of a chain of funeral homes from Kinney Services. Although the latter firm had operated funeral homes since the turn of the century, it was not a business which Kinney, an early conglomerate that evolved into Time-Warner, wished to continue to operate.

With the purchase of Kinney's operations in New York, New Jersey, and the greater Miami area, SCI added to its portfolio of establishments such well-known names as Walter B. Cook, Frank E. Campbell, and Riverside Memorial Chapels. The price paid by SCI for Kinney's 26 units, including real estate, was considered hefty at the time, but in retrospect it appears to have been a major coup for Waltrip and SCI. Sam Douglas, SCI's former president, told *Barron's* that the purchase was "a major milestone" for the company, which previously operated only 110 units (Edmands, April 2, 1971). Later the company acquired the second largest death care firm at the time, International Funeral Services, and in subsequent transactions it has used its considerable financial resources to pursue other private and public chains. In keeping with this pattern, SCI ventured outside the North American market in earnest in 1993 when it acquired Pine Grove Funeral Group, the largest chain of funeral homes in Australia. Following additional acquisitions there, it acquired Great Southern Group PLC and Plantsbrook Group PLC, both located in England, during 1994. This led to a major transaction during 1995 in which SCI acquired the death care operations of Lyonnaise des Eaux S.A., a French conglomerate company. Together, the acquired businesses perform approximately 30 percent of French funerals. The acquisition also included death care facilities in Belgium, Switzerland, Italy, the Czech Republic, and Singapore, setting the stage for further consolidation in those areas.

By demonstrating the effectiveness of a strategy of consolidation and internationalization of the death care sector, SCI has served as a model for others to emulate. Evidence of this is provided by Loewen's history; he first set out to build a large chain of funeral homes at about the same time as Waltrip did, in the early nineteen-sixties. By 1975 Waltrip's firm owned several hundred properties, but Loewen had acquired only a few establishments located in Ontario and British Columbia (Lubove, *Forbes*, June 22, 1992). After withdrawing from the role of consolidator to pursue careers in politics and then real estate, Loewen returned in the mid–nineteen-eighties to his earlier goal of developing a chain of funeral homes. As a beneficiary of conditions more favorable to consolidation, he soon acquired dozens of funeral homes in Canada and throughout the United States. In 1987 shares of his company were offered to the public for the first time. Hundreds of U.S. properties were then acquired, as the company demonstrated a highly effective acquisition approach emphasizing succession planning. On the strength of that program Loewen grew rapidly into the second-largest death care firm in North America, but it suffered a serious setback in late 1995 when a civil lawsuit was resolved in favor of a Mississippi life insurance company and related parties who claimed that Loewen had breached an earlier settlement reached in a related lawsuit brought in a Mississippi state court. The jury in the case awarded the plaintiffs $500 million in compensatory and punitive damages, a staggering amount which roiled the market for Loewen shares, sharply reducing the market capitalization of the company and raising questions about its credit worthiness and possible bankruptcy.

To avoid posting a $625 million bond required to appeal the jury award,

Loewen settled the Mississippi case in early 1996 for roughly $175 million in cash and stock. It then promptly reached an out-of-court settlement for another $30 million in cash and stock in a second breach of contract suit brought by a Pennsylvania insurance company. These large settlements stabilized the market in Loewen shares, but left major questions about its futures as an acquirer.

Views from the Top

So much for the history of each company. Where do their leaders stand on various aspects of the death care economy of today? It will be useful to listen to the views of their present or former chief executive officers, as expressed to the financial and trade press in recent years.

SCI

In a *Wall Street Transcript* article on SCI (June 6, 1992), Waltrip stated his positions on various issues.

On the prospective demand for death care:

> As far as SCI's position within the industry, we have done an exceptional job placing our growth in the communities that had the graying American population: People over 60, 65 years old. That population has shifted geographically rather drastically over the last 10 or 15 years, and we moved with that. So now we have a major presence in most every area where this over-65 population has moved, and therefore we'll be in a position to benefit from an accelerated death rate when it occurs.

On cremation:

> I think cremation will continue its growth of about 1 percent per year that it has experienced over the last decade. We're strong in the cremation business also, so we will be able to avail ourselves of the increase in that area.

On the impact of government regulation:

> I can't really see any governmental interference in our business other than some of the things that affect all businesses. I mean, certainly we're all affected by taxes and other governmental influences. But I can't really see where any government influence aimed directly at our industry, could come into play.

On SCI's acquisition and growth plans:

> We're still on an aggressive acquisition program. Last year was the largest acquisition year we've ever had in the history of the company. Now, we probably won't be able to duplicate that exactly in years to come as a percentage of size, because we're so large now to grow that much in one year is almost impossible. There are not that many large operations for us left to acquire. But, we're still acquiring at the same rate, or a little better, than we have in

the past, so it would not be uncommon for us to acquire 40 to 100 firms in one year, and we feel we can do that very easily.

We've been involved from time to time in ventures where we did not own 100 percent of a funeral firm or cemetery. That never has proven very effective for us, and over the last several years we have either bought those or sold our interest to the others we were involved with. So the majority of our acquisitions are and will be wholly-owned.

On SCI's intention to expand internationally, which later culminated in major acquisitions in Australia and the takeover of several large death care providers in Great Britain and continental Europe:

[SCI has made] various studies and looked into the possibilities of overseas expansion, and that certainly is a possibility.

On the stability of the death care sector:

If there is a recession-proof type of business, we have to be the closest thing to it that I can think of. The conditions of the economy have little or no effect on our business whatsoever. In fact, it almost seems like when we have recessionary times, or let's say, a flat economy, we have a tendency to do better. Most people have planned for monies to pay for their funeral.

The Loewen Group

In an interview with *Cemetery Management* (June 1993), an industry publication, Loewen replied to several questions which bear on issues raised at earlier points in this book.

Cemetery Management: What is the overall mission of the Loewen group?

Mr. Loewen: Our purpose is to provide a corporate vehicle which facilitates the orderly transition of ownership and management of funeral homes and cemeteries from one generation to the next in the interest of the principals and the communities we collectively serve. Our approach to quality succession planning is designed to enable cemetery owners and funeral home owners to retire with dignity and pride.

In order to ensure the provision of quality service, we believe it is essential to maintain a balance between people and service concerns, and sound planning and fiscal management. We also take seriously our responsibility to provide employees with opportunities to grow in their profession.

CM: Internecine warfare has marked this industry for a number of years, clearly demonstrated by lawsuits of one type or another between one segment of the industry vis-à-vis another. Again, as an interested party, how do you think this plays out to the consumer?

Loewen: The effects are very negative and abundantly transparent to the consumer. It is extremely easy to get the media or bureaucrats to investigate a competitor publicly. If the objective is dishonest and manipulative, it will always tarnish the reputation and integrity of all.

CM: State cemetery laws have been called a "crazy quilt" of regulation.

Would you favor greater uniformity in state laws or even the development of a model state providence cemetery law?

Loewen: The obvious answer to your question is yes. However, with our emphasis on succession planning and supporting the needs and interests of local and/or state regulations, our preference, apart from a general statement, is to support local culture.

Stewart Enterprises

Finally, here are the views of Lawrence M. Berner, former president and CEO of Stewart, as adapted from a *Wall Street Transcript* article (June 28, 1993).

On the use of combinations as a means of shifting market share in a community:

> The reason we do it, is that we can provide more services to property owners of that cemetery, we can substantially increase our revenue base and achieve some economies of scale. And we can dramatically alter market share in a given community ... in combination with the extensive selling of pre-planned funeral services.
>
> I'll give you an example. In 1991, Stewart developed two new funeral homes. One in St. Petersburg, Florida, at a cemetery called Memorial Park. The cemetery does about 1,300 burials annually. Within five years from the opening of that funeral home we would expect that 50 percent of the people using the cemetery will use the funeral home. If that happens, and we believe it will, then we will have developed a 650-plus funeral service business in St. Petersburg. Now those 650-plus calls ... will be coming from competition. So we will increase our market share in the funeral business dramatically in that location.

On dealing with the growing number of cremations:

> In the U.S. cremation is thought of principally as a low-cost alternative to traditional burial. In the U.K., there is a cremation rate of about 75 percent. Seventy-five percent of the people that die in the U.K. are cremated. But 90–95 percent of those cremations involve a traditional funeral service before the cremation and a memorialization after the cremation. So there is a completely different way of development in the U.K. and in other countries, compared to that in the U.S.
>
> On the positive side there is an opportunity, we believe, in this country for that sort of a trend to begin to take place, similar to the U.K. So Stewart offers full packages to people, of cremation plus traditional funeral services and memorialization. In 1992, 20% or so of the people dying in the United States were cremated, according to CANA [Cremation Association of North America] statistics.
>
> So, I see an opportunity for funeral services to really capitalize on this cremation phenomenon, which is no longer a trend, it's a reality, and be able to offer people more traditional funeral services, along with memorialization when they select cremation. There's a big part of the population out there that is not being served adequately by the funeral industry, principally because the industry is not doing a good job educating the public as to what's available to them.

Those are two major changes that are still taking place in the industry, and which will have a continued impact as we go forward into the 21st century.

On demographics:

Stewart's client mix, if you will, is heavily centered around the more elderly segment of the population. Those are really the most likely candidates for our products and services in the near future, and as that elderly population grows it will benefit us in several ways. The first and most obvious way is that the number of people in the U.S. dying annually will increase, although at a small rate. The death rate has been down in the past, but because of the aging of the population there's still an aggregate increase in the number of deaths that occur annually in the U.S. and this increase will likely continue into the 21st century.

But more importantly for us perhaps is that the elderly segment of the population is the prime market for our prearranged sales of funeral services and merchandise and cemetery space. So we benefit from the aging of the population in two ways: One, on an as-delivered, at-need basis for our products and services; but beyond that from an ability to market to this mature group those services and products on a pre-planned basis.

So, I don't think you'll see any change in the type of people that are going to be interested in our products and services. It's generally going to be people who are in the elderly part of the population. If we could figure out how to sell to much younger people, that would be just wonderful; but most people don't want to think about our products and services very much, and they don't until they reach a certain age. Most people consider buying cemetery space probably around age 50. The average age of the customer on the cemetery side would be between 50–60. On the funeral service side, it would be around 65 years old. Naturally, these statistics are from pre-need sales.

Views of an Analyst

As a small sector of the economy with few investor-owned firms, the performance of death care companies has not received much attention even from securities analysts. The major public death care companies have been followed by a few securities analysts, however, including Steve Saltzman and Gregory Capelli of the Chicago Corporation.

A recent article in *The American Funeral Director* (August 1994) recounted Saltzman's views as expressed during his presentation to a conference of the Casket and Funeral Supply Association of America, particularly his views on the strategies of the "Big Three":

"There are very different strategies when you look at prearrangements and combinations," Mr. Saltzman said. "What is striking to me is while SCI has the greatest number of combinations — about 85 — it represents only 10% of its base, while combinations are about one-third of Stewart's base. This is very significant because it indicates the ways these companies are looking at their markets.

"At the moment, Stewart has about a six-year backlog of [pre-need] funerals, whereas SCI's backlog is about 2.5 years, although in aggregate SCI's backlog is larger than Stewart's," Mr. Saltzman said.

He called the Loewen Group "the real sleeper" in marketing. "Historically, Loewen has done the least in prearrangements and combinations. But 1993 was a watershed year for Loewen with respect to these issues," he said.

"It has made a very aggressive thrust into cemeteries, virtually doubling the size of its cemetery base in 1993. Loewen also has put into place a very serious marketing program, and is moving into combinations by acquisition and internal development of them."

According to the article, Saltzman noted that the average size of each corporation's funeral homes affects their acquisition philosophies:

Loewen tends to acquire small funeral homes in small towns, suburbs, and rural communities. "That's a very interesting strategy," Mr. Saltzman said. "It partly explains why Loewen's funeral homes have the highest margins. ... In most cases, they're the only game in town, or maybe one of two."

At the opposite end of the spectrum is Stewart, which tends to acquire very large funeral homes and cemeteries in very competitive markets, while SCI is in the middle with a mix of operations.

"While [in some cases] the companies are stepping on one another's toes, bidding against one another for a funeral home, to a great extent the corporate acquirers are still after different types of funeral homes," he said.

After reporting on Saltzman's views on what is to be gained by clustering establishments, the article quotes his words and paraphrases them on the advantages of combined establishments:

Funeral home–cemetery combinations, said Mr. Saltzman, "are out of the playbook of new age retailers"—category killers like Home Depot. Combinations, he said, provide one-stop shopping for death care services and merchandise. When customers can go to one place to see the merchandise and facilities, they are more likely to make a commitment for purchases than they would be to a sales counselor calling on them at home.

Saltzman is described as enthusiastic about the stocks of the public consolidators based on the relatively low level of consolidation in the sector at this point:

More and more of his clients, he noted, see the death care group as a "dynamic growth industry," not as a "sleepy little" backwater of the economy. "There's still a long way to go for growth in this industry," Mr. Saltzman told the suppliers. "We're nowhere near what some investors feel is market saturation" by large investor-owned companies.

In Saltzman's view, consolidation is still in its infancy:

"For the moment, there are only four publicly traded companies. Collectively, they owned 6% of the country's funeral homes in 1993 and performed 14% of the country's funerals," he said. "A lot is written about their domination of the industry ... but this is still a relatively low degree of consolidation."

He said the big companies' next 14% share of the market will be "a little tougher and probably more expensive" to take. That's partly because not all independent funeral home and cemetery operations are desirable takeover candidates and not all independent operators want to sell.

Finally, Saltzman is said to believe that the year 2005 will usher in a "golden era of death care services" because of the increase in the population of people 45-65 years old, "which will overrun any increase in life expectancy, any advances in medicine, and increases in the availability of funds for medical care." This prospect of growing demand for death care due to an aging population in the U.S. and elsewhere will be the subject of the next chapter.

Similar Challenges, Different Strategies

With its large population of the elderly, Florida has been a magnet attracting the big death care providers like Stewart, which has the largest number of its facilities located there. California, where the largest number of U.S. deaths occurs each year, is the top state for both SCI and Loewen. In the U.S., Stewart has focused on areas where adherence to the so-called traditional funeral is strong. Less appealing are areas of the country where cremation and direct disposal methods are frequently chosen over more costly traditional death care. Nevertheless, all three of the leading companies have major presences in some areas where cremation rates are higher than the national average.

As a sign of the rising number of cremations performed in this country, all three companies operate crematories at many of their cemeteries, which often include columbariums. In 1992 Loewen pointed out in his company's annual report that the one percentage point per year increase in the cremation rate in the United States "in itself doesn't concern us because we are funeral service providers. Cremation is simply an alternative to earth burial. In Britain and Australia, the cremation rate is more than 50% and people continue to choose very traditional funeral services." Unlike in those countries, however, cremation was introduced to American consumers as a low-cost alternative to traditional death care frequently offered by alternative providers. It often has been accompanied by less-than-complete funeral services and less expenditure on final disposition (e.g., containment in a cardboard box followed by scattering, instead of inurnment followed by placement in a columbarium) and on memorialization. The gradual spread of cremation and direct disposal is a serious cause for concern to many smaller funeral directors, and at the very least it would seem to represent a marketing challenge for the large death care firms.

One of the most effective means of meeting this challenge would appear to be an aggressive strategy designed to add value by marketing cremation as a substitute for earth burial, offered within a complete package which includes a traditional funeral, final disposition of the cremains through inurnment and niche interment, and memorialization. This is a stated objective of Stewart's pre-need sales program in markets with high cremation rates, such as parts of

Florida. The success of such efforts, along with the tendency for the number of traditional funerals to be maintained by a gradually rising annual number of deaths, may reduce the severity of any negative impact due to the rising cremation rate in the United States.

Another challenge for death care providers has been the flat demand for their services. This is demonstrated by the experience of even large firms where "same-establishment" volume actually has declined year to year in some cases due to mortality trends in their key market areas. It is true that in the future the aging of the population in the United States is expected to spur the annual number of deaths in many markets where units of some major companies are concentrated. Even so, it seems unlikely that a slowly growing market of itself will ever enable the death care firms to deliver double-digit growth in revenues and earnings. Their respective abilities to do that will continue to depend primarily on the degree to which they are successful at increasing market share by acquiring additional units or taking business away from one another and the independent operators with whom they compete.

Pre-need selling is likely to play a key role in helping the large companies take business away from their competitors. Reflecting its cemetery origins, Stewart's annual reports cite a "steadfast commitment" to this strategy, and SCI reports that it "continues to expand" its pre-need sales effort, whereas Loewen has been less aggressive in this respect than the two firms that are more cemetery-intensive. Also to a greater extent than with Loewen, the expansion patterns of both SCI and Stewart appear to be aimed at forming or expanding local clusters of several funeral homes and a cemetery located near one another and operated together with shared personnel and equipment for greater efficiency. Moreover, the development of funeral homes within, or adjacent to, cemeteries creates an even more efficient set of physically unified and operationally integrated facilities. Evidence presented in Chapter 17 indicates that this approach has been highly effective in building market share at the expense of rival stand-alone funeral homes. The plot and crypt owners of an existing cemetery are a captive group of potential customers for a combined facility, on whom the cemetery's existing sales organization calls in order to sell pre-planned funerals along with its full line of cemetery products.

The belief of SCI in the competitive strength of combinations is indicated by its operation of as many as 100 such facilities at the end of 1995. Stewart, which began as a cemetery operator, had the highest percentage of combined facilities, and most of its cemetery acquisitions had been based on their prospects as combinations. Loewen, while historically uninterested in acquiring cemeteries and developing combined operations, had begun to show increased interest in this strategy.

Sector Changes

In some markets, clusters of establishments and combined facilities coexist with large numbers of family-owned "stand-alone" funeral homes, many of which are low-volume/high-cost establishments catering to an ethnic or religious niche within a limited, often changing, geographic area. Insulated from much competition, such firms have managed to survive in spite of the consolidation of those around them in many areas. Yet, despite their insulated status, the owners of funeral homes and cemeteries represent a large number of candidates for affiliation with a chain as a business and competitive matter or as a matter of personal tax, retirement, and succession planning.

For their part, the public chains have used their access to capital markets to raise funds with which to bid for attractive acquisition candidates. Although less than 10 percent of the death care sector's units have so far been acquired by the public companies, in some areas the competition for acquisition candidates has been intense. Choice properties which fit into the expansion plans of more than one national firm have sometimes become the object of spirited bidding contests, involving the considerable egos of those on both sides of the negotiations. Often it has been not only the purchase price that is the subject of negotiation, but also less concrete factors, such as the continuing family management contract with the successor company and the selling family's faith in its continuity. Family members who do not continue with the successor company are usually required to sign "non-compete" agreements which keep them out of the death care business for a specified period of time.

In search of new opportunities, executives of the major companies stalk the conventions of funeral directors and cemeterians. To cultivate relationships throughout the sector, each company has employed a different strategy. For example, SCI runs a finance arm which has made hundreds of loans, totaling hundreds of millions of dollars to independents over the years. Such loans, often used to finance the expansion of independent operators, establish financial ties which may lead to eventual acquisitions by SCI, usually of multiple units. Loewen has developed a network of geographic growth centers headed by former owners of key acquisitions who act as regional managers or "partners," whose role is to initiate further acquisitions within their respective areas. Stewart, from its previous experience as a cemetery developer and former builder of hundreds of community mausoleums in dozens of states, has knowledge of and contacts with a large number of cemeteries, enabling it to pursue those which fit into its strategy of acquiring facilities suitable for developing combinations.

Out of this networking has come a rapid pace of acquisitions. Where smaller operators have entered the game, such upstarts have often been gobbled up by the large ones in friendly or hostile takeovers. In particular, SCI has shown a penchant for this mode of bulk expansion, which sometimes involves contentious transactions and international activities. It often has purchased several regional chain operations during a single year. At times Loewen has adopted a similar strategy, and Stewart has used such an approach to acquire multiple properties. Family firms which previously sold to regional operators may thus become units of one of the largest companies after all. This factor may limit the appeal of small acquirors and encourage independent firms to choose directly among the largest ones.

Acquisition Tactics

It might seem in keeping with the calm exterior of the death care economy and the gentle demeanor of funeral directors that the negotiations leading up to the affiliation of a family firm with one of the national companies would be a polite affair. Perhaps with some of them it is, but in a rare glimpse at the process, the son of SCI's chairman provided the *New York Times* (Myerson, August 1, 1993) with a different picture of the negotiating technique employed by his company. The article first takes note of the manner in which acquisition candidates are identified: "To plan acquisitions or new homes, executives consult with the team in the demographic room. There, an NEC Multisync 4FG computer monitor displays neighborhood-by-neighborhood data on incomes, shopping preferences, ethnic groups, religion and age. And, most important, actual and predicted death rates."

The article next leads into a scenario in which the SCI negotiating technique is described:

> Once the company has targeted an area, it tries to buy the premier home. Its acquisitions tend to come with client families (known as repeat customers) who have been delivering up their members for generations.
>
> Often, the owners of the home initiate the talks. But even when they don't, S.C.I.'s starting approach is always friendly, especially since the same clans have often owned these homes since their founding. "We try to be very, very diplomatic," said W. Blair Waltrip, the chairman's son and executive vice president. He has a finance degree, not a funeral director's license, and the ways of a Wall Street merger baron.
>
> The younger Waltrip's first visit to a funeral home owner can seem like a mission of compassion — for the complications of passing the business on to children, the cost of complying with regulations and all the other work, work, work. If by the end of a second visit, the funeral director shows no desire to have S.C.I. lighten the burdens, then Mr. Waltrip might mention that he has also called on the home's leading competitor.
>
> Still no luck? "On the third contact we tell them we have property zoned and we are seriously considering building a funeral home," Blair Waltrip said. That might be on a cemetery that S.C.I. already owns, giving the new home a claim on everyone who has a plot. Targeting elderly plotholders has helped the company gather contracts for $1.3 billion in funeral arrangements, provoking rivals to demand tighter regulations.
>
> "Not that we are competing with you," Blair Waltrip continued, as if addressing a funeral home owner who was being unreasonable. "But we are interested in expanding."

Finally, the article describes the "makeover" of an acquired firm in terms which and SCI marketing manager says are "getting to be more and more of a science":

> After the acquisition comes the makeover. For $25,000, S.C.I. can install new carpeting, lighting, furniture and wallpaper, buying most items in bulk

from manufacturers. The former owners, or their children and assistants, are usually asked to stick around, most often as managers but sometimes merely to maintain ties to churches or clubs.

The new owners find ways to raise the average sale at least 5 percent, usually more. Major credit cards are accepted (and S.C.I. is thinking about issuing its own). The company also takes special care to freshen up the casket room, with market research and casket fashions coming into play [Myerson, *New York Times*, August 1, 1993].

One thing that does not change under SCI ownership, however, is the name of an acquired funeral home or cemetery. That stays the same, and customers may be unaware that the firm has changed hands, passing from a local family into the control of what the article calls "an invisible giant."

Capitalizing on a Family Image

All of the national firms have been loath to alter the face of an economic sector which has thrived on its reputation for providing personal, family-to-family service to the bereaved. Where local funeral homes have long since been acquired by one of the national companies, headquartered far away — even in another country — from the communities in which its units operate, this illusion is maintained meticulously. The names of acquired establishments are retained, and some previous owners are usually kept on as hired managers. To keep those who are not employed from capitalizing on their family names by opening a new funeral home or working for others, the acquirors incorporate "non-compete" agreements in their transactions.

This strategy has allowed the large firms to remain very much in the background, virtually unknown to consumers, but actively engaged in ridding their units of the slack tolerated by former nepotistic owner-managers. Management information and control systems have been changed or installed by the corporate staffs of the national firms. Clusters and combinations have greatly improved utilization of equipment and personnel. Resulting economies and efficiencies are reflected in the superior operating performance of the units of the public companies as compared with most of their family-run counterparts. Operating profit margins have consistently exceeded 20 percent at Loewen and SCI, where even higher results in the funeral service sectors have offset conventionally lower margins on the cemetery side. At Stewart, where the cemetery sector represents a larger share of total results, the operating profit margin has lagged behind the other two companies. Offsetting this impact of the lower-margin cemetery sector, however, is the potential represented by Stewart's large customer bases when higher-margin funeral homes are added to more of its cemeteries.

Operating efficiencies have contributed to strong margins at each company, but a key factor has also been the pricing flexibility that funeral homes possess. As mentioned previously, itemization requirements imposed on funeral providers by the FTC have had little impact on their ability to charge prices that more than keep pace with inflation. Based on average funeral service revenues of the three leading companies, it appears that as part of their consolidation strategies focused on lower volume establishments, Loewen and SCI have utilized pricing more aggressively than has Stewart. Given the premier status of the properties on which Stewart has focused, the company has also employed price increases as a part of its strategy to improve margins.

High Finance and Death Care

Various factors, including the extent to which death care expenses are covered by insurance proceeds, help to cushion the influence of the economy on the revenues and earnings of funeral homes and cemeteries. The resulting stability at their operating units has provided the public companies with healthy and reliable cash flows which have allowed them to use debt heavily to finance acquisitions. Debt/equity ratios are highest at SCI and Loewen, especially when intangibles are excluded from equity. The tendency of each company has been to supplement internally generated funds with occasional new issues of stock in order to reduce debt burdens accumulated as a result of a previous series of leveraged acquisitions. This strategy has allowed each firm to achieve continuous revenue growth which, combined with firm margins, has appeared on the bottom line, supporting stock prices and permitting additional stock issues.

This strategy has required SCI, Loewen, and Stewart to return repeatedly to the debt and equity markets to fuel their appetites for expansion. Issues of new shares (common or preferred) have been used by each company as a necessary means to reduce debt and support new rounds of borrowing. In this way the companies have obtained access to hundreds of millions of dollars in borrowed funds with which to finance still more acquisitions. For example, SCI raised as much as $1 billion from the sale of new debt and equity securities during 1995 alone.

Adding these sums to the undetermined amounts of funds at the disposal of the regional acquirors, some analysts are concerned that the trend toward consolidation in the sector has resulted in too much money chasing too few attractive acquisition candidates, for which the public companies have sometimes overpaid. Yet the game is afoot, and a slowing in the acquisition pace of any one of the public companies would force it to accept a slower rate of growth consistent with the gradually increasing number of people who die annually. For the two largest firms, this means that a very large number of acquisitions must be negotiated and consolidated year after year. Some large chains of department stores, drug stores, motels, and the like have eventually encountered financial or operational difficulties, or both, as they have continued to expand beyond some apparently optimal size. While at present this does not appear to be the case for the large death care firms, it has been pointed out that Loewen has recently encountered legal difficulties arising from its aggressive acquisition activities. Furthermore, the financial performance of SCI suffered from the effects of an ill-fated foray outside its core business during the 1980s. Following several reorganizations, the company now seems to be placing great emphasis on international expansion. This focus may reflect SCI's concern over increased competition for acquisitions within the domestic economy. In some local markets, the strategy of expanding clusters by acquiring multiple facilities in the same area could also eventually raise antitrust problems.

Stewart has also shown interest in international markets by acquiring a leading funeral provider in Mexico City and a group of Australian funeral homes. The development of funeral homes in more of its heritage cemeteries is likely to be a further contributor to continued growth at Stewart. Loewen's aggressive acquisition strategy has long appealed to investors, but the company's litigation woes have tarnished its outlook and damaged its reputation, at least for the moment. Finally, investors have generally applauded SCI's efforts to become a global company in spite of its costs and risks.

Clearly, the death care companies have attracted the attention of individuals and institutions whose interests lie in value-oriented stocks which offer highly reliable long-term growth prospects through all kinds of economic conditions. Investors attracted to death care stocks, of course, are not loyal family members devoted to running funeral homes and cemeteries with a view toward passing them on to the next generation. They are much more likely to focus on the ability of the death care companies to deliver short-term results, perhaps even at the expense of their reputations for service and value. Such pressure from Wall Street may eventually test the ability of the death care firms to live up to the responsibility they have assumed as successors to the hundreds of formerly family-owned businesses now under their control.

As the chain firms continue to woo investors with high margins and prospects for double-digit growth in revenues and earnings, they must cope carefully with the fact that funeral homes and cemeteries occupy a special place in the American business system which sets them apart from fast-food restaurants or supermarkets or even newspapers and television stations. The managements of the public companies must continue to balance their special status as death care providers and investor-owned companies whose shareholders can be a demanding interest group focused largely on short-term financial performance. Investors, whether individual or institutional, are unlikely to view death care as a calling, and they are unlikely to regard funeral homes and cemeteries as businesses which are to be managed sensitively with a view toward leaving them to the next generation.

To some extent investors and analysts have tended to view the death care firms as generators of cash flows which are augmented primarily through acquisitions. The valuations accorded to the companies are a function of their acquisition rates. With rare exceptions, analysts have not looked beyond the success of the acquisition programs of each firm for the underlying source of the cash flows generated by their operations. Yet it is the operations of any acquired or developed units, along with those of the existing units of a firm, that will expand market share and generate (or fail to generate) whatever cash flows are expected to justify current stock prices. By concentrating attention on the acquisition rates of death care firms, analysts have tended to assume that the acquiring firms benefit from having more and more units. Common sense suggests that growth in the number of units operated by a firm (due to acquisitions) will be accompanied by growth in the firm's revenues. Given stable profit margins, this implies more rapid growth in the earnings and cash flows of aggressive acquirors. Assuming that units are acquired at less than the present values of the incremental cash flows that they add to the acquiring firm, the value of that firm, and thus of each share of its stock, is enhanced by the acquisition. Analysts appear to believe that acquisitions by death care firms automatically satisfy these assumptions. But do they?

There are no obvious grounds for assuming that the managers of death care firms would deliberately acquire an additional unit for more than its present value, but a present value is a calculation based on assumed cash flows, which are in turn based on a number of assumptions about future earnings, on estimates of future market shares resulting in certain future revenues, and on future cases of certain types involving specific services and merchandise sold at certain prices and provided or acquired at certain costs. None of these things is certain of course. They are gross assumptions about future operations and operating conditions in markets subject to variations in all of the factors mentioned as well as in others — interest rates, tax rates, regulatory burdens, and so on. The eventual success of the acquisition program of a firm depends on the quality of such assumptions by its management. Yet if any consideration is given by analysts to the quality of such assumptions, it is usually limited to gross consideration of the stability of operations in death care markets and the pricing flexibility enjoyed by death care firms. One cannot escape the feeling that significant risks may be passed over by analysts who fail to look more closely at the operating characteristics of the acquisition targets and target markets of death care firms.

In particular, there are several factors affecting the operating conditions of some funeral homes which may raise concerns about their values as acquisitions. Among these are declining revenues due to fewer deaths or a less favorable mix of services and merchandise sold; pricing pressures due to low inflation and increased competition in some markets, especially from combinations; higher operating and regulatory costs; and the uncertainty of operating in foreign markets where death care practices differ and the economics of death care establishments are unlike those here at home. In spite of these concerns, there is greater competition for acquisitions and this tends to support or raise the prices of acquisition candidates, especially of those that become the objects of bidding contests between two or more potential acquirors. To some extent the particulars of any one of these acquisitions, even when it involves multiple units, are at the margins of the large portfolios of the national companies which consist of hundreds of properties. This substantially mitigates the impact of any misjudgments about the prospects and value of any single acquisition.

In the long bull market which we have experienced for more than a decade, perhaps there was no great need for analysts to concern themselves with anything more than the appearance of aggressive expansion. If a more circumspect attitude by analysts is due, however, perhaps it is time for them to begin to look beyond an aggressive acquisition strategy to the values of the operations of death care firms, which are what will sustain them through less sanguine periods and into the long-run future.

The Need for Caution

None of the remarks in the previous section are meant to throw cold water on the wisdom of acquisitions aimed at further movement toward consolidation, based on creating clusters of small units that can be more effectively and efficiently operated together. The case for this is strong, and its practical results have been demonstrated by the success of multiunit operations. Even beyond such benefits, there may be some advantages to the further growth of very large death care firms, although these seem less clear and harder to demonstrate. The international expansion paths of the largest firms seem to be driven by the search for markets just as in other industries which go abroad in order to export American products. The exportability of death care is yet to be demonstrated, but the efficiencies of the death care delivery systems developed by the large death care companies may well be exportable.

The favorable treatment of the stocks of the public companies has facilitated their rapid growth, and this will probably serve to attract others into their ranks, on their own or through affiliation with the existing companies. Public ownership is not an unmixed blessing, however, and some of the owners of regional operations may wish to remain private. It will be recalled that in the late nineteen-seventies under different conditions, SCI publicly admitted to having an interest in returning to its earlier status as a private company through a management buyout. There is also evidence from other industries that successful private companies have later regretted their decisions to go public. This is probably especially true of those whose owners were talked into it by those who wanted a piece of the action in the market for initial public offerings.

It must also be the case that there are individual families who have later regretted their decisions to sell to the regional or national firms, or at least regretted selling to the one to which they sold. It is hard to imagine the difficulties of making such a decision, not simply of whether to sell, but also to whom. The promises of the acquiring teams from the big companies and the testimonials of prior acquirees featured in the annual reports and promotional material of the acquirors must be hard to evaluate.

Management Compensation

One of the most vexing issues faced by the public death care companies is the inevitable scrutiny to which the salaries and other compensation of their senior managers is likely to be subjected by critics of death care providers. The compensation of management is often criticized, but in the case of death care firms it is especially sensitive. It is unlikely to allay criticism for any company to point out that when the management compensation of large companies is spread over thousands of cases, it amounts to a few hundred dollars per funeral service or interment. For what? critics may ask.

A more effective justification for the compensation policies of any public company is the extent to which its policy is comparable to that of firms in other industries which are similar in size and profitability. Presumably each of the public companies has established compensation committees at board level, whose members are outside directors. This is consistent with the way in which the compensation of senior management is determined in public companies of most types. There is no reason why this should not be an entirely acceptable standard for determining appropriate levels of compensation for death care firms. Unless, of course, it is held that such firms are to be treated differently for some reason. The present thesis is that they are not different in significant respects from other profit-oriented businesses. Accordingly, there are no reasonable grounds for singling out the compensation levels of death care firms for criticism. To say that there are no grounds for doing something is not, of course, to say that it will not be done, and it is ordinary wisdom for public companies to expect to be called upon to defend the compensation of their top managers.

In matters of management compensation generally, there has been a tendency for companies to adopt a performance-based incentive system to tie the pay of senior managers to the performance of their stock. The use of such a system by a death care company is illustrated by the plan adopted in 1993 by Stewart. It provided options to a number of key managers, not just the top few, and it was subject to two constraints: first, the stock price was required to increase at a rate of 20 percent compounded annually over four years; second, earnings per share were required to grow at a compound rate of 15 percent over the same period. This last condition insured that management was not rewarded solely by external factors affecting the price of the stock. The operating performance of the firm was required to justify any rewards under this system. Ironically, option plans which require the achievement of such performance objectives result in a charge to earning which is not required in connection with conventional options that vest over time irrespective of performance.

The reason usually cited for linking managerial compensation to the performance of a large company and its stock is to provide an incentive for managers to serve the interest of shareholders. This may seem to imply some neglect of the interests of other parties, but the opposite is true. Although it is only the shareholders of companies who are directly interested in their profits, maximum profit is the result of the effective and efficient operation of a firm. Operation in the most profitable manner therefore entails serving the interests of all those groups on whose continued support the efficient operation of the firm depends, whether they are customers who buy its goods or services, employees who work for it, creditors who lend to it, or suppliers who sell to it.

It is thus pointless to debate whose interest is more important, that of the stockholders or that of the customers, to mention only two of the groups associated with death care firms. Both are obviously important, and it is necessary for publicly owned firms to serve the interests of both. To what extent the interests of any particular group will be served is not up to the management of such firms; it is determined by conditions in the markets for the goods and services they provide, in the markets for their inputs such as caskets and labor, and in the financial markets. If management fails to satisfy any necessary group, the interests of all groups are threatened, including the interests of management (Chambers, 1986, Chapter 7). That is the nature of the conditions under which firms of all types operate in market economies, including the death care economy.

19. *Prospective Demand for Death Care*

Vital Statistics

Like births, deaths are reportable vital events. When a death occurs, a death certificate identifying the cause(s) is required. A permit must also be obtained before a corpse can be buried, entombed, or cremated. Usually the death certificate is prepared by the attending physician; in other cases it is prepared by a medical examiner, coroner, or other state official. The registration of death certificates permits the collection of vital statistics, enabling the mortality characteristics of different populations or communities to be prepared. Trends in such characteristics may be discerned in the same community over a period of years. Conventional measures of a variety of mortality characteristics have been calculated and made available by the Bureau of the Census, insurance companies, and other organizations. No extensive analysis of those data is presented here, but they are the basis for a series of observations about the prospective demand for death care goods and services.

The first such observation relates to the nature of age-specific death rates, which are the rates for various age groups within the general population of the United States. Characteristically, these rates "start at a rather high level in the first year of life, fall to a minimum near age ten, then move up slowly into midlife and finally rise rapidly at the older ages" (Spiegelman, 1968, p. 89). A second observation is that these age-specific rates have tended to decline during much of this century. Spiegelman attributes these reductions to several trends which began with "the birth of a public health movement for sanitary measures" during the late nineteenth century. This movement received great impetus from the discovery of the bacterial origins of communicable disease" (p. 88). Improved health and medical care, growing health awareness, and continued economic progress throughout the twentieth century eventually led to substantial reductions in death rates at all ages, but more so for some age groups than for others. "Quite generally, the reduction in mortality during this period has been relatively greater in infancy, childhood, and the early adult years, the rate of improvement thereafter falling off with advance in age" (p. 89).

As a consequence of these considerations, the number of Americans who live to old age has increased, leading to an increase in the number of deaths that are caused by or associated with aging: cardiovascular-renal disease, cancer, and other so-called "degenerative" diseases. This implies that a growing number of elderly persons in the U.S. population eventually will lead to an increase in the number of persons who die annually and to a higher average age at death.

The Annual Number of Deaths

As shown in Table 19.1, the death rate per 1,000 population steadily decreased from 17.2 persons per 1,000 population in 1900 to 9.6 per 1,000 in 1950. Although the death rate has continued to decline, but sharply, since 1950, to around 8.6 per 1,000, the population has increased steadily during the same period so that the annual number of deaths has risen from 1,452,000 in 1950 to more than 2,200,000 in recent years. Looking ahead, a more rapid increase in the number of deaths occurring annually in the United States is expected as the composition of the population becomes more heavily weighted with the elderly and the aggregate death rate rises.

Table 19.1
*Annual Numbers of Deaths and Death Rates
for Decennial Years Since 1900,
with Projections Through 2050*

Year	Number of Deaths[a]	Death Rate[b]
1900		17.20
1910		14.70
1920		13.00
1930	1,327,000	11.30
1940	1,417,000	10.80
1950	1,452,000	9.60
1960	1,712,000	9.50
1970	1,921,000	9.50
1980	1,990,000	8.70
1990	2,162,000	8.60
2000	2,712,000	10.01
2010	3,026,000	10.55
2020	3,397,000	11.32
2030	3,873,000	12.53
2040	4,213,000	13.37
2050	4,270,000	13.36

Source: Statistical Abstracts of the United States. (a) To the nearest thousand; data unavailable before 1930. (b) Per year per 1,000 population; death rates prior to 1930 are for death registration areas of the United States.

As mentioned before, advances in medical care and public health and safety in the twentieth century have tended to reduce mortality at all ages of the U.S. population. The most noticeable impact of these advances was a sharp decline in the death rates at young and middle ages, so that a much larger proportion of the people now lives into the sixties, seventies, eighties, and beyond. The average life expectancy at birth has thus increased from 47.3 years in 1900 to almost 76 years at present. Improvements in life expectancy have been distributed among various age groups, including the elderly. Thus in 1990 the life expectancy of men and women aged 65 in the United States was 15.1 years and 18.9 years respectively. These figures are based on the population as a whole and various cohorts within the population. They do not indicate anything about the life expectancy of any individual member of the population or changes in the human life span or maximum length of human life. According to authorities on aging such as Dr. Leonard Hayflick, the author of *How and Why We Age* (1994), a great deal of available evidence indicated that the potential "span of life" has been largely unchanged for roughly 100,000 years.

This view is based on biomedical research which indicates that aging and a fixed life span are biological characteristics of organisms which mature completely. In the case of man, the maximum life span appears to be 115 to 120 years, which is regarded as the range beyond which no one has lived. In practice, of course, relatively few people live beyond 100 or even 90, and a reasonable view appears to be that the potential increase in average life expectancy in the future is less than twenty years, and this increase will depend mostly on breakthroughs in the treatment of cardiovascular disease, renal disease, and cancer. The authority of Dr. Hayflick backs up this view.

> Finding a cure for the leading cause of death in the United States — cardiovascular disease — would add 13.9 years to the life expectation of newborns and 14.3 years to the life expectation of sixty-five-year olds. That would be spectacularly rewarding. But even if we became able to prevent *all* causes of death now appearing on death certificates, the resulting increase in life expectation would not come close to the twenty-five-year increase that has occurred since the turn of the century! The period of rapid increase in human life expectation in developed countries has ended [Hayflick, 1994, pp. 98–100].

Based on mortality data from the 1970s, Dr. Hayflick concludes: "if we succeeded in eliminating each of the leading causes of death written on death certificates, most people would live to be about one hundred years old" (p. 100). He then adds: "These centenarians would still not be immortal. But what would they die from? They would simply become weaker and weaker until death occurred. We could then either invent new terms to write on death certificates or return to using that old term, 'natural causes,' attributing death to the inexorable normal losses in physiological function that are the hallmark of aging" (p. 100).

As to the prospects of breakthroughs in dealing with natural causes resulting from aging, Dr. Hayflick comments as follows:

Most biomedical research is directed toward resolving causes of death currently written on death certificates, but the primary cause of death, the *increase in vulnerability* to what was written on the death certificate, is largely ignored. That vulnerability results from the normal aging process. Even if cures are found for all the "certified" causes of death, we will still be fated to die of the physiological losses of old age because so little research is now being directed toward understanding the aging process. More basic research into the biology of aging would serve a double purpose: by increasing our knowledge of the fundamental aging process we would also gain insight into how to reduce our vulnerability to the causes of death now appearing on the death certificates of older people.

Only a few biomedical research scientists are now working on the underlying causes of aging that increase our vulnerability to chronic disease and accidents. Unless more attention is paid to the fundamental processes of ageing, the fate of everyone fortunate enough to become old will be death on or around his or her hundredth birthday. And, despite what might be written on the death certificate, the true causes of those deaths will probably be unknown [1994, pp. 46–47].

In *How We Die*, Dr. Nuland provides a variety of evidence which supports the views expressed by Dr. Hayflick, whose work he also cites. In addition to the theory of finite cell division proposed by Dr. Hayflick, there is a "wear and tear" theory, a theory of "programmed cell death" called "apoptosis" involving a "death gene," and other theories which seek to explain senescence. Dr. Nuland concludes: "There is no lack of theories, no lack of champions, and no lack of concordances among concepts. What emerges from all the experimental data and the speculations they provoke is the inevitability of aging, and therefore of life's finiteness" (p. 78). In other words, death and the demand for death care are somehow pre-ordained.

In general, taking into account all causes of death (internal and external), Fader and Wade conclude:

> Future improvements in mortality will depend upon such factors as: the development and application of new diagnostic and surgical techniques, the presence of environmental pollutants, improvements in exercise and nutrition, the incidence of violence, the isolation and treatment of causes of disease, the development of new forms of disease, improvements in prenatal care, the incidence of abortion, the prevalence of cigarette smoking, the misuse of drugs (including alcohol), the extent to which people assume responsibility for their own health, and changes in our conception of the value of life [Health and Human Services, December 1983, p. 5].

After considering how these and other factors might affect mortality trends, Fader and Wade state the following:

> Further improvements for those under 65 are projected to be relatively small compared with past improvements because very little additional improvement in infectious diseases (such as poliomyelitis and influenza) is possible and because a small improvement in mortality from violent causes

(accidents, suicide, and homicide) is expected. Improvements for the aged are expected to continue at a relatively rapid pace, as further advances are made against degenerative diseases (such as heart and vascular disease). The gap between male and female mortality is expected to continue widening, but at a decreased rate as women become increasingly subject to many of the same environmental hazards and social pressures as men [p. 6].

After adjusting for anticipated changes in the age distribution of the population, mortality is projected to improve at an average rate of about 0.6 percent per year through 2058. This is about half the average rate of improvement observed during most of the twentieth century.

In view of these considerations, it appears that only modest improvements in life expectancies and virtually no increase in life span are reasonably expected in the near future. By directing its efforts toward the resolution of diseases which prematurely lead to death, research is producing a shift in the age distribution of the population in favor of the elderly, creating a much larger number of those 65 and over. This has obvious implications for the number of deaths occurring annually in the United States and thus the prospective demand for death care, which is tied directly to that figure.

Mortality Projections

As projected by the U.S. Census Bureau, the number of "oldest old" persons, those 85 and over, as a percent of the total population of the United States will increase steadily for many years, from 1.3 percent in 1990 to 5.1 percent in 2050, and the number of elderly, those 65 and over, will grow from 12.16 percent to 22.9 percent of the total population. Because the death rate among these groups far exceeds the average rate for the population as a whole, the aggregate death rate similarly will rise as shown in Table 19.1 from 8.6 per 1,000 in 1990 to 10.0 per 1,000 in 2,000 and eventually to 13.4 per 1,000 in 2050. The annual number of deaths will almost double from 2,162,000 in 1990 to 4,270,000 during the same period. All this will have an increasingly positive influence on the volume of cases handled by death care providers, who will no longer be subject to a stagnant demand for their services.

The effect of this growth will be to increase steadily the volume of cases handled by death care establishments, but the impact of this increase on the total revenues generated by the part of the economy they comprise will depend on trends in consumer expenditures for death care in future years. In recent years, during which the annual number of deaths has been flat, total personal consumption expenditures on death care goods and services have increased only modestly, and this increase was due largely to inflation. A restraining influence has been a persistent increase in the proportion of consumers who choose cremation, memorial services, or other nontraditional forms of death care. In the future, total death care expenditures are likely to continue to grow as the influence of nontraditional choices is offset by a more rapid increase in the

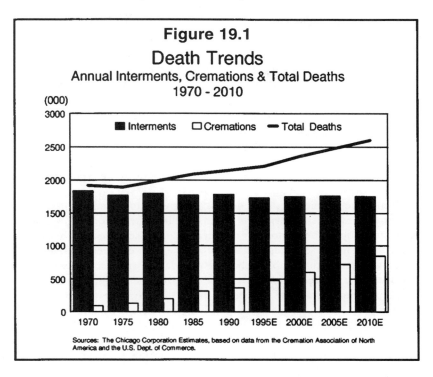

Figure 19.1

Death Trends
Annual Interments, Cremations & Total Deaths
1970 - 2010

(000)

■ Interments   ☐ Cremations   ▬ Total Deaths

Sources: The Chicago Corporation Estimates, based on data from the Cremation Association of North America and the U.S. Dept. of Commerce.

annual number of deaths, so that the number of traditional funerals remains relatively constant, in spite of a rising number of cremations. This is shown in Figure 19.1 which depicts the trends in traditional "casketed" interments (burials and entombments), cremations, and total deaths based on data and estimates of the U.S. Department of Commerce, the Cremation Association of North America, and the Chicago Corporation. These trends suggest that total death care revenues may be expected to increase at approximately the rate of growth in the number of deaths plus the rate of growth experienced per death care expenditures. Against this background of sector growth, the growth paths of specific establishments and firms will be influenced by changes in their market shares resulting from the effects of their pre-need sales efforts, changes in their product mixes, and the impact on them of the development of clusters and combinations. The growth of chain companies will be further influenced by the results of their acquisition programs.

Future Trends

From the aggregate mortality statistics discussed in previous sections, it is not possible to project the growth in volume which particular geographic markets will experience in the future. Rates of change in the number of deaths in each of these will depend on demographic characteristics such as the concentration of elderly persons in each. It is reasonable to suppose, however, that the number of deaths in most areas of the country will increase steadily into the first half of the twenty-first century. This will usher in a new era for death care providers, many of whom have experienced declining volume for years due to fewer deaths or greater competition in their markets. Some of them will continue to suffer the impact of negative demographic developments in their markets, even in those geographic areas expected to experience a growth in the total number of deaths occurring annually. Furthermore, the economic consequences of growth in this number for any particular market and for individual death care establishments depends upon future trends in the types of death care desired by those who die and their survivors.

It must be remembered that death care as we know it and as it is provided by death care establishments is the latest stage in an evolutionary process in the social conventions and customary practices of many segments of the American population. The present stage in this process is not to be regarded as the final stage, and it seems reasonable to believe that death care practices will continue to evolve in the future as they have in the past. In this continuing process, some traditional elements of those practices may be cast off because they no longer serve the purposes they once did under living conditions which prevailed in the past. For example, wakes and visitation are now held in funeral homes rather than in family residences as they once were, families do not always choose earth burial as they once did, and far more funerals are pre-planned today. In these respects and in others, death care has always been and will continue to be adapted to trends and developments in the larger society. Just as the urbanization and secularization of that society has resulted in changes over the past century, future social trends and commercial developments within the death care sector will produce further changes in the next century. In the anticipation of the effects on the sector of a continually rising annual number of deaths due to the aging of the population, it would be unwise to ignore the prospects for these changes and their implications for the fortunes of death care providers individually and collectively. As a part of the fabric of American society, however, American death care practices are highly resistant to criticism, and they are not subject to overnight changes of a revolutionary sort. Nevertheless, in the long run they will continue to be subject to the kinds of evolutionary changes observed in the past. It is instructive to consider any evidence which indicates the directions in which these changes may take place.

Cremation

Perhaps the most notable continuing change in death care practices has been the gradually increasing number of cremations performed nationally. The growing importance of cremation is clear because more than 20 percent of Americans who die annually are now cremated, compared with 4 percent in

1966. The cremation rate varies widely by region, ranging from as high as 70 percent in some geographic areas to virtually zero in others. According to the Cremation Association of North America (CANA), the rate is highest (30 percent to 40 percent or more) on the West Coast, in the mountain states, and in Florida. Rates are lower in the Central and Eastern states but are increasing in most areas. As shown in the table below, CANA projects a nationwide cremation rate of 32.5 percent by the year 2010, up from 6.6 percent in 1975. Based on the experience of other countries, the rate may eventually peak at between 50 percent to 60 percent later in the twenty-first century. If such estimates are correct, the U.S. cremation rate will approach the level in England, where the rate increased from the single-digit level immediately after World War II to its current 70 percent figure. In any event, it is clear from the general tendencies of the past that the U.S. cremation rate will continue to increase steadily but gradually well into the next century.

Percent of Deaths Followed by Cremation, 1975–2010

Year	Percent of Deaths
1975	6.6
1980	9.7
1985	14.9
1990	17.1
1992	19.1
1993	20.2
1994	20.8
2000	25.6 (E)
2010	32.5 (E)

Source: Cremation Association of North America. (E)=Estimate.

It is not necessary here to enter into any kind of debate over the relative merits of different forms of pre-final or final disposition of the body. It is sufficient for our purposes to point out that the main difference between a traditional funeral service followed by cremation and one followed by earth burial is the act of final disposition itself. In both cases the ceremonial content may be the same, involving the presence in a casket of the prepared and restored body. Visitation and desired funeral services may be held, requiring the use of funeral home facilities and services. Following these, the body is either transported to a cemetery for burial or to a crematory for cremation. In the latter case, there is no necessity for a grave marker or monument, but an urn for the cremated remains and a niche in a columbarium for the urn may be desired to complete the death care process. The cost of the cremation, including urn and niche, is comparable to the cost of traditional burial or entombment in many areas.

The result is that cremation as a part of complete death care is not necessarily a practice which leads to less spending by consumers, reducing the revenues of providers. On the other hand, it is inevitable that revenues in the sector will be affected adversely, especially within the mortuary services and memorialization industries, if the spread of cremation is accompanied by radical departures from the practice of including traditional ceremonies and permanent memorialization in the death care desired by consumers. Such departures may occur in connection with the choice of other forms of final disposition, but they have tended to be associated especially with the practice of cremation.

Departures from Complete Death Care

In regard to the last point, it is important to distinguish between the choice of cremation as a pre-final stage in the process of final disposition and so-called "immediate disposition" which involves cremation but does not incorporate the traditional elements of a funeral service or traditional memorialization in the death care process. In the case of immediate disposition, the extent of the mortuary services required to be provided by funeral homes is limited to the acts of conveying the remains from the place of death to the crematory in an appropriate container and attending to certain details required in connection with such arrangements. Since no funeral services are held, there is no reason to prepare the body for viewing during ceremonies held in the facilities of the funeral home. What is worse yet for funeral service providers, there may be no need for an expensive casket, which is often desired when a funeral service is held. There is thus a corresponding reduction in the revenues received by funeral homes in cases involving curtailed services.

For most funeral homes, the implications for their revenues of the increase in the number of immediate dispositions are severe inasmuch as most of their operations and facilities are geared to the provision of a complete complement of services, including visitation and the presence of a restored and casketed body. In other countries, it is not uncommon for consumers to purchase complete death care which involves cremation as the preferred form of pre-final disposition and includes the services of a mortuary and some form of memorialization. More so than in other countries, however, the practice of cremation in the United States was originally introduced and promoted as a means of reform of what was viewed by some as unnecessarily expensive and excessively elaborate death care practices. In the years since its introduction, it has also been advocated by critics of traditional funerals as a "logical and economical" alternative to traditional funerals. The upshot of these historical developments is that in this country cremation is considered a form of final disposition of the body and tends to be associated in the public mind with incomplete death care that does not include traditional ceremonies and rituals or memorialization. This is the way it has been presented by critics of American death care practices, with the result that cremation as a form of pre-final disposition has been linked to bodiless funerals involving curtailed services or none at all at the time of death. A memorial service may sometimes be held at a later time and without the services of a funeral home. In some cases, this link between cremation and bodiless services or no services has been reinforced by direct disposition firms who market their services in this way in some geographic markets. In general, however, the association of cremation with less-than-complete death care is reflected by the fact that more than 80 percent of cremations do not involve the use of a casket (*Federal Register*, January 11, 1994, p. 1598). Less than 50 percent of the cremains produced each year are interred in a cemetery as a means of providing permanent memorialization of them (Sloane, 1991, p. 228).

All of these circumstances surrounding the role of cremation in American death care have led many funeral directors to regard the practice as an actual or potential threat to their principal business as providers of the ceremonial component of complete death care. In general, those fears are well-based insofar as they relate to the potential effects of cremation — curtailed funeral services and memorialization. If they are concerned about their future, it clearly makes good economic sense for funeral directors and cemeterians, as death care providers, to exert considerable influence to emphasize among American consumers that cremation is a pre-final step toward final disposition and that it is not a substitute for, and is not to be confused with, funeral services or memorialization or even with final disposition itself.

It appears to be necessary to inculcate the view that final disposition and the ceremonial elements of mortuary services are complementary parts of a complete death care package which also includes appropriate forms of memorialization. To inculcate such a view is likely to require methods beyond the means and resources of individual funeral homes and even the trade associations of funeral directors. The task appears to require instead the methods of direct marketing and one-on-one salesmanship which have been used so effectively by cemeteries to sell their products directly to consumers. Reliance on at-need selling appears inadequate to the task; it seems that pre-need selling is required in order to reach consumers earlier rather than later, when further erosion of public support for traditional services is likely to have occurred.

Obviously, the large multiunit death care firms are better able than small, stand-alone funeral homes to support a strong pre-need sales effort of this sort, but by failing to lock potential consumers into traditional services before need, firms that depend primarily on at-need sales may find that they eventually will be confronted with changed case loads that include a much larger proportion of cases involving cremation, curtailing in some way the extent of mortuary services required or desired.

Curtailed Death Care

Several factors appear likely to strengthen tendencies to curtail the extent and expense of death care in the future. One of these is the increasing average age at death resulting from the greater proportion of those over 75 among the people who die annually. There is a natural tendency to regard the death of an elderly individual as a less tragic event than the death of a younger person. Often the elderly party possesses a smaller circle of relatives and friends of his or her generation for whom the ceremonial component of death care is a critical part of the process. The urge to ceremonialize and to memorialize are both likely to experience some loss of intensity on the part of survivors under such circumstances. Also, increasingly the institutionalization of elderly persons removes them from close contact with later generations, and thus their death is a less emotionally charged event. When the elderly person has suffered from a lengthy degenerative illness, the survivors — including children and grandchildren — may well experience "anticipatory grief," which reduces the impact of the death. Final disposition becomes the focal point of the survivors in such cases, diminishing their desire to spend on elements of death care which involve traditional ceremonies and memorials. Curtailment of those elements of death care may occur therefore in cases involving elderly decedents.

Prior to the imposition of the unbundling requirement on funeral homes (see Appendix), the opportunity for families to curtail the mortuary services selected in such cases was limited by the insistence of mortuaries on the purchase of a complete funeral service. Even now they may encourage such purchases. In the future, however, the wider availability of immediate disposition firms and discount establishments offering mortuary services consisting of graveside services only, or other forms of less-than-complete funerals, will provide greater opportunities for the public to curtail the death care selected, particularly in deaths involving the elderly.

Just as cremation has grown as crematories have become more widely available throughout the country, curtailed death care is likely to grow as the spread of discount operators occurs. Aside from this factor however, the effect of the FTC rule requiring the itemization of funeral home prices has created conditions under which it is easier for survivors to decline elements of traditional funeral services. While families may be disinclined to do so in cases involving nonelderly deaths, they may well be more inclined to do so in the future in cases involving the elderly. Economic factors may contribute to this inclination on the part of growing numbers of so-called "sandwich families" which are burdened with the costs of raising children and caring for elderly parents simultaneously.

In order to avoid the effects of this propensity, it would seem to be necessary and advisable for funeral homes to attempt to market their services to the elderly and the aging on a more extensive pre-need or near-need basis, giving them the opportunity to ensure that they are provided with complete death care of their choice. To fail to do this is to run the risk of a significant shift away from complete death care to curtailed services for the members of the most rapidly growing segment of the population. Moreover, there is a risk that public experimentation with immediate disposition firms and discount operators in elderly cases may acquaint them with such establishments, leading more of them to opt for curtailed services in other cases as well.

A potential spur to the consumer demand for curtailed funerals is likely to be the increased availability of such services by firms which specialize in providing them, perhaps through the units of a chain operated under a common name. By offering "direct disposal," "graveside services only," or other limited forms of death care goods and services, these discount operators avoid the necessity for investment in extensive facilities required to provide traditional services. So far there are only a few such "de-integrated" providers, but Porter points out that the concept of de-integrated firms has attracted consumers in other industries (pp. 244–45). There are likely to be more competitors attempting to apply this delimited retailing concept toward marketing specific death care products, perhaps on a regional or national scale. In fact, SCI appears to have toyed with the idea. In 1993, the *New York Times* reported that "SCI executives are discussing new ways to lure poorer families. 'We want to have a Macy's type of operation, but we want to have a Wal-Mart too,' SCI's chairman told the *Times*" (Myerson, August 1, 1993).

Implications for Providers

It is difficult, if not impossible, to assess precisely the future impact of a gradual trend toward curtailed death care on the revenues of death care providers. For one thing, it appears that there are differential effects to be expected on the different types of establishments. As discussed previously, the role of final disposition in the death care process appears to be the anchor to which the other parts are tied. The cemetery-crematory provider of final disposition goods and services is virtually exempt from the vagaries of demand for mortuary services, although shifts in the urge to memorialize have a direct impact on the sale of memorial products by such firms. Clearly, though, the greatest future impact of shifting preferences for death care goods and services will be upon the mortuary services component, which includes the ceremonial element to which the choice of a casket is directly related.

The failure of the operators of funeral homes to separate the sale of the ceremonial component of mortuary services from the sale of merchandise used in those ceremonies has tended to make their revenues dependent on the sale of caskets and to impede their adoption of rental caskets which encourage consumers to retain ceremonies in cases where cremation is the preferred form of final disposition. Yet it appears that the gradually increasing preference for cremation will require the adoption of the practice as a strategy for creating demand for ceremonies in conjunction with the choice. Proper pricing of the ceremonial component of funeral services would enable a funeral home to promote its sale regardless of the type of final disposition or casket selected. Moreover, it would appear to address past and potential criticism which has frequently attacked the sale of expensive merchandise by funeral homes; the sale of ceremonies has not been attacked. In fact, many critics of traditional death care practices have specifically recognized the importance of ceremonies in the form of memorial services, for example.

For various reasons discussed throughout, the prospective demand for death care is likely to be influenced by future criticism of traditional practices as the annual number of deaths rises sharply and the prices of death care goods and services continue to increase. Based on an analysis of the nature and influence of past criticism on consumer behavior, it is reasonable to assume that the strongest attacks will be based on the sale of expensive merchandise. For too long the role of the casket as the basis on which the revenues and profits of mortuaries depend has been allowed to obscure their nature as providers of death care, first and foremost. For the sake of the long-term health of the industry, it appears to be urgent that funeral directors acquire the nerve to abandon their role as casket merchants and recognize in their pricing practices that they are primarily providers of services — death care services.

A Suggested Strategy

Some of the historical reasons for emphasis on the sale of caskets by funeral homes have been mentioned, but all of them are clearly beside the point when seen in the light of such present conditions as federal unbundling requirements and the widespread and growing practice of cremation. It should be evident that funeral homes must adapt their practices to modern circumstances in which there is a need to promote, to sell, and to charge appropriate prices for the ceremonial aspect of the funeral services they provide, whether or not a casket is used and regardless of the quality of the casket selected.

There is in fact a strong case for articulating the value of the ceremonial content of funeral services. Although critics have cast doubt on the validity of arguments for promoting different qualities of caskets, there appears to be no doubt in the minds of sociologists, psychologists, anthropologists, and others outside of the death care sector that there is valid cause for preserving established institutions and rituals which have proven their worth over long periods in the past. Anthropologists have found that "certain repeated ceremonial forms — rituals surrounding birth, death, puberty, marriage, and so on — helped individuals in primitive societies to re-establish equilibrium after some major adaptive event had taken place" (Toffler, 1970, pp. 338–41). Sociologists have pointed out that in societies like ours, characterized as they are by rapid change, there exists a body of evidence for the benefits resulting from the maintenance of traditional observances surrounding random events such as death (Toffler, pp. 338–41). Social philosophers have long recognized that "It is the beginning of wisdom to understand that social life is founded upon routine. Unless society is permeated, through and through, with routine, civilization vanishes" (Whitehead, 1921, p. xiv).

Such evidence would appear to provide an interdisciplinary basis for the retention and augmentation of the ritualistic content of traditional funerals and memorialization processes within the framework of modern society. Often there are economic benefits from avoiding traditional funerals and memorialization, and these may appear to outweigh any social and psychological costs of eliminating the ritualistic elements of funerals. Such costs are usually ignored altogether by those who promote nontraditional death care as the "logical" and economical alternative, and critics of traditional American death care practices have completely dismissed the value of ceremony and ritual offered by such practices. To counterbalance this argument may require further proof by death care practitioners that traditional funeral services have potentially beneficial social and psychological effects.

In the death-related general interest literature and in material published by death care firms and trade organizations, there is a great deal of fragmentary anecdotal evidence of the social and psychological benefits of traditional and nontraditional ceremonies. There are also reports that those who forgo traditional rites and ceremonies may later regret their decisions to do so. No serious attempt has ever been made to marshal the evidence for these reports, to analyze it, or to assess the direct and indirect benefits of ceremonial observances. On the other hand, there is also no body of evidence which suggests that such ceremonies are in any way harmful. The only question surrounding them is therefore whether their benefits justify their costs, particularly when they involve the use of elaborate and expensive merchandise, namely caskets.

Unfortunately, it has not been possible for funeral directors to make a case for the benefits of funeral services, which are potentially psychologically satisfying social affairs, as long as their costs of rendering ceremonial services are recovered largely or even partially in the revenues produced from the sale of caskets. Indeed this method of pricing funeral services may have had the effect of encouraging some consumers to forgo potentially beneficial funeral services in order to avoid the costs of purchasing caskets which they do not desire to do. Moreover, the unbundling and itemization requirements of federal regulation encourages consumers to economize on such elements of traditional funerals as wakes, visitation, and other ceremonial elements having a potentially important psychological and social function. Yet the final report of the FTC staff, which recommended promulgation of those requirements, explicitly avoided any analysis of the "impact that the rule will have on the consumer's psychological and emotional welfare" (U.S. FTC, 1978, p. 500).

To counteract such effects of regulation and criticism, it may be necessary for death care providers to promote the view more effectively in the future that ceremonial funeral services facilitate the grieving process by creating an appropriate setting in which survivors confront the reality of loss of a family member in a comforting context while receiving expressions of support from as wide a circle of friends and acquaintances as possible.

Industry Views

There is some recent evidence in the comments of representatives of the national death care companies that their leaders are aware of the importance of establishing the view that the primary role of mortuaries is to provide services, especially ceremonial funerals, rather than to sell merchandise such as caskets. Reporting on the comments made by several sector leaders at a trade gathering, *The American Funeral Director* recently noted that the leading companies "are concerned about maintaining the funeral in the face of changing consumer needs and demographics, not only for their own survival but also because they believe the funeral has an intrinsic social value" (November 1993). David Fitzsimmons of Loewen indicated in the same article that his firm is concerned about what type of services a family selects and prefers that they choose a funeral incorporating a ceremony: "A lot of time, we try to define a traditional funeral as one with a casket. I think we need to begin to redefine a traditional funeral as to whether or not it incorporates a ceremony." John Morrow of SCI addressed the role of rental caskets as a means of promoting ceremonial services in cases of cremation: "SCI sees an opportunity in the area of merchandising with cremations, and we feel this area has been neglected. The rental casket should be seen as part of an overall cremation merchandising program that provides a customer with the full range of options. My hope is that the rental casket will be a step to having the cremation consumer go to a standard wood product."

Representing Stewart, Jerry Alexander said that "cremation is an 'untapped market'" for funeral homes. Stewart, he said, views cremation as a form of final disposition, just like burial, and not an alternative to funerals. Alexander asserted that Stewart would "aggressively deal with cremation through pre-need selling, and that does not exclude rental caskets." Speaking more generally, Fred Hunter, the president of Prime Succession, one of the largest privately owned chain companies, said, "increasing cremation rates should not be seen as a threat to the traditional funeral, but as an opportunity to create new markets." All of these panel members agreed that if the large death care companies do not properly address the needs of consumers regarding cremation, they run the risk that more of their customers will forgo ceremonial services as well as traditional forms of memorialization of the bodily remains.

Against this background of industry opinion about the importance of promoting the ceremonial content of death care, it is remarkable that this opinion does not appear to be universal. Thus, a recent book entitled *Reinventing Funeral Service* by Alton F. Doody, Jr., an industry consultant, was well-received by many death care providers, in spite of the fact that it is entirely devoted to the role of funeral homes as merchandisers of products rather than services. Indeed, the words *ceremony* and *services* do not appear in its index. To some extent, perhaps, this reflects the author's interest in merchandising as a business activity, but Doody makes clear his view that merchandising products, especially caskets, is the primary activity in which funeral homes are engaged. He defends this view by pointing out that "after all 50% to 60% of a funeral home's total revenue comes from the sale of funeral-related products" (p. 32). In a footnote, he explains this point in the following way:

> To arrive at the percentage, 50 to 60%, it is necessary to include prod-uct sales that are handled by funeral homes on an agency basis, such as vaults and monuments. Technically, in some funeral home accounting systems, vault sales, monument sales, and some other lines of products are not treated as "sales" but as "commissions earned" or "other income." The important fact is that funeral homes derive substantial revenues from these product lines. They are a basic part of the "economics" of the funeral service business. In this sense they should be thought of as sales. This is in contrast to "cash advances," which are typically handled without a markup (p. 32).

Since the historical focus in the operation of funeral homes has been on merchandising caskets, it is difficult to see how a description of new or better ways of doing this can be described as a "reinvention" of funeral service.

Moreover, it is difficult to see how a continuation of the historical focus on merchandising caskets is in the long-term best interest of an industry which is subject to the influence of a long-term shift in consumer attitudes away from earth burial toward cremation, for which a casket, especially an expensive one, is of questionable use or value.

In terms of the future, it may be wiser for funeral homes to consider "rein-venting funeral service" by focusing on their role as providers of services for which the public is willing to pay and which are in keeping with whatever forms of death care goods may be desired. As Jacquie Taylor, president of the San Francisco College of Mortuary Science, has noted, funeral homes provide con-sumers with more than cars and caskets. "It takes nearly 40 hours of labor for a modest funeral. Four, five, or six people go to bat for the family, from the time the phone rings. This is a chain of events the funeral service industry never communicates to the public, but it's a message we must convey" (*American Funeral Director*, January 1995). Earlier, she explained the modern role of the funeral director in the following terms: "What we're really doing now is event coordination — just like wedding planners" (Levine, *Forbes*, May 11, 1992, p. 163). Those who are not yet comfortable with this role may continue to behave as if they are primarily retailers of caskets for which the prospec-tive demand is limited in spite of the growing numbers of people who die.

If, on the other hand, funeral directors come to see themselves as providers of "care" in the true sense of the term "death care," they will be able to shift the focus of attention away from their roles as providers of merchandise to their roles as providers of care to families at a time of need. What does this imply for the future of casket sales?

Anticipations of Practitioners

Writing in *The American Funeral Director* (June 1993), Tom Ward of Aurora Casket Company recently foresaw a "casketless future" in America as a result of the continued spread of cremation. Rather than a "casketless future," it is more likely that what is to be feared by funeral directors is a "serviceless" future in which the ceremonial content of funerals is reduced or removed. To obviate this, it would seem necessary that the industry shift its focus away from the sale of caskets to the sale of services, no matter whether cremation or burial is chosen. Such services may include inexpensive caskets suitable for cremation or even rental caskets. To absorb the effects of this change, funeral homes must adopt a rational system of pricing their services that does not depend on the sale of expensive caskets and other merchandise.

The effect of the increase in cremation on revenues may be feared by stand-alone funeral homes, but it does not necessarily presage less consumer spending on death care as a complete process — including mortuary services, final disposition, and memorialization. For those firms that provide complete death care at combined establishments or via their operation of clusters, the sales effort whether at-need or pre-need may be expected to promote spending, particularly on memorialization, in ways which effectively compensate for any loss of revenues from the sale of less expensive caskets or the use of rental ones.

Perhaps the most fanciful view of the future presented by death care providers is that expressed by Aaron Shipper, a cemeterian from New Jersey who predicted in 1988 that "Burial in the earth will become unfashionable and will ultimately be banned by the government in 2030" (Cronin, *American Cemetery*, December 1993). No basis exists for such a claim, of course, and no purpose is served by it. Earth burial has a proven appeal as a form of final disposition to many segments of the population. Like traditional funeral services, burial and entombment are not fragile social institutions likely to fade away, and there is no reason to ban them.

The concept of a cemetery as a permanent "resting place" where bodies and cremains are interred or entombed in pleasant and peaceful surroundings is an ingrained part of the American heritage. The evolution of memorial parks has changed the landscape of the modern cemetery, but not its basic significance. The development of mortuaries within cemeteries has revitalized many of them and will continue to do so. New forms of operation which economize on land use, such as multiple and vertical interments and high-rise mausoleums, may arise in the future in response to changes in attitudes and commercial initiatives, but this is true of the development of any economic sector. No sector of the economy can escape the forces of change and none of its participants can afford to ignore the need to coevolve with changes occurring around them.

20. *Future Developments in Death Care*

Prognosis

In previous chapters some features of the anatomy and physiology of the death care economy have been examined. At frequent points in our examination, a variety of underlying problems were diagnosed, and in many cases treatment was proposed. Whether the diagnosis, much less the treatment plan, is acceptable to those in the sector is beyond the concern of this analysis.

Many of the problems of death care providers have been reinforced over long periods of time. For funeral directors these have included the following: (1) a widespread preference for at-need sales techniques which have invited criticism and regulation while leaving many establishments vulnerable to competition from firms which promote pre-need selling, (2) the use of casket-pricing formulas which have tended to make funeral homes overly dependent on the sale of merchandise rather than personal services, (3) the failure to accommodate the modern desires of consumers for death care alternatives of various kinds, (4) adherence to a tradition of "gentlemanly coexistence" which has left them ill-equipped to resist new forms of competition such as cemetery-mortuary combinations, (5) reliance on legal restrictions to protect themselves from competition, and (6) a tendency to depend on price increases to compensate for flat or declining demand for traditional funerals. Such practices are not likely to serve well the owner(s) of a funeral home in the twenty-first century unless it is the only establishment for miles in all directions. Not even that monopoly status will protect the financially unsound cemetery that is poorly maintained or ineffectively managed from slowly becoming a problem for its owners and ultimately the community in which it is located. What then is the prognosis for death care providers generally? It is not possible here to revisit all of the concerns raised in the course of our examination heretofore, but the summary treatment of some general themes and trends may provide the basis for some informed speculations about the future.

(1) *The future of mortuary services.* As we have seen, the extent of mortuary services desired by consumers has been subject to a series of influences tending

to curtail the role of funeral homes as providers of traditional services. The unbundling requirement of federal regulations and the development of direct disposition companies, memorial societies, and discount operators are factors favoring the curtailment of funeral services in the future. The trend toward curtailed services is likely to be spurred by pressure on consumers to opt for less-than-traditional services as a result of a higher average age at death, an increase in the number of pre-planned funerals, and the more frequent choice of cremation by consumers. Only counterpressure in the form of effective at-need and pre-need sales techniques appears likely to offset a tendency to trade down on the part of consumers to less-than-traditional funerals as a result of these factors. Growth in the numbers of Americans in the age groups which comprise the traditional markets for pre-planned funerals is a favorable trend, but improvements in the effectiveness of pre-need sales organizations at selling to younger age groups would further expand their potential markets. Such improvements may be facilitated by the growth of pre-arrangement and pre-funding as a practice embraced by increasing numbers of people in all age groups who are more accustomed to planning for future life events than were their predecessors in earlier generations.

(2) *The future of final disposition.* In the long run, the various forms of final disposition available from cemeteries are subject to further modifications in the future as vertical structures become high-rise, and upright burial, deep burials, and multiple interments are offered by some operators. Only timidity on the part of cemeterians will prevent their exploration of these options and the exploitation of those which appear worthwhile. More urgently, there is a need for cemeterians to address the tendency for their facilities to become isolated places during the twentieth century. The addition of mortuaries to suitable cemeteries has been of some help in this respect, but more effort is needed to relate the notion of the cemetery as a "final resting place" to the conditions of modern life. These conditions are different in significant respects from those which prevailed during the previous era, in which memorial gardens and memorial parks developed.

In particular, this is the age of mobility in which centrifugal forces commonly separate family members from one another. Many families no longer live out their lives in a single community in the way they once did. Under such circumstances, it may seem that the idea of a "family plot" has outlived its usefulness. But in fact just the opposite may be true. As families become geographically dispersed, the idea of returning to a common location after death may be appealing. The cemetery serves as such a common location. At least this is an idea which might be seriously promoted by cemeteries.

Even when cremation is incorporated into the final disposition process, the cemetery is a logical site for the permanent disposition of cremated remains. This includes inurnment followed by containment in a columbarium, as well as scattering of cremains in a memorial site. With the increasing number of cremations, indiscriminate scattering of cremated remains and cremains might eventually become an environmental issue of public concern. Clearly, cemeteries have proven their worth as effective and even sacred sites for the final disposition of human remains of all types. New forms of cemeteries may evolve in the future in response to evolution in forms of final disposition and memorialization.

(3) *The future of memorialization.* Even in the short span of the twentieth century, there have been major changes in the ways in which the memorial urge or impulse manifests itself in the demand for memorials of various types. Judging from past experience, there is every reason to believe that memorialization practices in the future will be different in some respects from accustomed forms, just as those forms are different in some respects from past forms.

While the use of traditional modes of memorialization may be expected to continue in the future, a wider use of new forms of memorialization (e.g., cyberspace memorials) may be anticipated as emerging technologies are adapted for use to express novel forms of the impulse to memorialize. The inherent appeal of (tax-deductible) financial or "living" memorials is likely to continue to grow in tandem with the promotion of their use by various types of non-profit organizations in their fund-raising campaigns. Some of this growth may come at the expense of spending on durable and perishable memorials unless more effective means of promoting these are devised and employed. To a large extent, the prospects for such promotional activities are tied to the success of efforts to encourage forms of final disposition which are complemented by durable (and perishable) memorials and to develop new final disposition and memorial products which complement cremation.

Bearing in mind these broad outlines of the future of death care, we turn now to a consideration of some specific forces at play as the death care economy enters the twenty-first century.

Trends in Attitudes

As discussed more fully in Chapter 19, the number of deaths occurring annually in the United States is destined to increase gradually in the next decade, and then more rapidly throughout the first half of the next century. The effect of this increase in the total number of deaths will be to increase the volume of cases handled by many death care providers, but the impact on the growth of their revenues and profits will depend on the types of death care desired in connection with cases handled by them in the future. So far it does not appear that a trend toward more variety in American death care practices has affected aggregate death care receipts adversely. Recent trends in the attitudes of Americans toward dying reveal an increasing acceptance of death as a part of everyone's normal life cycle. This is seen in a tendency for more people to wrest control over the way they die from members of the medical profession and from institutions in which they find themselves as death approaches. Living wills and advance directives have become increasingly popular among Americans in their attempt to exert a greater measure of control over their own dying process.

As a natural extension of these attempts, more individuals may also seek to exert greater control over the death care they will receive. Pre-need and near-need planning provide them with this opportunity. The death care firms which provide consumers with this opportunity are those which stand to benefit most from this trend toward greater interest in the process of dying and its aftermath. As mentioned earlier, the Open Society Institute announced in late 1994 that it would fund a $15 million program of study entitled "Project on Death in America." In a program announcement, the project is presented as follows:

> The experience of dying has changed over the past several decades, with many more people enduring prolonged deaths as a consequence of chronic and progressive disease. Needless suffering — physical, emotional, existential, and spiritual — too often accompanies these deaths, for both dying persons and survivors. The Mission of the Project on Death in America is to understand and transform the culture and experience of dying in the United States through initiatives in research, scholarship, the humanities, and the arts; to foster innovations in the provision of care, public education, professional education, and public policy. The Project on Death in America is funded by the Open Society Institute, a non-profit foundation that supports the development of open societies worldwide [*Request for Applications*].

In another program announcement directed primarily to scholars mostly allied with health institutions and universities, further detail is given on the project:

> Each scholar will propose and implement a significant project that addresses a critical issue in the care of the dying in his or her own institution or community. The project must have institutional support and the potential for integration into existing structures. In addition, the project should have potential generalizability to other settings, populations, and institutions, and should represent an innovative approach to care, education, research, and/or advocacy. Especially encouraged are projects that address access to care issues; development of culturally-sensitive services for patients at the end of life and their families; comprehensive educational programs for health professionals, especially those in primary care; out-comes of different care delivery models for patients near the end of life and for family members during bereavement; public education and advocacy; and development of models that help patients and their families achieve physical, psychological, and spiritual well-being and "gentle closure" in the face of impending death [*Faculty Scholars Program*].

Reference to any part of the death care process is conspicuously absent in both announcements, and no representative from the death care sector is a member of the project advisory board. This is so in spite of the fact that the death care process inevitably follows the event of death, and its form affects the bereavement of surviving families and their well-being. It would thus seem to be an important topic to be addressed by any comprehensive study of "Death in America." Clearly, there are significant issues which have long remained unresolved in connection with death care practices in America and elsewhere. Sloane (1991) suggests: "There needs to be more research about the ambivalence Americans feel about private and public expressions of death, and in comparing their feelings with those of Europeans, Asians, and people of all cultures" (p. 281). According to our own analysis, the value of grievous ceremonies of various types or of viewing a restored corpse are two such issues which might be investigated through interdisciplinary research, leading to a tangible contribution to the well-being of bereaved Americans in the future. The opposed claims of death care providers and their critics, based on personal convictions and anecdotal evidence, will never fully resolve basic questions about the value of traditional practices and alternatives to them. The cost of the kind of research that could help to resolve such questions is beyond the means of most providers and critics. Furthermore, the large death care companies and associations are unlikely to underwrite such disinterested research projects if they fear the results will undermine their vested interests. Independent sponsorship is indicated, but the Open Society Institute's program does not appear to be designed to provide it.

Also absent from the Institute's program announcements is any explicit mention of the issue of assisted suicide, even though the practice has become a topic of open debate in American society. Without entering into this debate, several points may be made. First, neither attempted suicide nor suicide itself is illegal in the United States. Second, although the act of assisting suicide has long been against state laws, changes in those laws have been proposed in some states. If they are adopted, the legality of assisted suicide is likely to spread. This may eventually lead to "death planning," and the resulting new attitudes will undoubtedly underscore public awareness of pre-planned death care. Further emphasis on death education arising out of programs like the Project on Death in America is also likely to draw attention to death care pre-planning as a device for reducing the anxiety experienced by aging and dying persons and their families over impending death care arrangements and expenses. These cultural trends are an invitation for death care providers of all types to expand their pre-need sales programs in the future.

Consolidation and Identity

Earlier chapters have described the process of consolidation of the death care sector of the U.S. economy in terms which leave no doubt about its continuation in the future. Even if the number of consolidators does not increase greatly, those which already exist represent the potential to extend in the twenty-first century into more and more areas of the country and the world. Of course, the growth paths of the resulting international, national, and regional companies are subject to various limiting factors, including a gradually declining number of acquirable establishments remaining in the sector.

As consolidation continues, it will probably follow the established pattern of retaining the different "local" names and reputations of separate death care establishments. The perceived importance of this strategy has precluded the promotion of any firm as a provider of a "national brand" of death care that might serve as a guarantee of the quality and value of services rendered by its units wherever they might be located. Thus SCI as the name of a parent firm that "stands behind" the quality of services provided by its units has no reputation among actual or potential consumers of death care. In New Orleans, Stewart advertises a variety of facilities under the umbrella of the name Stewart Enterprises, but it has not sought to identify any of its units in other areas as being "a Stewart enterprise." Nor does Loewen designate its units as "members of the Loewen Group of companies." Is it possible that in the future one or more of the large companies could profit by attempting to associate their units with a common affiliation?

Probably not, since it is generally believed that the operation of distinctive funeral homes and cemeteries as part of a chain is incompatible with the kind of personal services consumers desire from such establishments and with the interests of consumers who prefer to deal with providers whom they know and trust, directly or indirectly. On the other hand, there is a possibility that some standardized form of death care involving little or no variety could be marketed under a regional or national brand name such as the Telophase Society. This would more closely resemble the operation of chains engaged in the marketing of fast food or economical lodging. As with those units of chains, it is possible that the units of a national or regional chain of limited-service facilities might be composed of franchised crematories locally owned and operated under a brand name to assure the quality and value of the limited goods and services provided. Franchising might also allow independent full service establishments to achieve some of the benefits of chain operation while remaining locally owned and operated.

One hears it said repeatedly that local ownership and management are important to the customers of a funeral home. This makes sense insofar as consumers often wish to deal with those whose names they know and trust. But that is a matter of the name and personnel of an establishment rather than its actual ownership. It is difficult to believe that at this stage of the twentieth century American consumers are so committed to locally owned firms that the ownership of a funeral home or a cemetery by a national company—or a multinational one, for that matter—adversely affects their willingness to patronize it. If consumers patronized only locally owned businesses, then Sears, McDonald's, Wal-Mart, and other firms would never have achieved the success they have. Regardless of their ownership, firms employ local members of the communities in which they operate, and if they are public companies, their shares may also be owned by those in many communities.

Ultimately, the facade of local ownership and management is a holdover from the era of small, family-run businesses of all types. This, however, is the era of large national and multinational firms, as most of us know and accept. The tendency of American consumers to choose all types of goods, foreign or domestic, based on their superior quality and value is sufficient to indicate that it is those features, not the ownership of firms, which is the ultimate test of the willingness of consumers to support a product or service.

This discussion raises the question of whether the U.S. death care economy may be entered by more foreign companies in the future. The success of the Loewen Group in the United States and of SCI in Canada and elsewhere provides evidence for the view that foreign ownership is not an insurmountable barrier to success in the death care field. Attracted by the long-term prospects of the sector, other foreign firms may explore various means of participating in the U.S. death care economy. With American death care firms now engaged in expanding abroad, it would be foolish to claim that a foreign firm could not succeed here because of cultural differences in death care practices.

More Combinations

Entrepreneurial success stories of the sort represented by Lake Lawn Metairie Funeral Home and other cemetery-mortuary combinations provide a basis for predicting that more cemeteries will establish mortuaries in the years ahead. Stewart has said that every active, well-managed, financially sound, well-located growing cemetery is the potential site of a new funeral home. He contends that the resulting combined operation is sure to succeed if it is marketed effectively. With similar confidence in the concept of combined facilities, Waltrip has said that there will be a funeral home in every large cemetery by the year 2000. This may be true, give or take a few years, of the suitable cemeteries with the resources to develop funeral homes within them. It may take somewhat longer for the independent cemetery operators to take the necessary steps involved in becoming combined operations. Some of these may prefer to affiliate with the national companies as a means of accomplishing the transition. Even noncommercial cemeteries which are suitable candidates for combined operations may become targets of opportunity for the national or regional companies.

All of this will lead inevitably to further pressures on the stand-alone funeral homes with which combination establishments compete. As documented in the case of the New Orleans market, more stand-alone firms will choose to consolidate by forming or joining regional and national chains. The number of funeral homes and cemeteries owned by the national companies is likely to increase steadily for decades. Nevertheless, the loyalty of customers to established independently owned funeral homes is strong and some of them may be able to survive or even to prosper by exploiting their niches within markets where combinations exist or further consolidation occurs. In other industries, like food and hardware, which have consolidated and developed integrated "super stores," some independent operators have survived, but many have not. The loss of clients by small funeral homes to cemetery-mortuary combinations and clusters of units operated by the national companies may be a slower process, but the eventual outcome is likely to be the same. In the case of death care emporiums, aggressive pre-need selling to the existing customer base of the cemetery is likely to accelerate the process.

The effectiveness of cemetery-mortuary combinations in taking business away from established stand-alone funeral homes now has been demonstrated in many different markets where cemeteries have added funeral homes. The interesting dynamic in the future is likely to be the multiplication of combinations in a single market area, creating a "cluster of combinations," if you will. An example of one area where this is happening is the New Orleans metropolitan area, where Stewart Enterprises owns no stand-alone funeral homes. Instead, it owns two cemetery-mortuary combinations and operates a third mortuary which is located adjacent to a large fraternal cemetery. As described in Chapter 17, the impact of Lake Lawn Metairie Funeral Home has precipitated a rapid consolidation among most of the rival funeral homes with which it competes. The interesting twist in the case is that the cluster formed by the consolidated funeral homes includes a large cemetery which seems suitable as the site of a combination establishment. The dilemma for the cluster operator is that if it adds a mortuary to the cemetery, it will almost certainly draw a large number of cases away from its cluster units in which it has made sizeable investments, presumably on the basis of their existing volume levels. Meanwhile, Stewart's Lake Lawn Metairie Funeral Home — together with the new one — are a continuing threat to the stand-alone units of the cluster.

On a broader scale, SCI has hundreds of clusters which have been formed as acquisitions were made over the years. Many of them include cemeteries, some of which are presumably candidates for combinations, but again if the company attempts to develop some of them, it will create problems for its other units in the same cluster. The same is less true of Stewart, however, which has acquired many of its cemeteries with a view to their potential as combinations. As they are developed in more areas, they will draw volume primarily from rivals, not from the firm's other units. This differs from the situation of chains which are the result of acquisitions made long ago, before the creation of combinations evolved as a sophisticated consolidation strategy.

Coping with Combinations and Clusters

Considerations of the kind just discussed indicate how much the death care field has changed since Forest Lawn began operations in 1933. With so many such facilities now in existence throughout the United States, it is perhaps hard to believe that there are still a few states and the District of Columbia where combinations are prohibited. This is a tribute to the relative strength of funeral directors vis-à-vis cemeterians in those jurisdictions, but legal prohibitions are flimsy protection from the winds of fundamental change which raise the stakes for those eager to enter fields from which they are excluded. The large companies are unlikely to be deterred by such tactics.

Even in those states where combined operations are not prohibited by law, their development continues to engender hostility and bickering between the combination and rival stand-alone funeral homes in some areas. The result is protracted litigation from which only the lawyers ultimately will benefit. Whatever the outcome in any particular case, the age of the combination is here and stand-alone funeral homes must learn to live with them if they can. We will see more and more funeral homes emerge in independent cemeteries and in those owned by regional and national firms. We may also see more cases of funeral homes located adjacent to noncommercial cemeteries because this practice gains many of the advantages of a combination without burdening the owner of the funeral home with the investment required in a cemetery. It also expands the number of sites at which combined facilities may be developed.

As noted in Chapter 17, in order to compensate for a loss of volume to competitors, stand-alone funeral homes must reduce costs or raise prices, or both. But costs are difficult for small firms to cut, and price increases beyond the rate of inflation are difficult to sustain, even for funeral homes, in an increasingly competitive marketplace. For some of them, however, the impact of increasing deaths will continue to sustain casket sales in spite of the trend toward cremation.

Views of the Future

The trends discussed so far are extrapolations of established tendencies which have gained momentum in recent years and are destined to continue into the twenty-first century. As the turn of the century approaches, however, one hears a plethora of speculations. A recent article on the future of "The Cemetery in America" presented several of these, including the possible development of "a national death care program, not dissimilar in concept to Medicare" (Cronin, *American Cemetery*, December 1993). While this sounds extreme, it is a vision of the future which cannot be dismissed out of hand. Reference has been made throughout this book to various parallels between death care and health care. For obvious reasons both of these types of care are matters of great concern and expense for the elderly. With continued growth in the proportion of elderly people in the U.S. population, it is not a farfetched notion that an entitlement to death care exists along with an entitlement to medical care. With a modest death benefit already payable under Social Security, it would be a simple administrative task to implement a national death care program for the elderly. To enact such a program is another matter, given the present concerns about long-term solvency of the Social Security System and the intergenerational rivalry which probably would attend any proposal to expand benefits under the system.

For practical political reasons, therefore, it appears that any socialization of death care is not a viable prospect in the United States. This does not mean, however, that the interests of an aging population in the subject and cost of death care will go unexpressed. The AARP is a national outlet for expressions of those interests, as evidenced by active participation of that organization in the review of the funeral trade rule by the FTC. One area of likely interest to the elderly is the greater availability of pre-planning and cremation, both of which many funeral directors have resisted in the past but which have become the subject of promotion by chain companies.

Technology and Entrepreneurship

In some economic sectors, the changes which take place are driven by technology, but death care is a low-tech field. The basic technologies of mortuary services, final disposition, and memorialization are ancient. Only the engineering techniques involved in the construction of community mausoleums and lawn crypts stand out as significant technological improvements in the production process of cemeteries, although substantial improvements have occurred in the equipment used by both funeral homes and cemeteries. Such improvements probably will continue to be made, but it is hard to imagine any technological changes that are likely to alter the structure of the death care sector dramatically.

On the contrary, the driving force in the sector will continue to be gradual shifts in the style of mortuary services, final disposition, and memorialization that people tend to prefer. The cause for these shifts in this country is widely expected to be a gradual aging of the population accompanied by slowly changing ethnic demographics. Both of these imply inevitable changes in both total and per capita expenditures on death care. Also they imply future shifts in the goods and services which funeral homes and cemeteries will be called upon to provide not only to their new customers but also to their old ones. The most recent continuing shift of this kind is represented by the trend toward cremation, which has been going on for several decades now and is certain to continue. It is not enough to say that the spread of cremation is due merely to the changing preferences of consumers and leave it at that. This view rests on a common confusion between the roles of consumption and production, the two basic economic activities.

Consumer desires are involved in economic change, but the agents of change are new products made available to consumers. Consumers could not shift from earth burial to cremation until cemeteries (or other establishments) began to build crematories, making that option available to the public. This in turn created the further opportunity for cemeteries to sell final disposition space for cremains. That is what entrepreneurship involves: providing options to which consumers then respond. Commercial cemeteries historically have been more active in this regard than funeral homes, perhaps because cemeterians have been less encumbered by a "business or profession" dilemma that has limited funeral directors. Commercial cemeteries have accepted their status as commercial businesses and have acted like businesses in other industries, promoting themselves and offering options which create demand for new products.

History makes this clear. First came rural cemeteries, followed by lawn-parks, then memorial parks, all promoted through pre-need selling. In time, commercial cemeteries added community mausoleums, crematories, and columbariums. The latest phase has been for many of them to round out their offerings by building mortuaries.

Has there been any such pattern on the funeral services side of the business? Clearly not to the same extent to which commercial cemeteries have undergone change. To a large degree, this is a consequence of inherent differences between the two lines of business. Cemeteries located on large tracts of land were by nature suited to become sites for crematories and ultimately for funeral homes as conditions ripened. The local stand-alone funeral home, whether located in an urban or suburban area, could not easily surround itself with a cemetery, or even add a crematory. With a smaller customer base and annual volume than the typical cemetery, it was less economical for a funeral home to employ a pre-need sales force. Cemeteries were thus the beneficiaries of some favorable circumstances when compared with funeral homes. There also appears to have been a substantial difference between the mentalities of cemeterians and funeral directors. Cemeterians have seen themselves basically as real estate developers and salespersons. As such, they have been eager to have more products to sell and to sell them sooner, on a pre-need basis, rather than wait for the occasional at-need call. They have thought of their work not as a profession, but rather as a commercial enterprise.

Cemeterians never conceived of themselves as professional or quasi-professional counselors or grief therapists entrusted with the emotional welfare of deceased families. Funeral directors have so conceived of themselves, and this undoubtedly has limited their freedom and sense of entitlement to promote their businesses aggressively. Apparently, it has been felt that to do so would not be "professional." There was always the risk that such self-promotion might take business away from a fellow professional, causing him to retaliate or to criticize the promoter for some lack of professional ethics. But, in point of fact, there is no obvious reason why professional services or personal care of the highest quality and most sensitive kind may not be provided effectively and efficiently in a businesslike way. After all, doctors' offices and private medical clinics are operated as businesses. Law practices are businesses. Many leading hospitals are businesses. These seem to be capable of providing sensitive personal services of high quality while maintaining high professional standards.

Pre-Need and Near-Need Selling

What has brought about a greater business emphasis at some funeral homes is the development of more multiunit operations, regional chains, and the national companies in which the management structure is separated from the operational staff that renders professional services. In addition to focusing on further acquisitions, the managements of these firms have also become involved in improved cost controls and better sales techniques. In forming clusters, these operators have brought funeral homes and cemeteries under common ownership, rationalizing the relationship between these two traditionally separate businesses.

It has always seemed rather odd that people bought half their death care in advance of need, and the other half at-need. The only way to explain this is that the cemetery half has been sold aggressively on a pre-need basis, and the funeral service half has not. With more emphasis on selling the complete death care package on a pre-need basis, this will change, and pre-need sales of funerals eventually will exceed those at-need, just as pre-need sales of cemetery property exceed those at-need. Some analysts have estimated that as many as 40 percent of funeral services will be pre-planned by the year 2000. This development has the potential for counteracting the threat to funeral homes posed by the cremation trend, especially if the sales effort is focused on selling cremation as part of a complete package of death care goods and services including a traditional ceremony.

If death care providers promote their view that cremation should properly be preceded by an appropriate funeral service and followed by appropriate final disposition with memorialization, the popular American notion of cremation as a cheap alternative to a traditional funeral and final disposition and memorialization may eventually become a thing of the past. The cremation societies and direct disposal services will continue to promote such a view, no doubt, but their message is unlikely to offset the power of effective salesmanship directed at the broadest cross-section of the American public whose heritage favors complete death care. Demographic trends also may assist sales efforts of this sort, since religious adherence increases with age. Likewise, traditional death care is favored by several of the ethnic groups which are rapidly growing segments of the U.S. population. Saving and purchasing burial insurance to provide in advance for a decent funeral has long been a priority within some of these groups, and they represent a receptive market for a well trained and experienced sales force.

What seems to be required in the future is a greater willingness on the part of death care providers, especially the largest ones, and the associations, to promote the three components of death care as positive purchases on which it is reasonable for families to spend in keeping with their beliefs and in accordance with their means. This will require them to present a strong case for the value of complete death care and to view their operations as businesses which are entitled to promote and to extend their product lines like businesses in other sectors of the economy.

Innovation in Death Care

Most businesses seek to expand their product lines, and their owners and managers often boast that such and such percent of their revenues comes from products that did not exist, say, five years ago. By contrast, funeral directors are more likely to boast of the strength of the demand on the part of their customers for traditional funerals, the elements of which have remained largely unchanged for generations. Rather than promote change in their funeral practices, their tendency has been to resist it until it has been thrust upon them by forces beyond their control.

It is true that some funeral homes have been innovative about cost management. Often they have been forced to control costs due to regulatory burdens generally and due to increased competition from combinations, direct disposition companies, and discount providers in some areas. But cost management can go only so far. Once an establishment is an efficient provider with a stable profit margin, profits will increase only as revenues rise. Raising prices can help to keep revenues rising, but only within limits. Prices cannot be raised indefinitely by enough to compensate for a dwindling case load. Most funeral directors know this and they have been bothered by flat or declining volume due to unfavorable demographic trends, death rates, and increased competition from clusters or combinations in their areas. In some cases firms have sought to do more advertising and even to adopt pre-need sales techniques to attract new customers and to lock existing ones into traditional funerals. But such strategies are usually met by countervailing responses of the same sort by other firms, the net result of which is higher costs for all, which inevitably leads to a need to raise prices. And if this process goes too far, causing more customers to trade down in a given product line, it turns out to be a perverse strategy.

What funeral homes have not done is to seek to add value through innovation in the components of the so-called traditional funeral. This has been a significant failure of the mortuary services industry. For the record, this criticism applies across the board to the national companies, the regional operators of multiple units, and the local operators of single establishments. The national firms have been innovative in their methods of negotiating and financing a steady stream of acquisitions, and along with the regional operators they have improved operating efficiencies through forming clusters and developing combinations. Some of them have adopted innovative sales programs. But none of them has demonstrated any remarkable capacity for product innovation. This stands out in sharp contrast to the emphasis on product development in other sectors and on the cemetery side of the death care sector.

This may have something to do with the fact that funeral services are subject to the constraints of tradition. By definition, traditional practices are not subject to overnight changes of a revolutionary sort. But traditions do evolve and they are subject to modification or augmentation at the margin. Weddings have always been traditional ceremonies, but as technology permitted they began to include commemorative still photographs as a new product, then videotapes. Some may derisively, say that the American public would never go for videos at a funeral service. But history suggests otherwise. Death masks were once the vogue in Europe. As technology permitted, death photography became a flourishing business earlier in this century, but it does not conform with the modern focus on the life of the deceased. Why not then incorporate photographs of the living person in memorial products, such as monuments and markers? Photographs of this sort have become an established part of the memorialization process in other cultures, and they might appeal to a large segment of American consumers, including those comprising various growing ethnic groups.

Funeral services usually have been lost to posterity because no record is made of them. Videotaped records of the services might well appeal to consumers as a value-added product offered by funeral homes. The potential demand for a product of this sort designed for inclusion in the nascent market for memorialization on the Internet is virtually unlimited. With greater promotion and acceptance, the demand for such video memorial tributes is likely to increase. The practice might even become an established part of American death care in the future.

Memorial Television?

It will soon be the turn of the century, and vast changes are underway in our lives due to such developments as interactive TV and a communications "super highway." These changes will affect our customs and institutions. It is possible that the future will bring Memorial TV in which the public simply sits at home and tunes into funerals and memorial services for the people they know, or even those they do not know, for that matter. After all, we now have Court TV through which trials are exposed to the general public and Sports TV on which even low-attendance sporting events get a showing. People watch Congress deliberate on C-Span.

Like the idea of Forest Lawn, the idea of Memorial TV may sound like a gigantic joke, but any serious attempt to anticipate the future is worth taking seriously. It is not reasonable for death care providers of any type to assume that the future will be like the past. It makes sense for those interested in the future of an industry to anticipate pro-actively the ways in which its constituencies will coevolve with developments in other industries and lifestyles. It is certain that those in the retailing industries, the entertainment industries, and many other industries are actively engaged in preparing for the changes in our daily lives which developing technologies will bring. But who in the industries of the death care sector is so engaged? Who within the various trade associations and the large companies?

Urban Tombs?

There are innovators outside the death care sector who have conceived of fascinating projects representing new ways of delivering death care to the public in magnificent facilities which appeal to the desires of consumers in novel ways. Just such a project, designed by New York City architects David Tobin and Roger Robison, received the Lidster Trophy in the Total Concept Category of the 1993 Phoenix Awards, sponsored by the Memorial Advisory Bureau of London, England. The Tobin/Robison project proposed a design for a high-rise mortuary/mausoleum/columbarium structure in mid-town Manhattan.

According to Tobin and Robison, their design is significant because of its successful introduction of a historical archetype, the tomb, into a modern urban context. Their proposal, presented in the form of an artist's rendering depicted on page 394, can be regarded as having a potentially unique impact on high-density urban centers around the world. The memorial was developed as a modern metaphor of contemporary urban life, as Tobin and Robison explain:

> The problem with dying, for a New Yorker, is leaving New York. This city is the permanent and favored destination for the people who live here. They have come to the city for a life of liberty and the pursuit of uncommon dreams. Being in this metropolis among others who share the same idea defines their existence. For New Yorkers, a memorial structure must reflect the hopes and dreams of the life they have lived. Located on Broadway and the Southwest corner of Central Park, their souls will be able to be a part of the city forever.
>
> The voids between the walls are filled with chapels, memorials, terraces and a staircase which ascends from the ground floor to the roof. The tallest part of the memorial is an atrium open from the ground through the roof, extending 50 stories. In the void, plates of glass are projection screens which reflect the electronic images of those interred within the memorial. The street front provides retail space for flowers, kites, bells, chimes, books and magazines. The roof holds an open-air cafe overlooking the park and the city.
>
> The architecture of the memorial is defined by the symbols it evokes. The stone walls, the entrance with a monumental vertical sliding bronze door, the reflecting pool at the bottom of the largest atrium and the planting of trees in the front plaza symbolize the cliff, cave, spring and sacred grove, and always, the building rising above the city, offers its soul to the heavens.

The interesting thing about this idea is that it comes from outside the death care industries per se. And for this reason, it is perhaps detached from the practical conditions known to the greatest degree by those in the cemetery industry. For example, there are serious problems with incorporating crypts holding decaying bodies in a multiuse facility. A columbarium for cremated remains does not pose the same problems, but it serves only a segment of the market, limiting its potential scale. Perhaps the greatest obstacle to the construction of any new facility like the Urban Tomb is its lack of heritage. The ties of large segments of the death care consumers of any area to the existing cemeteries and funeral homes are so strong that the prospects of such a project, especially such a massive one, are likely to be viewed as risky.

Even though New York City is rapidly running out of cemetery space, the highly speculative nature of a novel facility is likely to deter investors. The prospects of new facilities are much more secure when they are associated with

An urban tomb. Rendering by Vladislav Yeleseyev. Copyright 1993 by David Tobin/
Roger Robison, Architects. Reproduced by permission.

established heritage facilities. Accordingly, the existing cemeteries in New York, such as Woodlawn in the Bronx, are presumably better suited as the site of new death care facilities, including high-rise mausoleums and perhaps funeral homes. The problem is that these are inconvenient locations at which to conduct funerals for those who live in Manhattan. It appears, therefore, that the death care process is likely to remain a fragmented affair for those who live there.

The Florida Pyramids

A different kind of project of sizeable proportions has been proposed by developers in Florida. In this case the project consists of two major structures in the form of a large and a small pyramid. Both structures are designed to serve as a community mausoleum and columbarium. According to press reports, one of the proposed pyramids is 495 feet tall, or about fifty stories, which would make it the second tallest man-made structure in all of Florida. That is taller than the Great Pyramid in Egypt (418 feet), but not quite as tall as the Washington Monument (555 feet). By comparison, the smaller pyramid proposed for the site is 171 feet tall. The interior of the large pyramid contains 300,000 burial vaults or crypts and one million columbarium niches. The small pyramid to be constructed first contains 10,000 crypts and 20,000 niches. Plans call for a glass-enclosed chapel to be located in the pinnacle of the large pyramid, the base of which is to be surrounded by a moat. Both structures feature natural lighting and are powered by solar energy. The project includes a crematory but not a funeral home, since the proposed location is a rural area (Stanfield, *Times-Picayune*, September 11, 1994).

In the latter respect, the conception behind the proposed project is unique in ways other than its huge size and pyramidal shape. It appears to be predicated on the notion that monumentation can replace proximity of location and heritage as objects of consumer desires, especially where cremated remains are concerned. Whereas consumers have traditionally preferred nearby facilities, the monumental nature of the pyramids is intended to appeal to consumers throughout an entire region rather than a local area. According to Stanfield's report, the developers of the proposed pyramids envisage "a time when people from all over the East coast will bury family members in the pyramid, then stop by to pay their respects while vacationing in the Sunshine State."

Perhaps. But the location of the project remains uncertain. The objections of residents in the neighborhood of the site initially selected in the small town of Wildwood, Florida, caused the developers to back away from that location. As a result, the project was stalled, and for this reason or others, it may never be built. Be that as it may, the concept is interesting for what it suggests about the prospects for a shift away from an emphasis on the local character of cemeteries to an emphasis on their status as regional or even national monuments of sorts. The would-be developers of the pyramids emphasize the importance of the "visibility" of the structures and the symbolic appeal of their pyramidal shapes. Quite apart from any mystical properties associated with pyramids, their lasting qualities as demonstrated by the Egyptian and other pyramids may appeal to the desires of many consumers for permanent interment and memorialization of remains.

To promote the Florida pyramids would presumably require a broadly based marketing program designed to appeal to consumer desires for permanence and symbolic memorialization in connection with a place of final disposition. The emphasis placed on these factors in the sales process would have to overcome the conventional preference for proximity. Because of the size of the facility, regional and national advertising could be used to encourage such a shift in public attitudes. This would represent a previously unrealized opportunity for persuasive media techniques to be used to influence consumer attitudes about final disposition and memorialization. Large-scale advertising has been considered uneconomical for use by small-scale establishments serving local markets to which consumers are assumed to be tied. The potential implications of such a project for traditional cemeteries must surely be obvious.

Parting Comments

Whatever criticism has been offered in these pages is not to be taken as anything more than a body of suggestions for improvement on a long history of dedicated service by death care practitioners of all types. Because of occasional reports of wrongdoing by individual funeral directors or cemeterians, it is understandable that questions have sometimes been raised about the general level of ethics of death care providers as a class. In response, it may be pointed out that specific instances of incompetence, dishonesty, noncompliance and even fraud occur in every industry, profession, vocation, and field of human endeavor.

Anecdotes involving the confusion or misplacement of bodies or cremains; the outright refusal to serve certain clients, and other bizarre incidents occasionally appear in the press. But these do not indicate a general lack of high standards and integrity throughout the sector. With more than 6,000 funerals held daily in the United States, it is inevitable that some mistakes and even abuses may occur. What is remarkable is that there are so few claims of malpractice or misconduct against death care practitioners. Excluding therefore the exceptions to the norm which exist in every industry in every part of the economy as a whole, it is doubtful that there is any group of men and women who have served their communities so long and so well as death care providers. We think we speak for a large majority of consumers when we commend those men and women for the work that they have done in the service of us all. It is our hope that they will continue to earn our appreciation and support in the future as they have in the past. To the full extent that death care providers are committed to high principles, the future of the death care economy is bright.

The future may not be so bright, however, for particular death care firms whose owners and managers continue to live in the past. There are always some firms in every industry that have to be dragged against their will into the future, but they are seldom if ever the firms which are the most successful in adapting to an industry's demands and challenges. There are those who expect the aging of the population to turn around their declining volume or who feel that prices can be increased ad infinitum. Good sense counsels against both attitudes. Repeated price increases have negative consequences involving serious risks for any firm or industry as a whole that employs them as a strategy for long-run survival. The fate of the health care sector confirms this. It is folly to believe that the prices of death care can increase for long at a higher rate than prices in general. This implies that higher volume is the only means of growth in the revenues and profits of death care providers in the long run. But higher volume for a particular establishment is unlikely to follow automatically from the rising annual number of deaths.

Some may believe that if all else fails, they can always sell out to a national or regional chain company because these companies appear to have an insatiable appetite for acquiring properties and a seemingly blank check from Wall Street with which to bid up their prices indefinitely. But history suggests that this process cannot continue indefinitely. There are notorious cycles in the stock market which affect acquisition activity generally and within particular industries. The values of businesses of all types are subject to the influence of these and other factors, such as interest rates, many of which are beyond the control of those who own and operate the companies involved on either side of acquisitions. Of the three large death care companies, only SCI has a record as a public company which extends back into an era of high interest rates, inflation, and generally bearish conditions in the stock market. The fluctuations in the price of its stock during those periods reminds us of the potential for variations in the valuation of the stocks of death care companies in the years ahead. Furthermore, the acquisition programs of the public and private companies will be subject to their capacity for obtaining resources with which to expand both domestically and internationally. It seems likely that the diversion of management's attention to international expansion in all the largest companies must involve a corresponding diversion of their resources.

Whatever the future holds for particular death care firms large and small, it is clear that the need and desire for death care will continue. Changes in these needs and desires may occur in the future, requiring changes in the operations of death care providers, but the desire for death care goods and services will remain. The production, promotion, and delivery of death care goods and services in the forms and varieties desired by consumers will constitute the means by which establishments of all types — whether large or small, family-run businesses or chain units — will secure their position in the death care economy of the future.

Afterword

This book has presented the case for adoption of the term "death care" to refer to the totality of activities associated with the event of death in contemporary society. At an earlier point, it was said that this term was not proposed as a replacement for the several terms we are accustomed to using for the various activities that come within the domain of death care as a total process. We have used "death care" primarily as a technical term to describe all those activities considered together. Until lately, there was no satisfactory technical expression in the language to encompass the full range of activities comprising death care or to describe collectively the various commercial and noncommercial providers of death goods and services. Out of this necessity, the term "death care" was coined by some providers. Now "death care economy" is here proposed as the name for the economic sector composed of establishments, firms, and industries providing death care goods and services of all kinds.

The previous lack of an adequate technical term of this sort is indicated by the awkward and confusing title of the latest exhaustive bibliography of books and articles on aspects of what we now call "death care." For lack of a comprehensive term at the time of its publication (1976), the book was entitled *Funeral Services: A Bibliography of Literature on Its Past, Present and Future, the Various Means of Disposition, and Memorialization*. With a comprehensive term available today such a book might more accurately be entitled *Death Care: A Bibliography of Literature on the Past, Present and Future, of Funeral Services, Final Disposition, and Memorialization*. This improves on the prior title by using "death care" as a unifying term designating, but not replacing, the separate and distinct, but closely related, parts of the complete process it denotes.

Although the term "death care" has not been proposed for use in the vernacular, it is possible that it will fall into popular use as a noun or adjectival phrase descriptive of the basic nature of goods and services provided by a set of interrelated activities demanded by consumers in the event of death. It may appeal to the American appreciation for the linguistic short cut. Already the term has crept into usage in the financial community, and it has been employed at times in the general press. It has been used extensively by Stewart Enterprises and other death care companies in prospectuses, annual reports, investment forums, and press releases.

So far the term has not acquired currency. For example, it is not included among the entries in *Death Dictionary*, a book which contains more than 5,500 clinical, legal, literary, and vernacular terms that refer to death and was published by McFarland in 1994. Nevertheless, the term has been used selectively for years by a number of providers and others, especially by advocates such as Frank B. Stewart, Jr., who defines it in his speeches as "the means for the fulfillment of the human desire to be remembered as having been significant, which is accomplished through ceremony and tribute, dignified disposal or burial, and appropriate memorialization." Whether he actually coined the term or not, he has called consistently for its adoption based on his conviction that it truly and precisely describes the basic nature of the business and that consumers are ready to use these actual words in order to deal with the reality of death.

Others in the business may oppose the idea of using the term "death care" in communicating with the public at large or even among themselves because of its inclusion of the word "death." That word is still taboo to many, including some death care practitioners. Yet a variety of benefits may accrue from wider use of the term by death care providers to refer to what they do and to describe the goods and services they provide. In response to their concerns about "negative connotations," it may be pointed out that the adoption of the term "death care" would represent a desirable reversal of the tendency toward the use of euphemisms by funeral directors — a tendency which so often has attracted criticism and even ridicule.

In this book, attention has been drawn to the problem of using such terms as "funeral services," "burial" or "remembrance" to describe the complete death care process because any such term actually describes only one part of the whole. It is difficult to conceive of a term not including the word "death" that fully comprehends the totality of activities, goods, and services comprised by death care. No one would take seriously a proposal that the terms "post-life care" or "posthumous care" be used instead of "death care." Furthermore, the latter term is in keeping with current social and cultural trends which bespeak a growing acceptance of death and dying as natural phenomena. The fact that *How We Die* could be the title of a best-selling book in the 1990s attests to a greater readiness on the part of the public to deal with death more realistically than it did in the past. This trend is broadly viewed as a healthy one by many psychologists, psychiatrists, social workers, theologians, and others as a sign of our culture's growth into realistic maturity. With the continued aging of the population, more Americans than ever before will face death in the future. They and their survivors will have no choice but to deal with the reality of death — not only as an emotionally distressing event but also as a significant economic event involving spending on a series of commercial transactions entailing mortuary services, final disposition, and memorialization.

To understand these transactions conceptually as "death care" is to integrate them into a unified whole, providing consumers with a proper context of choice allowing them to allocate their resources rationally among the three components of death care in the most satisfying way. This seems most likely to occur when death care is sold to consumers as a total package of goods and services by a single provider on a pre-need basis. We believe that in the future a growing number of consumers will purchase death care in this manner. Nevertheless, many will not, and the death care economy will remain highly fragmented. To embrace the whole of it, a classification system for death care goods and services was developed in Chapter 6, and a classification system for death care establishments was proposed in Chapter 7.

As mentioned in the Preface, an Economic Classification Policy Committee of the U.S. government is currently engaged in a "fresh slate" examination of the existing industrial classification structure based on criteria developed for the creation of a North American Industrial Classification System (NAICS). In addition to the development of a production-oriented industrial classification system, the ECPC is also charged with developing a market-oriented product grouping system. In the course of this book, a classification system of each type was devised for the death care economy.

Based on the analysis presented, it appears that those systems meet many of the criteria established by the ECPC. In particular, it appears that the proposed death care industries meet whatever reasonable "size and importance" criteria are likely to be applied for inclusion in NAICS. They clearly "include a sufficient number of companies so that Federal agencies can publish industry data without disclosing information about the operations of individual firms." The changes proposed are clearly such that they can be employed by government agencies to classify the data they collect and publish "within their normal processing operations." Finally, the death care economies of the United States, Canada, and Mexico are clearly sufficiently similar, if not identical, that the proposed classification of "death care" industries can be implemented in those countries as well as the United States (Federal Register, July 26, 1994, p. 38096). The large U.S. death care companies operate in Canada and Mexico, as well as elsewhere outside the United States, and the second-largest such company is itself based in Canada.

Along with the proposed production-based industrial classification system presented in Chapter 7, the demand-based product classification system developed in Chapter 6 seems to meet various ECPC criteria for a market-oriented economic classification framework. The proposed system groups together death care products which are close substitutes or which make up a marketing category as specified in ECPC working papers. By focusing on the use of goods and services in the death care process regardless of where they are produced, the market-oriented or demand-based system groups together the outputs of death care establishments and related enterprises. These desired features of a market-oriented system are specifically incorporated in ECPC working papers and in its call for proposals regarding a market-oriented product grouping system (*Federal Register*, July 26, 1994, pp. 38095–96).

No matter what provisions are made for the treatment of death care goods and services, establishments, and industries under NAICS, the argument and evidence of this book are complete. They provide the basis for further study and advancement of the subject and field of death care.

Appendix

"The Funeral Rule"
Federal Trade Commission
Final Amended Funeral Industry Practices
Trade Regulation Rule

PART 453-FUNERAL INDUSTRY PRACTICES
Sec.
453.1 Definitions.
453.2 Price disclosures.
453.3 Misrepresentations.
453.4 Required purchase of funeral goods or funeral services.
453.5 Services provided without prior approval.
453.6 Retention of documents.
453.7 Comprehension of disclosures.
453.8 Declaration of intent.
453.9 State exemptions.
   Authority: 15 U.S.C. 57a(a); 15 U.S.C. 46(g); 5 U.S.C. 552.

§453.1 Definitions.
   (a) *Alternative container.* An "alternative container" is an unfinished wood box or other non-metal receptacle or enclosure, without ornamentation or a fixed interior lining, which is designed for the encasement of human remains and which is made of fiberboard, pressed-wood, composition materials (with or without an outside covering) or like materials.
   (b) *Cash advance item.* A "cash advance item" is any item of service or merchandise described to a purchaser as a "cash advance," "accommodation," "cash disbursement," or similar term. A cash advance item is also any item obtained from a third party and paid for by the funeral provider on the purchaser's behalf. Cash advance items may include, but are not limited to: cemetery or crematory services; pallbearers; public transportation; clergy honoraria; flowers, musicians or singers; nurses; obituary notices; gratuities and death certificates.
   (c) *Casket.* A "casket" is a rigid container which is designed for the encasement of human remains and which is usually constructed of wood, metal, fiberglass, plastic, or like material, and ornamented and lined with fabric.
   (d) *Commission.* "Commission" refers to the Federal Trade Commission.

401

(e) *Cremation.* "Cremation" is a heating process which incinerates human remains.

(f) *Crematory.* A "crematory" is any person, partnership or corporation that performs cremation and sells funeral goods.

(g) *Direct cremation.* A "direct cremation" is a disposition of human remains by cremation, without formal viewing, visitation, or ceremony with the body present.

(h) *Funeral goods.* "Funeral goods" are the goods which are sold or offered for sale directly to the public for use in connection with funeral services.

(i) *Funeral provider.* A "funeral provider" is any person, partnership or corporation that sells or offers to sell funeral goods and funeral services to the public.

(j) *Funeral services.* "Funeral services" are any services which may be used to:

(1) Care for and prepare deceased human bodies for burial, cremation or other final disposition; and

(2) arrange, supervise or conduct the funeral ceremony or the final disposition of deceased human bodies.

(k) *Immediate burial.* An "immediate burial" is a disposition of human remains by burial, without formal viewing, visitation, or ceremony with the body present, except for a graveside service.

(l) *Memorial service.* A "memorial service" is a ceremony commemorating the deceased without the body present.

(m) *Funeral ceremony.* A "funeral ceremony" is a service commemorating the deceased with the body present.

(n) *Outer burial container.* An "outer burial container" is any container which is designed for placement in the grave around the casket including, but not limited to, containers commonly known as burial vaults, grave boxes, and grave liners.

(o) *Person.* A "person" is any individual, partnership, corporation, association, government or governmental subdivision or agency, or other entity.

(p) *Services of funeral director and staff.* The "services of funeral director and staff" are the basic services, not to be included in prices of other categories in §453.2(b)(4), that are furnished by a funeral provider in arranging any funeral, such as conducting the arrangements conference, planning the funeral, obtaining necessary permits, and placing obituary notices.

§453.2 Price disclosures.

(a) *Unfair to deceptive acts or practices.* In selling or offering to sell funeral goods or funeral services to the public, it is an unfair or deceptive act or practice for a funeral provider to fail to furnish accurate price information disclosing the cost to the purchaser for each of the specific funeral goods and funeral services used in connection with the disposition of deceased human bodies, including at least the price of embalming, transportation of remains, use of facilities, caskets, outer burial containers, immediate burials, or direct cremations, to persons inquiring about the purchase of funerals. Any funeral provider who complies with the preventive requirements in paragraph (b) of this section is not engaged in the unfair or deceptive acts or practices defined here.

(b) *Preventive requirements.* To prevent these unfair or deceptive acts or practices, as well as the unfair or deceptive acts or practices defined in §453.4(b)(1), funeral providers must:

(1) *Telephone price disclosure.* Tell persons who ask by telephone about the

funeral provider's offerings or prices any accurate information from the price lists described in paragraphs (b)(2) through (4) of this section and any other readily available information that reasonably answers the question.

(2) *Casket price list.* (i) Give a printed or typewritten price list to people who inquire in person about the offerings or prices of caskets or alternative containers. The funeral provider must offer the list upon beginning discussion of, but in any event before showing caskets. The list must contain at least the retail prices of all caskets and alternative containers offered which do not require special ordering, enough information to identify each, and the effective date for the price list. In lieu of a written list, other formats, such as notebooks, brochures, or charts may be used if they contain the same information as would the printed or typewritten list, and display it in a clear and conspicuous manner. Provided, however, that funeral providers do not have to make a casket price list available if the funeral providers place on the general price list, specified in paragraph (b)(4) of this section, the information required by this paragraph.

(ii) Place on the list, however produced, the name of the funeral provider's place of business and a caption describing the list as a "casket price list."

(3) *Outer burial container price list.* (i) Give a printed or typewritten price list to persons who inquire in person about outer burial container offerings or prices. The funeral provider must offer the list upon beginning discussion of, but in any event before showing the containers. The list must contain at least the retail prices of all outer burial containers offered which do not require special ordering, enough information to identify each container, and the effective date of the prices listed. In lieu of a written list, the funeral provider may use other formats, such as notebooks, brochures, or charts, if they contain the same information as the printed or typewritten list, and display it in a clear and conspicuous manner. Provided, however, that funeral providers do not have to make an outer burial container price list available if the funeral providers place on the general price list, specified in paragraph (b)(4) of this section, the information required by this paragraph.

(ii) Place on the list, however produced, the name of the funeral provider's place of business and a caption describing the list as an "outer burial container price list."

(4) *General price list.* (i) (A) Give a printed or typewritten price list for retention to persons who inquire in person about the funeral goods, funeral services or prices of funeral goods or services offered by the funeral provider. The funeral provider must give the list upon beginning discussion of any of the following: *(1)* The prices of funeral goods or funeral services; *(2)* The overall type of funeral service or disposition; *(3)* Specific funeral goods or funeral services offered by the funeral provider.

(B) The requirement in paragraph (b)(4)(i)(A) of this section applies whether the discussion takes place in the funeral home or elsewhere. Provided, however, that when the deceased is removed for transportation to the funeral home, an in-person request at that time for authorization to embalm, required by §453.5(a)(2), does not, by itself, trigger the requirement to offer the general price list if the provider in seeking prior embalming approval discloses that embalming is not required by law except in certain special cases, if any. Any other discussion during that time about prices or the selection of funeral goods or funeral services triggers the requirement under paragraph (b)(4)(i)(A) of this section to give the consumers a general price list.

(C) The list required in paragraph (b)(4)(i)(A) of this section must contain at least the following information:

(1) The name, address, and telephone number of the funeral provider's place of business;

(2) A caption describing the list as a "general price list"; and

(3) The effective date of the price list;

(ii) Include on the price list, in any order, the retail prices (expressed either as the flat fee, or as the price per hour, mile or other unit of computation) and the other information specified below for at least each of the following items, if offered for sale:

(A) Forwarding of remains to another funeral home, together with a list of the services provided for any quoted price;

(B) Receiving remains from another funeral home, together with a list of the services provided for any quoted price;

(C) The price range for the direct cremations offered by the funeral provider, together with: *(1)* A separate price for a direct cremation where the purchaser provides the container; *(2)* Separate prices for each direct cremation offered including an alternative container; and *(3)* A description of the services and container (where applicable), included in each price;

(D) The price range for the immediate burials offered by the funeral provider, together with: *(1)* a separate price for an immediate burial where the purchaser provides the casket; *(2)* separate prices for each immediate burial offered including a casket or alternative container; and *(3)* a description of the services and container (where applicable) included in that price;

(E) Transfer of remains to the funeral home;

(F) Embalming;

(G) Other preparation of the body;

(H) Use of facilities and staff for viewing;

(I) Use of facilities and staff for funeral ceremony;

(J) Use of facilities and staff for memorial service;

(K) Use of equipment and staff for graveside service;

(L) Hearse; and

(M) Limousine.

(iii) Include on the price list, in any order, the following information:

(A) Either of the following:

(1) The price range for the caskets offered by the funeral provider, together with the statement: "A complete price list will be provided at the funeral home."; or

(2) The prices of individual caskets, disclosed in the manner specified by paragraph (b)(2)(i) of this section; and

(B) Either of the following:

(1) The price range for the outer burial containers offered by the funeral provider, together with the statement: "A complete price list will be provided at the funeral home."; or

(2) The prices of individual outer burial containers, disclosed in the manner specified by paragraph (b)(3)(i) of this section; and

(C) Either of the following:

(1) The price for the basic services of the funeral director and staff, together with a list of the principal basic services provided for any quoted price and, if the

charge cannot be declined by the purchaser, the statement: "This fee for our services will be added to the total cost of the funeral arrangements you select. (This fee is already included in our charges for direct cremations, immediate burials, and forwarding or receiving remains.)" If the charge cannot be declined by the purchaser, the quoted prices shall include all charges for the recovery of unallocated funeral provider overhead, and funeral providers may include in the required disclosure the phrase "and overhead" after the word "services"; or

(2) The following statement: "Please note that a fee of (*specify dollar amount*) for the use of our basic services is included in the price of our caskets. The same fee shall be added to the cost of your funeral arrangements if you provide the casket. Our services include (*specify*)." The fee shall include all charges for the recovery of unallocated funeral provider overhead, and funeral providers may include in the required disclosure the phrase "and overhead" after the word "services." The statement must be placed on the general price list together with casket price range, required by paragraph (b)(4)(iii)(A)*(1)* of this section, or together with the prices of individual caskets, required by (b)(4)(iii)(A)*(2)* of this section.

(iv) The services fees permitted by §453.2(b)(4)(iii)(C)*(1)* or (C)*(2)* is the only funeral provider fee for services, facilities or unallocated overhead permitted by this part to be non-declinable, unless otherwise required by law.

(5) *Statement of funeral goods and services selected.* (i) Give an itemized written statement for retention to each person who arranges a funeral or other disposition of human remains, at the conclusion of the discussion of arrangements. The statement must list at least the following information:

(A) The funeral goods and funeral services selected by that person and the prices to be paid for each of them;

(B) Specifically itemized cash advance items. (These prices must be given to the extent then known or reasonably ascertainable. If the prices are not know or reasonably ascertainable, a good faith estimate shall be given and a written statement of the actual charges shall be provided before the final bill is paid.); and

(C) The total cost of the goods and services selected.

(ii) The information required by this paragraph (b)(5) of this section may be included on any contract, statement, or other document which the funeral provider would otherwise provide at the conclusion of discussion of arrangements.

(6) *Other pricing methods.* Funeral providers may give persons any other price information, in any other format, in addition to that required by §453.2(b)(2), (3), and (4) so long as the statement required by §453.2(b)(5) is given when required by the rule.

§453.3 Misrepresentations.

(a) *Embalming Provisions—*

(1) *Deceptive acts or practices.* In selling or offering to sell funeral goods or funeral services to the public, it is a deceptive act or practice for a funeral provider to:

(i) Represent that state or local law requires that a deceased person be embalmed when such is not the case;

(ii) Fail to disclose that embalming is not required by law except in certain special cases, if any.

(2) *Preventive requirements.* To prevent these deceptive acts or practices, as well as the unfair or deceptive acts or practices defined in §§453.4(b)(1) and 453.5(2), funeral providers must:

(i) Not represent that a deceased person is required to be embalmed for

(A) direct cremation;

(B) immediate burial; or

(C) a closed casket funeral without viewing or visitation when refrigeration is available and when state or local law does not require embalming; and

(ii) Place the following disclosure on the general price list, required by §453.2(b)(4), in immediate conjunction with the price shown for embalming: "Except in certain special cases, embalming is not required by law. Embalming may be necessary, however, if you select certain funeral arrangements, such as a funeral with viewing. If you do not want embalming, you usually have the right to choose an arrangement that does not require you to pay for it, such as direct cremation or immediate burial." The phrase "except in certain special cases" need not be included in this disclosure if state or local law in the area(s) where the provider does business does not require embalming under any circumstances.

(b) *Casket for cremation provisions*—

(1) *Deceptive acts or practices.* In selling or offering to sell funeral goods or funeral services to the public, it is a deceptive act or practice for a funeral provider to:

(i) Represent that state or local law requires a casket for direct cremations;

(ii) Represent that a casket is required for direct cremations.

(2) *Preventive requirements.* To prevent these deceptive acts or practices, as well as the unfair or deceptive acts or practices defined in §453.4(a)(1), funeral providers must place the following disclosure in immediate conjunction with the price range shown for direct cremations: "If you want to arrange a direct cremation, you can use an alternative container. Alternative containers encase the body and can be made of materials like fiberboard or composition materials (with or without an outside covering). The containers we provide are (specify containers)." This disclosure only has to be placed on the general price list if the funeral provider arranges direct cremations.

(c) *Outer burial container provisions*—

(1) *Deceptive acts or practices.* In selling or offering to sell funeral goods and funeral services to the public, it is a deceptive act or practice for a funeral provider to:

(i) Represent that state or local laws or regulations, or particular cemeteries, require outer burial containers when such is not the case;

(ii) Fail to disclose to persons arranging funerals that state law does not require the purchase of an outer burial container.

(2) *Preventive requirement.* To prevent these deceptive acts or practices, funeral providers must place the following disclosure on the outer burial container price list, required by §453.2(b)(3)(i), or, if the prices of outer burial containers are listed on the general price list, required by §453.2(b)(4), in immediate conjunction with those prices: "In most areas of the country, state or local law does not require that you buy a container to surround the casket in the grave. However, many cemeteries require that you have such a container so that the grave will not sink in. Either a grave liner or a burial vault will satisfy these requirements." The phrase "in most areas of the country" need not be included in this disclosure if state or local law in the area(s) where the provider does business does not require a container to surround the casket in the grave.

(d) *General provisions on legal and cemetery requirements*—

(1) *Deceptive acts or practices.* In selling or offering to sell funeral goods or funeral services to the public, it is a deceptive act or practice for funeral providers to represent that federal, state, or local laws, or particular cemeteries or crematories, require the purchase of any funeral goods or funeral services when such is not the case.

(2) *Preventive requirements.* To prevent these deceptive acts or practices, as well as the deceptive acts or practices identified in §§453.3(a)(1), 453.3(b)(1), and 453.3(c)(1), funeral providers must identify and briefly describe in writing on the statement of funeral goods and services selected [required by §453.2(b)(5)] any legal, cemetery, or crematory requirement which the funeral provider represents to persons as compelling the purchase of funeral goods or funeral services for the funeral which that person is arranging.

(e) *Provisions on preservative and protective value claims.* In selling or offering to sell funeral goods or funeral services to the public, it is a deceptive act or practice for a funeral provider to:

(1) Represent that funeral goods or funeral services will delay the natural decomposition of human remains for a long-term or indefinite time;

(2) Represent that funeral goods have protective features or will protect the body from gravesite substances, when such is not the case.

(f) *Cash advance provisions*

(1) *Deceptive acts or practices.* In selling or offering to sell funeral goods or funeral services to the public, it is a deceptive act or practice for a funeral provider to:

(i) Represent that the price charged for a cash advance item is the same as the cost to the funeral provider for the item when such is not the case;

(ii) Fail to disclose to persons arranging funerals that the price being charged for a cash advance item is not the same as the cost to the funeral provider for the item when such is the case.

(2) *Preventive requirements.* To prevent these deceptive acts or practices, funeral providers must place the following sentence in the itemized statement of goods and services selected, in immediate conjunction with the list of itemized cash advance items required by §453.2(b)(5)(i)(B): "We charge you for our services in obtaining: (specify cash advance items)," if the funeral provider makes a charge upon, or receives and retains a rebate, commission or trade or volume discount upon a cash advance item.

§453.4 Required purchase of funeral goods or funeral services.

(a) *Casket for cremation provisions—*

(1) *Unfair or deceptive acts or practices.* In selling or offering to sell funeral goods or funeral services to the public, it is an unfair or deceptive act or practice for a funeral provider, or a crematory, to require that a casket be purchased for direct cremation.

(2) *Preventive requirement.* To prevent this unfair or deceptive act or practice, funeral providers must make an alternative container available for direct cremations, if they arrange direct cremations.

(b) *Other required purchases of funeral goods or funeral services—*

(1) *Unfair or deceptive acts or practices.* In selling or offering to sell funeral goods or funeral services, it is an unfair or deceptive act or practice for a funeral provider to:

(i) Condition the furnishing of any funeral good or funeral service to a person arranging a funeral upon the purchase of any other funeral good or funeral service, except as required by law or as otherwise permitted by this part;

(ii) Charge any fee as a condition to furnishing any funeral goods or funeral services to a person arranging a funeral, other than the fees for: (1) Services of funeral director and staff, permitted by §453.2(b)(4)(iii)(C); (2) other funeral services and funeral goods selected by the purchaser; and (3) other funeral goods or funeral services required to be purchased, as explained on the itemized statement in accordance with §453.3(d)(2).

(2) Preventive requirements. (i) To prevent these unfair or deceptive acts or practices, funeral providers must:

(A) Place the following disclosure in the general price list, immediately above the prices required by §453.2(b)(4)(ii) and (iii): "The goods and services shown below are those we can provide to our customers. You may choose only the items you desire. If legal or other requirements mean you must buy any items you did not specifically ask for, we will explain the reason in writing on the statement we provide describing the funeral goods and services you selected." Provided, however, that if the charge for "services of funeral director and staff" cannot be declined by the purchaser, the statement shall include the sentence: "However, any funeral arrangements you select will include a charge for our basic services" between the second and third sentences of the statement specified above herein. The statement may include the phrase "and overhead" after the word "services" if the fee includes a charge for recovery of unallocated funeral provider overhead;

(B) Place the following disclosure in the statement of funeral goods and services selected, required by §453.2(b)(5)(i): "Charges are only for those items you selected or that are required. If we are required by law or by a cemetery or crematory to use any items, we will explain the reasons in writing below."

(ii) A funeral provider shall not violate this section by failing to comply with a request for a combination of goods or services which would be impossible, impractical, or excessively burdensome to provide.

§453.5 Services provided without prior approval.

(a) *Unfair or deceptive acts or practices.* In selling or offering to sell funeral goods or funeral services to the public, it is an unfair or deceptive act or practice for any provider to embalm a deceased human body for a fee unless:

(1) State or local law or regulation requires embalming in the particular circumstances regardless of any funeral choice which the family might make; or

(2) Prior approval for embalming (expressly so described) has been obtained from a family member or other authorized person; or

(3) The funeral provider is unable to contact a family member or other authorized person after exercising due diligence, has no reason to believe the family does not want embalming performed, and obtains subsequent approval for embalming already performed (expressly so described). In seeking approval, the funeral provider must disclose that a fee will be charged if the family selects a funeral which requires embalming, such as a funeral with viewing, and that no fee will be charged if the family selects a service which does not require embalming, such as direct cremation or immediate burial.

(b) *Preventive requirement.* To prevent these unfair or deceptive acts or practices, funeral providers must include on the itemized statement of funeral goods and services selected, required by §453.2(b)(5), the statement: "If you selected a funeral that may require embalming, such as a funeral with viewing, you may have to pay for embalming. You do not have to pay for embalming you did not approve if you selected arrangements such as a direct cremation or immediate burial. If we charged for embalming, we will explain why below."

§453.6 Retention of documents.

To prevent the unfair or deceptive acts or practices specified in §453.2 and §453.3 of this rule, funeral providers must retain and make available for inspection by Commission officials true and accurate copies of the price lists specified in §§453.2(b)(2) through (4), as applicable, for at least one year after the date of their last distribution to customers, and a copy of each statement of funeral goods and services selected, as required by §453.2(b)(5), for at least one year from the date of the arrangements conference.

§453.7 Comprehension of disclosures.

To prevent the unfair or deceptive acts or practices specified in §453.2 through §§453.5, funeral providers must make all disclosures required by those sections in a clear and conspicuous manner. Providers shall not include in the casket, outer burial container, and general price lists, required by §§453.2(b)(2) through (4), any statement or information that alters or contradicts the information required by this Part to be included in those price lists.

§453.8 Declaration of intent.

(a) Except as otherwise provided in §453.2(a), it is a violation of this rule to engage in any unfair or deceptive acts or practices specified in this rule, or to fail to comply with any of the preventive requirements specified in this rule;

(b) The provisions of this rule are separate and severable from one another. If any provision is determined to be invalid, it is the Commission's intention that the remaining provisions shall continue in effect.

(c) This rule shall not apply to the business of insurance or the acts in the conduct thereof.

§453.9 State exemptions.

If, upon application to the Commission by an appropriate state agency, the Commission determines that:

(a) There is a state requirement in effect which applies to any transaction to which this rule applies; and

(b) That state requirement affords an overall level of protection to consumers which is as great as, or greater than, the protection afforded by this rule; then the commission's rule will not be in effect in that state to the extent specified by the Commission in its determination, for as long as the State administers and enforces effectively the state requirement.

[Title 16, Part 453 CFR (REVISED JANUARY 1994)]

References

Aaker, David A., and George S. Day, eds. *Consumerism/Search for the Consumer Interest.* 2d ed. New York: Free Press, 1974.

Acsadi, G. Y. and J. Nemeskeri. *History of Human Life Span and Mortality.* Budapest: Akadimiai Kiado, 1970.

Adams, Walter, and James Brock. *The Structure of American Industry.* 9th ed. Englewood Cliffs, N.J.: Prentice Hall, 1995.

Adler, Sydney. "History and Financing of Cemeteries," In *Cemeteries: Legal and Business Problems.* New York: Practising Law Institute, 1972.

American Hospital Association. *Postmortem Procedures.* Chicago, 1970.

"American Practitioners at Beijing Symposium." *The American Funeral Director* (November 1993).

"Analyst Foresees a Golden Era." *The American Funeral Director.* (June 1994).

Ariès, Phillippe. *The Hour of Our Death.* New York: Alfred A. Knopf, 1981.

Arnold, Thurman W. *The Folklore of Capitalism.* New Haven: Yale Univ. Press, 1937.

Arvio, Raymond P. *The Cost of Dying and What to Do About It.* New York: Harper & Row, 1974.

Assail, Shaun. "Ten Things Your Funeral Director Won't Tell You." *Smart Money* (May 1994).

Bayo, Francisco R., and Joseph F. Fader. "Mortality Experience Around Age 100." *Transactions of the Society of Actuaries,* 1983.

Becker, Ernest. *The Denial of Death.* New York: Free Press, 1973.

Berger, Arthur, ed. *Perspectives on Death and Dying.* Philadelphia: Charles Press, 1989.

Bigelow, Gordon S. "Funeral Service Education: Background and Status." *The American Funeral Director* (October 1992).

Blackwell, Roger D. "Management Planning for Growth Oriented Funeral Firms." In *Funeral Homes: Legal and Business Problems.* New York: Practising Law Institute, 1971.

_____. "Price Levels in the Funeral Industry." *Quarterly Review of Economics and Business* (Winter 1967).

_____. "The Product of the Funeral Director." In *Funeral Homes: Legal and Business Problems.* New York: Practising Law Institute, 1971.

_____. "Professional Pricing by Funeral Firms," In *Funeral Homes: Legal and Business Problems.* New York: Practising Law Institute, 1971.

_____. "A Public Relations Program for Funeral Directors." In *Funeral Homes: Legal and Business Problems.* New York: Practising Law Institute, 1971.

_____. "Socioeconomic Variables Affecting Funeral Purchase Decisions." In *Funeral Homes: Legal and Business Problems*. New York: Practising Law Institute, 1971.

Brennan, Raymond Louis. "The Laws Relating to Cemeteries." In *Cemeteries: Legal and Business Problems*. New York: Practising Law Institute, 1972.

Brown, Raymond E. *The Death of the Messiah*. New York: Doubleday, 1993.

Brozan, Nadine. "F.D.R. Memorial Is Under Way." *New York Times*, October 14, 1994.

Bruck, Connie. *Master of the Game: Steve Ross and the Creation of Time Warner*. New York: Simon and Schuster, 1994.

Byrne, Harlan S. "Stewart Enterprises." *Barron's*, October 11, 1993.

Carlisle, Tamsin. "In Mexico's Naftalife, They'll Sing 'Swing Sweet, Loewen's Chariot.'" *Wall Street Journal*, December 9, 1993.

Carlson, Lisa. *Caring for Your Own Dead*. Vermont: Upper Access Publishers, 1988.

Casket Manufacturers Association of America. "Future Trends in Funeral Service." Panel discussion, audiotapes, 1993.

Chamberlin, E. H. *Theory of Monopolistic Competition*. Cambridge: Harvard University Press, 1947.

Chambers, R. J. *Financial Management*. Sydney: Law Book Company, 1986.

Cockerham, William C. *Medical Sociology*. 4th ed. Englewood Cliffs, N.J.: Prentice-Hall, 1989.

Colvin, Linda M. "The Creative Funeral." In *Grief and the Meaning of the Funeral*. New York: MSS Information Corp., 1975.

"Combinations — Two Businesses or One Process?" *Southern Funeral Director* (May 1992).

Cox, Meg. "Death Conquers Bestseller List as Boomers Age." *Wall Street Journal*, February 23, 1994.

Cressy, et al. v. Metairie Cemetery Association, et al. Report of the Commissioner and Judge Ad Hoc, Civil District Court for the Parish of Orleans, State of Louisiana (1980).

Cronin, Xavier A. "The Cemetery in America." *American Cemetery* (December 1993).

_____. "Regulation Tops ACA Agenda." *American Cemetery* (December 1993).

Curl, James Stevens. *A Celebration of Death*. London: B. T. Batsford, 1993.

Davis, Jo Ellen. "Bob Waltrip Is Making Big Noise in a Quiet Industry." *Business Week*, August 25, 1986.

Dolan, Carrie. "Burying Tradition, More People Opt for 'Fun' Funerals." *Wall Street Journal*, May 20, 1993.

Doody, Alton F., Jr. *Reinventing Funeral Service*. New Orleans: Center for Advanced Funeral Practice Management, 1994.

Douglass, Sam P. "Advantages and Necessity of Affiliation in the Funeral Service Industry." In *Funeral Homes: Legal and Business Problems*. New York: Practising Law Institute, 1971.

Eadie, Betty J. *Embraced by the Light*. Placerville, Calif.: Gold Leaf Press, 1992.

Economic Classification Policy Committee, *Issues Paper No. 1*, "Conceptual Issues," *Issues Paper No. 2*, "Aggregation Structures and Hierarchies," Bureau of Economic Analysis, U.S. Department of Commerce, January 1993, reprinted in *Federal Register*, March 31, 1993, pp. 16990–17004; *Issues Paper No. 3*, "Collectibility of Data," May 1993; *Issues Paper No. 4*, "Criteria for Determining Industries," October 1993; *Issues Paper No. 5*, "The Impact of Classification

Revisions on Time Series," July 1993; *Issues Paper No. 6*, "Services Classification," March 1994; Summary of Public comments to ECPC Issues Papers Nos.
1 and 2, October 1993.

Edmands, Michael J. "Undertaker to Entrepreneur." *Barron's*, April 2, 1971.

Ely, Richard. *Outlines of Economics*, 3d ed. New York: Macmillan, 1919.

Engel, James F., and Roger D. Blackwell. "Improving Funeral Firm Performance
Through Better Consumer Analysis." In *Funeral Homes: Legal and Business
Problems.* New York: Practising Law Institute, 1971.

Ettinger, Robert C. W. *The Prospect for Immortality.* New York: Doubleday, 1964.

Fader, Joseph F., and Alice H. Wade. *Life Tables for the United States: 1900–2050.*
U.S. Department of Health and Human Services, Social Security Administration, Office of the Actuary, Washington, D.C., December 1983.

Feifel, Herman, ed. *New Meanings of Death.* New York: McGraw-Hill, 1977.

Fiffer, Robert S. "Cemetery Land Use Problems." In *Cemeteries: Legal and Business
Problems.* New York: Practising Law Institute, 1972.

Flaherty, Francis. "Death Benefits Become Living Benefits." *New York Times*, October 16, 1993.

Foderaro, Lisa W. "Death Wishes." *New York Times*, April 3, 1994.

"France's Supermarket for the Bereaved." *Fortune*, March 8, 1993.

Frank, Stephen E. "Dear Mom and Dad: Today at College I Learned to How to
Spit Wine in a Spittoon." *Wall Street Journal*, October 5, 1994.

"Fred Hunter's Alternative to the Memorial Society." *The American Funeral Director.* (November 1993).

Freud, Sigmund. "Mourning and Melancholia." *Collected Papers of Sigmund Freud.*
Vol. 4. London: Hogarth Press, 1956.

Fulton, Robert. *Death and Identity.* New York: Wiley, 1956.

_____. "Death and the Funeral in Contemporary Society." *Death Education II: An
Annotated Resource Guide.* Washington, D.C.: Hemisphere Publishing, 1985.

"Funeral Industry Practices; Final Amended Trade Regulation Rule." *Federal Register*, January 11, 1994, pp. 1592–1613.

Gebhart, John C. *Funeral Costs.* New York: G. P. Putnam Sons, 1928.

Gentry, Dwight L., and Charles A. Taff. *Elements of Business Enterprise.* 2d ed. New
York: Ronald Press, 1966.

Goldberg, Jacob. *Pastoral Bereavement Counseling: A Structured Program to Help
Mourners.* New York: Human Sciences Press, 1989.

Goldberg, Vicki. "Death Is Resurrected as an Art Form." *New York Times*, May 2,
1993.

Goldman, Ari L. "For Funerals, a Female Touch." *New York Times*, February 13,
1993.

Gordon, Leland A., and Stewart M. Lee. *Economics for Consumers.* 6th ed. New
York: Van Nostrand, 1972.

Gould, J. P. and C. E. Ferguson. *Microeconomic Theory.* 5th ed. Homewood, Ill.:
Richard D. Irwin, 1980.

Greenberg, Erwin H. "The Legal Aspects of Death." In *Acute Grief and the Funeral*,
edited by Vanderlyn R. Pine et al. Springfield, Illinois: Charles C. Thomas, 1976.

Guyon, Janet. "British Funeral Firm Says It's Dead Set Against Bid from U.S."
Wall Street Journal, July 12, 1994.

Habenstein, Robert W., and William Lamers. *The History of American Funeral
Directing.* Milwaukee: Bulfin Printers, 1955.

Hackett, Thomas P. "A Psychiatrist Compares His Profession and Ours." *The Director* (July 1976).

Hancock, Ralph. *Forest Lawn Story*. Los Angeles: Academy Publishers, 1955.

Harmer, Ruth Mulvey. *The High Cost of Dying*. New York: Crowell-Collier Press, 1963.

Harrah, Barbara K., and David F. Harrah. *Funeral Services: A Bibliography of Literature on Its Past, Present and Future, the Various Means of Disposition, and Memorialization*. Metuchen, N.J.: Scarecrow Press, 1976.

Hartman, Bart P., and Joseph F. Cheleno. "Estimating Profit and Cash Flow for a New Funeral Home." *Management Accounting* (November 1979).

Hayflick, Leonard. *How and Why We Age*. New York: Ballinger, 1994.

Hendin, David. *Death as a Fact of Life*. New York: W. W. Norton, 1973.

Heskett, James L. *Managing in the Service Economy*. Boston: Harvard Business School Press, 1986.

Hinton, John. *Dying*. Baltimore: Penguin Books, 1967.

Hollingsworth, B. B., Jr., "Establishing the Purchase Price and Structuring the Transaction." In *Funeral Homes: Legal and Business Problems*. New York: Practising Law Institute, 1971.

Hopke, William E., ed. *The Encyclopedia of Careers and Vocational Guidance*. 8th ed. Vol. 2, *Professional Careers*, and Vol. 4, *Technical Careers*. Chicago: J. G. Ferguson, 1990.

"An Interview with Raymond L. Loewen." *Cemetery Management* (June 1993).

Irwin, Heather. "Virtual Memorial Garden Is Last Exit on Information Superhighway." *Times-Picayune*, July 27, 1995.

Jacob, Rahul. "Acquisitions Done the Right Way." *Fortune*, November 16, 1992.

Jacobson, David. "Video Memorials: The Latest in Funeral Home Offerings." *Times-Picayune*, January 3, 1993.

Judson, George. "Trying to Revive the Waning Business of Interment." *New York Times*, November 13, 1992.

Kalish, Richard A., ed. *Death and Dying: Views from Many Cultures*. New York: Baywood Publishing, 1980.

Kastenbaum, Robert. *The Psychology of Death*. New York: Springer, 1992.

Kavanaugh, Robert E. *Facing Death*. Baltimore: Penguin Books, 1974.

Kelley, Etna M. *The Business Founding Date Dictionary*. New York: Morgan and Morgan, 1954.

Kelly, Eugene W., Jr. "Religion in Family Therapy Journals: A Review and Analysis." In *Religion and the Family*, edited by Laurel Arthur Burton. New York: Haworth Pastoral Press, 1992.

Kieso, Donald E., and Jerry J. Weygandt. *Intermediate Accounting*, 8th ed. New York: John Wiley & Sons, 1995.

Kissel, G. "An Analysis of the Market Performance of the Funeral Home Industry of Philadelphia." Wharton School M.B.A. Project, 1970, cited in FTC 1978, p. 43.

Knapp, Martin. "Economies of Scale in Local Public Services: The Case of British Crematoria." *Applied Economics* (1982).

Kolatch, Alfred J. *The Second Jewish Book of Why*. New York: Jonathan David, 1985.

Kübler-Ross, Elisabeth. *On Death and Dying*. New York: Collier-Macmillan, 1969.

Lapin, Harvey I. "Cemeteries Offer Unique Opportunities for Tax Planning." In *Cemeteries: Legal and Business Problems*. New York: Practising Law Institute, 1972.

_____. "Funeral Homes Permitted on Cemetery Property." *Cemetery Business & Legal Guide*, January (1981).

Levine, Joshua, and Seth Lubove. "Cash and Bury." *Forbes*, May 11, 1992.

Levine, Stephen. *Who Dies*. New York: Doubleday, 1982.

Lough, William H., with Martin R. Gainsbrugh. *High-Level Consumption*. New York and London: McGraw-Hill, 1935.

Lubove, Seth. "Dancing on Graves." *Forbes*, February 28, 1994.

_____. "Death Stock." *Forbes*, June 22, 1992.

Lucas, Sam J., Jr. "How to Represent the Seller of a Funeral Service Firm." In *Funeral Homes: Legal and Business Problems*. New York: Practising Law Institute, 1971.

McGinnis, Michael, and William Foege. "Actual Cause of Death in the U.S. in 1990." *Journal of the American Medical Association* (November 1993).

McMillen, Glenn G. "Death Down Under." *The American Funeral Director* (January 1995).

McNaspy, C. J. *Our Changing Liturgy*. New York: Hawthorne Books, 1966.

Manual of Accreditation. Cumberland, Maine: American Board of Funeral Service Education, 1990.

Margolis, Otto S., et al., eds. *Grief and the Loss of an Adult Child*. New York: Praeger, 1988.

_____. *Grief and the Meaning of the Funeral*. New York: MSS Information Corp., 1975.

Martin, Judith (Miss Manners). "What's the Best Kind of Funeral?" Universal Features Syndicate, March 27, 1994.

Meltz, Barbara F. "Dealing with Death." *Honolulu Advertiser*, January 10, 1994.

Milgrom, Paul, and John Roberts. *Economics, Organization and Management*, Englewood Cliffs, N.J.: Prentice Hall, 1992.

Mitford, Jessica. *The American Way of Death*. New York: Fawcett World Library, 1963.

Moore, Joan. "The Death Culture of Mexico and Mexican Amercians." In *Death and Dying: Views from Many Cultures*. New York: Baywood Publishing, 1980.

Mortuary Administration and Funeral Management. Rev. ed. Dallas: Professional Training Schools, 1991.

Myerson, Allen R. "This Man Wants to Bury You." *New York Times*, August 1, 1993.

Naisbitt, John, and Patricia Aburdeen. *Megatrends 2000*. New York: William Morrow, 1990.

Neale, A. D. *The Antitrust Laws of the U.S.A.* New York: Cambridge University Press, 1960.

Nuland, Sherwin B., M.D. *How We Die/Reflections on Life's Final Chapter*. New York: Alfred E. Knopf, 1994.

Osmont, Kelly. "The Need for Viewing in Grief Resolution: A Counselor's Perspective." *Dodge Magazine* (March 1992).

Parker, Wallace M. "Laws Affecting the Sale of Merchandise and Merchandise Trusts." In *Cemeteries: Legal and Business Problems*. New York: Practising Law Institute, 1972.

_____. "Legislative Trends — Effects of Truth in Lending." In *Cemeteries: Legal and Business Problems*. New York: Practising Law Institute, 1972.

Paton, W. A. *Shirtsleeve Economics*. New York: Appleton-Century-Croft, 1952.

Pear, Robert. "Population Growth Outstrips Earlier U.S. Census Estimates." *New York Times*, December 4, 1992.

Petersen, H. Craig, and W. Chris Lewis. *Managerial Economics*. 3d ed. New York: Macmillan, 1994.

Phaneuf, Arthur. "Preneed Accounting." *The American Funeral Director* (June 1994).

Pine, Vanderlyn R., et al., eds. *Acute Grief and the Funeral*. Springfield, Ill.: Charles C. Thomas, 1976.

Plowe, Mort C., and Rudolph C. Kemppainen. *Funeral Director's Financial Handbook*. Englewood Cliffs, N.J.: Prentice-Hall, 1983.

Polson, C. J., R. P. Brittain, and T. K. Marshall. *The Disposal of the Dead*. Springfield, Ill.: Charles C. Thomas, 1962.

Porter, Michael E. *The Competitive Advantage of Nations*. New York: Free Press, 1990.

Pullins, Jerry. "The Merger Movement Within the Cemetery Industry." In *Cemeteries: Legal and Business Problems*. New York: Practising Law Institute, 1972.

Quigley, Christine, ed. *Death Dictionary: Over 5,500 Clinical, Legal, Literary and Vernacular Terms*. Jefferson, N.C.: McFarland, 1994.

Raether, Howard. "Funeral Service in the Seventies." In *Funeral Homes: Legal and Business Problems*. New York: Practising Law Institute, 1971.

Raether, Howard C., and Robert C. Slater. "Immediate Postdeath Activities in the United States." In *New Meanings of Death*, edited by Herman Feifel. New York: McGraw-Hill, 1977.

Rapp, Stan, and Thomas L. Collins. *Beyond Maxi-Marketing: The New Power of Caring and Daring*. New York: McGraw-Hill, 1994.

Rappaport, Alfred. "An Analysis of Funeral Service Pricing and Quotation Methods." Evanston, Ill.: National Selected Morticians, 1971.

Roberts, Sam. "Police Funeral: Sorrowful Rite and Potent Symbol." *New York Times*, March 20, 1994.

Rosenbaum, David E. "Economic Outlaw: American Health Care." *New York Times*, October 26, 1993.

Ruhl, Jack M. "Providing Advisory Service to Funeral Directors." *CPA Journal*, (March 1993).

Ryan, W. J. L. *Price Theory*. London: Macmillan, 1965.

Saffron, Morris H. "Thanatology: A Historical Sketch." In *Loss and Grief: Psychological Management in Medical Practice*, edited by Schoenberg et al. New York: Columbia University Press, 1970.

St. John, Adela Rogers. *First Step Up Toward Heaven: Hubert Eaton and Forest Lawn*. Englewood Cliffs, N.J.: Prentice-Hall, 1959.

Saltzman, Steven. "The Death Care Industry." Chicago: The Chicago Corporation, 1994.

Scherer, F. M., and D. Ross. *Industrial Market Structure and Economic Performance*. Boston: Houghton Mifflin, 1990.

Schlichter, Sumner H. *Modern Economic Society*. New York: Henry Holt, 1931.

Schmetzer, Uli. "Affluent Chinese Seek Lavish Ways to Leave World." *Times-Picayune*, September 10, 1994.

Schmidt, William E. "For Jostled British, Now Double-Decker Graves." *New York Times*, September 20, 1994.

Schoenberg, Bernard, ed. *Loss and Grief*. New York: Columbia University Press, 1970.

Schor, Esther. *Bearing the Dead*. Princeton, N.J.: Princeton University Press, 1994.

Schultz, Ellen E. "Survivors Find New Help with Financial Decisions." *Wall Street Journal*, September 16, 1994.

"SCI Challenging Wisconsin Anti-combo Law." *The American Funeral Director.* (June 1994).

Scott, Janny. "An Onassis Legacy: Facing Death on One's Own Terms." *New York Times,* June 4, 1994.

"Service Corporation International." *Wall Street Transcript,* June 6, 1992.

Shepherd, James, and George Wilcox. *Public Policies Toward Business.* Homewood, Ill.: Irwin, 1979.

Sherman, J. K. "Immortality and the Freezing of Human Bodies." *Natural History* (December 1971).

Silverman, Phyllis R. "Another Look at the Role of the Funeral Director." In *Grief and the Meaning of the Funeral.* New York: MSS Information Corp., 1975.

Sloane, David C. *The Last Great Necessity: Cemeteries in American History.* Baltimore: Johns Hopkins University Press, 1991.

Slud, Martha. "Fans Pay Big Bucks to Spend Eternity with Stars." *Times-Picayune,* August 14, 1994.

Smith, Adam. *The Theory of Moral Sentiments,* New York: Augustus M. Kelley, 1966. Originally published in 1759.

Smith, Richard L., Jr. "Some Current Cemetery Accounting." In *Cemeteries: Legal and Business Problems.* New York: Practising Law Institute, 1972.

Smith, Ronald G. E. "Are There Too Many Funeral Homes?" *Mortuary Management* (February 1980).

_____. "The Big Three." *The American Funeral Director* (July 1993).

_____. "Combinations Changing U.S. Burial Traditions, Part One." *American Cemetery* (February 1993).

_____. "Combinations Changing U.S. Burial Traditions, Part Two." *American Cemetery* (March 1993).

_____. "In Defense of Tradition." *Mortuary Management* (October 1978).

_____, and L. H. Falk. "The Relationship Between Cemeteries and Mortuaries." *Mortuary Management* (March 1979).

_____, and _____. "Caskets and Vaults." *Mortuary Management* (February 1979).

_____, and _____. "Cemetery/Mortuary Combinations." *Mortuary Management* (September 1979).

_____, and _____. "Competition and Regulation in the Funeral Service Industry." *Mortuary Management,* February 1978.

_____, and _____. "Funeral Directors and Casket Manufacturers." *Mortuary Management* (January 1979).

_____, and _____. "Funeral Homes: Values and Prospects." *Mortuary Management* (July/August 1979).

_____, and G. L. Schoen. "The Funeral Service Industry." *Mortuary Management* (December 1977).

_____, and _____. "Prices, Costs and Profitability in the Funeral Service Industry." *Mortuary Management* (April 1978).

_____, and _____. "Some Implications of the Chain Operation and Investor-Ownership of Funeral Homes." *Mortuary Management* (May 1978).

_____, and _____. "Trends in Funeral Services." *Mortuary Management* (January 1978).

Snyder, Keith D., and Richard E. O'Dell. *Veterans Benefits.* New York: Harper, 1993.

Solomon, Caleb. "Ghouls, No, but They've Dug Up Some Macabre Secrets of the Grave." *Wall Street Journal,* October 30, 1992.

Spiegelman, Mortimer. *Introduction to Demography*. Cambridge: Harvard University Press, 1968.

"Standard Industrial Classification Replacement Notice." *Federal Register*, July 26, 1994, pp. 38092–38096.

Stanfield, Frank. "Neighbors: Pyramid Tomb Won't Stack Up." *Times-Picayune*, September 11, 1994.

Steinfels, Peter. "Beliefs." *New York Times*, April 2, 1994.

Stephenson, John S. *Death, Grief, and Mourning*. New York: Free Press, 1985.

"Stewart Enterprises, Inc." *Wall Street Transcript*, June 28, 1993.

"Study of Named Cemeteries Finds a Puzzling Pattern," *The American Funeral Director* (July 1993).

Stueve, Thomas F. H., *Mortuary Law*. 7th rev. ed. Cincinnati: Cincinnati Foundation for Mortuary Education, 1984.

Szanton, Andrew. "Changing Styles Bring Cremation Industry to Life." *American Demographics* (December 1992).

Thornton, Emily. "Death Trends from Des Moines and Beyond." *Fortune*, March 8, 1993.

Toffler, Alvin. *Future Shock*. New York: Random House, 1970.

Toth, Susan Allen. "Venice's Isle of the Dead." *New York Times*, May 16, 1993.

"Trends in California." *The American Funeral Director*. (January 1995).

"The 200 Call Question." *The American Funeral Director*. (November 1993).

U.S. Department of Commerce. Bureau of the Census. *Current Population Reports*, Annual. Washington, D.C.

_____. _____. _____. *Guide to the 1987 Economic Censuses and Related Statistics* and *Census of Service Industries (1987)*. Washington, D.C., 1987.

_____. _____. _____. *Proceedings, International Conference on Classification of Economic Activities*. Williamsburg, Virginia, November 6–8, 1991.

_____. _____. Bureau of Economic Analysis, Economic Classification Policy Committee. Report No. 1, "Economic Concept Incorporated in the Standard Industrial Classification Industries of the United States," and Report No. 2, "The Heterogeneity Index: A Quantitative Tool to Support Industrial Classification." Washington, D.C., August 1994.

_____. Department of Labor. Bureau of Labor Statistics. *CPI Detailed Report*. Washington, D.C., March 1994.

_____. _____. Division of Consumer Expenditure Surveys. *BLS Handbook of Methods*, Bulletin 2414, Chapter 18, "Consumer Expenditure and Income," Washington, D.C.

_____. Executive Office of the President. Office of Management and Budget. *Standard Industrial Classification Manual*, 1987.

_____. Federal Trade Commission. *Report of the Presiding Officer on a Trade Regulation Rule Proceeding: Review of the Funeral Industry Practices Trade Regulation Rule*. Washington, D.C., July 1990.

_____. _____. Bureau of Consumer Protection. *Funeral Industry Practices: Final Staff Report to the Federal Trade Commission with Proposed Amended Trade Regulation Rule*. Washington, D.C., June 1978.

_____. _____. _____. *Funeral Industry Practices: Final Staff Report to the Federal Trade Commission with Proposed Amended Trade Regulation Rule*. Washington, D.C., June 1990.

_____. _____. Office of Impact Evaluation. *Report on the Survey of Recent Funeral Arrangers*. Washington, D.C., April 1988.

_____. National Center for Health Statistics. *Vital Statistics of the United States,* Annual. Washington, D.C.

_____. Senate. *Antitrust Aspects of the Funeral Industry,* Hearing Before the Subcommittee on Antitrust and Monopoly of the Committee of the Judiciary. Washington, D.C., July 1964.

Van Buren, Abigail. *And Now, Caskets Available for Rental.* Universal Press Syndicate, 1994.

Viscusi, W. Kip, John M. Vernon, and Joseph E. Harrington, Jr. *Economics of Regulation and Antitrust.* Lexington, Mass.: D.C. Heath, 1992.

Ward, Tom. "Casketless Future?" *The American Funeral Director.* (June 1993).

Warren, W. G. *Death Education and Research: Critical Perspectives.* New York: Haworth Press, 1989.

Wass, Hannelore, ed. *Facing the Facts.* Washington, D.C.: Hemisphere Publishing, 1979.

_____, et al., eds. *Death Education II: An Annotated Resource Guide.* Washington, D.C.: Hemisphere Publishing, 1985.

Waugh, Evelyn. *The Loved One.* Boston: Little, Brown, 1948.

Weisman, Avery D. *On Dying and Denying: A Psychiatric Study of Terminality.* New York: Behavioral Publications, 1972.

Whitehead, Alfred North. "On Foresight." *In Business Adrift.* New York: McGraw-Hill, 1921.

Woods, Alison. "Mourners Will Please Pay Respects at Speeds Not Exceeding 15 MPH." *Wall Street Journal,* September 23, 1993.

Index